México Between Feast and Famine

ENRIQUE C. OCHOA

México Between Feast and Famine

Food, Corporate Power, and Inequality

THE UNIVERSITY OF
ARIZONA PRESS

TUCSON

The University of Arizona Press
www.uapress.arizona.edu

We respectfully acknowledge the University of Arizona is on the land and territories of Indigenous peoples. Today, Arizona is home to twenty-two federally recognized tribes, with Tucson being home to the O'odham and the Yaqui. Committed to diversity and inclusion, the University strives to build sustainable relationships with sovereign Native Nations and Indigenous communities through education offerings, partnerships, and community service.

ISBN-13: 978-0-8165-5222-1 (hardcover)
ISBN-13: 978-0-8165-5221-4 (paperback)
ISBN-13: 978-0-8165-5223-8 (ebook)

Cover design by Leigh McDonald
Typeset by Leigh McDonald in Warnock Pro 10.5/14 and Bufalino (display)

Publication of this book is made possible in part by the proceeds of a permanent endowment created with the assistance of a Challenge Grant from the National Endowment for the Humanities, a federal agency.

Library of Congress Cataloging-in-Publication Data
Names: Ochoa, Enrique, author.
Title: México between feast and famine : food, corporate power, and inequality / Enrique C. Ochoa.
Description: Tucson : University of Arizona Press, 2025. | Includes bibliographical references and index.
Identifiers: LCCN 2024032656 (print) | LCCN 2024032657 (ebook) | ISBN 9780816552221 (hardcover) | ISBN 9780816552214 (paperback) | ISBN 9780816552238 (ebook)
Subjects: LCSH: Food industry and trade—Mexico. | Mexico—Economic conditions. | Mexico—Social conditions.
Classification: LCC HD9014.M62 O25 2025 (print) | LCC HD9014.M62 (ebook) | DDC 338.10972—dc23/eng/20241211
LC record available at https://lccn.loc.gov/2024032656
LC ebook record available at https://lccn.loc.gov/2024032657

Printed in the United States of America
♾ This paper meets the requirements of ANSI/NISO Z39.48-1992 (Permanence of Paper).

For all those struggling daily
for a just food system

CONTENTS

ILLUSTRATIONS

FIGURES

TABLES

ACKNOWLEDGMENTS

This book, like all labor, has been a collective endeavor that would not have been possible without the support of countless people. It has been inspired by the struggles and visions of grassroots organizers and communities struggling for a just food system rooted in their diverse histories, experiences, and knowledges. Movement organizers and critical scholars have produced a significant body of scholarship that is reframing how we understand the relationship between food, land, water, power, community, culture, and the future of the planet. *México Between Feast and Famine* draws from the work of numerous Mexican scholars and organizers who have been engaged in this struggle. Wherever possible, they are mentioned in the text, notes, and bibliography.

I especially would like to acknowledge the support of people who have helped me in a number of ways, including by providing comments, words of encouragement, recommendations of sources, invitations to present my work, and critical discussions. I am grateful to Carolina Bank Muñoz, Chris Boyer, Verónica Castillo-Muñoz, Rafael Chabrán, Lani Cupchoy, Juanita del Toro, Elizabeth Coonrod Martínez, James Mestaz, Juan Mora Torres, Julio Moreno, Tanalis Padilla, Jaime Pensado, Jeffrey Pilcher, Stefan Pohl-Valero, Suyapa Portillo-Villeda, Richard Roman, Claudia Serrato, Mike Soldatenko, Gabriela Soto-Laveaga, Frank Stricker, Steve Teixeira, Robert Weis, Martín Valadez, Victor Valle, and Edur Velasco

Arregui. My sincere gratitude to both Sandra Aguilar-Rodríguez and Alex Aviña for their important insights and feedback on the manuscript. I hope that I did their comments justice.

I have received support from several institutions throughout this project's gestation. Funding from the Latin American Program of the William and Flora Hewlett Foundation for a project on the social and political responses to globalization enabled me to research the transnationalization of capital in the 1990s and 2000s and the rise of popular movements resisting neoliberal plunder. I am grateful for the support of David Lorey, the foundation's former program officer, and for Celia Simonds who coordinated the project with me. This led to early conversations with officials of the United Food and Commercial Workers Union in Los Angeles (UFCW 770) as they were grappling with how to organize workers as Mexico's Gigante supermarkets expanded in the Los Angeles area. A Rockefeller-funded Humanities Faculty Fellowship at Cal State LA jump-started my research on transnational tortillas. I want to thank Alejandra Marchevsky, Ricky Rodríguez, and John Ramírez, the program directors, for their support. I also thank Lucila Chávez and Natalia Mazas for outstanding research assistance during this early phase of the project. A mini grant from the Pat Brown Institute enabled me to explore food sovereignty movements in Boyle Heights and East Los Angeles and I appreciate the long conversations that I had with Victoria Delgadillo, Fernando Meija, Carlos Ortez, and Irene Peña.

The idea for the book first germinated during my time as the Michi Nishiura and Walter Weglyn Endowed Chair for Multicultural Studies at Cal Poly Pomona (2006–2008). I would like to thank Mary Yu Danico, Jonnie Owens, Gilbert Cadena, Patricia de Freitas, Sandy Dixon, Terri Gomez, the late Toni-Mokjaetji Humber, Jocelyn Pacleb, Anita Jain, Estela Ballón, Dan Lewis, Cecilia Santiago, the staff of the Multicultural student centers, and Barbara Way for their support during my time at Cal Poly. I had the pleasure of working with several research assistants and students whose activism and scholarship continue to shape my thinking. In particular, I want to thank Melissa Tori Barreto, Oscar Márquez, Rocio Navarro, Rosa Portugal, Chris Rodriguez, Andrea Serrato, and Lisa Williams Moorhead.

My academic career has largely developed at Cal State University Los Angeles. The alma mater of my parents, it was always a lifelong dream to teach Latin American studies and history at Cal State LA given the community-centered focus of the critical Latin American studies program that developed under the direction of Louis DeArmand, Donald Bray, Marjorie Bray, Tim Harding, and Bill Bollinger. My parents spoke frequently about their time at Cal State LA and the various events they attended and the people they met. During the 1980s, Cal State LA was the place to go to hear speakers from Central America, Mexico, and Cuba. Since I joined the LAS program in 1995, I have been fortunate to have worked with passionate and caring scholars, including Don, Marjorie, Tim (even after he had retired), Bill, and then later, Beth Baker, Ericka Verba, Alex Villalpando, Gabriela Fried Amilivia, and Sandy Gutiérrez. In the history department, I have had a series of supportive chairs and colleagues, in particular Francisco Balderrama, Stan Burstein, Cheryl Koos, Mark Wild, Scott Wells, Choi Chatterjee, Chris Endy, Afshin Matin-Asgari, Pete Sigal, Angela Vergara, Eileen Ford, and Kittiya Lee. I want to particularly thank the support of Diana Balli, Nofoau Leau, Melody Singleton, Betania Santos, and Douglas Ramon, who have always generously helped me navigate the institution, even as their workload skyrocketed. I have benefited from three sabbaticals and two difference-in-pay leaves at Cal State LA that have provided time for me to write several chapters.

I have been nourished by my work with numerous Cal State LA students over the years. Their desire for a deeper understanding of the forces that have often expelled them and their families from their homelands to an often-hostile United States has transformed my approach to teaching and learning over the years. It is a privilege to watch them as they unlock the histories and experiences that schools, universities, and other institutions have taught them to forget.

Once again, the University of Arizona Press team has been a pleasure to work with. The enthusiasm and insight with which Kristen Buckles approached this manuscript was truly invigorating. I appreciate the work of the rest of the editorial team, especially Elizabeth Honor Wilder, Leigh McDonald, Abby Mogollón, and Amanda Krause. I am grateful for the thoughtful and careful copyediting work of Sana Rahman.

Nothing that I have accomplished would have been possible without the love and support of my small, tight-knit family. I dedicate this book to them. My parents, Henry J. Ochoa (1935–1989) and Francesca Palazzolo Ochoa (1941–2021), were outstanding parents and humane and passionate educators. They created a loving and supportive household and encouraged my sister and me to read and critically examine the world around us. They supported us in our education and in all that we did. After our father's death, my mother traveled with us on trips to Mexico, Nicaragua, and Europe. She was a treasured friend, mother, and grandmother who did whatever she could to support us. Her death to COVID–19 in early 2021 has been devastating.

My sister Gilda Ochoa read the entire manuscript and several drafts of individual chapters in her usual critical and supportive manner. Her invaluable feedback is reflected throughout the book. Over the years Gilda has been my closest academic and political collaborator, and I continue to learn from her.

Julie, Sebastián, Ricky, and Andy have lived with this project for far too long. They all endured hearing about it in different settings and protested when I went too far explaining the intricacies of the corporate food system. I thank them for their love, patience, insights, and support.

I am also grateful for the love and support of my mother's partner, Jesse Henderson, my aunts Luisa Smietana and Luce Palazzolo, my brother-in-law Eduardo Ruíz, my late in-laws Jack and Elizabeth Kaup, and my longtime friend Adrián Contonente.

While I have received much support, I alone am responsible for any errors or omissions.

México Between Feast and Famine

INTRODUCTION

Toward a Holistic Approach to Mexican Food Systems

In 2010 and 2011, the United Nations made two important statements about Mexican food and nutrition. In 2010, the United Nations' Educational, Scientific, and Cultural Organization (UNESCO) named Mexican cuisine as an Intangible Cultural Heritage of Humanity. In its citation, UNESCO acknowledged the complex regional and local cuisines that developed over the course of centuries and noted that "traditional Mexican cuisine is a comprehensive cultural model comprising farming, ritual practices, age-old skills, culinary techniques and ancestral community customs and manners."[1] In passing on this ancestral knowledge, "[c]ollectives of female cooks and other practitioners devoted to raising crops and traditional cuisine" express community identity, reinforce social bonds, and build stronger local, regional, and national identities. For the Mexican government, the UNESCO designation was a global recognition of the value of the nation's culinary traditions and cuisine. It hoped that a boom in tourism would follow.[2]

A little more than six months after the UNESCO declaration, the United Nations Special Rapporteur on the Right to Food, Olivier De Schutter, made a site visit to Mexico to study the nation's food situation. His report documented the dire state of nutrition for a significant portion of the Mexican population: "a total of 52 million people (46.2

percent of the population) lived in poverty while 28 million (24.9 percent) had insufficient access to food."[3] He underscored that one-third of Indigenous children suffered from chronic malnutrition compared to 10 percent of non-Indigenous children. De Schutter argued that food poverty and malnutrition were directly linked to government policies that hurt Mexico's rural and urban poor. These policies, the report showed, indirectly subsidized fast food and junk food and were a primary cause of obesity and skyrocketing diet-related illnesses.[4] The special rapporteur emphasized that the healthy traditional diets, developed over centuries, were increasingly out of reach for much of the population, exacerbating inequality and health disparities.

These seemingly contradictory pronouncements by UN agencies about Mexico's food system are part of the contradictions that have shaped Mexican history. The rise of foodie culture and celebrity chefs has made Mexico a "destination for the world's foodies."[5] Elite chefs from the United States and Mexico rummage through market stalls and forage for insects, larvae, and other "exotic" foods to add to their culinary repertoire and serve to their high-end customers. Chef Enrique Olvera is credited as a leader in this movement as a "young yet influential cook who has managed to modernize Mexico's pre-Hispanic food traditions in an elegant way."[6] The foodie fixation with Mexican food and culture is part of the long colonial and capitalist assault on Mexico's food system. As corporate chefs appropriate Indigenous and working-class foods and make them "elegant" while deepening Mexico's systemic inequalities, Indigenous and campesino communities have been forced into poverty with limited access to the rich cuisines that they and their ancestors are credited with creating. However, as Gustavo Esteva argued, "maize is one of our creations, and maize, in turn, created us."[7] Maize was first cultivated by Indigenous peoples at least ten thousand years ago, and since then they created complex knowledge systems based on maize and other crops, selecting and breeding seeds to adapt to different types of soils and geographic conditions, and for use in diverse maize-based foods, including tortillas, tamales, pozole, esquites, chichas, atole, and many others.

This deep history of Indigenous food systems, however, has been under assault since 1519, when Europeans first pulled into the harbors of Veracruz in what is now Mexico. Centuries of colonialism, capitalism, and patriarchy radically transformed community autonomy, landholding patterns, diets, knowledge systems, and living standards. Colonizers invaded the countryside, violently expropriating lands and the labor of Indigenous people, Africans, and mestizos. They used the legal system, private armies, and other forms of state power to enforce their control. New hierarchies of power and knowledge were constructed, and the complex Indigenous food systems and knowledges were caricatured, marginalized, and selectively appropriated to erase the cultures and communities that created them.

Since the 1980s, neoliberal capitalist globalization has taken this assault to new heights. As tariffs and producer and consumer subsidies were slashed, campesinos, workers, and small businesses have been forced to scramble for other ways to make ends meet. Neoliberal policymakers codified the assault through constitutional changes to begin privatizing the collective lands of ejidos in 1992 and through the 1994 implementation of the North American Free Trade Agreement (NAFTA). These legal shifts opened the countryside to increased foreign investment, land grabs, the creation of factories in rural areas, the growth of mega agribusiness, mineral extraction, illegal drug production, and environmental degradation. Global transnational capital now dominates the food system and is rapidly privatizing and transforming seeds and knowledge systems in unprecedented ways. The result has been devastating for rural communities whose members are often forced to migrate, abandoning the ways of life that their ancestors had been engaged in for centuries.[8]

Driven by Mexican and international capital in conjunction with shifting government policies, this process has led to a growing concentration of wealth as millions of Mexicans suffer from malnutrition and a growing junk food diet as poignantly noted by the cartoonist Eduardo "Rius" del Río in his 2000 book, *La basura que comemos: Transgénicos y comida chatarra (The Garbage We Eat: GMOs and Junk Food)*.[9] Mexico's population has the dubious distinction of having both high rates of malnutrition and diet-related diseases. In 2022, nearly one in four Mexicans, or 23.4 million people, suffered from a lack of access to nutritious food according to Mexico's official evaluation agency that measures poverty and the impact of social policies.[10] Despite repeated government statements that food poverty will soon be eradicated, the official total percent of food insecure people has hovered between 18 and 24 percent of the population for at least the past decade.[11] Independent estimates place this number at nearly half of the Mexican population.[12] In 2020, the COVID–19 pandemic exacerbated food poverty in Mexico, with millions falling into extreme poverty and many more on the precipice. Nevertheless, the government played down the extent of the crisis and President Andrés Manuel López Obrador went so far as to proclaim in a speech to the United Nations, "Despite the pandemic and crisis, there is no hunger in Mexico."[13]

While many Mexicans suffer from a lack of food, an increasing number suffer from the modern diet consisting of fast, salty, and carbohydrate-laden foods. Inexpensive ramen noodles and *comida chatarra* (junk food) have become increasingly popular as beans and tortilla consumption has declined. Food system scholars Alysha Gálvez and Gerardo Otero have independently demonstrated the connection between the rapid growth in these nutritionally related diseases and the shifting trade and social policies associated with NAFTA. Between 1990 and 2013, chronic kidney disease increased by 276 percent, diabetes by 41 percent, and coronary heart disease by 52 percent. The top three causes of death in Mexico are diet related, with diabetes being "the number one killer in Mexico."[14] Otero calls this dietary shift the "neoliberal diet."[15]

The transformation of Mexico's food system, however, has been an enormous source of wealth creation and concentration that has benefited a small number of families. Neoliberal economic expansion has made Mexico the home of some of the world's largest and most important food companies. According to *Forbes México*, in 2017 the assets of twelve out of fifteen of Mexico's billion-dollar families came from their involvement in the food, beverage, and food retail sectors.[16] Among the billionaire food industry clans are the González Moreno family, owners of the world's largest tortilla producer Grupo Maseca (GRUMA); the Servitje family of Grupo Bimbo, the world's largest baked goods and packaged bread producer; and the Robinson Bours family, owners of Bachoco, one of the world's largest poultry producers. In addition, the families of Mexico's top food retailers, Aurrerá, Soriana, La Comercial, Gigante, and Chedraui, made the list.[17] Since the 1990s, these companies have transformed the food system in Mexico and in much of Latin America. Most have multinational links and are expanding across the globe, making a small group of Mexican capitalists and their allies very wealthy, while the diets of millions deteriorate.

Economic and nutritional polarization falls heaviest on Indigenous communities. Indigenous women, creators and innovators of complex and nutritious cuisines, have been relegated to the margins in the era of corporatized Mexican foods. The most egregious example of efforts to erase Indigenous women's knowledge is in the production and marketing of tortillas. The major corporate tortilla producers seem to studiously avoid mentioning Indigenous women's crucial role in inventing the nixtamalization process. Nixtamalization adds niacin and other nutrients to maize, which made it the basis of the Mesoamerican diet for thousands of years. After the sixteenth century, in places where the nixtamalization process was not employed, such as the U.S. South and Midwest and southern Italy, poor farmers suffered the scourge of pellagra, a vicious disease characterized by diarrhea, dementia, dermatitis, and ultimately death.[18] Instead of celebrating Indigenous women's scientific innovation of nixtimalization, Europeans and elite Mexicans continually demeaned the knowledge and work of Indigenous women at the metate and considered Indigenous men in the field inefficient producers. These chauvinistic attitudes, however, did not prevent capitalists from appropriating their knowledge and technologies and making millions from the physical and intellectual labor of Indigenous people and campesinos and campesinas. Appropriation and erasure persist as industrial tortilla producers, such as GRUMA, center themselves as the innovators of the industry.

Poverty and malnutrition rates in Mexico are notoriously worse in the countryside, especially among Indigenous populations. In their award-winning book, *Morir en la miseria* (*To Die in Misery*), journalist Miguel Badillo and his collaborators documented life in the municipalities of Mexico where conditions were among the poorest on the planet. They demonstrated that eleven of the country's municipalities in the primarily Indigenous regions of the states of Chiapas, Oaxaca, Veracruz, and Guerrero are among the world's poorest. The journalists estimated that another 122 municipalities were only slightly better off and any small shift in the economy profoundly affects these communities.[19] Hunger affects all aspects of lives in rural areas, according to Abel Barrera, director of the Centro de Derechos Humanos de La Montaña Tlachinollan:

Here the problem is hunger. The government does not guarantee the nutrition of the people who live in the countryside. With what a family

in the mountain sows, it harvests 400 kilos of maize. And this is enough
food for a family of eight for three months; but this assumes that they
don't get sick, that they don't have to invest in clothing or in their children's schooling. And when this runs out, they don't have anything to
eat.[20]

Coupled with persistent hunger, the modern junk food diet has colo-
nized the countryside. Scholars have examined the ways that U.S. junk
food such as Coke and Pepsi have entered the markets and mixed with
local histories and cultures in the twentieth century.[21] However, since
the 1980s, cheap and nutritionally poor foods have flooded the markets
in epidemic proportions. In San Cristobal de la Casas, Chiapas, Cristina
Alonso, director of Luna Maya Birth Center, reported that "people can't
afford beans but they can afford Coke and chips."[22] This has led to the
growth in consumption of salt and carbohydrate-laden ramen noodles,
international chain fast-food restaurants, and a decline in traditional
food consumption.[23] The United Nations Special Rapporteur concluded
in his report of Mexico that the country's

> agricultural policies currently encourage the production of grains, rich in
> carbohydrates but relatively poor in micronutrients, at the expense of the
> production of fruits and vegetables. The result is that for many Mexicans,
> particularly in urban areas or in northern states, switching to healthier di-
> ets is becoming increasingly difficult. The trade policies currently in place
> favour an increased reliance on heavily processed and refined foods, with
> a long shelf life, which does not favour the consumption of fresh and more
> perishable foods, particularly fruits and vegetables.[24]

México Between Feast and Famine directly confronts these glaring
contradictions in Mexico's food system. It explores how a region with a
diverse, locally controlled food system that was embedded in millennia-
old ecological and cosmological systems transformed into an anthro-
pocentric, market-driven system that feeds some very well as it uproots
millions and leaves large segments of the population "to die in misery."[25]
Communities, however, continue to resist, maintain, and adapt their
ways of knowing even as the forces of colonialism and capitalism seek to
eradicate them and their ways of life.

Toward a Critical and Holistic Approach to Mexican Food Systems

The scholarship on Mexico's food histories and cultures has been as fragmented as the processes of colonialism and capitalism.[26] Beginning in the mid-twentieth century, scholars began to document the main political and structural features of Mexican food history. The initial studies, in the post–World War II period, focused on the colonial period to understand the historic roots of food crisis, popular mobilizations, and government grain regulation in order to shed light on the current period of food crisis and growing market regulation.[27] By the late 1960s and 1970s, studies influenced by dependency and Marxist debates about the role of agriculture in society explored food production within a framework of the development of capitalism and its impact on working Mexicans.[28] By the 1980s and 1990s, scholars increasingly studied food distribution and consumption, with many linking these to the creation of a national cuisine or to national economic development strategies.[29] At the same time, the essential role of women in food production began to be considered.[30]

In his now classic work, *¡Que Vivan Los Tamales! Food and the Making of Mexican Identity*, Jeffery M. Pilcher provides a sweeping history of Mexico from before the conquest through the late twentieth century.[31] Pilcher's focus on the formation of national cuisine provides an integrated understanding of the role of food in nation building. Pilcher's *Planet Taco: A Global History of Mexican Food* employs his cultural analysis to explain the rapid expansion and popularity of Mexican food across the globe.[32] The Mexican food historian José Luis Juárez López has written a magisterial three-volume culinary history of Mexico.[33]

Building on the works of Pilcher and Juárez López, recent scholarship has paid much more attention to diets, nutritional sciences, and state policy since independence. Through analysis of scientific and policy discourses, these studies demonstrate the ongoing efforts to transform diets in the name of civilization and modernity.[34] The work of Sandra Aguilar-Rodríguez is among the few to focus on the connection between food, state building, and gender in the 1940s and 1950s. She examines policymakers' efforts to use women to transform working-class diets and the ways women negotiated this process. Aguilar-Rodríguez's blending of analysis of institutional records and life food histories with women assesses how reformers "questioned the nutritional value of the working-class diet and considered it a threat to the construction of modern Mexico" and "how the state implemented modernization discourses among the working class and how women became central to their interpretation."[35] Aguilar-Rodríguez is able to effectively demonstrate how racial and gender ideologies and discourses influenced institutional policies and the daily practices of women in the kitchen.[36]

Social scientists have noted the transnational dimensions of food and agricultural policies. Most of these studies have centered on the countryside, agricultural labor, and food production, significantly complicating our understanding of commodity chains and the social, political, and gendered impacts of food production and processing.[37] Carolina Bank Muñoz has demonstrated the power of capital to take advantage of national, racial, and gendered divisions of the workforce to expand markets.[38] Others have demonstrated how the kitchen and the community garden represent epistemic sites and sites of resistance, opening up many new avenues for understanding the complexities of food in Mexican societies.[39]

Alysha Gálvez's *Eating NAFTA* centers neoliberalism and NAFTA in the deterioration and polarization of Mexican diets, and the epidemic growth of chronic diet-related diseases since the 1990s. Gálvez demonstrates that the laws and economic transformation ushered in with NAFTA fundamentally shifted the relationship between the state and citizens: in which the state absolved itself of its social role and unleashed the forces of the market on the population. State, private sector, and medical discourse were recalibrated to blame individuals and communities for obesity, as measured through newly created tools of the body mass index (BMI), and other deleterious health-related effects that this nutrition transition has on communities.[40] Instead, Gálvez argues that "the massive proliferation of diet-related illness" is "a kind of structural violence—a result of policy decisions and priorities."[41] Through her structural and holistic analysis, Gálvez demonstrates the destructive effects of free trade policies on Mexican diets, campesino ways of life, and the ways that "imperialist nostalgia" works to re-create maize-based milpa cuisine as haute cuisine.

Scholars of food systems and food regimes have helped theorize food systems over the longue durée. Placing the development of food systems within the larger context of capitalist world systems, Harriet Friedmann and Philip McMichael periodize different "food regimes" that characterize the manner in which food has been produced, distributed, and consumed.[42] McMichael argues that, since World War II, the world has seen a corporate food regime dominated by centralizing transnational corporations that engulf the world food systems into a global marketplace.[43] Gerardo Otero has applied the food regime approach to Latin America by demonstrating a distinct neoliberal food regime characterized by market liberalization and deregulation and the gutting of the social safety net in favor of an explicit alliance with transnational agribusiness corporations and biotechnical firms that accelerate campesino displacement.[44]

That complex and nutritious foods developed over centuries in Mexico are directly being undermined by capitalist-driven markets reflects the broader history of coloniality and capitalism in Mexican history. While conquest and colonization began in 1519 in Mexico and nominally ended with Mexican independence in 1821, generations of scholars have demonstrated that the process set in motion in 1519 continues to this day. Coloniality of power scholars argue that we must examine not only political systems but also epistemological systems. For the Peruvian intellectual Aníbal Quijano, the practices and legacies of European domination persisted long after the systematic repression of Indigenous people and the end of formal colonialism. These practices persist in the hierarchies, knowledges, and cultural systems in addition to the basic sociopolitical and economic structure of Latin America.[45]

Walter Mignolo, building on Quijano's notion of coloniality, argues that there is a colonial matrix of power that connects economic and political power to knowledge and subjectivity and that creates physical and epistemological hierarchies about race, gender, and sexuality.[46] Similar to Patricia Hill Collins's discussion of a matrix of domination, these hierarchies are intersectional and undergird the ideologies, knowledge systems, and structures of inequality throughout the Americas.[47] Drawing on Quijano and Mignolo, Zilkia Janer and Vanessa Fonseca have independently applied these concepts to food in the Americas. Janer focuses on the colonial processes of the "degradation of Indigenous culinary knowledge as a response to the challenge that American nature and Indigenous culinary practices posed to Europe."[48] In her analysis of the advertising and marketing of Mexican foods in Texas, Fonseca demonstrates that "coloniality of power will evidence how in late capitalism, the commodification of culture and the colonization of life results from the implementation of marketing practices as neocolonial forces leading to the reconfiguration and transformation of subjectivities, both Hispanic and non-Hispanic through consumption."[49] According to analysts of both food regimes and coloniality of power, we can begin to see how food is transformed from that which sustains life to just another commodity uprooted from its historical context.

The attempts by foodies, chefs, and corporate interests in the Global North to untangle this richness and complexity of Mexican foods and package it and market it to a broad audience is the latest in a series of colonial endeavors. María Elena García's *Gastropolitics and the Specter of Race* critically explores the coloniality of Peru's vaunted culinary revolution where elite chefs appropriate Indigenous foods and foodways and stylize them for the jet-set foodies in fine dining establishments. This extractive process fits into broader projects of mestizaje and capitalist extraction where "the emphasis on fusion (the 'happy encounter' between the Andes and Europe) and on dialogue, unity, and the ability to 'overcome any difference' glosses over the brutality of the colonial encounter and ongoing experiences of violence, dispossession, and marginalization."[50]

Campesinos, food sovereignty activists, and scholars, especially in the past two decades, have advanced our understanding of the importance of campesino agricultural systems and their resiliency despite centuries of assault. Building on the work of Alexander Chayanov and through close work with communities, a number of studies have challenged the modernization paradigm that posits large-scale private agriculture to feed growing urban centers. Works by scholars Kirsten Appendini, David Barkin, Armando Bartra, José Luis Calvo, Gustavo Esteva, Gerardo Otero, Blanca Rubio, Steven E. Sanderson, and Blanca Suárez, to mention but a few, emphasize the impact of neoliberalism on the countryside and the ways communities have resisted the plunder and developed agroecological methods coupled with struggles for autonomy.[51] Esteva has emphasized the "battle for rural Mexico" and voices and ways of knowing that colonial and capitalist sources have sought to obliterate. Esteva reframes our understanding of food not as a commodity but as *comida*, reflecting a more holistic vision of food and the relationships with people, the land, other sentient beings, and the knowledges that have been centuries in the making. Through "re-embedding food in agriculture," he calls for the restoration of these relationships as the just way to nurture the planet and the pluriverse of communities who live on earth.[52]

Global Capital and Mexico's Food System

México Between Feast and Famine addresses the history and transformations of Mexico's food system within the larger contours of Mexican history. There are relatively few books in print and in English that address the political and social underpinnings of wealth, inequality, and poverty within the broad sweep of Mexican history. Among the works published over the past two decades in English that seek to provide an analysis of the development of capitalism and inequality in Mexican history are Ramón Eduardo Ruiz's *Mexico: Why a Few Are Rich and the People Poor* (University of California Press, 2010) and John Tutino's *The Mexican Heartland: How Communities Shaped Capitalism, a Nation, and World History, 1500–2000* (Princeton University Press, 2018). Both studies are sweeping works of interpretation that provide unique insights into capitalist development and inequality throughout Mexican history. Both Ruiz's nation-focused analysis and Tutino's regional study examine Mexico's insertion into the global political economy and the social and economic consequences of capitalist transformation. Both works, however, are overwhelmingly focused on the period prior to World War II and consequently are unable to fully capture the ways that political and economic power are developed, exercised, and transformed and how they shape Mexico today.

This study is based on my more than thirty years of study and research of Mexico's food system, poverty, and social programs. My first book, *Feeding Mexico: The Political Uses of Food Since 1910*, examined the ways that Mexico's postrevolutionary governments used food as a political tool in creating a hegemonic nation-state and in creating social peace.[53] Through the analysis of popular struggles for better living conditions, the political economy of food, and developmentalist state policy, I argued that the expansion of state intervention in the food economy and the creation of a network of state-owned food stores and industries from the 1930s to the 1980s subsidized workers and campesinos to quell worker demands for increased wages and campesino demands for control of their land and their labor power. Social and economic policy supported Mexican capitalists and fostered the transformation of Mexican agriculture away from campesino-based production toward an agribusiness model of development.

This current study, *México Between Feast and Famine*, centers the shifts in Mexico's food system since the 1980s and sets them in the context of the long history of coloniality and capitalist expansion and their class, racialized, and gendered impacts. This book examines the multiple expulsions and forced displacements that colonial and capitalist policies have caused in the region now known as Mexico since the sixteenth century. Beginning with violent resource extraction, land grabs, and genocide of Indigenous peoples, this process has deepened over the years as nature became natural resources, and labor, land, food, water, and even life have been commodified. As capitalist growth concentrated resources and disposed of Indigenous peoples, campesinos, and workers, Western racialized discourses and science blame them for their impoverishment and disparage their foodways and cultures. Using the tools of nutrition science, modern colonial forces have reduced food to calories and body shapes and sizes to weight scales and BMI, alienating food and bodies from nature, cultural contexts, communities, and knowledge systems. Modern companies, many owned by Mexican capitalists, innovate colonial practices that reinforce racial, ethnic, class, and gender hierarchies to expand the market. These companies also actively transform the idea and image of Mexican food and often work to variously delink it from Mexican history and from Indigenous women. They play on the nostalgia of an imagined Mexican past, and they appropriate and modernize traditional foods such as tortillas to connect to tropes of modernity, hygiene, and whiteness. Other companies hold up their products and businesses as paragons of modernity, culture, and sophistication, premised on Mexico as a forward-thinking modern nation. Many position their businesses as progressive and socially responsive and highlight their promotion of good nutrition, gender equity, and environmental responsibility. By co-opting the rhetoric and language of social movements through corporate social responsibility programs, corporations have shifted discussion of inequality, poor working conditions, environmental degradation, and malnutrition away from their businesses and the workings of capitalism and instead position themselves as the solution to inequality, environmental destructions, racism, and sexism.

By titling the book *México Between Feast and Famine*, I recognize the polarization of Mexican society and the nuances and complexities of historical processes. Famine, which has led to widespread death over a large area, has been a relatively rare phenomenon in Mexican history, only recorded on a few occasions during the eighteenth century and at various times during the heights of the fighting in the Mexican Revolution.[54] However, chronic hunger and shortages connected to colonial and capitalist policies have resulted in the slow grind of poverty and malnutrition that has left millions of Mexicans "to die in misery."[55] Some scholars of famine take a more expansive view that emphasizes a continuum of mass death on one side and chronic hunger on the other such that malnutrition might be seen as "slow-burning famine."[56] Gálvez has recently argued chronic diet-related "disease is a slow-moving disaster, more deadly than earthquakes and infectious outbreaks, and especially insidious for its slow and sometimes invisible work."[57] In the first decade of the twenty-first century, one Mexican think tank using official statistics found that "hunger caused more deaths than drug cartels," with 85,343 people dying of hunger compared to 49,804 dying due to violence connected to the cartels.[58] However, this slow death is hidden in Mexico, as economic polarization grows and the media perpetuates the myth that "in Mexico, nobody dies of hunger," as a popular Mexican anchorman argued in 2014.[59] Six years later, President López Obrador declared to the United Nations General Assembly that "despite the pandemic and economic crisis, there is no hunger in our country." Mexico's fact-checking journalists immediately labeled the president's statements as false.[60] Meanwhile, Mexican and international capitalists and foodies feast.

México Between Feast and Famine is based on my research in archives, libraries, newspapers, magazines, internet publications, government studies, corporate records and reports, multilateral and nonprofit studies, advertisements and public relations websites and materials, cookbooks, and interviews. I am also fortunate to be able to draw upon the works of numerous organizers, community activists, and scholars who are working to create a more just food system in Mexico and throughout the world. These works form a veritable treasure trove of archival material that documents foodways and food systems throughout Mexican history.

This study, however, does not pretend to be a comprehensive history of Mexican food, foodways, or the food system. Instead, *México Between Feast and Famine* aims to construct an analysis that links political economy, coloniality, cultural knowledges, and nation building to capitalist inequality, government policies, forced displacement, malnutrition, and their class, racial, and gendered impact. Through a systemic power analysis of Mexico's food system over the years, this book builds on the above works and does the following:

1. Provides a historically rooted analysis of the political, economic, social, and cultural factors that have transformed the Mexican food system over time;
2. Directly addresses the contradictions of Mexico's polarized food system. It unpacks how Mexico's celebrated complex cuisine that was developed and nurtured by Indigenous and campesino communities over centuries is now virtually inaccessible to these same communities that continue to suffer from high rates of food poverty and malnutrition. These contradictions are placed within the long history of coloniality characterized by an interlocking matrix of domination that systematically seeks to appropriate and erase Indigenous histories and gendered knowledge in Mexico for profit;
3. Explores the connections between public policy and the expansion of private enterprise and the roles of Mexican and international capitalists in shaping the Mexican food system;
4. Provides the first in-depth and historical study of key agribusiness and food corporations that dominate and shape the food system in Mexico and throughout Latin America—from production, to distribution, marketing, and consumption;
5. Analyzes the social and cultural impact of neoliberal food systems and the ways that communities have sought to resist, maintain, and adapt their ways of knowing even as the forces of colonialism and capitalism seek to eradicate them and their ways of life.

This book is divided into seven chapters and a conclusion that examine Mexican history through the lens of food and food systems, their transformation, and the deepening of coloniality and inequality through-out Mexican history. Chapter 1 provides a historical analysis of the complex food systems that were developed in the region now known as Mexico in the thousands of years prior to Spanish conquest and colonialism. It then examines the repeated efforts of Spaniards and Mexican elites to render Mexico's complex food system into a homogeneous modern capitalist food system. Chapter 2, "A Better Diet for Our People': The Persistence of Inequality in the Postrevolutionary Food System," demonstrates that despite campesino efforts to resist the ongoing encroachment on their lands and labor, postrevolutionary governments, with a few notable exceptions, opted to accelerate their control over the countryside. As communities resisted, mechanisms of violence and control were escalated through the tried-and-true tactics of authoritarian reformist policies.

Chapter 3, "Corporate Power and the Neoliberal Assault on Mexico's Food System," examines how neoliberal policies of the 1980s initiated a process of corporate takeover of the Mexican food system. By examining the political economy behind the corporate assault on the Mexican food system, this chapter tracks how policy shifts benefited many of the companies that were already doing well during the second half of the twentieth century. Chapters 4 through 6 examine the rise of dominance of four transnational food companies (GRUMA, Bimbo, Grupo Aurrerá / Walmart, and Oxxo). All were politically and economically well positioned to benefit from neoliberal policies and quickly became regional and world leaders in the food industry. These chapters demonstrate the ways the leaders of these corporations strengthened their political and economic power to increase their market share by drawing upon and reinforcing racial and gender hierarchies while positioning themselves as socially responsible corporations. Chapter 7, "Paradise of Junk Food': Popular Struggles, Corporate Power, and the Social Costs of Mexico's Food System," examines how Mexico's colonial and capitalist assault on the food system has exacerbated inequality. Further, it illustrates some of the ways the campesino and Indigenous communities, grassroots movements, and intellectuals have resisted neoliberal policies and are rearticulating a vision of food sovereignty rooted in the histories and cultures of Mexico's Indigenous and working-class communities. We then turn to the ways that both the state and corporations have worked to demobilize resistance through massive expenditures in public relations campaigns that seek to co-opt social justice discourse, recenter corporate power, and reinforce social hierarchies.

CHAPTER 1

COMMODIFYING A WAY OF LIFE

Food, Capitalism, and Coloniality in Mexican History

*Maize is a way of being and living, that at the same time connects us to Mother
Earth, the gods and with everything else, with the living and with the dead.*
—MARCOS SANDOVAL, TRIQUI ELDER AND FORMER DIRECTOR OF THE
MUSEO NACIONAL DE CULTURAS POPULARES E INDÍGENAS

For millennia in the Americas, food has been a way of life and a way of
being that has connected people to the world around them. As Triqui
elder and scholar Marcos Sandoval argues for maize, food defines and
shapes relationships to the land, to ancestors, to nature, and to the people
who cultivate and prepare it.[1] The Chicana food studies scholar Meredith
Abarca has theorized that the *sazón* (flavor) of food prepared by Mexicana cooks is based on a multisensory knowledge involving touch, tex-
ture, smell, taste, sight, and hearing, developed through learning based
on generations of work, experimentation, and experience in the field and
around metates and comales.[2] These complex and multilayered understandings of food and life developed over millennia have been under
assault since 1492.

For more than five centuries, the expansion and hegemony of Western
scientific knowledge systems, fueled by colonialism, capitalism, and patriarchy, have sought to study, name, classify, and commodify nature. By
separating cultivation from its social and cultural context, colonial and
capitalist forces render food into a mere commodity—a disembodied
delivery system of calories and nutrients to increase the productivity of
workers. Instead, Gustavo Esteva argues that *comida* (meal) is not *alimento* (food product) but instead includes "the social context, the whole

human world which *comida* embeds, the very heart of *comida*."[3] The struggle between *comida* and *alimento* is at the heart of the battle for Mexico's food system.

This chapter examines the repeated efforts to render Mexico's complex food system into a homogeneous modern capitalist food system. The processes of coloniality laid the foundations for transforming Mexico's food system and the knowledge systems that undergird it. By exploring this process over the course of Mexican history, we can see how dominating forces of coloniality and capitalism have developed, expanded, and deepened in different regions and succeeded in violently dispossessing campesinos of land and impoverishing much of their population. In the face of these multiple assaults, communities resisted and adapted their diets to maintain their community-based food systems. Campesino resistance has shifted policy in often contradictory ways. After providing a brief overview of the food system prior to the conquest, I examine the ways that colonizers sought to reshape the economy, the diets and lives of Indigenous communities, and the flora and fauna throughout the colonial period. The final section examines the ways that capitalist expansion and Eurocentric, patriarchal, and racist ideologies deepened the assault on Indigenous, campesino, and working-class diets.

Food as a Way of Being and Living

For thousands of years, the country now known as Mexico was a complex mix of diverse regions and societies. The numerous communities and civilizations that developed over millennia formed distinct ways of life, languages, cultures, and ways of knowing. Food sources, cooking methods, and even concepts of food varied regionally, contributing to the formation of different cuisines. The cultivation of maize shaped many regional and community identities in central and southern Mexico, fostering the creation of sedentary communities. Nevertheless, the diversity and autonomy of local communities and cultures remained strong. While scholars have recognized this diversity, the power of centralizing nation-states, capitalist markets, and conventional scholarship have obscured the history of this México *profundo* rooted in diverse Indigenous histories and constructed an imaginary Mexico that appears as a unified whole, in the words of Mexican anthropologist Guillermo Bonfil Bata-lla.[4] This México *imaginario* undermines and erases the pluriverse of cultures, communities, and knowledges.

Beginning approximately eight to ten thousand years ago in Meso-america, including present-day central and southern Mexico and the Central American countries of Guatemala, Belize, Honduras, El Salvador, Nicaragua, and Costa Rica, food and cuisine were closely connected to the development of sedentary agriculture and the cultivation of maize. Maize was cultivated from wild grasses, known as teosinte, at least eleven thousand years ago (between 10,000 and 9,000 BCE). The earliest ar-chaeological evidence of maize cultivation has been found in the current state of Guerrero, Mexico, dating back to 8759 BCE and in the Tehuacán Valley in Puebla (7900 BCE). The oldest "distinctly recognizable, un-equivocally dated maize cobs" were found in the Valley of Oaxaca dated from approximately 6,230 years ago.[5] It is believed that maize cultivation spread throughout Mesoamerica and then to North America and South America such that by 1700 BCE maize was found as far north as Ohio and as far south as Chile.[6]

Maize cultivators developed the knowledge of which seeds do better in which soil depending on climatic conditions over generations. This knowledge and way of reading the land and the elements was central to how communities developed their worldviews. The taming of teosinte and the cultivation of larger ears of maize for various uses was the re-sult of intentional seed saving, experimentation, and breeding processes developed over the course of millennia. The holistic science of maize cultivation that emphasized quality over quantity has persisted despite colonial and capitalist obsession with quantity above all else.[7] At pres-ent, scholars identify at least fifty-nine landraces of maize in Mexico and thousands of different varieties.[8]

The care with which communities cultivated and prepared maize and other crops reflected their importance both as ways of life and sources of nutrition. Maize developed as the basis of Mesoamerican cuisines and was consumed in numerous forms, including solids (tortillas, tamales, *memelas*, *tlacoyos*, *totopos*, gorditas, *pinole*, *rosetas*, and *palomitas*), and semi-solids and liquids (pozole, atole, tejate, *rescalate*, *esquiate*, chicha, *tesgüiño*, tepache), to name but a few.[9] There were significant regional variations in the preparation of these foods. Tamales, for example, with masa (maize dough) as their base, included different ingredients reflecting on local history and agro-ecological factors, such that "the choice of tamale fillings was endless."[10] Hence tamales varied widely by region, as cooks creatively adapted them for different occasions.

The innumerable uses of maize are also reflected in the multiple names in Indigenous languages for maize in its different forms and stages of development. Early Spanish conquerors remarked on the diversity of names in Nahuatl, "when it is on the cob (*mazorca* in Spanish) it is called *centli*; after it has been taken off the cob it is called *tlaullii*; when the seed sprouts until it is an arm's length it is called *tloctli*. . . . When the cob is . . . young it is called *xilotli*."[11] The numerous varieties of maize and the complexities of breeding maize for different uses, soils, and climatic conditions, naming different types of maize, and preparing it in innumerable ways attests to the centrality of maize in Mesoamerican communities.

Many Mesoamerican origins stories link maize to the creation of humans. According to the the Popul Vuh, the K'iche Maya book of creation, after searching for a good material to make humans, the gods decided on masa: "From yellow corn and white corn his flesh was made; from corn dough the arms and legs."[12] In Mexica or Aztec creation stories, humans were created five different times. On the fifth attempt, humans were nourished with maize, which helps explain why the world has lasted so long. Variants of Mexica lore explain that maize was introduced by the god Quetzalcoatl and served as the basic building block of Mexican civilization.[13] Alfredo López Austin documented several Mesoamerican origin stories that center maize at the beginning of civilization: "many of these myths concerning maize have been passed down from a remote and imprecise time in ancient Mesoamerican history up to our present day, making it evident that rural maize has been of vital historic concern to rural communities."[14] Thus, the presence of maize created a common food history and culture throughout Mesoamerica despite the great diversities of peoples, histories, and cultures.[15]

Human knowledge, invention, and ingenuity have been central to the process of maize cultivation and its daily transformation into *nixtamal* and then tortillas, tamales, and other foods. Indigenous women who prepared maize used their deep knowledge of the properties of maize to develop important culinary and scientific innovations. Key to this knowledge was the process of nixtamalization, transforming maize kernels into masa in a way that adds key amino acids (lysine and tryptophan) and niacin, part of the vitamin B complex, that enhance the protein value of maize.[16] The releasing of niacin prevented Mesoamericans from the scourge of pellagra, which would develop when un-nixtamalized maize became the main source of food following European conquest and colonization of the Americas.[17] While archaeologists have yet to date when this nixtamalization process was first developed, archaeological evidence shows that metates, the grinding stones on which maize is milled, have been around since before 3000 BCE. However, widespread use of grinding stones and nixtamalization probably occurred approximately 2,000 years ago.[18]

In sedentary areas, women devoted many hours each day to the art and labor of food preparation. Given their centrality within the food preparation process, it is likely that women developed important food technologies that created a varied, complex, and enduring cuisine "that could unleash maize's nutritive capacity."[19] The act of creation and innovation in food preparation is a complex process. As scores of recent food histories now demonstrate, while we may be able to document ingredients and dishes, how they are prepared cannot be easily reduced to a recipe. A cook's sazón is part of an epistemological process. Embedded in sazón is the knowledge that women preparing the food have passed down to each other and how particular cooks add to this knowledge. For Meredith Abarca, "the kitchen and the sazón represent a form of a '*sitio y lengua*,' to quote Emma Pérez, that offers a site of power (the kitchen) and a discourse of empowerment (the sazón) to those historically silenced by colonialist, imperialist, and patriarchal social mechanisms."[20] The important roles of multisensory knowledge and love in preparation of foods are often intangible; however, they are essential to the cultural processes that shape individuals and communities over generations.

The Mesoamerican milpa system, the cultivation of the "three sisters"—maize, beans, and squash—was widely practiced and provided a nutritious food base. Milpa crops are highly complementary; they receive light at different heights. Squash shades the ground, reduces weed growth, and conserves moisture. Bean vines climb the maize stalks, keeping the beans out of the reach of insects in the soil and at the same time replenishing soil with nitrogen. The milpa system, which also included the cultivation of other crops, is considered one of the most successful and sustainable systems of agriculture. There were at least five different types of beans consumed in Mesoamerica and they provided essential protein, fiber, vitamins, and minerals.[21]

While maize was and remains a crucial staff of life in Mesoamerica, it was accompanied by a diverse supply of fruits, vegetables, and legumes that provided complex nutrients to Indigenous diets. It has been estimated that prior to the conquest, communities in central Mexico cultivated at least eighty different plants, nearly all of which were used for food.[22] An array of cacti and succulents provided fruits such as the tuna and beverages such as pulque. Fruits such as avocados and tomatoes added flavor and crucial nutrients to the Mesoamerican diet.[23]

The diet for most Mesoamericans was largely vegetarian and occasionally supplemented by meat. Domesticated animals in Mesoamerica, such as turkeys, were generally used for meat along with hunted quail and deer, and a variety of insects.[24] Mesoamericans had long developed secondary food sources from the natural environment in preparation for times of drought and scarcity when crops did not produce at the expected rates. The knowledge and gathering of roots, seeds, fruits, herbs, and nuts developed over the course of centuries and provided for the population in times of scarcity. They were seen as "famine foods by the Maya." The Franciscan friar Toribio de Benevente commented in the 1530s that, because of their knowledge of roots and the edible landscape, the Indigenous population "could endure barren years more easily than other races."[25]

Mesoamerican diets were nutritious and rich in vitamins and minerals. In his detailed study of Aztec health and diet, Bernardo Ortiz de Montellano demonstrates that they met or surpassed modern nutritional requirements by the United Nation's Food and Agricultural Organization (FAO).[26] The Mexica diet included many nutrition-rich foods that were ignored by Spanish chroniclers after the conquest or eliminated from cultivation and the diet. Amaranth, a nutritious grain that has been cultivated for approximately eight thousand years, was a staple of the Mexica diet and flourished in conditions of high temperature and dry soil. After only five weeks or less, this prolific plant produces a weekly crop of edible leaves for up to six months after planting. Amaranth, rich in lysine and containing 16–18 percent protein, was more nutritious than wheat. Because it was widely used in religious ceremonies, however, it was banned by the Spaniards after the conquest and was only used secretively.[27]

Tecuitlatl , a blue-green algae that grew on Lake Texcoco, was widely consumed by the Mexica. Harvested from the lake and sold in markets, it was often eaten with maize or with a sauce made of various chiles and tomatoes. Contemporary scholars believe that tecuitlatl is what is now referred to as spirulina and is a highly nutritious algae that thrives in salty lakes like those in the Valley of Mexico. While it grew abundant and was available year-round, repeated efforts by Spanish and Mexican elites to drain the lake virtually eliminated its consumption.[28] As with many other Indigenous foods, spirulina was recently "discovered" by foodies and nutrition conscious elites in the Global North who have extolled it as a wonder food, while ignoring the communities that nurtured its use.[29]

The complex and diverse food systems in Mesoamerica fostered the creation of large sedentary communities with populations in the millions on the eve of the Spanish conquest in 1519. According to Woodrow Borah and Sherburne Cook,

> This diversity is one key to the survival of a huge population. If we forget the esthetic aspect of the matter, we see that the Indians as a whole were exploiting in an amazingly efficient matter the total biomass of the environment, and that in terms of essential elements, vitamins, and protein they probably had enough, except in years of complete crop failure. Even then the deficiency was quantitative, not qualitative.[30]

México profundo developed a complex food system and mechanisms for feeding its population. This was central to how communities saw themselves and their relationship to the land, to the earth, to their gods, and to the world.

The Beginnings of the Assault on Indigenous Diets and Food Knowledges

With the arrival of the Spanish in Mexico in 1519, life for Indigenous peoples was radically transformed. While this transformation may not have occurred overnight for all populations, it significantly impacted life for millions of people and set the basis for colonial control that has thus far lasted more than five centuries. While communities resisted European imposition and adapted to the new laws and ideas imposed on them, European colonization led to land grabs, forced expulsions, displacements, and concrete efforts to erase Indigenous ways of living and knowing.[31]

With the European conquest came what Alfred Crosby has referred to as the Columbian exchange. The biological exchange that occurred with the conquest led to centuries of colonization that profoundly marked the Americas and the rest of the world. However, the use of the term "exchange" downplays the often violent and asymmetrical nature of this process. Disease and the introduction of Eastern hemispheric plants and animals upended the lives of Indigenous communities in ways that European communities did not experience.[32] The conquest unleashed genocidal violence, the appropriation of lands, the destruction of histories and cultures, and ecological transformations.

Within the first century of conquest, Spaniards brought diseases to the Americas that would turn the world upside down. New changes in the labor regime and diets coupled with the lack of exposure to diseases that Europeans introduced led to widespread death. The scale and scope of this death cannot be underestimated. Borah and Cook estimated that on the eve of European conquest there were approximately 25.2 million people in central and southern Mexico; by 1546 this number dropped to 6.3 million, bottoming out at 900,000 in 1650. While estimates vary, most scholars agree that wherever Europeans went in the Americas, within decades the Indigenous population plummeted by 80–90 percent. With this genocide, we cannot begin to imagine what was lost in terms of food knowledge and cultures.[33]

From the moment of their arrival, Europeans praised the diversity of foodstuff, the quality of the land, and the abundance in the markets. When describing the markets in Tlatelolco, Spaniards were stunned by "the extraordinary variety of the enormous market . . . and all agree as to its orderliness." Among foodstuff there were "maize, beans, oil-bearing seeds, cocoa, peppers, onions, a thousand kinds of green-stuff, turkeys, rabbits, hares, venison, ducks, and little mute hairless dogs that the Aztecs liked to eat; fruit, sweet potatoes, honey, syrup from maize-stalks or the juice of agave."[34] Marveling at Indigenous abundance only fueled the Europeans' desire to control it and extract wealth. While there was abundance, the Spaniards were not familiar with most of the food, and it often challenged their notions of good and nutritious food. According to Rebeca Earle, Spanish "chroniclers felt compelled to list in detail the European foods the Americas lacked." After all, to live well by European standards meant to consume bread, meat, and wine and not tortillas and pulque, the fermented drink from the maguey plant.[35]

The Spanish sought to cultivate wheat on the best lands and in less than a decade, by the late 1520s, they instituted a bread-processing system, in which wheat was grown on local haciendas, transported to Mexico City mills, processed, and baked into bread. By the late 1530s, this process led to declining prices and widespread wheat consumption by the European population and those living and working closely with them.[36] Very rapidly, most of the best lands in and around Mexico City were usurped for wheat production and maize was increasingly relegated to poorer lands. This pattern, facilitated by the massive death of Indigenous peoples, was repeated throughout Mexico.[37]

To incorporate the Indigenous population into Spanish society as "*gente de razón*," missionaries poured their efforts into learning about Indigenous societies so that they could transform them. That meant that Indigenous diets had to be transformed. Thus began the colonial process, as Zilkia Janer argues, of the "degradation of Indigenous culinary knowledge as a response to the challenge that American nature and Indigenous culinary practices posed to Europe."[38] Central to this process would be the devaluing of maize and all its by-products.

The Franciscan friar Bernardo de Sahagún lectured the Indigenous people he was seeking to convert; he suggested they eat

> that which the Castilian people eat, because it is good food, that with which they are raised, they are strong and pure and wise . . . raise Castilian maize (wheat) so that you may eat Castilian tortillas (wheat bread). . . . Raise sheep, pigs, cattle, for their flesh is good. . . . You will not eat what the Castilian people do not eat, for they know what is edible. . . . You will become the same way if you eat their food.[39]

However, some early Spanish writers such as the physician and botanist Francisco Hernández, who traveled to New Spain between 1570 and 1577, marveled at maize: "They call it Tlaolli, which we call Wheat from the Indies and the Haitians call maize. . . . I praise it highly and do not understand how the Spanish, always diligent imitators of all things foreign . . . have neither adapted (it) for their own use, nor attempted to plant and cultivate (it)." He lavished praise on the maize-based foods such as tortillas, atole, and tamales: "This food has begun to be pleasing to the Spanish, as well as to those who have been born of Spanish and Indian parents." In discussing the method for cooking tamales, he remarked, "This method began to catch on among the Spanish residents of Mexico, so I was able to experiment a bit myself; it is no secret that it is delicious."[40] While Francisco Hernández may have enjoyed tacos, as Rafael Chabrán writes, Spanish tastes and chauvinisms made it difficult for other Europeans to accept Indigenous foods.

The state of European knowledge of medicine and how the body worked emphasized the careful balancing of bodily humors. While Europeans were worried about going to lands that did not have bread, they also thought that eating Indigenous foods would weaken their constitution. Spaniards feared their bodies would be transformed into Indigenous bodies that were "delicate and feminine and of weak complexion."[41] Therefore, when possible, Spaniards felt that it was essential to eat Spanish foods.

Beginning at the onset of colonization, Europeans brought the food crops and animals necessary to remake Europe in the Americas. By bringing the basis for the food, Europeans were addressing both their comfort and their deeply held Eurocentric ideas about the superiority of their foods and their ways of life. The introduction of domesticated animals had a profound impact. The Western Hemisphere had none of the animals that were domesticated in the Eastern Hemisphere, such as sheep, cattle, and pigs. By the 1540s and 1550s, the population of pigs, sheep, and cattle multiplied exponentially as Spaniards of all classes sought to reproduce their diets. With these animals came more sources of protein but also a strain on the ecosystem. Grazing animals ate grass and vegetation down to the dirt, loosening the topsoil only to be washed away during the next downpour. The erosion of rich soil disturbed the ecosystem and had a profound impact on Indigenous communities, leading the historian Elinore Melville to term this process "a plague of sheep."[42]

Grazing animals encroached on Indigenous milpas. In and around Mexico City, cattle herds doubled in fifteen months and ate Indigenous milpas, forcing Indigenous people from their lands, "completely depopulating the region."[43] In Oaxaca, the destruction of Indigenous communities by large herds led the viceroy Antonio de Mendoza to ban cattle ranching in three valleys. As the viceroy wrote to his successor, "The Spaniards are crying that I have ruined them, they are right, for I assure Your Lordship that it is a pity; but I could not do otherwise. May Your Lordship realize that if the cattle are allowed, the Indians will be destroyed."[44] Cattle were a direct threat to Indigenous communities throughout the early colonial period. As lands were depopulated through force and death, Spaniards and mestizos usurped them for their own use. The growth of cattle, sheep, and pig populations also meant that communities would have to compete with the animals for maize and other foods. It would not be long before "grazing displaced agriculture and sheep displaced humans," further pushing Indigenous communities to marginal lands.[45]

Missionaries also worked to suppress Indigenous foods, especially those used in festivals. Friars compiled lists of festival foods, in their Christian war against Indigenous religions or idolatry, as Christians disparagingly referred to it. Amaranth was often shaped into religious figures and eaten during communion. The priests issued bans on amaranth but to no avail as it grew prolifically. Maize was also widely used in Indigenous festivals and religious ceremonies, but given its importance in Mesoamerican diets, priests tried to introduce European foods as substitutes for Indigenous foods.[46]

Even as Mexico's creole elite, those Spaniards born in the Americas, began to reluctantly accept some of the region's historic Indigenous foods, they tended only to complement or add spice to Spanish cuisine. They continued their predecessors' penchant to distinguish the food of the elite from that of the poor. While the creole elite began to adapt to some of the Indigenous foodstuff, according to the Mexican food historian José Luis Juárez López, "they displayed a lack of knowledge of American food . . . and an almost complete absence in their cookbooks."[47] Foods that were the basis of Indigenous cuisines were seen as inferior. Writing in in the midst of a famine in 1786, José Antonio Alzate betrayed the European bias toward wheat bread, whereas tortillas, "which constitute the principal staple of the poor cannot provide such as perfect nutrition as leavened bread."[48] Indeed, he argued that "it should not be eaten too much since one cannot eat it two days in a row without experiencing indigestion and it sitting heavily in the stomach."[49] These elites would only reluctantly begin to eat the foods of Mesoamerica beginning in the eighteenth century and not fully adopt this practice until the end of the nineteenth century. However, they consciously disassociated the food that they were adopting from the Indigenous population.

Capitalism, the Commodification of Food, and Nutrition Inequality

The late eighteenth and nineteenth centuries were periods of intensive capitalist expansion throughout Mexico. Economic growth was spurred by the shifts in the world economy and Mexico's increasing integration into the global market. By the eighteenth century, Mexico developed important regional economies and increasingly supplied the world economy with agricultural products in addition to silver. During the dictatorship of Porfirio Díaz (1876–1911), capitalist expansion extended to numerous areas that had hitherto been on the fringe of Mexican economy and began to transform the lives of campesinos and workers in those regions. Scholars often refer to this period in Latin American history as the second conquest, characterized by usurpation of lands, forced dislocation of communities, militarization, market integration, and loss of autonomy in many regions.

The transformations in Mexico that came with the ongoing colonization of lands, foods, and ways of life continued to impact generations of Indigenous peoples and poor mestizos. Studies of the late colonial period demonstrate the toll that colonization and shifting dietary patterns had. Throughout the eighteenth century, the domestic market favored wheat and cattle, making maize increasingly inaccessible to urban poor and campesinos. The price of maize steadily increased, indicating a growing scarcity.[50] As markets integrated smaller producers, campesinos were driven out. Grains flowed to the cities while maize prices became highly volatile, leaving campesinos to starve during periods of shortages.[51] The greater integration of agricultural markets favored urban dwellers who had greater access to food grains, especially during periods of scarcity.

Economic growth and market integration in the late colonial period resulted in increased inequality. This was especially prevalent during periods of food scarcity, exacerbating chronic malnutrition and significantly impacting health, nutrition, and living standards. Periodic food shortages reached crisis-level proportions on several occasions, and in 1785–86 a famine known as the "Year of Hunger" plagued Mexico's productive agricultural regions, causing the death of tens of thousands of people.[52] In his study of heights of soldiers during the period, Amílcar Challú finds that the height of literate soldiers declined in the first half of the eighteenth century and then stagnated for the next several decades, for an overall reduction of two centimeters. However, during the same period, the heights of illiterate soldiers declined four centimeters. Challú's analysis demonstrates that there was a widening gap between health and nutrition during the late eighteenth and early nineteenth centuries that especially affected poor and Indigenous peoples.[53]

Growing inequality led to the loss of community autonomy in areas of transformation and fostered the mobilization of communities, spurring Mexico's struggle for independence. Scholars have demonstrated how the increased usurpation of community lands pushed many communities to the margins as they lost their autonomy. Their lives became subject to labor exploitation and the whims of the market. The insurrection against Spanish rule that emerged in the Bajío, north of Mexico City, was directly connected to economic growth and inequality and precipitated by famine and drought in the region (1808–1810); however, as the early independence's armies got closer to Mexico City, where famine and drought were not as severe, fewer joined the rebel ranks and the conservative forces tied to Spanish empire held on to power.[54]

The wars for independence led to sharp declines in silver production and commercial agriculture in much of central Mexico, thus opening the way for increased production of maize. Autonomy was restored in many communities. According to John Tutino, "[W]hile commercial cultivators failed, Mexicans were well nourished from 1820–1850. Maize became available and affordable as estate production declined and family cultivation flourished. Tenant families ate first and marketed small surpluses in the Bajío. In the heartland, villagers pressed estates to pay more and to lease land. Estate owners lamented village and tenant autonomies."[55] On haciendas in Zacatecas and San Luis Potosí, families that were full-time employees were paid in food rations of maize that covered about 75 percent of the family's calories and were supplemented with beans, rice, and meat, which provided adequate nutrition. Temporary laborers, however, had a more precarious diet, subject to the availability of labor.[56] Nevertheless, families were able to supplement their diets with a rich diversity of highly nutritious foods that people consumed in the area, including agaves, cactuses, *flor de izote*, and many types of insects that, one historian optimistically concluded, made hunger relatively unknown for working people in the region.[57]

The economic downturn of the late eighteenth century, the wars for independence, and the breakdown of the central government led to a fragmented Mexico vulnerable to foreign intervention and regional caudillo rule for the first half of the nineteenth century. While the sharp increase in wealth inequality seemed to have alleviated, especially since market integration and capitalist growth faltered during the first few decades of the nineteenth century, evidence points to a decline in GDP per capita and the persistence of inequality.[58] While it may be true that food was available for many in different regions of the countryside, diets varied widely by class and region. In urban areas, growing wealth inequality exacerbated food inequality. Commentators at the turn of the nineteenth century pointed out the frequency and quantity that the elite of Mexico City ate since it was not uncommon for people to eat different meals four or five times a day. According to a 1791 report commissioned by the viceroy, "In Madrid they don't make as many meals as they do in the colony where they drink one or two chocolates, they breakfast copiously, they have the main meal, they again drink chocolate, have a snack, and then eat dinner . . . which was very different from in Madrid where there wasn't such gluttony."[59] On the contrary, travelers reported Mexico City's poor "eat tortillas and drink atole as their regular breakfast and dinner." The scholarly priest José Antonio Alzate, in his report to the viceroy, commented that "there is not a more common sight than to see numerous Indians satisfy their hunger with some tortillas, a little salt, and chile."[60]

Porfirio Díaz's thirty-five-year-long dictatorship (1876–1911), at a time of the expansion of the world economy, led to the transformation of Mexico. In a matter of three decades, Díaz militarized the countryside, deposed some regional leaders and forged alliances with others, courted foreign investors, and encouraged elites to ally with foreign business interests to propel a massive capitalist development strategy. This led to the

construction of a national railway system, built by U.S. capital, that connected Mexico to markets in the United States. Díaz's strategy fostered
capitalist development throughout Mexico through the opening of new
mines, the launching of the oil industry, the expansion of export agriculture, and the development of nascent industries. In the process, Mexico's
regions were integrated into a national market as Mexico became further integrated into the world market.[61] U.S. capitalists in alliance with
Mexico's political leaders played a leading role in the transformation of
Mexico.[62] By 1910, foreigners held some 35 percent of all Mexican surface
area and more than 60 percent of the nation's borderlands and coastlines.
Overall, fifteen thousand U.S. landowners controlled approximately 27
percent of the nation's land.[63]

Export capitalist growth had a devastating impact on Indigenous and
campesino populations in many regions of Mexico. The expansion of the
railroads opened the way for new lands to be incorporated into the national and international markets. As the railroad was being planned, land
speculators sold lands held by Indigenous and campesino communities,
alienating them from their traditional lands. Regional riots and popular
rebellions by affected communities were met with violence and increased
militarization.[64] In a brief time, regions shifted away from producing for
the domestic market to producing crops, such as cotton, sugar, hene-
quen, and coffee, for an expanding world market.

Haciendas grew and took advantage of economies of scale to increase
production for export. In the state of Morelos, a once diverse system of
landholding and agriculture production became a region controlled by
large sugar haciendas within two decades. Communities saw their historic lands usurped, and former landowners had little option but to work
as seasonal laborers on the new plantations. Nearly two dozen villages
that were on the map of Morelos in 1870 were swallowed up by haciendas
and no longer appeared on the map by 1910. Landholding became deeply
polarized as eighteen land-owning families came to control the majority
of the state's territory. By 1910, only 13 percent of Morelos lands were
communal pueblo lands and most of these were in mountainous areas.[65]

With the upheaval in the Mexican countryside and the expansion of
export agricultural production, basic food production maintained its per
capita levels throughout the Porfiriato.[66] The increase in production of
basic staples—maize, beans, rice, chile, etcetera—seems to have been a

result of sharecropping systems that enabled producers to feed themselves while providing hacienda owners with a significant share of their production in return for use of the land. Given the low profit rate of maize, since it was not a money maker for haciendas, this provided haciendas an important way of meeting internal production needs while at the same using better lands to produce more profitable crops.[67]

Increased maize output and economic growth, however, does not mean that working Mexicans lived or ate better. On the contrary, this violent primitive accumulation strategy alienated thousands of villages from their community lands and forced hundreds of thousands of rural Mexicans to sell their labor power with little else to fall back on. Industrial development exacerbated inequality, reducing wages and dislocating major segments of the artisanal classes. The historian Moramay López Alonso found that the height of Mexico's working-class laborers declined precipitously during the Porfiriato and then stagnated during the first decades of the twentieth century. This correlated with adverse impacts that economic growth of the Porfiriato had on the diet and living standards of working Mexicans.[68] Social and political discontent was expressed in numerous ways, most dramatically through organized rebellion, leading one scholar to conclude, "[I]t appears that Mexico's rural people asserted their rights and defended their interests with unparalleled combativeness in the two centuries from 1700 to 1900."[69]

Accompanying the assault on Indigenous lands and labor was a more concentrated cultural assault on Indigenous diets and foodways. While elite attitudes of cultural superiority existed since the conquest, the rise of social Darwinism and eugenics in the late nineteenth century provided the justification for racist conclusions of Indigenous inferiority. The most well-known progenitor of this view was the Porfirian senator and intellectual Francisco Bulnes. Bulnes's 1899 study correlates the protein content of maize, wheat, and rice with the strengths and longevity of civilizations. Bulnes argued that the Indigenous diet was an obstacle to national progress: "Maize has been the eternal pacifier of America's Indigenous races and the foundation of their refusal to become civilized."[70] Thus, as one historian has concluded, "for Bulnes, racial superiority was a question of diet."[71]

Bulnes was not alone in connecting traditional diets to Mexican poverty and so-called backwardness. In general, Mexican intellectuals and policymakers saw Indigenous bodies as inferior and their brains less developed than mestizos owing to their perceived inferior diets based on beans, corn, and chile.[72] In his 1888 study of hygiene in Puebla, Dr. Samuel Morales Pereira focused on popular eating habits and attributed what he characterized as the heavy consumption of maize and tortillas as part of Mexico's poor nutrition.[73] Mexican criminologists also widely underscored a false connection between poor diet and eating traditional Indigenous foods with racial inferiority and crime.[74]

The conclusions made by Mexican elites and policymakers about diet and racial inferiority were echoes of controlling ideologies developed in Europe and by U.S. travel writers routinely mischaracterizing Indigenous and working-class diets. One writer, who gushed about "the luxurious life at a gold mine" operated by U.S. capitalists, reflected the racist and anti-Indigenous views of elites:

> It is pitiful to think of such wonderful land remaining in the hands of the shiftless Indians. In a country where nearly every description of fruit cereal and vegetable can be raised, they are content to live on tortillas and beans; their little farms are crudely cultivated; they reap one large crop of Indian corn and then let the ground lie idle for the rest of the year. . . . Give him enough tortillas and beans, a little sugar, coffee and tobacco, his wants are satisfied, and he cares not a jot about the world and its progress . . . he is undoubtedly an obstacle to progress and to the best interests of his lovely land.[75]

Another prominent contemporary U.S. visitor to Mexico, Wallace Thompson, wrote of the need to understand this "grievously sick nation." In a chapter on Mexican foods, he described at length the basis of the diet, which, although he recognized its nutritious value, his cultural chauvinism led him to conclude was "rather strange and unpalatable," with spicy chile that caused digestive problems and contributed to malnourishment.[76] Through altering foodways and other cultural habits, social Darwinists and eugenicists argued that Indigenous people could become productive workers.[77] Thompson and other travel writers became influential interpreters of Mexican culture and society and their books would become widely consulted by U.S. educators and policymakers working with Mexican immigrants in the first half of the twentieth century.[78] Their ethnocentric perspectives on Mexican communities and diets would then be perpetuated by Americanization teachers who continued to wage war on Mexican foodways and cultures in the United States.[79]

The Mexican government took steps to change the diets of Indigenous people and the working classes. Policymakers focused their reforms on the growing number of public institutions that were created and expanded during the Porfiriato, such as prisons, state hospitals, and asylums. Wheat bread and French rolls (*bolillos*) began to be served in prisons and hospitals. In the kitchens of the growing Porfirian prison system, bakers were trained to meet the shifting food needs of the prison.[80] However, given the relative weakness of the state, there were few avenues to penetrate the homes and traditions of most Mexicans. Nevertheless, pseudoscience and these early policy implementations would constitute a crucial step in the war against the millennial diets and foodways created by Indigenous men and women.

The Porfirian elite looked to France for its cultural and culinary cues. The influence of French cooking pervaded most of Mexico City's elite restaurants. One U.S. traveler noted, "Of the few restaurants where the cooking can be relied upon, the best are the Café de Paris, the Café de la Paix, Sylvain's and the Café Chapultepec. In all these the cooks are French, and one can order a dish with a quiet mind and the certainty that it will be eatable."[81] Mexico City's finest restaurants sought out French chefs and their popularity led several to open their own restaurants.[82] Porfirian cookbooks were filled with recipes that were adapted from French cookbooks. Salvador Novo noted that the publication of *Nuevo cocinero mexicano en forma de diccionario* in 1883 demonstrates "just how far, in fifty years, French cooking has taken over Mexican homes."[83]

The popularity of French culinary traditions coupled with the pseudoscientific devaluing of Indigenous foods and the rise of Mexican nationalism led to elite adaptations of Mexican foods. These dishes were published in new cookbooks aimed at elite households and women overseeing meals. José Luis Juárez López and Jeffrey Pilcher have both written about the numerous journals and publications documenting this modernized cuisine throughout the second half of the nineteenth and early twentieth centuries and how they contributed to the forging of a bourgeois national cuisine.

Industrialization and Creating a National Food System

The transformation of Mexico during the Porfiriato led to the growth of industrialization in key sectors of the economy. As the national infrastructure of railroads developed and the commodification of lands and labor expanded throughout the country, a national market slowly began to emerge. Family-owned and operated companies producing for local and regional markets began to get access to financing that allowed them to employ technological innovations to expand into large, capital-intensive, vertically integrated firms producing for a national market. This happened in several industries, including beer, cement, steel, textiles, paper, explosives, and glass production industries, which led to the displacement of small, local, and regional producers without access to capital.[84] While the development of a national market for industrialized food products was still decades away, several sectors of the food industry, such as meat-packing, bakeries, and public markets, were able to obtain the required capital to transform the industry.

In Mexico City's meat industry and butcher shops during the later Porfiriato, a Mexican *Jungle*, to quote the title of Upton Sinclair's popular 1906 novel, was unfolding. The cattle boom of the late nineteenth century coupled with railroad construction and economic growth led to an increased consumption of beef, pork, and other meats. Reformers sought to minimize the number of injuries and deaths in butcher shops and overhaul Mexico City's meat distribution system.[85] In one of the first efforts, the politically powerful Terrazas-Creel family, with their hundreds of thousands of heads of cattle and the packing plants they controlled in the meat industry in Chihuahua, was granted the right to build and operate a modern slaughterhouse in Mexico City. With Chicago and Paris as models, foreign producers led by North American Beef Producers from Chicago also entered the market hoping to construct a national network of packing houses connected through the railroads, as had been done in the United States. However, these efforts were doomed. As food historian Jeffrey Pilcher demonstrates, "Proletarian slaughterhouse workers, petty bourgeois retailers, and wealthy livestock merchants forged a cross-class alliance that also counted on tacit support of consumers."[86] Consumer tastes and small butcher shops rebelled, demanding that modern innovations be adapted to fit the particularities of Mexico's market. This led to the expansion of small butcher shops and the growing demand for meat was met by the hiring of more workers in existing shops and by pressuring workers to produce more with little pay.[87]

Beginning with the French invasion of Mexico in 1862 and the rule by Maximilian, Austrian and French pastry chefs were part of the invading forces and quickly came to acquire most of Mexico City's downtown bakeries. These pastry chefs introduced various European-style breads and pastries, including individual-sized rolls such as bolillos.[88] Over the next several years, Spanish immigrants, mainly from the Basque region, arrived in Mexico and by the 1890s came to own most of the city's bakeries.[89]

Bakery workers faced grueling labor conditions and were poorly paid. Historian Robert Weis demonstrates that as the number of bakeries increased and the demand for bread grew, more workers were crammed into bakeries that were in desperate need of repair. The heat of the ovens and petroleum lamps made these overcrowded conditions even more difficult to work in. Workers frequently suffered burns from the ovens and from spilling the burning petroleum used to light the shop. The pressure of meeting demand often led to fights among workers and disputes between workers and owners. It was not uncommon for owners to lock workers in the backroom of bakeries until the shift was over, forcing workers to take their breaks and relieve themselves in the hot and crowded workshops. It was in these conditions that workers labored through the night to meet the growing demand for bread.[90]

Mexico City's public markets were overhauled during the Porfiriato to increase their efficiency and more effectively regulate the distribution of Mexico City's food supply. Through building and refurbishing market halls in the city's historic market areas, the Mexico City council hoped to accommodate more vendors in public markets. Porfirian officials hoped that this would limit the street vending, attract wealthier merchants to rent spaces, and make Mexico City's streets safer for the Porfirian elite. By containing market sales to the market halls, officials sought to better regulate sales, increase government revenue, and create a more modern and hygienic public market that would exude "culture and civilization." In addition to increasing market efficiency, historian Ingrid Bleynat argued that "markets and vendors became the target of a cultural crusade to reshape collective and individual public behaviors."[91] Despite these efforts at modernization, officials were unable to fully contain and control vendors.

Indigenous communities and working-class Mexicans resisted the prolonged assault on their ways of life that began during the colonial period and accelerated during the long nineteenth century. This resistance took multiple forms. In both the city and the countryside, workers and communities sought to maintain their autonomy and improve their living and working conditions. Despite the ongoing land grabbing by elites and the expansion of haciendas, the milpa was maintained even if it was relegated to poor and marginalized lands. The hardy nature of maize enabled it to grow in areas where few other products could. Communities adjusted their diets to eat what was available to them and made good use of what different ecosystems provided, such as wild eatable plants. While Europeans and elite Mexicans disparaged these foods, the economic and cultural system that they imposed on Mexico was directly responsible for the living conditions of rural and urban working populations.

Among the combination of factors that led to the popular uprising in 1910 was one of struggle for control over communities and lives and the polarizing economic system. Emiliano Zapata's uprising under the banner of *"tierra y libertad"* (land and liberty) best exemplifies this movement as communities argued that freedom could only be won with restoration of community lands. In other regions, there were popular demands for land reform—while these movements varied based on the local conditions, campesinos and rural workers demanded access to these lands.

The onset of colonialism and capitalist expansion radically altered the diverse food system and diets of the Indigenous peoples of the region now known as Mexico. Colonialism brought new racial, class, gender, and knowledge hierarchies. Throughout the nineteenth century, the second conquest of the Mexican countryside and its deeper integration into the world market created a new food regime that was increasingly dominated by mestizo capitalists seeking to profit while appropriating Indigenous women and men's labor and knowledge systems for their own gain.

CHAPTER 2

"A BETTER DIET FOR OUR PEOPLE"

The Persistence of Inequality in the Postrevolutionary Food System

*The improvement of the nutritive elements contained in the seed would lead to
a better diet for our people, a desirable objective from all points of view, because
an individual's ability for physical labor, as well as for intellectual development,
are so much better when the diet is better. It is evident that the selection of the
richest seed will result in the improvement of our population.*
—ANTONIO RIVAS TAGLE, DIRECTOR OF THE CAMPAÑA EN PRO DEL
MAÍZ AND AUTHOR OF *EL CULTIVO RACIONAL DEL MAÍZ* (1929)

For agricultural engineer Antonio Rivas Tagle, the answer to creating
a better diet for Mexicans in the twentieth century was rooted in the
transformation of campesino farming techniques.[1] Campesino farming
practices, he and other reformers argued, were outmoded and needed
the help of rational scientific practices. Rivas Tagle's Campaña en Pro del
Maíz (Campaign in Favor of Maize), established by Mexico's Secretary
of Agriculture and Development, aimed to improve maize cultivation in
order to improve the nutrition and therefore the productivity of working classes. Rivas Tagle's views represented the arguments of numerous
agronomists, who less than two decades after Emiliano Zapata's cry for
land and liberty argued that it was only science that could improve the
nutrition of Mexicans. However, this science was inflected with "Porfirian prejudices about the impact of climate, diet and race [that] still
influenced the agrónomos, as did their urban apathy towards peasants,"
as the historian Joseph Cotter has argued.[2]

This chapter examines how Mexico's food system was organized
throughout the twentieth century, emphasizing the postrevolutionary

state's role in structuring the feeding of Mexico. Despite the popular uprising of campesinos and campesinas during the first decades of the twentieth century, postrevolutionary governments, with a few notable exceptions, opted to accelerate their control over the countryside and facilitate capitalist expansion. Revolutionary policymakers reinforced paternalistic beliefs that local communities, campesino farmers, and campesina cooks were unable to feed the nation and contribute to the creation of a modern industrial country. They used state intervention-ist policies to create a capitalist market rooted in gendered, class, and raced-based nationalist and mestizaje ideologies that devalued Indige-nous and working-class knowledges. Policymakers, like Rivas Tagle, ar-gued that the state intervention could transform working-class Mexicans into modern efficient producers and good consumers. The first part of this chapter examines the popular uprising of the Mexican Revolution and the ways that revolutionary elites consolidated their control in the 1920s and 1930s by employing coercion, manipulation, consent, and co-optation of the campesinos through land reform policies, rural reforms, and the creation of new institutions. These new institutions, by the late 1930s and 1940s, were shifted away from redistributive policies and toward subsidizing private producers, with the support of the United States and the Rockefeller Foundation, to increase agricultural yield and output to provide inexpensive food for Mexico's growing cities. As peas-ants resisted, successive government-employed methods of violence and control coupled with reformist policies, which often crushed organizing attempts while instituting reforms that alleviated the worst effects of poverty, bolstered the power of the state. At the same time, foreign cap-ital entered Mexico in key sectors of food processing, challenged private capital, and accelerated the unequal access to nutritious foods, healthy diets, and public health.

From Land and Liberty to Legibility, Institutionalization, and Hegemony

With the slogan of land and liberty, Emiliano Zapata and his revolution-ary forces rose up in the state of Morelos to take back the lands that had been stolen from campesinos by capitalists and colonizers. Throughout Mexico, campesinos and workers heeded the call of Zapata and other revolutionary leaders to confront capitalist usurpation of their lands and labor and to regain control and autonomy over their lives. The bloody battles that ensued led to the death and migration of millions of Mexicans.

Death and destruction throughout Mexico had a profound impact on the production and distribution of foods. Revolutionary and government forces routinely seized lands and food stocks to feed their troops. Military leaders captured railroad cars and trains came to a grinding halt, hampering distribution of foodstuff. During the most intense periods of revolutionary upheaval, 1913–1915, crop harvests plummeted. The biggest decline came in 1914, according to official data, when maize production dropped by almost 70 percent and wheat by 144 percent.[3] As a result of production shortages, crop hording, and speculation, prices skyrocketed throughout the nation. In Mexico City, a region that was not particularly impacted by fighting, maize prices increased by 88 percent between 1910 and 1918, while bean and bread prices jumped by nearly 200 percent, and rice by 247 percent.[4] Between July 1914 and July 1915, the prices of basic foodstuff increased fifteen-fold.[5] Shortages and price surges occurred through Mexico during the 1914–1917 period, resulting in widespread grain speculation and food riots. In the state of Puebla, maize prices rose 500 percent between 1910 and 1920.[6] In San José de Gracia, Michoacán, "a severe drought began in 1915 and lasted until 1917. For three years running the corn crop was lost. The bones of cattle bleached in the fields." Those who had money had to travel more than three hundred kilometers to purchase grain at "fifteen times what corn had cost in 1910." Infant mortality skyrocketed and many families were forced to leave the region. These years of scarcity had an enduring impact on collective memory.[7]

Local governments and military and revolutionary leaders used a variety of methods to ameliorate the situation, but these were largely ineffective. Women, as they always have, played a crucial role in feeding communities and fighters during battle and amid massive food shortages. Whether it was procuring foods and cooking for men as soldaderas or feeding their families, women had to be inventive in acquiring scarce foodstuff, when at all possible. This often meant sacrificing their own nourishment for those they cooked and cared for. People ate what they could find during the most severe famines of the revolutionary period.

During this scarcity, epidemic diseases spread through many regions, killing tens of thousands.[8]

As new and old elites reconquered areas and imposed order toward the end of the decade, they worked to construct a more integrated nation-state. To do so, ruling elites killed and neutralized the more radical revolutionary elements, including Emiliano Zapata in 1919 and Pancho Villa in 1923, and implemented reforms to nominally address the issues raised by campesinos and workers. Revolutionary food shortages and famine remained deeply imbedded in popular memory, prompting revolutionary governments to constantly debate how best to spur production and ensure adequate distribution of basic foodstuff. For governing elites, however, this meant finding ways to balance the popular will of campesinos who had fought for "tierra y libertad" with their imperative of building an integrated, hegemonic, capitalist nation-state.

Mexico's 1917 Constitution set the basis for both addressing campesino and working-class demands and creating an integrated national market. Article 27 called for state guardianship over Mexico's lands and natural resources and gave the state the ability to seize and distribute land based on national priorities and the public good, laying the basis for an agrarian reform. Article 28 of the constitution prohibited monopolies and set the basis for government intervention in the economy to protect consumers. According to Article 28, "the law will severely punish, and authorities will prosecute with efficacy all concentration or hording of basic foodstuffs in the hands of one or a few who have as their objectives the increase of prices."[9] Article 123 laid the basis for labor reform, including the right to organize and the setting of minimum wages.

The full implementation of these articles, however, did not come immediately. Instead, enabling legislation was timed to increase the government's ability to integrate the revolutionary nation-state under its control. This required that government officials carry out a detailed mapping of the country to make the various regions of Mexico legible to state builders. Only by doing so would they be better able to control them as they centralized power in Mexico City.[10] Under the guise of revolutionary nationalism, this process was the continuation of the colonial project started four hundred years earlier. Now, however, with tools of modern social science and political and economic urgency, broader swaths of Mexico would be studied and incorporated in the nation based on the

designs of Mexico's ruling party.[11] The discourse centered around integrating diverse regions into the nation-state; creating a national market
was often couched in terms of nationalism, modernity, and social justice.
Through assimilating rural regions, campesinos, and Indigenous peoples,
government officials argued that they could protect peasants from rapacious landowners, speculators, and caciques.[12]

In the 1920s, under the leadership of José Vasconcelos, the Secretary
of Public Education (SEP) was charged with the task of building a national education system throughout Mexico. During this decade federal
educational expenditures jumped from 1.3 of a percent of actual federal
expenditures in 1920 to nearly 9 percent in 1922, and by the end of the
decade it accounted for 10 percent.[13] A major venture of the SEP was
the creation of rural schools throughout the nation to educate Mexico's
campesinos into the ways of modernity and national identity. Through
the rural schools, the state expanded its reach into regions that had hitherto little contact with the broader nation. Rural schoolteachers became
missionaries who taught campesinos basic education skills, hygiene, and
their rights in postrevolutionary Mexico, and helped forge national identity often on the terms of local communities.[14] As some of the few government officials with ties to the central government, teachers were often
charged with collecting data on the communities in which they worked.

During this same period, Mexican policymakers began conducting
censuses and organizing information about the nation's resources, lands,
food production capability, weight and price system, labor systems, regional power dynamics, and customs.[15] Jesús Rulfo, an extension agent
with the agricultural ministry, wrote in 1922, "Although it appears to be
a lie, our country is currently unknown; there are regions that remain
completely forgotten, due either to their distance or to communications
difficulties."[16] The government's Department of National Statistics significantly expanded the number of personnel, from 45 employees in 1921
to 453 in 1929. Graduates of the National School of Agriculture were
critical to the collection of basic information on the Mexican countryside. During the Censo Agrícultura y Ganadero de 1930, the government
sent out an army of employees into the countryside to collect data on
rural Mexico. Many of the state agents felt that they were "'travelers' in
a strange land." They were seen as outsiders by campesinos and viewed
with suspicion. Campesinos often resisted their efforts and told them lies

out of fear, as one agent wrote in his thesis for the National Agricultural School: "statistics collection aimed to find out what each person possessed in order to determine his corresponding taxes."[17] The cultural gulf between government employees and campesinos was often enormous and led them to blame campesinos for not being able to "pay attention for long, and the many ideas presented in a lecture go by rapidly and leave no trace in his mind."[18] The resistant attitudes of peasants were attributed to their "cultural level" and high percentage of illiteracy, which made government propaganda efforts, written or in films, ineffective. Officials complained that the "psychology of the rural population is naturally distrustful, and they provide inaccurate data or fail to show up to scheduled meetings."[19] Even as they reinforced stereotypes of campesinos, the invading force of agronomists collected information that led to the creation of the first map in the nation's history that listed every state and municipality.[20]

Census agents surveyed the regional weights and measures of basic grains throughout the countryside. As weights and measures emerged from community histories over the course of centuries, policymakers wanted to identify these different units to impose a national standard unit of weights and measurement. The census documented at least 217 different ways of measuring the weight of maize with names and units varying widely from community to community. For example, a *fanega* in one region of Zacatecas was the equivalent of seventy kilograms, whereas in another region it was sixty-five kilograms. Other units of measurements in Zacatecas included the *bulto* (65 or 70 kg), *carga* (130 kg), and *costal* (30 kg). States with larger Indigenous populations, and therefore longer histories in the region, had significantly more names for units of measurements. Oaxaca had at least thirty-nine different weight measures for maize, Veracruz had thirty-one, and Chiapas had at least twenty-three.[21] In the eyes of the state, as described by agronomists, the countryside was disorganized, and it needed to be studied so that it could be changed to forge a national market within an integrated nation-state.[22]

The expansion of the technocratic administrative state also extended to the growth of agricultural extension programs to teach campesinos new farming, marketing, and pricing techniques. Agronomists refused to acknowledge the complex systems that Indigenous communities had with respect to seed and seed selection. Proposals to the Banco

Nacional de Crédito Agrícola to study campesino agricultural systems were repeatedly denied; campesinos were taught scientific seed selection methods and urged to use imported seeds instead of using their traditional knowledges and methods. As one agronomist argued, "We use seeds that, without exaggeration, they would not even use to feed pigs in other countries."[23] In his 1937 book, *El cultivo del maíz*, dedicated to Mexico's ejidatarios, agricultural engineer Miguel Schultz exhorted campesinos to "select their maize seeds!" and provided a detailed listing of the most important commercial varieties, the majority of which were U.S. varieties.[24] The faith that agronomists had in their expertise served to reinforce racialized knowledge hierarchies that saw Indigenous and campesino methods as obsolete at best.

The struggle for land and liberty that initially led to popular land seizures resulted in agrarian reform programs connected to the national elite's goals of state building and market integration. Beginning in the 1920s, land reform policies were slowly initiated but it was not until the administration of Lázaro Cárdenas that a massive distribution of lands went into effect. Cárdenas hoped to distribute land in a way that did not disrupt agricultural production, allowed for producers to take advantage of economies of scale, and reflected communitarian principles in Indigenous and campesino communities. This translated into distributing lands as grants to communities in the form of ejidos, giving community members usufructuary rights but not allowing for the sale, renting, or mortgaging of the land. Given the long history of land grabbing and community dislocation and exploitation, especially in the recent period of the Porfiriato, Cardenistas felt that this structure could help strengthen communities, supply food for the nation, and make the nation self-sufficient in basic grains. Between 1930 and 1940, ejido lands increased from 13.4 percent of total cropland to 47.4 percent in 1940, and ejidatarios came to comprise half of total agricultural producers.[25] Throughout Cárdenas's presidency, 18.8 million hectares were distributed to approximately 800,000 Mexicans.

Cárdenas also used the land reform program to encourage workers and campesinos to organize offsetting the power of rural caciques, large landowners, and regional merchants who held virtual monopolies on the purchase of campesino harvests. For Cárdenas, the power of the state was needed to free campesinos from the tyranny of regional caciques who exploited campesinos through labor and commercial practices and who then manipulated the grain markets to sell at high prices to consumers. In his inaugural speech in November 1934, Cárdenas proclaimed, "It is fundamental to see the economic problem in its entirety and to observe the connections that link each of its parts with the whole. Only the State has the general interest, and because of this, only it has the unified vision. State intervention has to be greater, more frequent, and deeper."[26] This intervention would further tie local producers to the state to foster national unity and break the control of local caciques.

Public officials and scholars were often commissioned by state governors to conduct detailed economic and social studies of their states. While government censuses and statistics provided a general picture, more detailed field research was essential to understanding the complexity and diversity of Mexico's regions. Moisés de la Peña, an economist often contracted throughout the 1940s, argued there was a great "need for Mexico to know itself: to discover how it is, to identify and underscore its problems, and to study them based on what was actually occurring in order to become familiar with what can be done, so that it is possible to adopt measures that can help overcome the obstacles that retard national development in both the social and economic realm."[27] De la Peña was hired to produce detailed studies with his team of researchers that included economists, ethnologists, geographers, and geologists. Often on horseback, de la Peña's team scoured the regions of the vast and diverse states of Baja California, Campeche, Chihuahua, Chiapas, Guerrero, Oaxaca, Veracruz, and Zacatecas and wrote detailed and often multivolume reports on each state and territory.

While campesinos in many regions had access to land, following the land reform program, the state established other institutional mechanisms to construct campesino identity, provide technical support, credit, and marketing services to both aid producers and ensure a steady flow of food to the growing urban areas. The creation of a national campesino confederation helped establish the institutional framework for campesino integration and other mechanisms of state control throughout the Mexican countryside.[28] The government had communities create ejido committees that oversaw the governance and operation of the ejidos and served as officials that interacted with the new institutions created to serve the ejidos, including the Banco Nacional de Crédito Ejidal (BNCE) in 1936, Almacenes de Depósito Nacional (ANDSA), and the marketing agency through its various name changes: Comité Regulador del Mercado de Trigo (CRMT) in 1937 and Comité Regulador del Mercado de las Subsistencias (CRMS) in 1938.[29] In the process of land reform, Mexico's agricultural sector became increasingly centralized.

It was under Cárdenas, then, that efforts to create a centralized food system were initiated. Creation of the CRMT and CRMS was meant to purchase basic grains (wheat, maize, beans, and rice) from small producers and ejidatarios at fixed prices so that campesinos would be free from the exploitative grip of speculators. While small producers were the agency's initial target, spiraling food prices during the late 1930s and throughout World War II helped the government focus more on alleviating food prices for urban consumers and less on aiding small producers. Panic purchasing and food crises in the cities led to riots and organized labor began to demand higher wages to offset declining purchasing power. Women lined up early each morning to buy staples, only to see stores run out of food. It was during this period that the State Food Agency opened stores in working-class neighborhoods, often in conjunction with the union Confederación de Trabajadores de México (CTM) to provide low-cost staples as a hedge against inflation. Popular mobilizations and union advocacy led to greater intervention in the market, importation of food from the United States, and the opening of more stores. By 1944, there were nearly four hundred stores throughout Mexican cities that sold basic foods at approximately 10–25 percent of the price of the same goods at private markets. Price controls were implemented on all basic foods and a corps of inspectors was hired to enforce prices in both private and public markets.[30]

Government agencies had begun to systematically track price and production information during the Mexican Revolution. Cognizant of the food shortages and food riots in many regions in 1913–1915, municipal staff were asked to collect data on a weekly basis on twenty-five basic items that officials determined were indispensable to working-class households; about half of the price information collected was for food items.[31] These studies were essential in the construction of a national market. The Secretaría de Industria, Comercio y Trabajo began to collect price data on the Cost of Living for Workers (Costo de la Vida Obrera) in different municipios in the late 1910s and early 1920s. In doing so, officials calculated the number of calories workers should be eating, broken down by the type of occupation.[32] Real wage studies also begin to develop during these years to track wages during the period of rapid inflation in the late 1930s and 1940s.[33] By studying the situation of production, distribution, and prices, the government hoped it could head off crises. In 1935, the Secretary of the National Economy explained, "The action of the government had to be directed in some cases to remedy certain dangerous situations, such as the case of maize, indispensable cereal for the feeding of the people, and that, because of special circumstances had been being exported with the danger of excessively increasing its price." The government saw the need to keep a firm handle on production, prices, sales, and trade "to ensure that workers receive the most out of their labor and that merchants do not resort to unfair competition that drives up prices."[34] In 1933, the Secretaría de Agricultura y Fomento started to publish a monthly bulletin detailing crop production data and studies of specific crops, and in 1938 the Secretaría de Economía began publishing a monthly statistical magazine.[35]

Government agencies made this data more widely available in the late 1920s and 1930s through the publication of annual statistical yearbooks and reports. As Mexico City grew throughout the first half of the twentieth century, officials continuously worried about the provisioning of the city. In one of the first major studies on consumer prices and government regulation efforts, Guillermo Martínez Domínguez, a former director of the Comisión de Vigilancia de Abastecimieno del D.F., sounded the alarm of potential disaster:

> This monster with three million stomachs depends, then, for a large part of its food, on the transport of the daily supply of products. It lives day by day. It does not have reserves or stocks of food to deal with contingencies caused by any failure in the general system of production and distribution of merchandise.[36]

He called for more systematic and holistic government intervention that focused on satisfying the needs of the people and not only focusing on violations of laws and petty infractions.

Martínez Domínguez explained the results of a study completed in Mexico City based on surveys of 289,834 workers that demonstrated that most did not earn enough to meet their basic needs. Based on an average of 5 household members and 2,500 calories per person, Martínez Domínguez broke down the basic caloric intake of each food, calculated its cost per person, and then compared it to average salaries. He found that the average daily cost of basic foods in 1948 in Mexico City was 18.33 pesos—way above the average wage of a family of five, which fluctuated between 5.50 and 11.95 pesos a day. He concluded, "The result inevitably means that their nutrition is deficient and insufficient in quality and quantity . . . and they live in a state of permanent deficiency."[37] In fact, his calculations and conclusions are even more ominous when one considers that his household budgetary data did not include rent, clothing, and other household expenditures.

In a matter of three decades following the outbreak of the Mexican Revolution, the new ruling classes consolidated their power and began to construct social peace through the expansion of the state and social programs. While the social peace under Cárdenas was built through alliances with workers and campesinos, it established institutional structures that in the hands of more conservative presidents would lead to the disciplining and control of campesinos and workers to further extract wealth, keep wages and prices low to subsidize industrialization, and maintain their allegiance to the official political party (the Partido Revolucionario Institucional, PRI, after 1946).[38]

Transforming Diets, Consumers, Women, and Household Economies

As state officials sought to control the countryside and regulate what was produced and distributed, they implemented social policies to shape working-class diets and consumption. Nutritionists and anthropologists argued that poor nutrition among Mexico's campesinos and working classes was a result of individual decisions and a lack of education. Social reformers in the 1940s and 1950s "questioned the nutritional value of the working-class diet and considered it a threat to the construction of modern Mexico."[39] This supposed threat to a modern industrial nation was rooted in racialized and gendered hierarchies that were rapidly modernizing. Government officials explored ways to change and improve diets by targeting women as agents of change, without fundamentally challenging the underlying causes of poverty and malnutrition.

Postrevolutionary constructions of feminine modernity centered the role of mothers in creating a modern Mexico. Influenced by eugenics and the nutrition sciences, officials and reformers worked to stabilize the Mexican family following the disintegration of families and communities after a decade of revolutionary tumult. They encouraged heterosexual two-parent households so that men and women would work to maintain a stable household based on their gendered roles. Reformers saw the importance of focusing on women as mothers raising the next generation of citizens and as acting as stabilizing forces in the household.[40] To support mothers, government officials created a corps of female social workers, who "would serve as investigator, educator, counselor, and social engineer" and be able to make connections with poor mothers, enter their homes, and transform their practices in a seemingly caring manner.[41] In the introduction to *Libro para la madre mexicana*, a free manual written for expectant mothers at the suggestion of First Lady Sra. Aída S. de Rodriguez, the authors wrote of the moral obligation of women in raising children and the impact of motherhood on the nation:

> Through the sacrifice of an intelligent and active mother can make a weak and sickly child healthy and strong, useful to society and to her family; and there is no doubt that a robust and normal child could degenerate and become sickly and inferior through the negligence and ignorance of the mother, resulting in a both moral and economic failing for her family.[42]

Women were cast as revolutionary mothers who had the duty and privilege of raising the next generation of Mexicans and who could nourish well-disciplined citizens and productive workers.[43]

This nutritional educational approach, however, reinforced traditional elite views of Indigenous people and campesinos not having the knowledge to raise modern children. In rural schools, according to the historian Mary Kay Vaughn, the SEP in the 1920s and 1930s carried out a "campaign to transform campesina mothers into modern, market-oriented homemakers. If the school inspector had his way, women teachers would plunge through the doors of peasant homes to demand that children be inoculated against contagious disease, cured with modern medicines, fed more nutritious food, and bathed regularly."[44] Teacher education focused on the importance of nutrition and the education of women to nurture the next generation of Mexican citizens. The book *Alimenación normal del mexicano* exhorted, "As the family constitutes the main nucleus of every civilized society, housewives are responsible for solving the problems of daily nutrition for children, young people, adults, and the elderly."[45]

Social workers and visiting nurses hoped to enter the kitchens of working-class Mexicans and steer women into improving the diet and hygiene of their families. Public institutions, including schools, public health agencies, social welfare institutions, and new institutions such as public dining halls (*comedores públicos*), all aimed at improving the nutrition of working-class Mexicans by modeling what constituted healthy foods, "proper" hygiene, and table manners.[46] The historian Nichole Sanders explains that social workers went door to door in Mexico City's working-class community of Tepito to urge women to have their families go to the comedores públicos.[47] The goal, according to one social worker, was "not about heads of family spending less on food; rather, it is about allowing them to improve the quality of food their families consume while spending the same amount of money."[48] They also visited homes to provide mothers with instruction on nutrition, and according to historian Sandra Aguilar-Rodríguez, "[i]n this way, postrevolutionary governments sought to transform private family life of working-class families, with the goal of having more control, in the name of progress and modernity."[49]

Public family dining halls were established in 1941 by the Secretaría de Asistencia Pública. Officials argued that the project "constitutes a transcendental effort that will achieve the most favorable transformation of the physical health of the country's inhabitants strengthening their bodies so that they can provide the maximum amount of work and effort for themselves and for the country."[50] The menus in Mexico City's public dining halls were crafted by doctors and nutritionists. They often added the word "Mexican" to make foods seem familiar and to help shift the notion of what constituted Mexican food. Meals were accompanied by wheat bread and not tortillas since wheat bread was seen as more nutritious and the technology for mass-produced tortillas was still in its infancy.[51] Cooking lessons geared toward working-class women emphasized recipes that used "milk, sugar, eggs, meat, vegetables, and cereals, as these staples, doctors said, were missing from the average working-class diet."[52] Government officials argued that once women learned of the nutritional importance of these foods, they would use them in their daily cooking.

With funding from the Rockefeller Foundation, the Instituto Nacional de Nutrición (INN) was established in 1943 and headed by Dr. Francisco Miranda. The INN began a systematic study of Mexican diets.[53] Studies during the 1930s and 1940s continued to argue that Indigenous diets were lacking in basic nutrients. While several studies did recognize that inadequate Indigenous diets were linked to social conditions, policymakers continually emphasized artificially adding nutrients to foods and then ultimately changing Indigenous diets. Whenever possible, protein from meat and dairy products was recommended. The Instituto Indigenista Interamericano recommended adding protein-rich soybeans to maize to increase the nutritional value of Indigenous diets. Manuel Gamio, the director of the Instituto Indigenista Interamericano, argued that this was a culturally sensitive way to transform Indigenous diets:

> Inasmuch as corn dough tortillas are the basis of the indo-mestizo diet, a new dough has been prepared with a 33 per cent content of soybean. This mixture, as well as the fat released by the soybean, gave an agreeable taste to the tortilla, which was readily accepted by Indians and Mestizos, thus providing a starting point for the inclusion of soybean in other diet items.[54]

Such efforts to transform diets through adding soybeans or vitamins to traditional diets would be often repeated, but few programs were ever actually carried out.

Amid these deep-seated prejudices against Indigenous Mexican diets, contemporary empirical studies demonstrated that traditional diets were nutritious and balanced. A landmark Rockefeller Foundation–funded study of Indigenous Otomi communities in the Mezquital Valley, considered one of the nation's economically poorest regions, found that the community members spend 75 percent of their income on foodstuff. However, they maintained a diverse diet through eating "almost every conceivable edible plant" and a variety of insects.[55] The ability of communities to maintain diverse and healthy diets even in hard economic times demonstrated their knowledge of local plants and animals in the ecosystem and their understanding of nutrition. The Rockefeller Foundation scientists studied the nutritional value of local foods consumed, including Malva, a plant that grew wild and was consumed like spinach; charral, a local abundant fish; queso de tuna, made from the fruit of the prickly pear cactus; and pulque, the fermented beverage made from the maguey plant. The study concluded, "through the eating of tortillas, the drinking of pulque (the fermented unfiltered juice of the century plant), and the eating of every conceivably edible plant available, a fairly good diet is maintained."[56] The scientists were further surprised by their findings that good nutrition could be sustained without milk and other dairy products. As one scientist concluded,

> Our sense of preference or superiority and their inordinate respect for our prestige position tempts us to believe that ours is the preferred way of living. Thus we may be deluded into believing that good nourishment cannot be achieved unless milk, meat, eggs and certain designated vegetables are a part of the daily dietary.[57]

Modern prejudices even led well-meaning government officials to abandon programs that built on Indigenous diets. In her study of Mexican nutrition policy, the historian Pilar Zaueta argues, "The interpretive framework of doctors and nutritional experts was influenced by ideas about poverty developed in the social sciences, particularly the notion that poverty in Mexico was deeply rooted in stubborn self-reproducing cultural practices and psychological characteristics."[58] This model, then, reinforced the colonial hierarchy of foodstuff and nutrition even as studies revealed the nutritional importance of Indigenous foodways. The persistence of a multipronged assault on the foodways and diets of Indigenous and working-class communities did not improve nutrition or access to foods, but, coupled with high rates of urbanization, it did succeed at reducing the percentage of the population that regularly consumed tortillas as opposed to wheat bread from nearly 55 percent of the population in 1940 to approximately 31.5 percent in 1960.[59]

The Mexican "Miracle," Campesino Displacement, and Industrial Foods

Between 1940 and 1970, Mexican presidents prioritized industrialization, private sector investment, and large-scale private agriculture. This period, known as the Mexican Miracle, was characterized by high rates of economic growth often at the expense of Indigenous and campesino communities in central and southern Mexico. Building upon the corporatist state that Cárdenas institutionalized, presidents Manuel Ávila Camacho (1940–1946) and Miguel Alemán (1946–1952) tightened their grip on the political system through the Partido Revolucionario Institucional's monopolization of power. They shifted economic policies in the countryside to emphasize large-scale public works projects, such as roads and irrigation and dams, to spur private sector agriculture production and de-emphasize land reform and investment in ejidos and small producers.[60] The ejido system was increasingly used by the state to control peasant communities, deliver votes for the PRI and local politicos, and deepen the state's control in the countryside. This bifurcated agricultural system was characterized by highly capitalized large farms producing for a growing market and a poorly funded campesino-based agriculture that produced for local and regional markets. Thus, inequality was exacerbated by the push to address consumer demand and to subsidize urban consumption.[61]

The Green Revolution, funded by the Rockefeller Foundation and supported by the Mexican state, sought to bring modern scientific agricultural practices to Mexico. Mexican agricultural scientists had long been working to modernize farming practices and many welcomed the funding and support from U.S. scientists.[62] The emphasis on modern agricultural policies and "the marginalization of traditional wisdom did not start with the Rockefeller Foundation in 1943 but with the creation of the national School of Agriculture in 1854. . . . From then on peasant knowledge started to be marginalized," according to agricultural scientist Efraím Hernández Xolocotzi.[63] Hernández Xolocotzi was rare among the Rockefeller-supported scientists as he "developed a profound respect for traditional subsistence agriculture—so much that he considered campesinos as sources of agronomic knowledge."[64] While many recognized the merits of campesino agriculture, "the majority of the Mexican agricultural science community also did not believe that they were worthy of study."[65] In fact, many Mexican agronomists sided with the Secretary of Agriculture in their condemnation of the centuries-old Indigenous practices of intercropping corn and beans and thus were complicit in the "marginalization of a rich variety of knowledge systems."[66] Instead, wheat

and maize hybridization programs spurred the growth of mass production and monocultures. By selecting and breeding maize and wheat to
adapt to a variety of local conditions and adding chemical fertilizers and
pesticides, capitalist-oriented farmers reaped enormous profits at the
expense of campesino production.

Throughout the 1950s, policymakers sought to integrate the control
over campesino production of basic crops by linking loan policies and
finding ways to compel campesinos to sell to the state through expanding
the sites where the State Food Agency (CEIMSA in the 1950s and then
CONASUPO after 1961) would purchase crops.[67] Although the government's guaranteed price system was initially started to support ejidatarios and small producers, it quickly began to benefit larger and better
capitalized producers. The neglect of ejidos and rain-fed lands opened
the door for local caciques to dominate the government programs and
channel funds away from the majority of ejidatarios. In 1945, only 14
percent of Mexico's ejidos received credit from the national ejidal bank.[68]
Hewitt de Alcántara calculated that an average of 13 percent of ejidos
received credit between 1940 and 1970.[69] The new politics of the ejido
reinforced the bifurcated agricultural structure. Writing about Morelos,
Gladys McCormick found that "[t]he ejido and the cooperative thus sub-
merged the maize-based economy—one that Emiliano Zapata had hoped
to enshrine in his version of agrarian reform—and instead reinforced
the exploitative effects of capitalist development."[70] The illegal renting of
ejido lands to private farmers further exacerbated the impact of Mexico's
growing bifurcation of agriculture.[71] In effect, campesinos were increasingly forced to abandon their lands for part of the year in search of work
in Mexico's cities or in the United States.

As governments deemphasized the revolutionary demands for land
and liberty, food policy was used to subsidize capitalist industrialization
and urbanization during the 1940s and 1950s. As inflation cut into industrial workers' wage gains, unions fought for wage increases and for union
democracy. While demands for union democracy were often crushed by
the state, state control over the unions was often accompanied by wage
increases and an increase in the number of subsidized State Food Agency
stores. This authoritarian responsiveness enabled the governments to
forge social peace by maintaining control of the unions while keeping
food prices down and relieving wage pressures for industrialists.[72]

To keep food prices down in the city, policymakers subsidized large producers and then deepened state control over production and producers. In Nayarit, land reform and the growth of ejidos under Cárdenas initially led to increased maize production to feed local markets. However, during the period of maize scarcity in the 1940s and 1950s, Nayarit's maize was sent throughout Mexico and the state became one of the largest producers of maize in Mexico.[73] Martínez Domínguez noted, "The subsidy that the federal government pays has a double function: to sustain the price of masa and tortillas in the Federal District, and to stimulate the production of this grain in Colima and Nayarit."[74] By 1950, Nayarit accounted for more than one-third of all maize entering Mexico City by rail.[75] This process squeezed campesinos off their lands and especially hurt highland Indigenous communities who had received land and support under Cárdenas but were forced to abandon their lands for seasonal work in the Nayarit lowlands or migrate to the United States during the 1940s. According to the historian Verónica Castillo-Muñoz, "the 1950 census recorded the highest number of abandoned communities in the Sierra."[76] This massive displacement occurred in numerous places throughout Mexico as people were forced to migrate, initially seasonally but often permanently, to help support their families and communities in the countryside.

As a result of this agrarian transformation during the 1940s to the 1970s, campesinos in many areas were stretched thin. Rural to urban migration in the 1940s and 1950s was initially encouraged to meet the growing labor demands of industrialists. However, it was not long before the limited nature of Mexican industrialization led to the proliferation of "lost cities," characterized by makeshift constructions without basic services and populations that had little access to the formal labor market. The anthropologist Lourdes Arizpe explained that "the forces of attraction for migrants were substituted by the forces of expulsion of dispossessed campesinos," and migrants "went from the misery of the countryside to the new urban misery, without an improvement in their access to employment, welfare and services."[77]

Many campesinos experienced these policy shifts as a betrayal of the promises of the revolution. Throughout Mexico, campesinos organized to demand land, increases in resources, and independence from the PRI and its official Confederación Nacional Campesina (CNC) organization.

In Morelos, Rubén Jaramillo organized campesinos to demand a renewal of agrarian reform and the ideals of land and liberty for which campesinos had fought in the land of Zapata. They employed numerous tactics, from grassroots organizing to electoral participation, and as state repression radicalized the Jaramillistas challenged federal control through guerrilla movements until Jaramillo was assassinated in 1962.[78] Other groups formed the Confederación Campesina Independiente to rival the PRI-controlled CNC. A wave of land invasions in northern Mexican states began in 1958, with two thousand campesinos occupying lands in Sinaloa; others occupied lands in Nayarit, Colima, and Baja California.[79] The largest occupation was in Sonora, where Jacinto López and members of the Unión General de Obreros y Campesinos Mexicanos (UGOCM) occupied the lands of the Cananea Cattle Company, owned by U.S. capitalists.[80] These acts of resistance were generally met with repression, often followed by reform efforts on government terms.

State violence and co-optation in the countryside, coupled with the marginalizing of ejido and campesino agriculture, led to the radicalization of many in rural communities. Student movements joined with campesinos in many regions to demand meaningful land reform. Movements for land were often met with state repression, which led communities to scale up their mobilizations by joining and supporting the growing number of guerrilla organizations in the Mexican countryside.[81] During the 1960s and 1970s, active guerrilla movements emerged in numerous regions; the most well-known movement occurred in Guerrero and was led by rural schoolteachers Lucio Cabañas and Genaro Vásquez. State surveillance of rural movements grew over the late 1940s and evolved into a "laboratory of state-sponsored violence" to break rural autonomy, resulting in the murder and disappearance of thousands of Mexican citizens.[82]

This war against poor people in the countryside was coupled with reform policies that strengthened clientelism and control in the countryside.[83] During the 1970s, Mexican presidents renewed rural development programs. Using CONASUPO as its main tool, the government expanded stores throughout urban and rural areas and not just in working-class neighborhoods. Between 1970 and 1976, the number of stores doubled to 3,001, while rural stores expanded from 43 to 920 and came to account for nearly one-third of all CONASUPO stores. During the administration of José López Portillo, flush with petroleum earnings, the number of stores grew to more than 11,000 in 1982 with 9,000 stores in the countryside. To stock these stores, CONASUPO acquired factories that produced noodles and pastas and expanded its maize flour and rehydrated milk production and distribution. By 1982, CONASUPO received 65.4 percent of federal government transfers to state entities, up from 23 percent in 1970.[84]

The expansion of the state's presence in the purchasing and selling of basic grains and foodstuff was a direct response to social mobilizations. With the creation of the short-lived Sistema Alimentaria Mexicana (SAM) in 1980, for the first time in nearly forty years a concerted effort was made to support campesino production through a holistic and integrated approach to address the numerous factors that hindered campesino agriculture. As Jonathan Fox demonstrates, a portion of SAM reformists were university-trained intellectuals who had been shaped by the 1968 movement, and although they worked for the state, they had significant contacts with independent and popular organizers in the countryside. Pro-campesino officials in SAM worked with independent campesino organizations to mobilize their resources. They were able to raise the guaranteed price to sell maize and increase the acreage of funding for the amount of maize and beans from 1.8 million hectares in 1979 to 4.2 million hectares in 1982, greatly expanding the number of ejidatarios that had access to government loans by more than one-third.[85]

Pro-campesino officials worked with community organizers to establish community-controlled State Food Agency stores (DICONSA), which differed from other DICONSA stores that often were run by local power-brokers. They urged organizers and campesinos to organize community food councils to oversee the new stores. These councils created spaces for autonomist community organizing to flourish, especially in Indigenous communities. In Oaxaca, the strategy was so successful that the communities formed a statewide Food Council Coordinadora in October 1983, after SAM had been discontinued.[86] The Coordinadora organized a meeting of regional peasant organizations the following year, which was eventually formalized as UNORCA, or National Union of Autonomous Regional Peasant Organizations. They also organized a national network of food councils, which had "over three hundred delegates, representing

110 regional councils and over 4,200 communities from eighteen states, at that time approximately one-third of the food councils nationally."[87] DICONSA officials and other bureaucrats were not pleased with this campesino organizing and began to withhold supplies from the region, undercutting the Coordinadora. Some communities then created their own autonomous producer organizations.[88] When the food councils lost steam in the mid–1980s, they emboldened a new form of distributive reform that "was not conditioned on clientelistic political subordination" but instead "created a meaningful electoral process and encouraged the emergence of new representative social actors."[89]

The State and the Private Sector in Mexico's Food System

While the public sector played a significant role in driving Mexico's food policies in the postrevolutionary period, the role of the private sector should not be underestimated. Some regional food stores and processing plants emerged and several expanded into centers throughout Mexico. As national firms grew, so too did transnational corporations (TNC). Many began to invest in Mexico and established subsidiaries beginning in the 1930s. During the Mexican Miracle, TNCs deepened their reach, and by the 1970s, food TNCs played a significant role in overall sales in both burgeoning supermarkets and corner markets. Industrialized foods began shaping consumer tastes among upper- and middle-income Mexicans.

U.S.-based transnational food companies gained a firm foothold in Mexico between 1930 and the 1960s. Early U.S. investors saw Mexico as a source of production of tropical fruits and cooking oils. By the late 1940s, foreign companies saw opportunities for their products in Mexico's burgeoning consumer market. These early companies in Mexico, as table 1 illustrates, included some of the most important companies in the agribusiness and food markets, such as Corn Products Co. International, Anderson Clayton and Co., Nestlé, Pillsbury, Quaker Oats, and Chiclets Adams. By the 1940s, Coca-Cola, Pepsi Cola, and McCormick began operating in Mexico. The 1950s and 1960s saw major growth in transnational food investment, especially in fruit and vegetable packing, candy and confections, concentrated beverages, milk products, and the meat

TABLE 1 Major Food and Agribusiness Transnational Investment in Mexico, 1930–1978

	Country of Origin	Year Entered Mexico	Products
1930–1940			
Corn Products Co. International	U.S.	1930	corn starch, soups
The Carlox Co.	U.S.	1931	bread and cakes
Quaker Oats	U.S.	1935	cereals
Pillsbury	U.S.	1933	produced cookies and pastas
Anderson, Clayton and Co.	U.S.	1934	
Nestlé	Swiss	1935	
Beatrice Foods	U.S.	1938	milk-based products
Warner Lambert Co. (Chiclets Adams, S.A.)	U.S.	1936	candies, chewing gum, and confections
Agroaliment International	Lux	1940	candies and confections
1941–1950			
Coca-Cola	U.S.	1944	concentrated syrups and food coloring
Pet Incorporated	U.S.	1946	frozen fruits, vegetables, and juices
McCormick	U.S.	1947	manufacturing condiments
Northon Norwich Products	U.S.	1947	condiments
Carnation Co.	U.S.	1947	condensed milk
General Mills	U.S.	1948	cookies, pastas, wheat flour
PepsiCo	U.S.	1949	concentrated syrups and food coloring
1951–1960			
Kellogg Corp	U.S.	1951	breakfast cereal
Del Monte	U.S.	1953	popcorn, potato chips, fruits

TABLE 1 *continued*

	Country of Origin	Year Entered Mexico	Products
General Foods	U.S.	1953	
Nabisco	U.S.	1955	cookies, crackers
Stange Co.	U.S.	1956	condiments
Bayer For Invest	Canada	1956	concentrated syrups and food coloring
Ralston Purina	U.S.	1957	manufacturing pet foods
Campbell's Soup Co.	U.S.	1959	soups
Bristol Meyer International	U.S.	1958	*cajetas*, yogurt, and other milk products
Norton Simon	U.S.	1959	concentrated syrups and food coloring
Minute Maid Club	U.S.	1959	concentrated syrups and food coloring
North and South American Co.	U.S.	1959	puddings, gelatins, related products
Laurener Lea	U.S.	1959	frozen fruits, vegetables, juices, preserves
Marriot Corp.	U.S.	1960	other food products
1961–1970			
Davis Flavor Co.	U.S.	1961	concentrated syrups and food coloring
Stablishment	Italy	1961	preparation and meat packing
Seven Up International	U.S.	1962	concentrated syrups and food coloring
Delaware Lay Co.	Swiss	1962	cream, butter, and cheese
Miles Laboratories	U.S.	1963	concentrated syrups and food coloring
Anjinomoto Co.	Japan	1968	manufacturing condiments

TABLE 1 *continued*

	Country of Origin	Year Entered Mexico	Products
ITT Continental Baking	U.S.	1964	bread
Cargill Incorporated	U.S.	1964	sugar milling
Warner Jenkinson Co.	U.S.	1964	concentrated syrups and food coloring
Santa Fe Driscolls Packers	U.S.	1965	frozen fruits, vegetables, juices, preserves
Standard Brands	U.S.	1965	candy and confections; popcorn and chips
MacKenzie Angus B.	U.S.	1966	frozen fruits, vegetables, juices
Urthy Peck & Co.	U.S.	1966	concentrated syrups and food coloring
Beech-Nut Life Savers Co.	U.S.	1967	candy and confections
Tootsie Roll Industries	U.S.	1968	candy and confections
Canned Meats	U.S.	1968	preparation and meat packing
DeWied International	U.S.	1969	preparation and meat packing
United Brands	U.S.	1970	frozen fruits, vegetables, preserves, juices
Standley Sheluy Gent	U.S.	1970	ice cream, popsicles
1971–1980			
W.W. Underwood	U.S.	1971	condiments
Moxie Industries	U.S.	1971	candy and confections
Societé Financiere de Develop Ind.	Swiss	1971	frozen fruits, vegetables, juices, preserves
Societá Participazioni Alimentari	Italy	1972	preparation and bottling of seafood
Borden	U.S.	1972	milk and dairy
Di Giorgio Co.	U.S.	1972	food products

TABLE 1 *continued*

	Country of Origin	Year Entered Mexico	Products
Samuel Landson	U.S.	1973	frozen fruits, vegetables, juices, preserves
Topps Chewing Gum	U.S.	1973	chewing gum
Mallin C. Inc.	U.S.	1973	concentrated syrups and food coloring
The Wilfrom Co.	U.S.	1973	bread and cakes
Marubeni Co.	Japan	1974	frozen fruits, vegetables, preserves, juices
Citricos Tropicales	Panama	1978	frozen fruits, vegetables, preserves, juices

Sources: Adapted from Rosa Elena Montes de Oca Luján and Gerardo Escudero Columna, "Las empresas transnacionales en la industria alimentaria mexicana," *Comercio Exterior* 31, no. 9 (September 1981); and Hall, "Five Multinational Food Processing Firms in Mexico."

industry. By the 1950s, ten of the top twenty food processing companies in the United States had plants in Mexico.[90]

Many food TNCs began to become leading producers in their sector of the food industry. Overall foreign company participation in the food industry grew from 4.9 percent in 1962 to 8.6 percent of the total industry by 1970.[91] The number of transnational subsidiaries in Mexico grew significantly during this period, from approximately twenty-three before 1950 to thirty-one in the 1950s; ninety-three in the 1960s; and forty-one between 1970 and 1975.[92] One study demonstrated that in 1972, 20 percent of Mexico's largest food-processing firms were under U.S. control, and another 6 percent under the control of other foreign firms, 7 percent controlled by the state and 67 percent by Mexican private companies.[93] In 1975, of the forty-three leading U.S. transnational food companies operating in Latin America, thirty-three were active in Mexico, far eclipsing TNC activity in other Latin American counties.[94]

The growth of foreign firms began to drive out small national businesses.[95] There was a relatively high degree of concentration in Mexico's food sector. High tariffs kept food imports out and made it difficult for small entrepreneurs to break into the market, reducing competition. In a 1981 study, Montes de Oca and Escudero Columna found that thirty-one of the forty industrial classification categories in the food sector were dominated by the top four companies in that classification. Many of these industrial classification categories were controlled by foreign transnationals.[96] For example, in 1971 foreign capital controlled approximately 35 percent of the candy industry, 100 percent of the baby food industry, 95 percent of the breakfast cereal market, 85 percent of canned foods, 75 percent of the powdered chocolate milk, 100 percent of evaporated and condensed milk, and 30 percent of the cookie, cracker, and pasta market.[97]

The rise in transnational food processing in Mexico was largely owed to the burgeoning middle classes and the Americanization of Mexico's consumer tastes.[98] U.S. advertising agencies worked with transnational companies to shape their image to play to Mexican nationalism, creating "a sense of ambiguity that allowed Mexicans to embrace revolutionary and nationalist values while welcoming American culture which they considered necessary for entering the modern industrial world," in the words of the historian Julio Moreno.[99] Food TNCs cultivated and shaped consumer habits and taste, engineering food with added sugars and colorants, and "in some specific cases they have influenced consumers to purchase and consume products that have no nutritional value," as a 1976 study concluded.[100] According to Montes de Oca and Escudero Columna, "one can conclude that transnational companies impose the food habits of the industrialized countries through offering products differentiated by brand and using new methods of presentation and marketing." Through integrating Mexico in the global food economy, the TNCs "consolidate a deformed industrial structure following the logic of capitalist accumulation."[101]

The rapid growth of transnational food companies in Mexico during the 1960s alarmed many observers. In an *El Día* column in 1966, the popular journalist Manuel Buendía pointed out the potential disaster for small Mexican businesses by the entry of powerful U.S. companies such as Wonder Bread with its various snack foods. He admonished Mexican business owners:

You will try to defend yourselves but there is nothing that you can do. You and many other Mexican small businesses are impotent to fight against the enormous force of a North American consortium that has a hundred factories in almost every part of the world.

First, they will wage a price war against you. The North American company can reduce their costs since they have a factory process that is highly technical. Besides they don't care if they lose money at first . . . because once they have displaced the competition and they feel they are absolute owners of the market, they can fix the price at whatever pleases them. . . . But first you and your colleagues will be the object of a negative publicity campaign.[102]

Buendía's warning was a direct reference to the entry of ITT Continental Baking, the large conglomerate with Wonder Bread and Hostess as its lead brands, into the Mexican market in 1964. The industry was dominated by Bimbo Bread and its cake division, Marinela, which controlled nearly the entire sector. Between 1966 and 1967 Continental Baking made a major play for Bimbo's market share by selling Wonder Bread at half the price of Bimbo bread. With the financial backing of the Mexican government, Bimbo purchased the Mexican rights to the U.S.-branded Sunbeam Bread to curry to Mexican demands for foreign products.[103] As we will see in chapter 5, while Mexican capital staved off the threat of a U.S. corporation, they would be the leading drivers of Americanizing consumer tastes.

The rise of supermarkets facilitated the growth of the distribution of national and transnational processed foods. While family-run neighbor grocery stores (*abarrotes*) have existed for decades, in the late 1930s state-run stores began to operate to counter speculation and high prices. The State Food Agency stores rapidly expanded in large cities throughout the 1970s, growing from 3,001 in 1970 to 11,000 stores in 1981. While most were in working-class and lower-middle-class areas, there were several large-scale stores that rivaled the size of national chains. For example, the CONASUPER in Mexico City's Perisur was described as a modern supermarket where everything that a middle-class housewife wanted could be purchased. Critics pointed out that state-run stores should be promoting local products, not transnational products. In 1978, *Excélsior* reported that "transnational companies manufacture more than 80 percent of the products sold in CONASUPO's distribution system."[104] While CONA-SUPO began to produce its own packaged and canned goods in the 1970s under the LICONSA and Alianza labels, its production paled in comparison to the domination of transnational food corporations.

The rise of private supermarkets in Mexico followed the initial growth of the state supermarket chains. Super Mercados, S.A. (Sumesa) from Monterrey was established by Monterrey entrepreneurs in 1945 for upper-income groups and slowly expanded its chain. Throughout the 1950s and the 1960s, supermarkets grew steadily with the establishment of discounted Aurrerá (1959), Comercial Mexicana (1959), Soriana (1962), Gigante (1962), and Superama (1963).[105] Supermarkets and self-service stores were largely filled with packaged food items, many of which were supplied by transnational food companies and often had names in Spanish and brands that soon became well-known household items, including Nescafé, Salsa Maggi, Carlos V chocolate bars, Knorr consommé, and Sabritas potato chips.

The great disparity in wealth in Mexico meant that working-class Mexicans and middle- and upper-class Mexicans continued to have very different ways of purchasing foods in different types of markets. The working poor continued to rely on public markets, the large numbers of small family vendors, CONASUPO neighborhood stores, and itinerant markets (*tianguis*). In areas where families earned between one and two daily minimum wages, which accounted for at least 35 percent of the population in the Mexico City region, they purchased their food principally from street vendors and then from neighborhood CONA-SUPERs. In 1975, 63 percent of supermarkets were concentrated in upper-income neighborhoods and accounted for 40 percent of all stores in middle- and upper-income neighborhoods.[106] Of the nearly sixty-five thousand retail stores and shops that sold food items, 99.2 percent were either family operations that employed on average one person or small retailers that employed 1.7 people. Both categories accounted for only 43 percent of all the food sold in retail stores. On the contrary, the rest of the 0.8 percent of shops were classified as medium-sized, large, and giant retailers, including supermarket chains, which accounted for 57 percent of the retail market.[107] Although both state-run stores and private markets were not the major way that the working poor purchased foodstuff, they were a constant and growing threat to small vendors who sold in Mexico's network of public markets and open-air tianguis that were found throughout cities and the countryside.[108]

The transformation of Mexican urban diets in the 1970s was characterized by growth in the consumption of soft drinks, such as Coca-Cola and Pepsi. Medical doctors and government officials began to note the growth of type 2 diabetes within the Mexican population caused by the increased consumption of processed foods, carbohydrates, and sugar, considered cheap calories. The director of the Pediatrics Hospital argued that "[w]orking class fathers were malnourished and that is why they drank 'excessive quantities of soft-drinks.'"[109] Soft drinks filled bellies and delivered energy through sugar and caffeine to work throughout the day. Eduardo del Río, whose pen name was Rius, blasted junk-food diets and the foreign companies that produced them. He argued, "The danger of drinking coke is that people ignore that this soft drink is a true drug." Artists such as the band Los Nakos made a parody of the Coca-Cola commercial titled Droga-Cola. Growing consumer awareness about Coca-Cola's empty calories and growing ubiquity in the Mexican countryside led government policymakers to find ways to address the critiques.[110]

The response to popular critiques followed previous government responses and focused on consumer education and nutrition campaigns during the Luis Echeverría and López Portillo administrations. The National Consumer Institute published a bulletin and ads that tried to counter the growth of food corporations advertising and inflationary pressures.[111] CONASUPO developed a pamphlet series showing working-class housewives how to use CONASUPO products such as maize flour, pastas, beans, dried fish, and other products in making traditional dishes, with the technical consultation of Josefina Vásquez de León, Mexico's leading cookbook writer and food personality. The recipe booklets were distributed for free in CONASUPO stores and later compiled into a book, *Platillos Populares Mexicanos* (*Mexican Popular Dishes*), in 1971. Each pamphlet had thirty recipes that were developed taking into consideration the cost of items, ease of preparation, a balanced diet, attractiveness, and taste.[112] Nearly all recipes used CONASUPO products, incorporated regional dishes, and emphasized the Mexican-ness of the ingredients and the meal. Analysts praised the use of the state agency to counter the growing dominance of food corporations; however, many pointed out that even in these stores, transnational food products were sold widely. The amount spent on these campaigns paled in comparison to private advertising. The real issue had little to do with the lack of knowledge of workers and campesinos; these inequalities were built into the nation's political and economic system.[113]

Despite these critiques and attempts at reform, the growth of industrial foods and markets shored up private capital's growing role in the food sector. Except for some programs, such as the short-lived SAM, government policies spurred the industrialized food system. Production of industrialized foods items required greater resources (inputs of land, labor, water) that privileged capitalist production schemes over campesino production systems and set in motion a chase for modern industrial diets that commodified food and disassociated it from producers, communities, and the land.

CHAPTER 3

CORPORATE POWER AND THE NEOLIBERAL ASSAULT ON MEXICO'S FOOD SYSTEM

"Food business is booming south of the border."
—*BAKERY & SNACKS*, NOVEMBER 21, 2013

"NAFTA is starving Mexico."
—LAURA CARLSON, *FOREIGN POLICY IN FOCUS*,
OCTOBER 10, 2011

Beginning in the 1980s, neoliberal free trade policies began to open Mexico's food economies to the world market. In a relatively brief period, foreign and domestic capital captured key sectors of the food industry in what *Bakery & Snacks* called a booming business south of the border.[1] Officials transformed public policies to support the expansion of oligopolies that produce industrialized foods. The boom in agro-export specialization, as Guadalajara-based researcher Humberto González demonstrated, led to environmental degradation, severe exploitation of campesinos and Indigenous workers and communities, increased dependence on transnational companies and foreign governments, and an accentuation of the deprivation of access to healthy, nutritious, and culturally appropriate food for domestic customers.[2]

This chapter examines the political economy of the corporate assault on the Mexican food system. Capitalist domination of the food industry, of course, is not new. As the previous chapters have documented, there were a few weakly enforced checks on private and transnational capital's influence in transforming land use and (mis)shaping diets. Through examining the rise of the neoliberal food regime in Mexico, this chapter tracks how policy shifts benefited many of the companies that were already doing well and accelerated their national and global expansion by the turn of the twenty-first century. Many of these companies became regional and world leaders in the food industry through employing the tools of modern marketing to publicly frame their companies as socially responsible, while working behind the scenes to shape policy in their interests, radically reshaping Mexico's food landscape.

Neoliberalism and the Capitalist Consolidation of the State

With the fall in the price of oil in the early 1980s, Mexico's political and economic rulers, under the pressure of the World Bank and the International Monetary Fund (IMF), began to restructure the Mexican economy. The economic crisis provided Mexico's neoliberal elites with the opportunity they had been waiting for. By slashing social spending, privatizing state companies, and liberalizing trade, neoliberal policymakers hoped to attract foreign investment. By further integrating Mexico into the word economy, they argued that Mexico would achieve high rates of economic growth and that the lives of all Mexicans would be improved.[3] Mexico's neoliberal response to the economic downturn strengthened Mexico's capitalist class at the expense of large segments of the Mexican population.[4]

In a few short years, Mexico's business elite would come to exercise a profound influence throughout the country such that they would be the true *Amos de México* (masters of Mexico).[5] While Mexico's capitalists have a long history of organizing in their respective sectors, in 1975 they organized into a multisectoral business organization, the Consejo Coordinador Empresarial (CCE), to exert pressure on the Mexican government.[6] The CCE included eight of Mexico's business organizations representing a wide sector of the economy and included the Consejo de Hombres de Negocio, an elite group founded in 1962 that included Mexico's wealthiest and most powerful business leaders. The CCE organized to counter President Echeverría's urging of Mexico's official unions to form an umbrella labor organization, the Congreso de Trabajo, to strengthen their economic and political position. Half of the CCE's budget came from a few dozen of Mexico's largest firms, and by the 1990s about 350 firms were contributing to the budget. Among the top five contributing firms, two were food companies (Bimbo and Grupo Herdez), one was a conglomerate that was the main Coca-Cola bottler and distributor (Grupo Visa), and the other two were among Mexico's oldest corporations (Alfonso Romo Garza and Grupo Vitro).[7] The CCE played a critical role in lobbying the Mexican government to liberalize the economy through trade liberalizations, privatizations, and the negotiation of free trade agreements such as NAFTA.[8]

This class organizing occurred as Mexican capitalists were consolidating their control over their respective sectors and diversifying through investment in the stock market. Between 1974 and 1982, companies were able to take advantage of government credits and other opportunities that came with Mexico's booming oil sector to consolidate their oligopolistic control over their industries through buyouts of smaller companies, with Mexico's leading economic group ALFA acquiring thirty-six companies.[9] Many of these companies also expanded their position through diversifying their activities and creating alliances with foreign capital. Mexican banks began to acquire control of leading businesses in specific industries; for example, BANCOMER purchased Cementos Anáhuac and BANAMEX acquired the hotel chain Hoteles Camino Real.[10] With the crash of the economy in the early 1980s, these companies began to invest in Mexico's emerging stock market. This infused capital into several of Mexico's economic groups, leading many to go on buying sprees of stock brokerage firms, which would help them raise capital for future purchases and expansion.

The other main boon for Mexico's large capitalists came through the privatization of state-held companies in the 1980s and 1990s. Mexico's state sector began to divest of "nonessential" government enterprises in accordance with the structural adjustment strictures of the World Bank and the IMF. During the presidency of Miguel de la Madrid (1982–1988), the government began dis-incorporating government-owned businesses and entities that were deemed to have minimal overall impact on the economy or the social structure. During his six-year presidency, the number of state enterprises dropped from 1,155 to 449.[11]

With the low-hanging fruit of state enterprises gone, the administration of President Carlos Salinas de Gortari (1988–1994) sold many of Mexico's largest and most lucrative state entities, further enriching a small group of capitalists. Within the first two years of his administration, Salinas disincorporated 215 state companies, of which ninety were sold to private groups. These included six CONASUPO industrial plants (including maize and wheat flour milling operations), the phone monopoly Teléfonos de México, steel plants, twelve fertilizer plants, and Mexico's banks, which were nationalized in 1982. By 1994, only 216 state enterprises remained, including strategic and historically symbolic entities such as Mexico's oil monopoly, PEMEX.[12]

The privatization process was aimed at modernizing the state by turning over many of its historic functions to the private sector. The business elite found an ally in Carlos Salinas de Gortari and, in the words of the Mexican sociologist Elvira Concheiro Bórquez, "a grand accord" was reached between the government and Mexico's business class, and together they set out to transform the role of the Mexican state in the national economy. As business leader Josué Sáenz remarked at the time,

> Maybe the solution is a new State that is a promoter not an actor, a coordinator and not a director, a stimulator and financier but not a businessman: a State that helps private initiative to grow and innovate, and fill holes and identify opportunities; that does not operate directly in the economy but that does not permit the creation of private or government monopolies. A State that continues its work in developing infrastructure, social welfare and activities that cannot be developed by the private sector.[13]

The "grand accord" strengthened Mexico's financial groups such that the "lost decade" of the 1980s "was won by financial capital," as the economist Jorge Basave Kunhardt concluded.[14]

The close ties between the PRI and Mexico's capitalist class strengthened during the administration of Salinas de Gortari. It was widely reported that at a dinner at the home of former Secretary of the Industry and Commerce Antonio Ortiz Mena in February 1993 that included Mexican billionaires and multimillionaires, the president, and leaders of the PRI, the host solicited $25 million from each of the top businessmen for the 1994 presidential campaign. Since many of these millionaires had significantly bolstered their wealth through the privatization process and favorable public policies, many agreed on the spot.[15] According to one report, Emilio Azcárraga, owner of TELEVISA, stood up and said, "I, and all of you, have earned so much money over the past six years that I think we have a big debt of gratitude to this government. . . . We owe it to the president, and to the country."[16] By the end of the night, each pledged an average of $25 million for a total of approximately $750 million. As news of the meeting and the pledges leaked to the press it was correctly reported that "the PRI was setting financial quotas for the wealthy businessmen."[17]

By the mid–1990s, Mexico's business elites were in the economic driver's seat. Judith Teichman found that "[t]he ruling group now consists of a homogeneous circle of finance sector political bureaucrats who must be open like never before to the policy preferences of the country's biggest business interests."[18] The connection between personal ties and the growth of wealth and power during the Salinas administration is underscored by an owner of an export firm: "My company has very good relations with the current administration. A cabinet secretary will call me to arrange a meeting, and I speak with Carlos Salinas every two or three weeks or so. . . . Formal business organizations exist just to give a show of democracy."[19]

Mexican private firms' share of revenue among Mexico's fifty largest companies grew from 18 percent in 1984 to 58 percent in 1996, as the share of state-owned companies plummeted from 75 percent to 25 percent.[20] The number of Mexicans on the *Forbes* billionaire list grew from one when the list began in 1987 to twenty-four in 1994, for a combined net worth of $2.4 billion, and by 2011 there were ten Mexicans on the list who had a combined net worth of $124.1 billion. In 2015, there were sixteen Mexicans on the *Forbes* billionaire list, with a combined net worth of $144.5 billion. The 2015 list included Carlos Slim Helú, whose net worth equaled that of the other fifteen billionaires, with $77.1 billion.[21] Following a decline in the number of billionaires and their total wealth due to a weak peso, the COVID–19 pandemic, and economic recession, by 2023 Mexico's billionaires had an estimated combined net worth of $224.7 billion.[22]

A notable number of Mexico's billionaires derive their wealth from the food industry. This group accounted for one-third of the Mexicans on the *Forbes* 2015 billionaire list and even more when the wealth of family groups is considered. Table 2 illustrates that between 2015 and 2017 there were at least seventeen billionaire families in the food sector with a combined estimated net worth of $47.45 billion. These families were all well positioned economically and politically to take advantage of the shift toward neoliberal policies.

TABLE 2 Mexico's Food and Drink Billionaires on the *Forbes* List, 2015–2017

Family	Business	Est. Net Worth B$
Eva Gonda de Rivera and family	Widow of former chair of FEMSA Latin America's largest Coca-Cola bottler and Oxxo convenience stores	6.7
Maria Asunción Aramburuzabala and family	former owners of Modelo Breweries	6.5
González Moreno family	GRUMA (Maize Flour, Tortillas)	5.0
Servitje family	Grupo BIMBO (Bakery Goods, Snacks)	4.2
Jerónimo Arango family	Aurrerá retail store founders sold to Walmart and stake in Walmart de Mexico	4.3
Robinson Bours family	Founders of Industrias Bachoco Poultry Processing	3.2
José and José Francisco Calderón Rosas	Sons of the cofounder of FEMSA	2.1
Martin Bringas family	Controlling Shares in SORIANA Supermarkets	2.1
Barragán Morales family	Arca Continental—second largest Coca-Cola bottler and third largest snack food business	2.0
Calderón Rojas family	Sons of FEMSA's cofounder, 7% stake in Coca-Cola bottler and Oxxo stores	1.9
Max Michel Suberville	Major shareholder in FEMSA and family member of founders of Liverpool retail chain store	1.45
González Zabalegui family	Controls La Comercial Supermarket Group	1.6
Losada Moreno family	Grupo Gigante Holding Group—supermarkets, restaurants, and real estate	1.5
Cynthia and Bruce Grossman	Grupo Continental Coca-Cola bottling factories	1.4
Jorba Servitje brothers	Sons of BIMBO cofounder and members of the Board of Directors	1.3
Chedraui Obeso family	Grupo Comercial Chedraui Supermarkets	1.3
Martin Soberón family	Shareholders of Soriana Supermarkets	1.0
Total	17	47.45

Sources: Compiled from "World's Billionaires List," Forbes, 2015, http://www.forbes.com/billionaires/list/#version:static_country:Mexico; and Dolia Estevez, "Mexico's 15 Billionaire-Dollar Clans," Forbes, May 24, 2017.

With Mexico's economic restructuring came the privatization of Mexico's food system. Over the course of three decades, Mexico's food system infrastructure, which for nearly fifty years had, in theory, emphasized self-sufficiency and support of small and consumer producers, shifted to opening the food sector to private industry with the goal of increasing production to lower prices.

Radical Restructuring of the Countryside

Central to the transformation of Mexico's food industry were the policy shifts that transformed the Mexican countryside. Neoliberal policies were aimed at freeing up land and labor in the countryside to develop the institutional framework for private capital investment. Neoliberal reformers hoped to undo social and agrarian reforms to pave the way for Mexico's increased integration into the global marketplace.

Much of the groundwork for this restructuring had its beginning in the 1980s as the governments of Miguel de la Madrid and then Carlos Salinas de Gortari aggressively abandoned postrevolutionary policies that sought, albeit erratically, food self-sufficiency and encouraged national production of basic grains. With the economic crisis of the 1980s and the World Bank and IMF prescriptions for economic growth, policymakers shunned subsidizing small farmers and campesinos and instead urged privatizing the ejido and fostering the growth of economically efficient enterprises without much thought to the social costs.

State investment in small producers plummeted. Between the economic crisis of 1982 and 1990, state investment in the countryside dropped by 68 percent. The amount that the federal agricultural bank loaned to ejidatarios declined in real terms from 334 billion pesos to 60 billion pesos a year.[23] The state significantly reduced and then eliminated CONASUPO's guaranteed price program, further signaling their abandonment of small producers. By eliminating these subsidies, neoliberal policymakers sought to force out smaller producers and ejidatarios who could not compete with them by leaving the prices of agricultural products to market forces.

Early in his term, Salinas sought to find ways to create private-public partnerships between large food companies and ejidos with the hope that such alliances would modernize ejido production, making it directly responsive to markets and large private firms. While historically prohibited by Article 27, several companies had been lobbying for a change in policy so that they could produce their inputs on ejido lands. For example, in 1979 the owners of Gamesa, Grupo Visa, and Grupo Maseca along with the entrepreneur Pablo Livas Cantú approached President José López Portillo with a plan for the government to build basic infrastructure to help both producers and the private sector. But it proved too politically contentious to link ejidatarios and their lands with entrepreneurs according to Alberto Santos, known as Don Galleta (Mr. Cookie). However, seventeen days after taking office, Carlos Salinas de Gortari asked a group of PRI-affiliated entrepreneurs from Monterrey including Santos and Livas Cantú to develop a plan for modernizing the countryside. After fifteen days of discussions, "Gamesa proposed an initial project of integrated rural development using 4,500 hectares of land with an ultimate goal of using 50,000 hectares throughout the nation with the participation of the public sector, producers, and industry (Gamesa)."[24]

One of the early model experiments to begin to privatize the ejidos and circumvent Article 27 was developed by Gamesa and carried out in the Vaquerías region of eastern Nuevo León. In 1990 the ejidatarios from three ejidos, the largest and most established of which was San José de Vaquerías, entered into an agreement with the cookie giant Gamesa to use 5,000 hectares of land for the company's inputs. The company provided modern equipment and worked with government entities to expand irrigation works. In turn, the ejidatarios and other workers grew sorghum, soy, wheat, maize, and other crops for the market, thus eliminating much of their subsistence production.[25] Other proposals, by Herdez, Del Monte, and PepsiCo, emerged with the Vaquerías plan as a model. The Mexican economist José Luis Calva captured the sentiment of many critics, arguing that it was an illusion to think that these associations would be able to solve the problems of a decapitalized countryside since the private sector will only funnel resources where they will earn profit. Vaquerias was only viable for Gamesa because of the large subsidies and state support that the project received. Even Gamesa said, "It wouldn't be affordable to plant grains if there was no support."[26] By 1994 the project dissolved after Gamesa was bought out by PepsiCo.

However, Vaquerías was an important precursor to the reforms that Salinas was planning. On November 7, 1991, President Carlos Salinas, standing in front of a backdrop of the bust of the symbol of the land struggle, Emiliano Zapata, at the presidential palace of Los Pinos, signed the initiative to change Article 27 of the Constitution of 1917, effectively ending land reform policies. With approximately 2.5 million campesinos still waiting to receive land, Salinas's actions signaled that land reform was over and that Zapata's call for land and liberty was complete. With the stroke of his pen, ejido lands could now be sold, with the consent of ejido members, and private and foreign investors could begin to develop agribusiness ventures with ejidos.[27] After the president signed the reform package to send to congress, Luis Tellez, Undersecretary of Agriculture and architect of neoliberal policies in the countryside, held a press conference where he stressed the importance of creating a flexible land tenure system that would address the inefficiency of small landholding and ejidos and allow individual ejidatarios the right to sell their land, equal to other owners.[28] Tellez proclaimed, "We must have institutions that are compatible with free markets. There is a need for well-defined property rights, enforceable through the judicial system. The lack of such security has hindered agricultural investment in Mexico."[29]

As Tellez stressed the benefits of capitalist investment in agriculture, others in the administration sought to frame the reforms around modernization and social justice. Speaking to campesinos in Ucareo, Michoacán, the Secretary of Agrarian Reform Víctor Cervera Pacheco told the three thousand people in the audience that Salinas was the heir to Lázaro Cárdenas and that the new reform would revitalize the Mexican Revolution and not lead to the elimination of the ejido but, instead, could strengthen it. Banners proclaimed in Spanish: "The modernization of the countryside is social justice" and "The countryside demands a new attitude/reality and new mentality." According to Salinas and his team, the modernization of the countryside was paramount to the nation's economic growth and prosperity. While Cárdenas's land reform was seen as historically necessary, now they had to address the new reality that the land reform created, which led to "stagnation, technical deterioration which results in insufficient production, low productivity, and unfavorable terms of trade, and unacceptable living standards."[30] Salinas framed the end of land reform in terms of social justice and fighting poverty. He mobilized support from several government-aligned producer organizations to silence opposition from independent campesino organizations. These shifts in policy were made during Mexico's negotiation with Canada and the United States as part of the North American Free Trade Agreement (NAFTA), which was agreed to by the three presidents in October 1992. NAFTA created a free trade area between the three countries that would eventually eliminate tariffs and other market barriers with the hopes of increasing foreign investment.

Between Salinas's liberalization policies, reforms to Article 27, and NAFTA, the institutional frameworks were in place. As Kirsten Appendini has argued, "In less than six years, from 1989 to 1994, the institutional framework in rural Mexico was completely transformed in order to promote a model of economic growth based on the market and private investment."[31] Beginning in 1994, the door was opened for increased imports and efforts to modernize the countryside. The parallel purpose of government policies in the countryside, according to Appendini, was to both increase the globalizing project for large producers and businesses and modernize the operations of small producers and the peasantry. These policies, while at times contradictory, were meant to maintain a modicum of social peace as the livelihoods of campesinos were under assault.

Throughout the 1980s and 1990s, CONASUPO, Mexico's principle state food agency, was gradually privatized, dismantled, and repurposed to provide relief for the rural poor and to integrate some small producers in the emerging agribusiness complex.[32] The federal government first began to reduce its operation in the countryside, restricting the grains that it purchased at guaranteed prices at the same time that agricultural credit was significantly reduced so as to stimulate private sector investment in the countryside. Between 1989 and 1994, CONASUPO's food processing operations (ICONSA and MICONSA) were privatized, and funds were transferred from subsidies for consumption to providing foodstuff to the "truly needy."[33] By the late 1990s, guaranteed prices were eliminated and CONASUPO ceased operation as prices were liberalized for nearly all foodstuff. The remaining CONASUPO operations (DICONSA and LICONSA) were transferred to other agencies for more targeted social welfare programs.[34]

The transformation of the countryside, characterized by the reforms to Article 27, the dismantling of CONASUPO, and the decapitalization of the ejido, was aimed at reducing subsistence production. With the agrarian reform declared over, neoliberal policymakers argued for a reform aimed at helping peasants become market oriented. By focusing on production for the market, neoliberals sought to prioritize production and efficiency as determined by the market over a holistic view of the peasant and Indigenous food system and foodways.

Export Agricultural and the Loss of Self-Sufficiency

Integrating larger sectors of the Mexican countryside into the world market has had a profound impact on land usage in the countryside, forcing large numbers of campesinos to search for work in the cities to supplement their farm income through other economic activities. There has been a notable decrease in area of land used for basic grain production as the land for exports and feed crops increased significantly. In 1980, the amount of land planted in basic grains (maize, wheat, rice, and beans) was about half of Mexico's cultivated lands, and by 2011 that amount dropped to nearly 39 percent. At the same time the amount of land planted in feed crops grew from 14.5 to 30 percent and winter vegetables and fruits grew from about 25 percent of the value of Mexican agricultural crops to nearly 40 percent.[35]

The transformation of the countryside made Mexico a net exporter of food products while at the same time more dependent on imports of basic grains. According to Laura Carlson, "Before NAFTA, the country spent 1.8 billion dollars on food imports, it now [in 2011] spends a whopping 24 billion dollars."[36] A decade later, Mexico's food imports were more than $37 billion.[37] As part of the comparative advantage framework, policymakers worked to boost the production of export crops. While since the 1970s Mexico had been producing for the U.S. demand for winter vegetables, beginning in the 1990s there was notable export growth of other crops. By 2021, Mexico's five leading agricultural exports accounted for significant percentages of the world trade in these products: beer (33%), berries (15%), avocados (48%), tequila (48%), and tomatoes (28%).[38] Tomato and avocado production growth and exports have been especially notable. Between 1990 and 2010, the value of tomatoes and avocados as a share of national production doubled to nearly 10 percent of total production.[39] While avocados originated in Mesoamerica and have long been recognized as a nutritious fruit in Mexico, until 1997 the United States protected its market from Mexican avocados.[40] With NAFTA, Mexican producers gained access to the U.S. market and consequently Mexican avocado production and exports boomed. During the first decade of the twenty-first century, "Mexican avocado exports grew more than 25%, going from US$73 million in 2000 to $672 in 2010."[41] Between 2016 and 2021, avocado exports grew from $1.9 billion to $3.5 billion.[42]

Central to this transformation of the countryside has been the loss of self-sufficiency in maize. While the trend toward the loss of self-sufficiency in maize was well underway by the 1970s, it has only intensified with the neoliberal opening of the economy.[43] As table 3 indicates, although maize production has increased over the past several decades, it has not kept up with demand, causing Mexico to increase imports. Mexico's average yearly imports by decade have grown consistently since the 1940s. Between 1970 and 2020, this growth amounted to nearly a ten-fold increase, making the total amount of maize imports more than 32 percent of what the nation produces. Maize imports increased sharply with the liberalization of the prices of maize and tortillas that began in the 1980s and accelerated with the implementation of NAFTA.

The liberalization of the countryside has been coupled with the growing use of genetically modified seeds dominated by large multinational corporations such as Monsanto and Syngenta. As Gerardo Otero argues, the biotechnology revolution and neoliberal reforms in the countryside are linked as the liberalization of laws opened the way for biotech companies to operate within Mexico to the benefit of larger producers.[44] With the introduction of genetically modified maize in the early 2000s, Mexican campesinos' historic production of maize has been severely eroded. The neoliberal maize regime both drives communities to migrate and leads to greater importation of maize.[45]

The neoliberal transformation of the countryside was meant to drive campesinos off the land so the lands could be used for more profitable export crops. In 1991, Undersecretary of Agriculture Luis Tellez predicted that the market-oriented reforms would lead to the migration of

TABLE 3 Average Yearly Maize Production, Imports, and Consumption by Decade, 1940–2019

	A Production T Tons	B Imports T Tons	C=A+B Consumption T Tons	D=B/C Imports as a % of Consumption
1940–49	2,294	23	2,317	1.0
1950–59	4,217	240	4,457	5.4
1960–69	7,761	219	7,980	2.7
1970–79	9,034	1,312	10,346	12.7
1980–89	12,162	2,848	15,010	19.0
1990–99	17,239	3,269	20,508	15.9
2000–09	23,198	6,840	30,038	22.8
2010–19	24,405	11,775	36,180	32.5

Sources: Calculated from Aída Mostkoff and Enrique C. Ochoa, "Complexities of Measuring the Food Situation in Mexico"; Servicio de Información Agroalimentaria y Pesquera (SIAP) of the Secretaría de Agricultura, Ganaderia, Desarrollo Rural, Pesca y Alimentación (SAGARPA), http://www.siap.gob.mx/index.php?option=com_wrapper&view=wrapper&Itemid=350; and *Panorama Agroalimentario: Maíz 2019* (Mexico City: Fideicomisios Institutos en Relación Con la Agricultura, Dirección de Investigación y Evaluacion Económica y Sectorial).

about half of rural Mexicans over the course of the next two decades.[46] While migration did noticeably increase, Tellez's predictions did not materialize, much to the chagrin of elite pundits, like Jorge Castañeda, who laments Mexico's inability to evict its peasants from the land at a faster rate due to the "Mexican peasant's passionate attachment to the land, barren, inaccessible, almost useless land."[47] While neoliberal intellectuals Tellez and Castañeda hoped for a campesino exodus to make way for private capital, campesinos struggled to hold on to their land and liberty.

Mexico's rural population adjusted their livelihoods to the economic transformations in the countryside. Forced migration has a long history in the Mexican countryside but has sped up since the 1990s as the number of agricultural jobs dropped by 20 percent. According to Xóchitl Bada and Jonathan Fox, "Annual rates of cross-border migration more than doubled from an estimated 295,000 in 1991 to a peak of 725,000 in 2000."[48] This included growing numbers of migration from Indigenous communities from Oaxaca, Guerrero, and Puebla who often had little choice but to leave their communities.[49] According to Miguel Martínez Peralta, a Guerrero native who worked for twelve years in the fields of Sinaloa, "It's the truth: it is migrate or die. We are forced to go to work in Sinaloa."[50] These patterns of labor migration have significantly increased, especially in the states of Sinaloa and Baja California, where export agriculture has rapidly expanded.

Despite the initial rapid rates of migration following the liberalization of the economies and the implementation of NAFTA, migration has leveled off and the size of the rural population has grown. Between 2000 and 2010, the rural population dropped from 27 percent of the national population to 25 percent; however, it grew in absolute numbers. Most of the rural population is concentrated in ten states in central and southern Mexico and is disproportionately Indigenous.[51] Through the political and economic transformation of the countryside, Mexican campesinos have been forced to find multiple income streams to survive and maintain their ways of life. This new rurality has led to most rural residents earning only a portion of their income from farming and becoming integrated into regional labor markets.

The Rise and Global Growth of Mexican Food Oligopolies

With the onslaught of foreign multinational capital into the Mexican market following the deregulation of the economy and the transformation of global agriculture, large Mexican food companies had to expand domestically and internationally if they were to continue to exist. A small number of Mexican food companies were well positioned to take advantage of Mexico's neoliberal reforms. The 1995 economic crisis further strengthened many large Mexican corporations that were able to take advantage of the economic reforms and increase their concentration of the domestic market (figure 1).[52] By the end of the 1990s, each of these companies dominated the national market as virtual monopolies or as oligopolies by building on their longevity in the market, their distribution networks, their political ties, and marketing strategies. One business

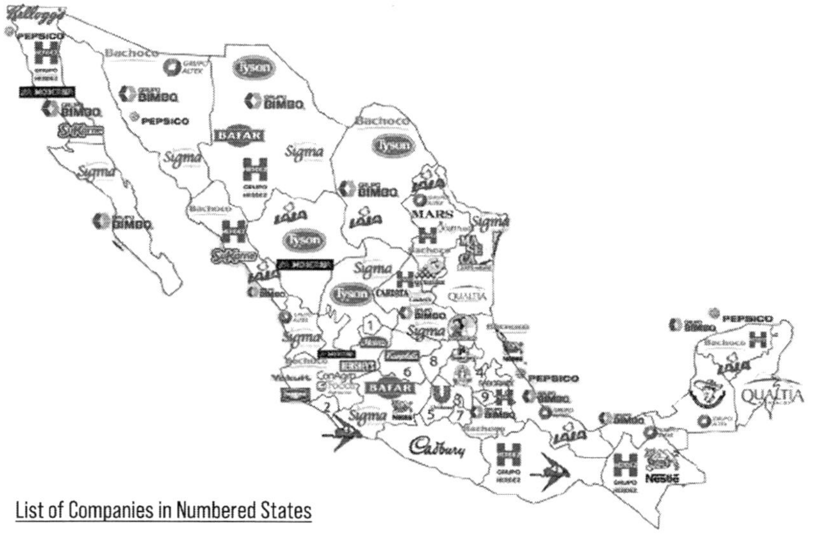

List of Companies in Numbered States

1. Aguascalientes: Grupo Lala, Industrias Bachoco, Sara Lee de México, Tyson Foods
2. Colima: Grupo Marítimo, Sigmas Alimentos, Marindustrias, Danisco Mexicana
3. Mexico City: Grupo Lala, Grupo Herdez, Grupo Bimbo, Pepsico, Kraft,
   Grupo Danone, La Costeña, ConAgra Foods, Gruma, Grupo Mac'ma, Grupo Turin
4. Hidalgo: Grupo Bimbo, Productos Santa Clara, Sigmas Alimentos, Pilgrim's Pride
5. Estado de Mexico: Unilever, Grupo Bimbo, La Moderna, Grupo Altex, Sigmas Alimentos, Kraft, Nestlé,
   Alpura, Yakult, Pepsico, Chocolates Turin, Grupo Herdez
6. Guanajuato: Industrias Bachoco, La Moderna, Grupo Altex, Grupo Lala, Grupo Herdez, Grupo Bimbo,
   Grupo Danone, Sigma Alimentos, Pepsico, ConAgra Foods, Campbell's
7. Morelos: Unilever, Pepsico, Givaudan de México, Ingenio Emiliano Zapata
8. Querétaro: Mars, Nestlé, Kellogg's, Qualitia Alimentos, Pilgrim's Pride, Nutec, Procesadora de Alimentos Mexicanos
9. Tlaxcala: Nestlé, Comercializadora Gonac, Productos Alimenticios La Morena

FIGURE 1 Food Processing Companies in Mexico by Region, 2018. (PROMÉXICO, *Industrias de Alimentos procesados: Unidad de inteligencia de negocios, 2015* [Mexico City: Secretaría de Relaciones Exteriores, 2015], https://www.gob.mx/cms/uploads/attachment/file/75325/150727_Alimentos_ESP.pdf.)

scholar triumphantly proclaims these companies "national champions."[53] The way was paved for them to forge alliances with foreign investors and aggressively expand abroad.[54]

The expansion of Mexican food and agribusiness followed global patterns.[55] During a period of two decades, several Mexican food companies were able to expand rapidly in Mexico's domestic market through a combination of merging and acquiring their immediate competition (horizontal combination) and through vertical integration. Many of these companies then were able to begin to control the entire supply chain from inputs to the marketing and distribution of their products.[56] The leading food companies that expanded abroad included: Grupo Bimbo—the world's largest baked goods and packaged bread company and fourth largest food company; Grupo Maseca (GRUMA)—the world's largest tortilla and flat breads producer; Grupo LALA—Latin America's leading dairy company; and Oxxo—Latin America's largest chain of convenience stores.

Beginning in the late 1990s and early 2000s, Mexican companies aggressively sought markets in other countries and forged alliances with large transnational companies. While in the 1980s Grupo Bimbo purchased an affiliate in Chile and started a plant in Guatemala, its big move came in 1992 when Bimbo made a deal with the Sara Lee company in the United States to become mutual distributors of their respective bakery products in their respective countries.[57] Similar deals and acquisitions were made with other companies in the United States and then in India. In 1997, Bimbo expanded into other Latin American markets, starting in Colombia and Peru, to begin their expansion and domination of the hemisphere's packaged bread markets.[58] Grupo Herdez began to export to the United States and then expanded its relationship with foreign companies, which it began with McCormick in 1947, to include Barilla (2002), Ocean Spray (2006), and Nestlé (2015).[59] Grupo Cifra, with its Aurrerá discount warehouses and its Superama supermarkets, forged an alliance with Walmart in 1991. The alliance helped Grupo Cifra consolidate its operations and edge out competitors Gigante, and Comercial Mexicana. Walmart took advantage of Mexico's peso crisis in 1995 and bought out Grupo Cifra fully in 1997.[60] GRUMA then expanded into the U.S. market in the 1980s and in 1997 forged a strategic alliance with Archer Daniels Midland, one of the world's leading grain traders, thus setting the stage for its global domination of the maize flour market, tortilla, and flatbread markets during the first decades of the twenty-first century.[61]

Similar rapid expansions occurred in the milk industry. Over the past two decades, Grupo LALA has quickly become Mexico's first dairy company to operate nationwide and expand into the U.S. market. Founded in 1949 in Torreón, Coahuila, as a regional dairy, LALA began purchasing regional Mexican dairies in 2000, including key brands Nutrileche,

Mileche, and Boreal. By 2013 LALA controlled more than 50 percent of the Mexican milk market, up from 37 percent a decade earlier.[62] LALA also expanded into the U.S. market, taking advantage of the economic recession of 2008–2010, and acquired Farmland Dairies, National Dairy, and Promised Land Dairy, and other milk product companies. The 2009 acquisition of National Dairy gave LALA one of the largest milk companies in the United States with the recognizable national Borden brand. In October 2013, LALA raised more than a billion dollars, selling its shares on the stock market to deepen its operations in Central America, where it already had plants in Guatemala and was building a new plant in Nicaragua.[63] In that year, LALA was ranked by the business magazine *Expansión* as number thirty-four on its annual list of the five hundred most important companies in Mexico. CEO Eduardo Tricio Haro was listed as the fifteenth most important businessman in Mexico.[64] In recent years, LALA has continued to grow, with purchases in Nicaragua in 2015 and the development of distribution networks in Honduras, Costa Rica, and El Salvador.[65] By 2023, LALA had a total of thirty-one factories: sixteen in Mexico, nine in Brazil, three in Central America, and two in the United States.[66]

Grupo FEMSA, Latin America's leading Coca-Cola bottler, has helped give Mexico the dubious distinction of being the number one consumer of soft drinks in the world. Founded by Mexico's Grupo Visa, whose history goes back to the founding of Cerveceria Cuauhtémoc in 1890, they created Oxxo in 1978 as a convenience store and a distribution point for their beer and Coca-Cola production. Oxxo rapidly expanded throughout Mexico, cutting into Mexico's small retail market and edging out Mexico's neighborhood markets (abarrotes); as one abarrote store owner explained, "when Oxxo opens a store, five abarrotes close."[67] In the process, Oxxo developed a sophisticated network that in 2015 had nearly thirteen thousand stores in Mexico and Colombia with more than nine million customers daily.[68] This growth has significantly enriched FEMSA and its owners, who made it to the *Forbes* billionaire list: Eva Gonda de Rivera and her family ranked number 201 with $6.7 billion; José and José Francisco Calderón Rosas ranked 894 with $2.1 billion; and Max Michel Suberville ranked 1,312 with $1.45 billion (table 2).

Mexican food processing companies continue to expand their operations in the second decade of the twenty-first century (figure 1 and table 4). These large food corporations have transformed what Mexicans

TABLE 4 Top Mexican Food Processing Companies, 2011–2022

Year	Company Sales M Dollars	Number of Employees	Sector and products
Grupo Bimbo			
2011	9,550	91,355	
2017	13,330	137,000	Bakery products, snacks, and confectionary
2022	22,150	139,631	
GRUMA			
2011	4,940	21,318	
2016	3,610	20,500	Corn flour, tortillas, flat breads
2022	6,250	23,506	
LALA			
2011	4,220	35,006	
2017	3,280	34,884	Dairy products
2022	5,187	40,315	
Industrias Bachoco			
2011	3,020	25,326	
2017	1,520	25,000	Chicken, eggs, convenience meats such as ground meat and chorizo
2022	5,494	34,098	
Ganaderos Prod. de Leche Pura (ALPURA)			
2011	864	10,000	
2018	n/a	11,700	Dairy products
2022	1,414	10,281	
Grupo Herdez			
2011	692	6,000	
2016	960	9,100	Salsas, canned fruits and vegetables, dry pasta
2022	1,758	10,587	
Grupo Bafar			
2016	581	10,000	Manufacturing and distribution of cold cut meats
2022	1,673	13,346	

TABLE 4 *continued*

Year	Company Sales M Dollars	Number of Employees	Sector and products
Keken			
2018	481	5,000	Exporter of pork to Asia
Conservas la Costeña			
2017	800	2,250	Preserved fruits, vegetables, canned foods, soups, sauces, jelly
2022	1,000	4,200	
SuKarne			
2022	3,911	14,510	Beef

Sources: USDA, "Mexico's Food Processing and Ingredients Report," GAIN Report Number MX 3321 (December 31, 2013); and USDA, "Mexico's Food Processing and Ingredients Report," GAIN Report Number MX 9303 (March 27, 2019); various company annual reports.

eat and are among the greatest traffickers of processed, calorie-laden foodstuff. Marketers have exclusive deals with producers and sell much of their products through the large retail outlets like Walmart, with its nearly three thousand stores in Mexico and its operations in four hundred cities in Mexico and Central America. Oxxo, with its more than twenty thousand stores throughout the country, is the largest distributor of Coca-Cola products and serves as a major distributor of Bimbo products, including its numerous bakery goods such as Gansitos and Pingüinos. In addition, Bimbo's highly developed marketing routes throughout the country place its products on the shelves of even the most remote stores. The long shelf life of processed foods and their relatively low price ensure that they are the foods to which working people have access.

The rapid expansion in meat-packing companies (table 4) is another telltale sign that the nation is quickly adopting a modern Western industrial diet. While meat consumption was relatively minimal prior to the Spanish conquest, it grew steadily over the next four hundred years.[69] Since the 1990s, per capita yearly rates of meat consumption have accelerated from thirty-four kilograms per capita in 1990 to sixty-three kilograms by 2009, and nearly seventy-three kilograms in 2020, a 147 percent increase.[70] Although nearly half of U.S. consumption, Mexico's per capita consumption has grown by more than 10 percent in all major meat categories since the 1990s and most analysts argue that the market has room for significant expansion.[71]

The leading meat producers in Mexico are a combination of Mexican and transnational firms. Alimentos SIGMA, the leader in frozen and processed meat and dairy production, is a subsidiary of Grupo ALFA, one of Mexico's largest and oldest industrial groups. SIGMA was established in 1980 when ALFA acquired Grupo Brener, which since 1939 was a leader in the small frozen meat market. SIGMA grew through forging alliances with transnational companies such as Kraft Foods, Oscar Meyer, and Yoplait to distribute their products in Mexico and throughout Central America and the Caribbean.[72] SIGMA, taking a lead from the frozen dinner revolution in the United States in the 1970s, began to market ready-made dinners. While these at first did not fit within middle-class Mexican notions of proper meals, an active campaign was launched by the company through a cooking show that aimed to show middle-class and working housewives how to cook quick and nutritious meals. During two decades of the twenty-first century, SIGMA acquired several local firms and through its main brands of FUD and Bar-S in the United States, and Campofrío in Europe, it is now one of the world's leading frozen meat producers.[73] Between 2011 and 2022, company sales nearly tripled as its number of employees grew from 27,923 to 45,150 (table 4). In 2023 it operated in eighteen countries in North America, South America, and Europe with sixty plants and acquired a majority share in Los Altos Foods, a large Mexican cheese producer in the United States.[74] It is rapidly expanding into vegetable protein by funding innovative start-ups.[75]

Grupo VIZ with its major brand SuKarne, acquired in 1997, is Mexico's leading producer of cattle and beef and the sixth largest producer in the world. Grupo VIZ was established in Sinaloa in 1969 by José Isabel Vizcarra Rodríguez and María Calderón de Vizcarra and is now operated by their son Jesús Vizcarra Calderón, who was recently ranked sixty-eighth on *Expansión*'s list of the top one hundred businessmen in Mexico. Vizcarra Calderón, the "Meat Czar" (El Zar de la Carne), is politically active and has been the mayor of Culiacán for the PRI; he also made two unsuccessful bids for governor of Sinaloa.[76] Since 1986, Grupo VIZ has been a vertically integrated company and now operates six self-contained production units that have feed lot, feed plant, slaughterhouse, and packaging and distribution sections.[77] It was well placed to expand its operations after the implementation of NAFTA. According to one SuKarne official, "We made a pivotal decision to embrace free trade and quickly became one of Mexico's largest marketers of imported meats. We started to export to the US in 1996, and the fact that Mexico had no BSE [mad cow disease] or foot-and-mouth was a reason for our success."[78] At the end of 2023, SuKarne had eight processing plants in Mexico and one in Nicaragua.[79] Their Durango plant, opened in 2016, is the world's largest beef processing plant and can feed up to 300,000 head of cattle daily on more than one thousand acres.[80] SuKarne imports meat and sells it under its name at over 386 points of sale in Mexico. In 2010, approximately 17 percent of its production in 2010 was exported to the United States, South Korea, Japan, and Russia. Two-thirds of its exports went to the United States in 2010 and by 2019 the share jumped to ninety-six. By 2019, SuKarne accounted for 75 percent of all Mexican beef that was exported.

Mexico's poultry industry has significantly higher rates of market concentration than the beef industry. Until recently, three companies dominated the poultry industry: Industrias Bachoco, a Mexican company based in Sonora, and the foreign transnationals Pilgrim's Pride and Tyson Foods. These three companies accounted for approximately two-thirds of the market share. Industrias Bachoco was established in 1952 in Ciudad Obregón, Sonora, by the Robinson Bours family and expanded throughout Sonora and Sinaloa beginning in 1962 and then exponentially expanded its operations in the 1990s, becoming a public company in 1997. Bachoco is Mexico's leading poultry producer and it is the number two producer of eggs. In 2014, it controlled 35 percent of the market share for chickens and 6 percent of the egg market. In the United States, through OK Foods that it acquired in 2011, it is one of the top twenty poultry producers with a 2 percent market share.[81] Pilgrim's Pride, owned by the Brazilian transnational corporation JBS, the largest meat producer in the world, has operated in Mexico since 1999 and is the number two producer of chicken with a market share of approximately 14 percent. Tyson Foods in Mexico, until it was acquired by Pilgrim's Pride in 2015, held the number three position in poultry production in Mexico with 12 percent of the market share.[82] Through its vertically integrated plants it processed 2.7 million chickens a week (approximately 140.4 million chickens a year).[83] With the acquisition of Tyson's poultry operations, Pilgrim's Pride has more than a quarter of the market share.[84]

Pork production in Mexico has been historically dominated by small producers; however, with NAFTA and the neoliberal opening there has been a growing concentration of the industry and a rise of large factory farming led by foreign firms. Between 1990 and 2005, pork production doubled in Mexico and imports of pork increased four-fold. By 2009 more than fifteen million pigs were raised and slaughtered in Mexico.[85] The U.S. Department of Agriculture is also looking to greatly expand pork exports to Mexico. The growth in pork consumption has led many to look to Mexico to intensify its production; however, the costs are very high.[86] In 1993, Virginia-based Smithfield Foods, the world's largest pork producer at the time, cooperated with Agroindustrias Unidas de México to create Granjas Carroll de México to raise and slaughter pigs in the Perote Valley of Veracruz and Puebla. Granjas Carroll quickly became the largest pork producer in Mexico and in 1999, Smithfield bought its partner out to become the sole owner. Granjas Carroll's production exploded, and Smithfield and other big firms increased their pork imports to Mexico. This combination rapidly drove smaller producers out of business.[87]

The rapid growth of factory farm pork production has had severe consequences for the Mexican environment and public health. Granjas Carroll's rapid growth led to environmental consequences that included poor handling of the wastewater, which was facilitated by Mexico's very low environmental standards and led to the pollution of groundwater. At the same time, the improper disposal of diseased pig carcasses led to an overwhelming stench that greatly affected the region's population. Incidents and complaints of vomiting and respiratory problems linked to the putrid smell of the pig factory farm were numerous.[88] In 2009, the outbreak of swine flu (H1N1) shook the industry and demonstrated to all that the community's complaints were indeed valid. Consequently, the community was able to halt Smithfield's plans for the expansion of Granjas Carroll. In 2013 Smithfield was acquired by W.H. Group (Shuanghui International Holdings, Ltd.) the Chinese state company that is a global leader in meat production.[89] After the acquisition, Granjas Carroll got the green light to expand. By 2024, in the midst of a regional drought, it had received fourteen concessions by Mexico's water authority to increase its expansion in Puebla, five of these since 2020. Campesinos and environmentalists in Veracruz and Puebla continue to protest Granjas Carroll's overexploitation of the water and its contamination of groundwater, in the face of threats and police repression.[90]

Despite the numerous complaints and problems that have beset the industry, the growing demand for pork in Mexico as well as China's acquisition of Granjas Carroll make the industry poised for growth.[91] Over the past decade, the industry had a strong recovery from the H1N1 fiasco. Mexican pork producers have expanded their exports to Asia and have been able to take advantage of U.S.-China tariff wars that were initiated during the Trump administration.[92] Pork exports more than tripled between 2016 and 2020, making China and Japan the two largest recipients of Mexican pork.[93]

Mexican food processors and retailers have radically transformed Mexico's food system in the past several years. This growth has been facilitated by neoliberal policies and tied to the political connections of Mexican capitalists. They have been able to take advantage of the economic and political transformations in Mexico and become major national producers, as figure 1 so starkly illustrated. In addition, most of these processors and distributors have developed a global reach and in some cases are the industry leaders. These processors have also been greatly facilitated by the rapid expansion of fast-food chains in Mexico.

From *Comida Corrida* to American Fast Food

While Mexico has always had an important tradition of street food and *comida corrida*, corporate-controlled fast-food chains and U.S. based casual restaurant chains, coupled with U.S.-style diners, have proliferated in Mexico since the late 1980s. These chains have come to rival small independent family-run restaurants that serve traditional Mexican fare and have led to the ongoing war against street food and street vendors. Led by U.S. fast food chains such as McDonald's, Burger King, KFC, and Domino's, held by Mexican and transnational companies such as Alsea, the leading restaurant franchise holder, and convenience stores such as Oxxo, these companies play an important role in Americanizing diets, shaping tastes, and Mexico's nutrition-related public health crisis.

Fast food arrived in Mexico well before McDonald's golden arches were planted on Mexican soil in 1985. The first fast-food restaurant chain to open in Mexico and in the Third World was Kentucky Fried Chicken, with its iconic image of Colonel Sanders, in 1963. Kentucky Fried Chicken opened its first restaurant in the city of Monterrey. Shares in the new restaurant were owned by Distribuidoras Bega, a part owner of José Cuervo Tequila. Kentucky Fried Chicken did well in Monterrey and soon restaurants were established in Guadalajara, Mexico City, and Cuernavaca. As with most foreign businesses in Mexico during this time, the businesses' inputs were sourced within Mexico. By 1969, Pizza Hut also entered the Mexican market and became the second foreign fast-food chain in the country.[94]

Mexican capitalists, however, were already developing their own fast-food chains. Burger Boy was one of Mexico's first successful chain hamburger restaurants modeled after U.S. fast-food chains. Established in 1968, Burger Boy emerged and thrived at a time when U.S. chains were not yet ready to expand into other countries and government policies protected Mexican businesses. Acquired by GRUMA in 1974, at a time when its growth in the tortilla market was limited by Mexican policies, Burger Boy grew to nearly fifty restaurants in the country, though it was principally concentrated in Mexico City. It became one of the very few places to serve a stereotypical U.S. meal of a hot dog, hamburger, French fries, and ice cream. Burger Boy clearly drew from McDonald's fame, with "Supermacs" and fish sandwiches and special promotions that gave away toys to kids and linked the promotions of particular television characters. Catchy television commercials with popular Mexican stars caught the imagination of Mexicans.[95] In 1973, Mexican entrepreneurs established Tomboy to compete with Burger Boy. Tomboy restaurants were drive-in restaurants with large parking lots and room for eating on outdoor tables under umbrellas. The first Tomboy was established on Insurgentes Sur, a principal Mexico City thoroughfare, in the middle-class neighborhood across from the Parque Hundido. Another branch soon was established in Acapulco.[96] Targeting families and especially children, Burger Boy and Tomboy's popularity set the stage for transforming middle-class tastes by making them more accustomed to U.S.-style fast food that would enter Mexico in the 1980s with free trade and NAFTA. These early chains also sold American-style modernity in the names of the establishments, the food, and the overall notions of modernity at a time of a growing middle-class youth and consumer culture.

While McDonald's opened restaurants in Brazil, Puerto Rico, and Central America in the 1970s, it was not until 1985 that the first McDonald's arrived in Mexico.[97] McDonald's flagship operation in Mexico was in the upscale Mexico City neighborhood of Pedregal just outside the famous U.S.-style shopping mall the Perisur. While it initially avoided operating in Mexico, given the heavy regulation on foreign businesses, McDonald's proceeded cautiously in the 1980s, hoping to take advantage of the devaluation of the peso and the liberalization of trade restriction. The first McDonald's in Mexico City was 49 percent owned by the U.S. corporation and 51 percent owned by Saul Kahn, a young Mexican entrepreneur. McDonald's was required to use beef, buns, and potatoes that were produced in Mexico. In the days following the restaurant's opening, cars were backed up a mile or more on Mexico City's Periférico beltway and sales reached approximately $10,000 a day. A month and a half after its initial opening, McDonald's owners were greeted by picket lines of demonstrators who were members of the PRI-affiliated restaurant and workers union who protested the hiring of part-time and non-union workers. The union also protested that McDonald's seemed to be only hiring lighter-skinned workers who were middle class in appearance. Two months after the Mexico City restaurant opened another opened in the northern city of Monterrey.[98]

Unlike in the United States, where McDonald's acquired a mass market of middle-class and lower-middle-class customers, in Mexico it became a symbol of upper-middle-class prosperity during the boom of free trade in the 1990s. McDonald's restaurants opened in upper-middle-class neighborhoods since its products were much more expensive that traditional tortas and tacos.[99] McDonald's growth over the 1990s and early years of the twenty-first century has resulted in its opening of more than four hundred restaurants in eighty-six cities in all thirty-two Mexican states. In addition, McDonald's opened several McCafés and Dessert Centers, bringing its total food outlets to well over five hundred, making it the leading chain restaurant in the country.[100]

In 2007, the McDonald's corporation decided to divest itself of its international holding and auctioned them off in a bidding process. Regional operators under the leadership of Woods Stanton, a Colombian businessman who worked with McDonald's first as an employee and then as a partner since the 1980s, formed Grupo Arcos Dorados and won the exclusive rights to operate and franchise McDonald's restaurants in twenty countries in Latin American and the Caribbean.[101] As of June 2019, Arcos Dorados controlled 2,200 restaurants with 90,000 employees in the region and was the largest McDonald's franchiser in the world.[102] This included nearly all of Latin America, with the exception of Central America, where the Cofiño family opened the first McDonald's in Guatemala City in 1974 and now controls McDonald's Mesoamérica, which operates in Guatemala, Nicaragua, Honduras, and El Salvador.[103]

Other U.S. fast-food and restaurant changes have also expanded throughout Mexico. Grupo Alsea has become Mexico's largest U.S. fast-food and chain restaurant franchiser in Mexico. Founded by the Torrado Martínez family in 1997, Alsea operated nearly two thousand restaurants in Mexico at the end of 2014, which was 20 percent greater than in 2013 (table 5).[104] Burger King, Domino's Pizza, and Starbucks are Alsea's most important fast-food franchises. In addition, Alsea operated a growing number of U.S.-style restaurants, including Chili's, California Pizza Kitchen, and the Cheesecake Factory.[105] In 2013, Alsea purchased the VIPS restaurant chain and its Mexican-style spin-off El Portón from Walmart. VIPS was the second largest full-service chain restaurant in 2010 with 13.4 percent of the market, second only to Carlos Slim's Sanborns Chain, which had 15.5 percent of the market.[106] Alsea is also rapidly growing in other countries and currently has restaurants in five other countries (Colombia, Chile, Spain, Brazil, and Argentina). This rapid growth of U.S. fast-food restaurants has led Alsea's growth in the Mexican economy. According to *Expansión*, in 2013 Alsea was ranked number 151 out of the top 500 Mexican companies and its CEO Torrado Martínez ranked fifty-ninth on the list of Mexico's top 100 business leaders.[107] In July 2015, Alsea announced that it was expanding its investments by one billion pesos with 70 percent of that amount aimed at opening new restaurants in Mexico.[108] Between 2013 and 2017, its net sales nearly tripled to 42,529 million pesos.[109]

By 2023, Alsea held 4,455 restaurants in eleven countries: five in Latin America and six in Europe. Slightly more than half of its restaurants were owned in Mexico. Alsea's diversification of countries and global growth is indicative of the globalization of Mexican corporations and their responsiveness to market demands. This global emphasis is best represented by Alsea's focus on the growth of Starbucks in Mexico. Opening its first franchise in Mexico in 2002, by 2005 it had 76 stores and 786 at the beginning of 2023. By the beginning of 2023, Alsea had 1,673 stores in nine countries in Latin America and Europe.[110] In April 2023, Alsea announced that it planned to open three hundred more Starbucks locations in Europe by 2028, which would bring the total number of its operations of Starbucks in Europe to 834.[111]

Neoliberal Food Structures and Neoliberal Diets

Transnational Mexican and international companies continue to dominate and transform the basic food market in Mexico, Latin America, and the United States. They all have deep multinational links and have been expanding across the globe, making a small group of Mexican capitalists and their allies very wealthy and strengthening their position within Mexico's political system. In the process they are accelerating the rates of transformation of Mexican diets, and this is contributing to long-term cultural, political, social, and environmental consequences. The capitalist transformation of the food industry has radically transformed the eating habits and diets of Mexicans in ways that colonizers and Mexican elites have dreamed about doing for centuries. In the process, much of the frozen, canned, and processed food sold in Mexico's burgeoning supermarkets and convenience stores differs radically from what Mexico and the world associate with Mexican food.

Several recent studies have drawn the direct link between the neoliberal transformation of Mexico's food system and the deterioration of Mexican diets. Studies demonstrate that rates of obesity and diet-related diseases increased precipitously with the liberalization of the economy and the flooding of the market with low-cost and ultra-processed foods. One recent study found that "retail food environments with higher densities of convenience stores were significantly associated with higher BMIs, even after adjustment for diverse sociodemographic variables."[112] Other studies have demonstrated that excessive access and exposure to unhealthy foods deeply influence their consumption.

These foods bear little resemblance to what the diverse peoples of Mexico have been eating for centuries. While industrialized food is being churned out in factories in the city and on the farms, it still has not

TABLE 5 Grupo Alsea's Restaurant Holdings in Mexico, 2001–2023

Name of Restaurant	2001	2005	2010	2014	2019	2023
Domino's	425	529	584	604	768	845
Pan Caliente	14					
Burger King	78	109	438	417	174	
Starbucks		76	300	456	737	785
Popeyes		5				
Chili's	11	31	47	73		70
California Pizza Kitchen			4	22	0	
P.F. Chang's		9	19	24	28	
Pei Wei				2	0	
Italianni's			66	95	74	
Cheesecake Factory				1	4	7
VIPS				259	288	244
El Porton				85	57	15
Corazón del Barrio						2
Total	439	728	1,037	1,999	2,463	2,244

Sources: Menú Alsea, *Informe Anual*, 2001, 2005, 2010, 2014; https://www.alsea .net/nuestras-marcas.html, https://www.alsea.net/somos-alsea.html.

been equally distributed. Instead, food production based on an industrial growth model has a devastating impact on small producers, the environment, the diets of the majority of Mexicans, and Mexico's cultural heritage. The shifts in government policies have, however, enriched a few and more closely integrated Mexico's capitalist classes and governing classes, strengthening the hand of capital while exacerbating political, cultural, and social inequality. In the following chapters, we examine how some of Mexico's leading food corporations have come to dominate the national and international food markets.

CHAPTER 4

MEN WITH MACHINES

GRUMA and the Transformation of the Tortilla Industry

From 2001 until 2011, the Mission Tortilla Factory was an attraction where visitors of Disneyland's California Adventure theme park could learn about the history of tortillas and see them being made. Touring the factory, Disney parkgoers first entered a room with a video monitor where they watched a short cartoon video about the Indigenous roots of maize and saw a mural depicting the Mayan god of maize giving maize to the Mayan people. On the walls of the next room was a brightly painted mural divided in two by a highway with an eighteenth-century Mission period scene on one side and a modern cityscape on the other. The mural contained inserts with four small dioramas containing holographic projections of kitchen scenes showing women cooking and making tortillas in each era (figure 2). The next room led to the production line where a large mural depicted the modern industrial tortilla production process led by GRUMA men and machines (figure 3). Visitors then entered the factory where glistening machines and conveyor belts showed the modern form of tortilla making as workers dressed in white chef clothing with Mission Tortilla baseball caps oversaw the process and gave visitors a sample of the modern tortillas.[1] Disneyland parkgoers were to come away from the exhibit with an idea of how this ancient food source was modernized by technical innovation and a part of Californian history through its Mission period past. Further, GRUMA's retelling of the history of tortillas centered its role in tortilla history, explaining that its founders, Roberto González Gutiérrez and Roberto González Barrera, "achieved a five-thousand-year technological leap in the industry of tortilla, by changing entirely the traditional manner to prepare the tortillas in Mexico."[2]

FIGURE 2 GRUMA's Appropriation of the Tortilla Story, Disney's California Adventure. (Yester California Adventures at Yesterland, "Mission Tortilla Factory Hosted by Mission Foods," http://www.yesterland.com/tortilla.html. [a] "Peek-in vignettes." [b] "3-D tortilla vignette." Photos by Werner Weiss [2010].)

FIGURE 3 Mission Tortilla Mural at Disney's California Adventure. (Photo by author.)

While tortillas were celebrated throughout the Mission Tortilla Factory exhibit, there were few indications that maize and tortillas are the primary staple of people from Mexico and Central America. Nor was there any indication that the Mission brand is a subsidiary of the Mexican GRUMA (Grupo Maseca) corporation, the largest tortilla producer in the world established in 1947. While fields of maize were shown in one mural and one room showed the connection of maize to Mexico's Mayan and Aztec past, visibly absent was the role of Indigenous peoples in the cultivation, innovation, and consumption of maize and tortillas since the conquest. The essential role of women in transforming maize into tortillas and the scientific and technological innovation that Indigenous women pioneered was almost nowhere to be found. Other than the cartoon and mural at the beginning of the tour, modern tortillas were portrayed as an innovation of men in Western modern society. In its tour, GRUMA reframed the history of the tortilla, making itself central to a thousand-year tortilla history and effectively erasing Indigenous women from the process.[3]

The appropriation of the history of tortillas by GRUMA is part of the systematic assault on Indigenous knowledges and foods that began with the onset of European colonization of the Americas and has only accelerated over the course of five centuries. As we have seen in previous chapters, settler colonial efforts to transform the diets of Indigenous peoples included the appropriation, commodification, and redefinition of these foods to fit the broader nation-state building project. Public health, nutrition, and social welfare campaigns aimed to improve nutrition through westernizing the Mexican diet. Capitalist development strategies fostered the expansion, industrialization, and mass marketing of food. Together, the Mexican state and GRUMA appropriated tortillas from the hands of Indigenous women and turned them over to men with machines—Mexican capitalists who in turn have reshaped tortillas for national and global markets.

Over time, GRUMA constructed a masculinist, individualistic, and modern construction of tortillas in opposition to gendered, collectivist, community-centered approaches rooted in Indigenous histories and cultures. Starting his company during the business-friendly administration of Miguel Alemán, González Barrera cultivated relationships with political bosses in Nuevo León who introduced him to key national leaders who opened the doors to Mexico's power elite for him. These relationships would enable GRUMA to grow throughout Mexico, expand into Central America and the United States, and survive Mexico's devastating economic crisis of the 1980s and its neoliberal transition. GRUMA would emerge stronger than ever and by the beginning of the twenty-first century would be poised for global growth.

This chapter explores the rise of GRUMA from a small local business in Cerrevalo, Nuevo León, through its integration into Mexico's power elite and its subsequent development into the global giant that it is today. This chapter pays particular attention to the ways that GRUMA and the Mexican state reshaped the tortilla narrative and how its development and expansion was facilitated by state policy and González Barrera's ties to Mexico's power elite. We then examine how these ties to the power elite helped catapult GRUMA into being the nation's largest maize flour producer during Mexico's neoliberal transformation and then facilitated its global expansion. The chapter concludes with a discussion of GRUMA's marketing strategies in the United States that simultaneously play on Mexican nationalism and disassociate tortillas from their Indigenous history.

GRUMA's Appropriation of the Tortilla Origin Story

While the history of tortillas began between five thousand and seven thousand years ago when Indigenous women developed the process of nixtamalization, GRUMA's tortilla narrative centers on its founder, Roberto González Barrera. According to the company's website,

> Mr. Roberto Gonzalez Barrera during a trip to Reynosa Tamaulipas found a rustic artifact that was used to grind dried "nixtamal." It was a mill that produced 18 tons per month of corn flour to prepare tortillas. He had an impulse and from the moment he had it in his hand he felt it could be a great industry. He took a test of this to his father, a man of work, engineer and born researcher, Mr. Roberto M. Gonzalez Gutierrez and together they achieved a five-thousand-year technological leap in the industry of tortilla, by changing entirely the traditional manner to prepare the tortillas in Mexico.[4]

In GRUMA's narrative, the tortilla production process was taken from the remnants of the stone ages and advanced five thousand years because of the ingenuity, foresight, and labor of González Barrera and his father. González Barrera's grandson, Carlos Hank González, explains,

> GRUMA is a Mexican company with a global reach, of which we all should be proud. My grandfather Roberto González Barrera created it; he began to sell tortillas in the U.S. when nobody thought that it could be successful. Now it is the most popular food.[5]

GRUMA's reshaping of the tortilla narrative centers the hard work and ingenuity of one man who advanced technology five thousand years and made it the most popular food in the United States. Throughout its literature and websites, GRUMA systematically erases the long history of maize cultivation and its daily transformation into nixtamal and that tortillas were the result of gendered Indigenous knowledges, science, and ingenuity developed over the course of thousands of years.

GRUMA's narrative fits the larger gendered and racialized arc of Mexico's postrevolutionary state-building process. As a mestizo nation, industrialist and nation builders constructed an alternative analysis of

Mexican foods, such as tortillas, that saw them as having the potential to be important and nutritious items but that they needed to be modernized, taken out of the hands of Indigenous women and campesinos, and infused with technical innovations. From the perspective of the modernizing Mexican state, traditional maize preparation was inefficient, too time consuming, unhygienic, and not sufficiently nutritious. According to the historian Aurora Gómez-Galvarriato, the introduction of mechanized mills and the mechanization of the tortilla industry led to the marginalization of women from the tortilla-making process. By 1924, women in the tortilla industry were earning 27 percent of what men earned. While many women had their own *tortillerías*, with mechanization and women's lack of access to capital, "these businesses became increasingly controlled and operated by men."[6]

Spurred by World War II food shortages, policymakers and entrepreneurs began to seek ways to increase food supply and modernize production. Shortages during World War II had at least as much to do with distribution as with production. For most periods, Mexico seems to have had enough maize and wheat to supply the country but due to transportation bottlenecks and regional hoarding, some regions experienced scarcity as grains remained in warehouses in one part of the country, far from urban areas. Consequently, it was often easier to import grains from the United States.[7] Another possible solution to shortages and resultant price hikes would be to find a way to store masa produced by *molinos de nixtamal*. However, storing masa was out of the question since it dried quickly and had to be used the same day. The same was true of tortillas as they dried out after several hours and could not be used the following day.

To address the fluctuating supply, GRUMA would adapt the maize flour production method that was used in the United States to create dehydrated masa that would be shelf stable. The making of maize flour was pioneered in San Antonio, Texas, with the patenting of a maize-dehydration technique by José Bartolomé Martínez in 1909.[8] This process was widely known in the U.S. Southwest during the first few decades of the century and stimulated the commercialization of Mexican food in Texas.[9] While the process most likely existed in Mexico, since a patent was filed in 1912, there is no record of commercial masa dehydration during these years. Not until 1949 with the opening of Molinos Azteca with its MASECA brand by Roberto M. González in Cerralavo, Nuevo León, did the commercialization of maize flour begin in earnest. In 1950, MASECA (Masa Seca or dry masa) was followed by the establishment of a state enterprise, Maíz Industrializado (MINSA), with a large factory in Tlanepantla outside of Mexico City.[10]

The industrialization of maize dehydration took off once greater technological innovation was developed. In the 1950s, GRUMA worked to improve the initial corn flour machine purchased by González Barrera and find ways to make the reconstituted flour, after water was added, look more like traditional masa. Initially, it did not stick together well and had a chewing gum–like appearance or it "looked too synthetic."[11] It was rejected by González Barrera's customers in his hometown as "not authentic because it was not milled at the metate, that the tortilla came out black, and that they did not have a good taste."[12] Through trial and error, they were able to develop an acceptable flour color and consistency. They opened a second mill in Acaponente, Nayarit, in the 1950s and then six more in the 1960s (Sinaloa, Nuevo León, Jalisco, Chihuahua, Veracruz, and Tamaulipas).[13]

"It Was the PRI That Created Me": Mexico's Power Elite and the Rise of GRUMA

While company literature makes much of the enterprising talents of Roberto González Barrera, GRUMA's success is intimately tied to González Barrera's cultivation of political connections over the years that catapulted him into Mexico's power elite. Year later, González Barrera noted the importance of these political connections, in his interview with Alberto Bello, the editor of *Expansión*: "I have always been an empresario connected to the government, the PRI and I are almost the same age, and it was the PRI that created me."[14]

GRUMA's rise occurred during the Mexican Miracle, from the 1940s to the 1970s. During this period, individual businesses prospered if they played by the political rules and incorporated themselves into the political system.[15] While the relationship between the business and the government could be volatile, conflicts were often expressed through business organizations and the PRI's corporatist structure. The private sector was always a significant political player that strongly influenced all governments. According to Antonio Ortiz Mena, the architect of the Mexican Miracle and political godfather to González Barrera, "our contact with the private sector was constant during when I was in government. We would call them, give them our ideas about a policy, wait for their reaction, and then we would analyze their reactions, take them into account, and incorporate them into our final policies."[16]

Roberto González Barrera honed his economic and political entrepreneurial skills from an early age. Beginning at the age of seven, under the tutelage of his grandfather, he became a shoeshine boy and began to make and rent shoeshine boxes to his cousins. Soon afterward he started selling eggs, vegetables, and maize, and at the age of eleven he left school to work in a neighborhood store. At the urging of his grandfather, he began to specialize in the vegetable market and sold his products in the underground market during the shortages of World War II. His lucrative trade took off. During the late 1940s, Roberto González Barrera worked in Veracruz for PEMEX, Mexico's state-owned oil monopoly, as a driver and assistant to Francisco Hewitt, a French oil driller who sold explosives in the oil fields, enabling him to establish important political connections.[17] He also began a side business selling coconuts and returned home after two years with 200,000 pesos saved.[18] With that money, González Barrera purchased his first maize flour mill in Reynosa and transported it to Cerralvo. His father at this time owned several businesses in Cerralvo, including a local bus service to the capital city of Monterrey and the town's first cinema. He also developed close connections to local politicians and caudillos. With the González family political and business contacts, GRUMA would be born. It was not a Mexican Horacio Alger's story, as company lore would have it. As Roderic Camp has demonstrated, "private-sector leadership is no more open to Mexicans of humble origins than political or cultural leadership."[19] While González Barrera did not start out with the wealth of many entrepreneurs in the postrevolutionary period, he nevertheless came from some local prominence and between him and his father, he had amassed tens of thousands of dollars.

These political connections were essential for GRUMA's growth and future development. A crucial relationship for the early growth of GRUMA was the González family's ties to the most prominent political leader in Nuevo León, General Bonifacio Salinas Leal. Salinas Leal fought in the revolution with Venustiano Carranza's troops and rose in the military ranks after attending National Military College after the revolution. During the 1930s he was a cavalry commander and between 1939 and 1943 served as the governor of Nuevo León.[20] General Salinas Leal built a strong political base while governor and imposed his own successor despite resistance from Mexico City. He then rejoined the army and soon became the zone commander for the Tamaulipas region from 1946 to 1951 and then a regional commander until 1959, after which he became governor of Baja California Sur.[21] A major power broker in the region and nationally, General Salinas Leal was known as an enterprising general involved in numerous business deals, some hidden and others more visible.[22] He lent Roberto González Gutierrez and his son "two million pesos for their maize flour business without any strings attached."[23] González Barrera would later say that the governor was like a second father to him and his first political godfather. Salinas Leal opened doors within the Alemán administration for the agile González Barrera to use his skills to make important deals. During this time, he developed important relationships, including his relationship with José Vivanco, who would become governor of Nuevo León (1952–1955) and then later the head of CEIMSA (1956–1958), the state food agency that had a monopoly on maize importation. Vivanco would help facilitate GRUMA's purchase of subsidized maize and its sale of maize flour to the federal government.[24]

At the end of the 1950s, González Barrera went to live in Mexico City to develop GRUMA's political connections and strengthen its national position. General Salinas Leal directed his political godson to meet with Raúl Salinas Lozano, a fellow Nuevo Leonese and friend of González Barrera's father.[25] Salinas Lozano, the head of the National Investment Commission in the Ruiz Cortines administration, who would soon become Secretary of Commerce under Adolfo López Mateos (1958–1964), was at the height of his power and became González Barrera's tutor in the circles of Mexico City's governing elite. Salinas Lozano, who wrote his 1944 thesis at UNAM's School Economics on price controls and government intervention, was a key policymaker overseeing prices of maize and tortillas during the 1950s and 1960s.[26] This relationship would prove crucial for GRUMA's growth during the 1960s and beyond. Once Salinas Lozano left the Secretary of Commerce, he became a GRUMA consultant. According to Alberto Bello, the editor of Mexico's leading business journal *Expansión*, González Barrera gave Salinas Lozano several loans throughout the 1970s totaling between 1.5 and 2 million pesos.[27] During this time, González Barrera would meet Salinas Lozano's sons Carlos Salinas de Gortari, the future president, and Raúl Salinas de Gortari, who became a key CONASUPO official during the 1980s and 1990s. González Barrera developed a very close relationship with the Salinas family and served as a witness during Raúl Salinas de Gortari's wedding.[28] These key extended familial relationships enabled GRUMA to thrive in a period of heavy government intervention in the maize-tortilla complex.

During this period, González Barrera met Carlos Hank González, an entrepreneur and up-and-coming political player, who would soon become a dominant force in Mexican politics. The economic and political power of both grew together over the next several decades as their relationship developed into a mutually beneficial one personally, politically, and economically. The two first met in Nayarit at the end of the 1950s, when González Barrera was overseeing the construction and operation of GRUMA's new plant in Acaponeta. They deepened their relationship in all-night conversations when their mutual political godfather, General Bonifacio Salinas Leal, was appointed governor of Baja California Sur and Hank González, a young congressman from the state of Mexico, was charged with setting up Salinas Leal's government in eight days. During this time, González Barrera worked with Hank González and the two became fast friends as he saw Hank González's political "genius."[29] Hank González would also be a key player in Mexico's grain markets, working for the state food agency CONASUPO, first as assistant sales manager and later as CONASUPO's director from 1964 to 1969. His political and economic fortunes would continue to grow during Carlos Salinas's presidency; Hank González would serve as Secretary of Agriculture.[30] The two developed a close personal, political, and familial relationship and González Barrera often referred to Hank González as his "hermano de alma" or soul brother.[31] This close relationship was solidified with the marriage of Hank's son, Carlos Hank Rhon, to González Barrera's daughter, Graciela González Moreno. Carlos Hank Rhon has served on the GRUMA board of directors and their mutual grandson, Carlos Hank González, was closely mentored by both magnates.[32]

By 1961, at the age of thirty-one, González Barrera had already developed close relationships with politicos who were at the upper echelons of Mexico's political system, and he began to contemplate running for political office. General Salinas Leal arranged a meeting for him with the head of the PRI, General Alfonso Corona del Rosal. The meeting was also attended by González Barrera's other backers, including Antonio Ortiz Mena (Secretary of Hacienda), Raúl Salinas Lozano (Secretary of Commerce), Carlos Hank González (congressman from the State of Mexico), Leopoldo Sánchez Ceres (governor of Sinaloa), and Eduardo Livas (gubernatorial candidate from Nuevo León). According to González Barrera, the president of the PRI told him that "he had never seen someone recommended by such godfathers. You have it made, my friend."[33] Although he was not chosen by the PRI to run for political office, González Barrera was fully integrated into the political establishment. This would bode exceptionally well for GRUMA and its future.

González Barrera's political web of connections within the PRI was crucial to GRUMA's survival and expansion in the late 1970s. At the end of the Gustavo Díaz Ordaz presidency (1964–1970), the government offered to buy GRUMA's plants and operation for 400 million pesos.[34] Mexico faced a deep political crisis following the government massacre of student demonstrators in 1968 and its subsequent crackdown on political dissent. The rise of urban and rural guerilla movements led the incoming government of Luis Echeverría to both launch a repressive dirty war and expand its populist social programs by building food stores and increasing its control of food supplies to keep food prices down as a way of ameliorating the social conflict.[35] Purchasing GRUMA would have been an important step in this process and it would have merged with the government's own milling operation, MINSA, giving the government effective control of the maize flour industry.[36]

However, González Barrera was dissuaded from selling by members of his politically powerful circle. The outgoing Secretary of the Treasurer, Antonio Ortiz Mena, the leading economic architect of Mexico's Stabilizing Development strategy, offered to help him secure a loan to expand his operations if he rejected the government's offer, telling him, "I don't think you should sell. It is an error. Mexico needs businessmen, people like you."[37] After hearing Ortiz Mena's offer, González Barrera went to the nearby house of his good friend Carlos Hank González, the past head of CONASUPO, the state company that would be acquiring GRUMA, and the current governor of the State of Mexico. During a conversation that lasted until dawn, Hank González pointedly advised him not to sell: "It is stupid to sell, Roberto. . . . You have the best business, something that no one has. The technology for processing coffee, sugar, wheat or rice is already invented, but you are developing the product that Mexicans eat the most. How are you going to leave that?"[38] Ultimately, González Barrera took the advice of two of Mexico's most powerful politicians of the second half of the twentieth century. With a million-dollar line of credit from Mexico's national development bank NAFINSA, secured with the support of Ortiz Mena, GRUMA began to expand its operations in Mexico.

Throughout the 1970s, GRUMA received opportunities for growth, even as the Echeverría government increased government regulation of the maize and tortilla industry. Since Mexico's populist governments used food policies as a mechanism for delivering on the faltering social promises of the revolution, the state was heavily involved in the marketing of maize and subsidizing traditional millers and tortillerías to keep the price of tortillas down while promoting small industry. At the same time, the governments of Echeverría and his successor, López Portillo, were expanding CONSAUPO's maize flour production operations.[39] González Barrera would later indicate frustration with the Echeverría government since it "imposed controls over private food companies that didn't allow us to grow. That is why we went to Costa Rica."[40] However, because of González Barrera's loyalty to the PRI, government officials in Echeverría's administration facilitated GRUMA's expansion internationally.

Although González Barrera felt limited by Echeverría's policies, the expansion of CONASUPO's maize flour production would also benefit GRUMA. Between 1970 and 1980, corn flour production increased from 2.9 percent to 7.3 percent of the nixtamal industry in Mexico. As the government poured more resources into corn flour manufacturing capacity, it set the basis for changing consumer tastes and tortilla production.[41] GRUMA dominated the market during this period but the expansion of CONASUPO and the development of its industrial technology and operations limited GRUMA's ability to grow. Between 1970 and 1976, CONASUPO created subsidiaries to mill maize flour (MICONSA and ICONSA) and wheat flour (TRICONSA) and another to produce packaged foods (ICONSA). During this period, overall federal government subsidies to CONASUPO increase nearly four-fold, accounting for 46.5 percent of total federal government transfers to state agencies.[42]

TABLE 6 Mexican Corn Flour Production, 1975–1980

	Total Production Tons	GRUMA Tons (%)	MINSA Tons (%)	ICONSA Tons (%)
1975	560,521	416,464 (74.3)	107,605 (19.2)	36,452 (6.5)
1976	348,750	185,632 (53.2)	74,576 (21.4)	88,542 (25.4)
1977	591,069	375,729 (63.5)	139,675 (23.6)	75,665 (12.8)
1978	724,637	474,649 (65.5)	179,604 (24.8)	70,384 (9.7)
1979	674,268	395,000 (58.5)	209,098 (31.0)	70,170 (10.4)
1980	803,700	500,000 (62.2)	234,000 (29.1)	69,700 (8.7)

Source: Nacional Financiera, *La industria de la harina de maíz* (Mexico City: NAFINSA, 1982), 17.

By 1980, GRUMA was Mexico's sixth largest food company, with net sales of 4,163 million pesos. It was followed by the state-owned Industrias CONASUPO. ICONSA, MICONSA, and CONASUPO would all be slimmed and then dissolved at the end of the century in a process of liberalization and privatization of the food markets.[43] GRUMA, with its close political ties to Mexico's power elite, its access to capital, and the growing success of its international operations, was well positioned to take advantage of market liberalization. In a very short time it would reap huge profits in Mexico that would help catapult Roberto González Barrera to the *Forbes* list of billionaires.

GRUMA's Neoliberal Tortillas

While GRUMA continued to grow steadily in Mexico during the 1970s and 1980s, the neoliberal reforms of the de la Madrid (1982–1988) and Salinas de Gortari (1988–1994) administrations helped catapult it to new levels. As noted in chapter 3, during the 1980s and 1990s state subsidies to social welfare programs were slashed, markets were liberalized, tariffs were reduced, and state-owned industries were privatized to foster private investment. These policies culminated with the implementation of the North American Free Trade Agreement in 1994.

Presidents Miguel de la Madrid and Carlos Salinas de Gortari put into action plans that had long been limited by previous governments to overtly favor the maize flour industry over the traditional nixtamal industry. As Kirsten Appendini has demonstrated, "[f]rom the point of view of cost and marketing, nixtamalized maize flour offered more advantages than traditional masa since it does not decompose (spoil), it can be stored, and tortillas made from it can be packaged and preserved."[44] The Mexican government promoted the maize flour's efficiency, citing government and industry studies. A NAFINSA study of the maize flour industry argued that the overall cost savings of tortillas made from maize flour were approximately 20 percent and that one kilogram of maize yielded 23 percent more tortillas than traditional nixtamalization.[45] Therefore, 42 percent of nixtamal mills added maize flour in the milling process while 64 percent of tortillerías did this to help reduce their costs.[46] In addition, policymakers saw the possibility of enriching maize flour with soy to increase the protein content of tortillas. NAFINSA concluded its study by touting the possibility that "this would make the tortilla the most nutritious protein-rich food, even superior to milk."[47] While the taste of maize flour–made tortillas was still an issue for consumers, state subsidies and corporate monopolies would soon trump taste.

Throughout the 1980s and 1990s, subsidies to corn and tortillas plummeted and were eliminated by the end of the decade.[48] Before they were eliminated, however, President Salinas began diverting state corn stocks away from forty-five thousand subsidized nixtamal tortilla factories and to the ready-mix tortilla industry, openly favoring GRUMA, by far the largest producer of maize flour.[49] Of the maize that went to maize milling, between 1978 and 1989, the amount going to the traditional nixtamal mills fell by 18.6 percent from 2.7 million tons to 2.2 million tons. By comparison, maize going to maize flour mills tripled from 745,000 tons to 2.4 million tons, thus surpassing the actual amount given to the nixtamal mills by 190,000 tons or 8.7 percent.[50] The reduction of maize going to traditional mills meant that the country's approximately 45,000 small millers had less to work with and were forced to buy on the free market.[51] Consequently, many were driven out of business as maize flour mills, led by MASECA and CONASUPO, MINSA, and MICONSA's operations, significantly increased their operations.

While the 1990s were a period of transition from CONASUPO's dominance of the maize and tortilla markets to the private market that significantly benefited GRUMA, the end of the tortilla subsidy heralded an important shift in GRUMA's operations. GRUMA's role in the market would now shift from fulfilling government contracts to developing and promoting its own brand in anticipation of further liberalization, including the end of the tortilla subsidy in 1999. In 1994, GRUMA began, for the first time in Mexico, producing packaged tortillas and expanding its operation. In 1995, GRUMA announced that it planned to double its capacity to produce maize flour by 1998. It also built plants in Chiapas, Oaxaca, Veracruz, and in the State of Mexico.[52] Maize flour producers increased their share in the production of tortillas from 21 percent in 1991 to 50 percent by 1998. By 2003, GRUMA controlled 71 percent of the maize flour industry, followed by MINSA with 25 percent and Hamas and Agroinsa with 4 percent.[53] Between 1991 and 2005, GRUMA's sales nearly tripled from $808 million to $2.45 billion.[54]

GRUMA also benefited in other ways from its close relationship to those in power. During the Salinas administration, the Mexican government agreed to pay GRUMA a total of $7 million in addition to a prior settlement of $17 million that was agreed to by GRUMA and the government's food agency CONASUPO. That the Salinas administration gave extra money to GRUMA, beyond what even the company agreed to, caused many to decry the payment as corruption when evidence of the deal first surfaced during a congressional investigation of CONASUPO and Raúl Salinas de Gortari in 1995. Salinas de Gortari was director of planning of CONASUPO during the early years of his brother's presidential administration and argued that MASECA was owed an extra $7 million after a settlement for $17 million was already reached. The $7 million extra given to GRUMA occurred against the wishes of the CONASUPO board, which disagreed with Salinas de Gortari's claim.[55] Many pundits and critics argued that this deal was political payback.

Since accusations of González Barrera's receipt of presidential favoritism were rampant, GRUMA was not allowed to purchase MINSA when it was privatized in 1993. According to the editor of *Expansión*, "[a]s much as he (González Barrera) tried to get it, the government decided to give priority to competition."[56] Had GRUMA acquired MINSA it would have had a monopoly of the burgeoning maize flour industry and possibly the tortilla industry. Instead, MINSA was sold to another major bene-ficiary of the Salinas era, the Gómez Flores family. The Gómez Flores family from Guadalajara, led by brothers Raymundo and Armando, also acquired Banco Cremi and Diesel Nacionales (DINA) during the privat-ization process.[57]

GRUMA's Global Tortilla Empire

GRUMA's international expansion began in 1972, when at the sugges-tion of Mexican government official Arsenio Farell Cubillas, director of the National Electricity Commission, the company was invited by President José Figueres to open a plant in Costa Rica.[58] According to González Barrera, President Figueres wanted MASECA to restart the maize industry since the custom of eating maize had been virtually elim-inated among the working classes due to the large amounts of wheat that entered the country through the U.S Food for Peace program.[59] While González Barrera complained that MASECA had limited opportunities for growth within Mexico, because of Echeverría's investment in the growth of CONASUPO, GRUMA's political allies armed the company with a line of credit from NAFINSA and set GRUMA up to be a trans-national corporation.

GRUMA began its operations in Costa Rica by importing maize flour from its Mexican operations and then developing technology to produce, package, and distribute shelf-stable tortillas from the corn flour process. Between 1972 and 1973, GRUMA's Costa Rican subsidiary Derivados de Maíz, SA (DEMASA) pioneered the process of converting maize flour to tortillas by, as it explains on its website, "importing 47 tortilla-making machines that use extrusion technology and we began producing 60 tor-tillas per minute made with maize flour imported from Veracruz Mex-ico."[60] GRUMA sold its tortillas under the TortiRica label and, since there were relatively few traditional tortillerías, it quickly became an important local industry. Beginning in 1979 and 1980, DEMASA began producing chips and other snacks made with maize flour under the Tosti brand and began to compete with the local Jacks brand.[61] In 1979, GRUMA was producing enough tortilla and other maize flour products that it built a maize flour plant in Costa Rica.

Despite its success in Costa Rica, GRUMA saw limited opportunity for expansion in Central America. The market for tortillas was still rather limited in Costa Rica and consumer studies showed that tortilla consumption dropped from 16.85 kilograms per person per year in 1966 to 10.82 in 1976 and then to 4.62 in 1982.[62] Reflecting on the period, González Barrera said, "We couldn't continue growing in Central America owing to the guerilla wars that lasted many years. We also couldn't grow in Mexico since the tortilla was controlled and the price subsidized. In addition, the unions for masa and tortilla producers opposed our growth."[63] Therefore GRUMA looked to the United States.

Beginning in the late 1970s, GRUMA entered the U.S. market and over the next two decades became a leader in the U.S. market. Its U.S. operations became the mainstay of its overall operations. In Los Angeles, it purchased two prominent local companies, Mission Foods in 1977 and then Guerrero tortillas in 1989. Guerrero was purchased from Verónico and Marina Trujillo, who started their factory in Los Angeles in 1973. The Trujillos expanded their business by adding flour tortillas to the corn tortillas that they started with, and by 1986 they had four factories and began to advertise on television. The Trujillos were also known for delivering hot and fresh tortillas to retail grocers.[64] GRUMA would take these important local brands and transform them with its maize flour tortilla–producing operations using the model it developed in Costa Rica.

With Mission and Guerrero as its key brands, GRUMA aggressively expanded in the 1980s and 1990s and transformed the two regional Los Angeles brands into national brands. By 1998, Mission and Guerrero tortillas came to account for approximately 24 percent of the tortilla market and GRUMA controlled 83 percent of the maize flour market in the United States.[65] Regionally, GRUMA brands accounted for more than 50 percent of the tortilla market in Denver, Los Angeles, Miami, Phoenix, Portland, San Diego, San Francisco, and Seattle and nearly reached the 50 percent mark in Dallas and New York (table 7). Just four years later, in 2002, GRUMA brands comprised more than 50 percent of U.S. supermarket tortilla sales and controlled approximately 70 percent of the market in Southern California. By 2003, GRUMA operated thirteen industrial plants in the United States, including the largest tortilla factory in the world in Rancho Cucamonga, California, and employed more than five thousand people.[66]

TABLE 7 GRUMA Brands Share of Regional Tortilla Market in 1998

City	Percent of Market Share
Dallas	48
Denver	53
Houston	28
Los Angeles	84
Miami	58
New York	47
Phoenix	53
Portland	56
San Antonio	24
San Diego	78
San Francisco	56
Seattle	86

Source: GRUMA, *Informe Anual*, 1998, 11,
http://www.gruma.com/media/149789/informe_anual_1998_esp.pdf.

GRUMA's growth during this period occurred through the help of a strategic alliance with Archer Daniels Midland (ADM), one of the leading agribusinesses in the world and a key recipient of U.S. corn subsidies. In 1996 ADM purchased $74.3 million worth of GRUMA stock, giving it 22 percent of the company and two of the eleven seats on GRUMA's board of directors. In exchange, ADM transferred two wheat mills in Mexico to GRUMA, creating La Molinera de México (40 percent owned by ADM), making use of its wheat-milling technology, and $258 million and 80 percent of its combined maize flour operations in both countries.[67] In 1997 and 1998, La Molinera de México purchased five additional wheat flour mills in Mexico.[68] In 1999, it purchased controlling interest in Venezuela's Molinos Nacionales, C.A. (MONACA), making it the number two producer of wheat and corn flour in that country, a position it held until 2010 when leftist president Hugo Chávez expropriated GRUMA's holdings.[69]

Throughout the 1990s, GRUMA expanded its operations in Central America from its Costa Rican base that dominated the Central American maize and maize flour markets and began to produce and market other food products. As Central American countries implemented neoliberal policies in their agricultural sectors in the 1980s, maize imports increased. In 1987, GRUMA established a plant in Honduras and then in 1999 began operations in El Salvador and Guatemala, following the civil wars in both countries.[70] In each of these countries, GRUMA became the leading importer of maize as overall maize imports skyrocketed, and in less than ten years imports were nearly two-thirds the amount of national production in Honduras, El Salvador, and Guatemala. GRUMA expanded its Costa Rican operations after Mexico and Costa Rica signed a free trade agreement in 1995. In 1996, GRUMA opened a plant to produce and can hearts of palm, making it the largest producer of this important crop in Latin America. In addition, GRUMA produced the Luisiana brand of rice and beans in Costa Rica, expanding into the nation's Caribbean rice and bean culture. The signing of free trade agreements and especially the implementation of the Dominican Republic-Central America Free Trade Agreement (CAFTA) in 2006 fostered the consolidation of the agro-export model at the expense of campesino producers, leading to increased rural social dislocation and forcing many to migrate to cities, Mexico, and the United States.[71] GRUMA's 2005 purchase of MINSA's Central American holdings gave it a virtual monopoly of the Central American maize economy. By 2005, GRUMA controlled 80 percent of the maize flour market in Guatemala and Honduras and approximately 70 percent in El Salvador and Costa Rica. In El Salvador and Guatemala, the volume of maize imports was, respectively, 70 percent and 65 percent of the total maize supply, up from 15 percent and 8 percent in 1990, while in Honduras the volume of maize imports reached 90 percent, skyrocketing from the less than 10 percent in 1990. Costa Rica, historically a small maize producer, by 2005 imported nearly all its maize.[72] GRUMA historically had fewer operations in Nicaragua, since it had been self-sufficient in maize and many of GRUMA's products were imported from neighboring El Salvador and Costa Rica. However, in 2011 it constructed a maize flour plant in Nicaragua.[73]

GRUMA expanded into the European market, opening and acquiring plants in England, Italy, Holland, Spain, Russia, and in Asia and Australia

TABLE 8 GRUMA Production Plants Throughout the World, 2023

Region/Country	Number of Plants
Americas	62
Mexico	25
United States	26
Costa Rica	5
Guatemala	2
El Salvador	1
Nicaragua	1
Ecuador	1
Honduras	1
Europe	9
United Kingdom	2
Spain	2
Italy	1
Russia	2
Turkey	1
Ukraine	1
Asia	2
China	1
Malaysia	1
Oceania	1
Australia	1
Total	74

Source: "Global Presence," GRUMA, accessed March 23, 2020,
https://www.gruma.com/en/we-are-gruma/global-presence.aspx?sec=8836.

TABLE 9 GRUMA's Global Expansion, 1973–2011

Country	Year	Type of Activity	Company Names and Brands
Costa Rica	1973	Flour, tortillas, snacks	Tortiricas, La Cima, Rumba, Tosty, Masa Rica, Luisiana
United States	1977	Tortillas, maize flour	Mission, Guerrero
Honduras	1987	Maize flour	DEMAHSA, Maseca
El Salvador	1993	Maize flour, tortillas	DEMASAL, Maseca
Guatemala	1993	Maize flour	DEMAGUSA, Maseca
Venezuela	1993	Maize flour production	Juana, La Comadre, Robin Hood
England	2000	Tortilla production	Maseca, Mission
Italy	2004	Maize flour production	Maseca, Mission
Holland	2004	Tortilla production	Maseca, Mission
Australia	2006	Tortillas, maize flour	Maseca, Mission
Spain	2006	Tortillas, maize flour	Maseca, Mission
China	2006	Tortillas, maize flour	Maseca, Mission
Malaysia	2007	Wraps, flat breads, naan	Maseca, Mission
Ukraine	2010	Maize flour	Maseca, Mission
Turkey	2011	Maize flour	Maseca, Mission
Russia	2011	Tortillas, maize flour	Maseca, Mission, Delicados

Sources: Adapted from Gustavo Vargas Sánchez and Luis Pérez Osnaya, "Gruma: Un análisis microeconómico," *Economía Informa*, no. 386 (May–June 2014): 36–37; and "History," GRUMA, accessed August 26, 2024, https://www.gruma.com/en/we -are-gruma/history.aspx?sec=8836.

with plants in Melbourne, Shanghai, and Malaysia (table 8).[74] Five years after launching its Asia and Australia divisions, GRUMA became the principle supplier of tortillas in the booming fast-food industry of these regions.[75] By 2020, GRUMA proclaimed that "it has visibility in **112** countries of the world through our global brands Maseca and Mission, as well as local leading brands of the markets which we participate: Guerrero in the United States, TortiRicas and Tosty in Costa Rica and Robin Hood in Venezuela, among others," and seventy plants worldwide (table 9).[76]

Roberto González Barrera, GRUMA's founder and the self-proclaimed "tortilla king," used his GRUMA success and political connections to purchase one of Mexico's largest banks during the bank privatization process, thus adding to his family's fortunes and securing financing for his tortilla operations. In 2011, GRUMA sold its shares in BANORTE, but González Barrera kept it in the family. GRUMA used the funds from the sale to pay off its debt, and it purchased four major regional milling and tortilla plants to take advantage of the increases in the price of maize and expand its international reach.[77]

De-Indigenizing and "Saving the Tortilla"

GRUMA's national and global expansion is predicated on transforming the narrative and imaginary origins of the development of maize and tortillas. This modernized narrative credited men with machines who made "a 5,000-year technological leap."[78] In the process, GRUMA emphasized modern hygiene and health discourses that connected to a gendered mestizo discourse tied to Mexican nationalism and capitalist development. A key aspect of transforming the tortilla narrative to center men with machines has been the delinking of the tortilla from Indigenous culture and society. To do so, GRUMA builds on the racialized discourses that cast Indigenous foods as valuable yet ultimately nutritiously inferior to European cuisine. At the same time, it develops complex marketing strategies to reach a broad market for maize flour and tortilla products. In the process, maize flour is cast as healthier and more hygienic than both traditional household nixtamalization at the metate and at the neighborhood Molino de nixtamal.

GRUMA argues that its achievement is revolutionary. As González Barrera said in 1999, "what we have achieved, is that of the tortilla of forever that now incorporates the best nutrition possible."[79] Without GRUMA's innovation, according to González Barrera, it was very likely that the consumption of maize tortillas would have disappeared as it nearly did in Costa Rica. According to González Barrera,

With all its importance and nobility, the technology to transform maize
into masa and tortillas had been stagnant for centuries. For this reason,
the beginning of Grupo Maseca, fifty years ago, had the goal of achieving
an important technological change, to modernize the way that masa and
tortillas are made and sold, to achieve a stable quality, an absolute hygienic
process, and a very competitive cost structure with other basic grains, like
wheat and rice, thanks to the greater efficiency of our productive process.[80]

The work of GRUMA, in its founder's appraisal, has both saved maize
and tortilla consumption in Mexico and reinvigorated its consumption
in Latin America and the world.

GRUMA worked for decades to find ways to enrich maize flour to
increase its protein content. Building on the coloniality framework that
maize was nutritiously inferior compared to wheat that was implanted
with the conquest and modernized and propagated by priests and intellectuals, GRUMA began experimenting with ways to increase protein
content soon after it was established. In the 1970s, it picked up on the
idea of adding protein-rich soy to its maize flour and began intense laboratory testing. In the second half of the 1990s, it conducted "three years
of test trials through the National Nutrition Institute and with the collaboration with Governor Vicente Fox in Guanajuato, piloted its sale in
Guanajuato, using technology of enriched maize flour that has a protein
quality equivalent to 88 percent that of milk, with cost advantages, easy
handling and transport that do not modify food habits."[81] The enriched
product has been sold in Costa Rica and Mexico.

In its efforts to rebrand the tortilla, GRUMA developed creative marketing strategies in Mexico and in the U.S. market that appeal to nostalgia, popular culture, and dietary and culinary trends. In Mexico, these
strategies include television marketing and the creation of paid shows
such as "MASECA en la cocina con las estrellas" on Azteca TV. Mexican
television stars host cooking shows using MASECA to make a variety
of dishes and show how easy it is to cook. For example, in one episode,
the popular singer Mijares describes how he makes carrot cake using
MASECA and explains that MASECA can be used in more than four
hundred dishes.[82] In another spot, Mijares's wife, the multiplatinum
singer and Televisa star Lucero, explains "how tasty the MASECA-made
tortillas are. Look at how soft they are," as she rolls the tortilla between

her two hands and coos alongside the show's host, "Wonderful. Rich in calcium and fiber and it doesn't make one fat!"[83] In these advertisements, mestiza women and men are reintroduced into the tortilla and masa cooking process by light-skinned Televisa stars, not as innovators and inventors but as recipe followers.

Within Mexico, GRUMA's rebranding of tortillas erases Indigenous agricultural and culinary knowledges, labor, and the larger political economic context. As with Mexican television in general, Indigenous women are absent from GRUMA's cooking shows. Their cognitive and sensory knowledges developed over centuries are ignored or erased as GRUMA appropriates and commodifies maize and normalizes the use of its product. While there is little doubt that GRUMA's soy additive improves the nutritive value of the product, this narrow technological focus ignores the larger political economic factors that have reduced the consumption of the poor to tortillas without squash, beans, meat, or the panoply of foods that used to accompany the historic tortilla.

Within the United States, GRUMA's marketing strategies have several dimensions, including marketing to both Latinos/as and non-Latinos/as by appealing to the nostalgia of Mexico or to a Spanish fantasy past and to the whims of U.S. dietary trends.[84] Guerrero and Mission are marketed separately, and an average consumer would be hard-pressed to find a link between the two companies. With Guerrero, GRUMA continued this process, working to appeal to Mexican and Latino consumers in particular through its use of the name—Guerrero, the surname name of both a famous Mexican independence leader (Vicente Guerrero) and a Mexican state. For the first decades of the company, the clear packaging was adorned with red and green lettering of the Mexican flag with drawings of ears of corn. Underneath the brand name, all written in Spanish, was the company's trademarked slogan, "*un pedacito de México*" (a little piece of Mexico).[85] The tortilla is reminiscent of the look and feel of tortillas made in the traditional fashion. The Guerrero website reinforces its ties to Mexico with the slogan "Pure Mexican Tradition."[86] Guerrero explicitly appeals to the consumers' nostalgic remembrances of their homeland and Mexican nationalism.

With Mission Foods, GRUMA made a direct effort to cultivate a non-Latino market, attempting to situate itself within the context and history of the U.S. Southwest. The brand name is a direct reference to the

Spanish Mission Period (1769–1833) and evokes a nostalgia for what scholars have termed the Spanish fantasy past that celebrates Spanish colonization and ignores the genocide of at least a hundred thousand of the region's Indigenous inhabitants.[87] GRUMA uses the glorification of this period to appeal to a non-Latino market by playing up Californian history and disassociating tortillas from Mexicans, Indigenous communities, and Mexican immigrants. Mission tortillas, in contrast to Guerrero, are packaged in clear bags with brightly colored lettering in English. The Mission label package is adorned with a mission bell and above the logo the package brags that Mission sells the "World's Best Selling Tortillas." On the bottom of the package, it proclaims, "No Lard-No Cholesterol" (figure 4). Mission distributes both corn and flour tortillas. The corn tortillas, however, do not look exactly like the Guerrero tortillas. Instead, they are smoother and lighter and look much like flour tortillas.[88] Beginning in 2004, Mission began to produce "wraps" to cater to their popularity and has developed low-carb tortillas to appeal to health-conscious consumers.[89] In late 2008, Mission unveiled its Life Balance Tortillas fortified with calcium and twenty-three vitamins and minerals, including omega–3 fatty acid DHA.[90] On Mexican Independence Day in 2021, Mission launched its "Better for You" line of products with tortillas that are low-carb, gluten free, organic, and whole wheat.[91] Earlier that year it unveiled its "Fresh Signature" line of flatbread, naan, pita, and roti, building on its experience with making and selling flatbread in Europe, Australia, Singapore, and Malaysia.[92] The following year it announced its new "Zero Net Carbs" tortillas that are keto-certified, high fiber, and low in calories. They come in many flavors, including original, sundried tomato basil, and herb garlic.[93] Mission has helped make the

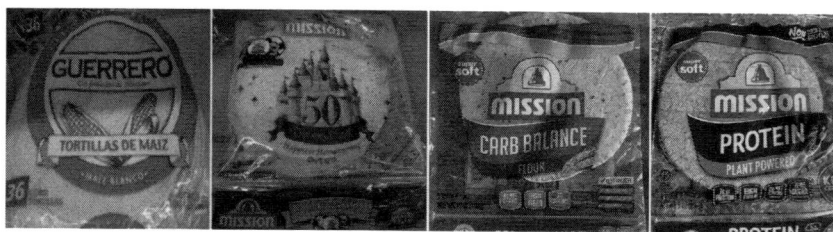

FIGURE 4 GRUMA Products in the United States. (Photos by author [left] and world .openfoodfacts.org [right])

tortilla industry the fastest-growing sector of the U.S. baking industry and in the process has contributed to the de-indigenizing and whitening of the tortilla.

Neoliberal Tortillas, Traditional Tortillas, and Consumers

During its neatly seventy-five years of operation, GRUMA has reshaped the tortilla and radically transformed its production, disconnecting tortilla production from Indigenous men and women who carefully cultivated the knowledge, the land, and the maize and created the process of nixtamalization. Throughout its expansion of production and its rationalization of the tortilla-making process, GRUMA and its supporters have argued that its capitalist production process coupled with the restructuring of the Mexican countryside would produce an abundance of maize and tortillas that would feed Mexico. That has not been the case. Instead, GRUMA's mass-produced tortillas have succeeded in deskilling the tortilla industry and transforming what a tortilla is.

During this period of the deregulation of the tortilla and the growth of GRUMA, there has been a polarization in the tortilla industry. As UNAM economists Enrique Dussel Peters and Samuel Ortiz Velásquez demonstrate in their Tortilla Meter (figure 5), the collapse of the purchasing power of the minimum wage and the liberalization of tortilla prices meant that the tortilla purchasing power of working-class families declined by 42 percent between 1984 and 1994, then by another 45 percent following Mexico's economic crisis of 1994–1995, and then another 40 percent during the worldwide rise in maize prices in 2007. All told, a daily minimum wage could purchase nearly six times fewer tortillas between 1984 and 2014, putting the basic food basket out of reach for millions of Mexicans.[94]

Since 2014, this trend remained the same until 2019 when the minimum wage increased, strengthened purchasing power. From 2019 to 2023, President López Obrador increased the minimum wage notably and this accounted for the increase from 6.3. kilograms in 2018 to 9.8 at the beginning of 2023 in the amount of tortillas that a daily minimum wage could purchase (figure 5). However, the general inflationary trend of these years has not been fully offset by the increases in the minimum

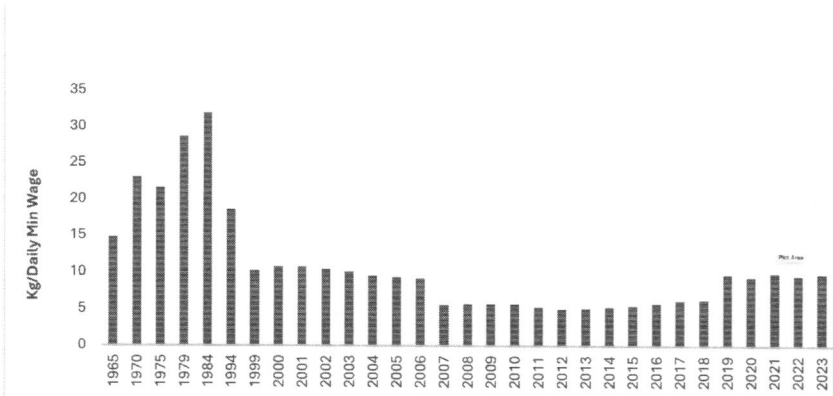

FIGURE 5 Kg of Tortillas That Can Be Purchased with a Daily Minimum Wage in Mexico, 1965–2023. (For 1965–2013, Enrique Dussel Peters and Samuel Ortiz Velásquez, eds., *Monitor de la manufactura Mexicana* 10, no. 11 (February 2015): 49; 2014–2023, calculated from the Comision Nacional de los Salarios Mínimos, "Tabla de Salarios Mínimos Generales," https://www.gob.mx/conasami/ documentos/tabla-de-salarios-minimos-generales-y-profesionales-por-areas -geograficas; and Sistema Nacional de Información e Intregación de Mercados, "Información Mensual de Precios Diarios de Tortilla en Tortillerías y autoservicios de México," http://www.economia-sniim.gob.mx/TortillaAnualPorDia.asp ?Cons=D&prod=T&Anio=2023&preEdo=Amb&Formato=Nor&submit=Ver +Resultados.)

wage. During this same period, 2019–2023, the prices of tortillas in tortillerías increased by nearly 44 percent, which led to a decline in the per capita consumption of tortillas by 22 percent.[95] The increased prices of grain, exacerbated by the 2022 Russian invasion of Ukraine and the general inflation, have been a major blow to the traditional nixtamal and tortilla industries.

As with the 2007 increase in tortilla prices, in this most recent crisis small producers have been driven out of business and maize flour producers and supermarkets have been the big winners. After considering the increased minimum wage, supermarkets sold tortillas at 58 percent less than the price that local tortillerías were selling at (figure 6). Given the large volume with which GRUMA operates and its domination of the importation of maize from the United States and its ability to store its product, it has not had to increase its prices higher than the artisanal tortillerías. Therefore, at the beginning of 2023, the price of a kilogram of tortillas at supermarkets or other stores that sold maize flour tortillas was 13.98 pesos, compared to 22.12 pesos at the local tortillería.[96] According to Rubén Montalvo, the head of the Cámara Nacional de la Industria de Producción de Masa y Tortillas (CNIPMT), "The tortilla industry is decapitalized. . . . There are many producers that are disappearing, closing their doors, and prices had to continue to climb because after all it is a business . . . and the price of maize is increasing."[97] Supermarkets are able to use their tortilla prices as loss leaders and make up the loss on the mark-up of other goods that customers purchase, something that small tortillerías are unable to do. Montalvo argues that the poor quality of the maize that is used by the maize flour company is also a factor in the differential prices. "We are worried that people buy that which they call a tortilla, and it really isn't. Supermarket tortillas have better prices because of their poor quality."[98]

The question of quality and declining nutritional value and taste has been raised by proponents of small producers and the knowledges held by campesinos and campesinas. As the head of the Fundación de Tortilla Maíz Mexicana argued, "[t]here's an enormous knowledge, but the

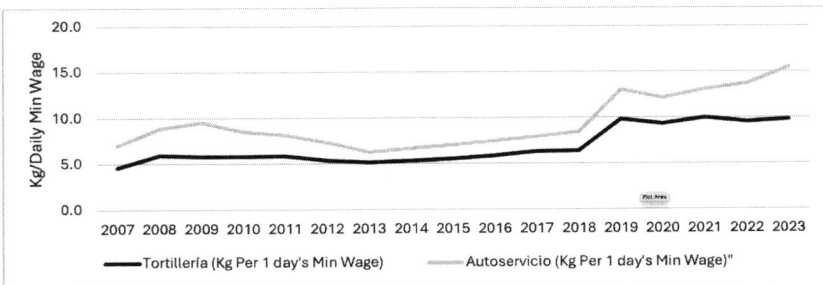

FIGURE 6 Kg of Tortillas That Can Be Purchased with a Daily Minimum Wage by Type of Outlet, 2007–2023. (Calculated from the Comision Nacional de los Salarios Mínimos, "Tabla de Salarios Mínimos Generales," https://www.gob.mx/conasami/documentos/tabla-de-salarios-minimos-generales-y-profesionales -por-areas-graficas; and Sistema Nacional de Información e Intregación de Mercados, "Información Mensual de Precios Diarios de Tortilla en Tortillerías y autoservicios de México," http://www.economia-sniim.gob.mx/ TortillaAnualPorDia.asp?Cons=D&prod=T&Anio=2023&preEdo=Amb& Formato=Nor&submit=Ver+Resultado.)

market doesn't recognize it. . . . The know-how exists. We simply need the will so it doesn't disappear, the will to transmit it to new generations."[99] According to the Alianza por Nuestra Tortilla, "producing and consuming a high-quality tortilla with different varieties of corn is a great challenge." It argues that monocultural production of maize coupled with the industrialization of tortilla production is detrimental to healthy and varied tortillas.[100]

Traditional tortillerías have been significantly impacted by GRUMA and tortillería owners argue that they are also "on the verge of disappearance."[101] An industry association, La Gran Alianza de Industriales de la Masa y la Tortilla en México, argues that fewer people are purchasing tortillas in tortillerías because of the large quantity of maize flour and rehydrated tortillas supplied by GRUMA and sold in supermarkets cheaply. Traditional producers cannot compete. According to their statistics, 15 percent of all tortillas are purchased in tortillerías, while 30 percent are sold door to door, and 55 percent of tortillas are sold in supermarkets.[102] They cite the fact that tortilla prices have escalated over the past decades, pricing out small producers and favoring large producers like GRUMA. Large retail stores, which have grown exponentially over the past two decades, sell tortillas made from maize flour mostly supplied by GRUMA. As figure 6 demonstrates, tortillas can be purchased for significantly cheaper in self-service supermarkets and the gap between tortillería prices and supermarket prices has especially increased after 2020.

GRUMA's production method, as with most modern industry, is focused on scale and efficiency with profound social consequences. While GRUMA is a relatively large employer because of its size (72% of the market), the maize flour-tortilla industry employs far fewer people than the traditional masa-tortilla industry and is detached from the concerns of Mexico's neighborhoods and rural communities. In 2010, the maize flour industry employed approximately five thousand people throughout Mexico, a significant increase from its 2003 amount of about three thousand people.

The nixtamal masa and tortilla producers, however, still comprise more than half (approximately 53%) of the overall tortilla industry and employ at least twenty times the number of workers in the maize flour sector. The approximately 78,852 masa and tortilla establishments in operation in 2008 employed 214,728 people, with 94 percent of these establishments employing between one and five people.[103] The major-ity (51%) of traditional masa and tortilla production is concentrated in seven states: the state of Mexico (14%); Mexico City (11%); Jalisco (7%); Veracruz (6%); Michoacán (5%); Guanajuato (4%); and Puebla (4%).[104] Given the size of the industry and its linkages with small agricultural producers and communities, the shrinking of this sector has profound consequences on the social fabric of these regions.

With the growth of mass-produced rehydrated tortilla production, quality, taste, variety, and traditional knowledges have been sacrificed. As the *New York Times* reported in 2018, "Quality has suffered in the race for the cheapest tortilla; nearly half the supply is now made with indus-trially produced masa harina, or corn flour, like MASECA."[105] That same year *Taste*, a James Beard award-winning online magazine, referring to GRUMA as the Tortilla cartel and argued that "the rise of industrial in-stant corn flour, masa harina, represents not only a gastronomic loss (the stuff tastes lousy), but a death blow to Mexico's corn heritage."[106] Writer and tortilla enthusiast Gustavo Arellano in 2012 wrote "Five Reasons to Hate GRUMA, Makers of Mission and Guerrero Tortillas, Maseca and Other Tortilla Evils." He later called out GRUMA for tortilla-washing and compared it to a famous anime character that is a "seemingly innocuous nothing-taco that slowly eats its competitors, assumes its charms, and gets more powerful with every fight . . . but is ultimately a fraud."[107]

In the United States, GRUMA-Mission has been even more successful at pushing out small producers and midsize producers, many of whom had deep roots in the community. Many of their critics charge that GRUMA-Mission has forged deals with the markets that give their products supe-rior placement in supermarkets. While buying shelf space, known as slot-ting, a common practice in the U.S. supermarket industry, in July 2001, eighteen U.S. tortilla makers filed a lawsuit against GRUMA seeking $70 million in damages and alleging that it "conspired to monopolize the sale of tortillas in various markets by using its dominant size to extract con-cessions from retailers."[108] Many supermarkets have specific sections lo-cated in the middle of the stores on the end of the isle where tortillas are located. However, only Mission and Guerrero products are placed there and other tortillas, if they are sold in the store, are placed in an ethnic foods section. Plaintiffs in the lawsuit argued that GRUMA paid specific chains millions of dollars for space and to deny competitors space, thus illegally working to restrain and monopolize the industry. The lawsuit was dismissed, and the Houston judge argued that slotting is common practice in the industry.[109]

The GRUMA lawsuit, however, indicated that its practices and growth and alliances had a profound effect on traditional Mexican American tortilla producers in communities from Los Angeles to Detroit. The tortilla industry had always been popular in the United States in largely Mexican American and Latino neighborhoods but by the 1960s it began to spread to the non-Latino population. So rapid was the growth that in 1965 the *Los Angeles Times* reported that tortillas were "selling like hotcakes in U.S. market."[110] Los Angeles was referred to as the tortilla capital of the United States since it was estimated that between one and two million tortillas were consumed daily. Tortilla consumption moved beyond the Mexican American community as supermarket chains throughout the city sold tortillas. For example, Von's Markets had nearly a hundred stores and sold more than five hundred thousand dozen-tortilla packages in 1964.[111] The development of the frozen food industry and the beginning of the fast-food industry created other markets for tortilla products beyond the Mexican population.[112] With the rapid growth of Mexican migration since the mid–1970s, the market grew exponentially. With this population growth, tortillas are the fastest-growing sector of the baking industry, with sales reaching $6.1 billion in 2004 and more than $8 billion in 2009. In 2009, tortillas outsold white sandwich bread for the first time in history.[113]

GRUMA's entrance into the U.S. tortilla market in the late 1970s scaled up the competition. The expansion of GRUMA has greatly impacted Los Angeles's tortillerías. While by the second decade of the twenty-first century, there still were about ninety tortillerías in California, they have had to scramble to find new niches to survive. Fernando Ruiz, the general manager of La Gloria, one of Los Angeles's leading producers, states that the competition has become fierce: "We're working harder and longer for a lot less money than we used to."[114] Los Angeles–based La Reina, once the largest producer of flour tortillas in the nation, shifted its operations to make up for market share loss. Its president, Ricardo Robles, cited GRUMA's growth and monopoly practices for the reason his business was shrinking.[115] La Reina looked for new niches to survive, such as expanding its participation in Mexican

food business by adding frozen foods, chips, moving into organic tortilla production and adding other specialty items to its product line. Nevertheless, La Reina's revenue in the early 2000s was nearly 20 percent
less than it was in 1983.[116] This mirrors the experience of other tortilla
producers that have been able to maintain their business—they had to
diversify their production or shut down. Tumaro's Gourmet Tortillas,
based in Santa Monica, developed its product low in fat and using organic products to appeal to health-conscious consumers. It has also
worked to create numerous flavors to sell the tortillas as "wraps," as
tortillas are consumed in many guises on a global basis.[117]

Over the past decade, the industry has seen the development of high-
end tortillerías that claim to be reclaiming traditional tortilla production using "heirloom corn" with the "foodie" and good food movement
among upper-middle-class communities in the United States.[118] One of
the leaders in this industry is the Los Angeles–based Masienda, founded
and operated by Jorge Gaviria, who works with farmers in Mexico: "In
Mexico there are about 3 million subsistence farmers producing heirloom corn. . . . They are protecting the biodiversity of corn, but they can't
compete with the prices of subsidized commodity corn from the U.S."[119]
Through partnering with celebrity chef Rick Bayless, Masienda provided
tortillerías and molinos de nixtamales with heirloom corn, and then
tortillerías like Popocapetl in Chicago provided tortillas to fine-dining
restaurants. High-end tortillerías have emerged in Los Angeles, such as
Kernel of Truth that opened in 2014 and specializes in using non-GMO
maize, "pushing back against a tortilla-making process that became industrialized in the 20th century, particularly through the domination of
Maseca, a producer of dehydrated tortilla flour."[120] These high-end tortillerías, however, are focused on the booming Mexican cuisine industry
that is geared to elite and largely non-Mexican consumers.

High-end tortillerías producing tortillas for elite restaurants operated
by celebrity chefs, even if in reaction to the industrialized tortillas, is a
further appropriation of Indigenous food knowledges and the labor of
Indigenous and campesina women. Much like GRUMA, in these operations the labor and knowledge developed by Indigenous women are
often erased. Instead, they are replaced by men with machines who see
themselves as "rescuing authentic food" from the clutches of both women
and the GRUMA tortilla cartel.

Men with machines armed with deep political connections and access to capital have transformed the tortilla industry and created what
Elizabeth Fitting has referred to as "the neoliberal tortilla regime." While
neoliberal agricultural policy dislocated campesinos and communities,
GRUMA's political ties and production process transformed the tortilla
industry. GRUMA placed itself and its founder at the center of the history of the tortilla. In the process, it has reinforced colonial hierarchies
that privilege men with machines at the expense of Indigenous men and
women who have nurtured maize and fed generations of Mexicans. Mexico's historic and delicious tortilla that was accessible to working Mexicans and campesinos has almost become a thing of the past as GRUMA
tortillas are priced to capture more and more of the market and normal-
ize its tortillas as authentic and improved for the domestic market. In
its global market operations, GRUMA disassociates tortillas from their
Indigenous context and even, at times, from Mexico by shape-shifting
the tortilla into new forms to reach consumers. GRUMA has contributed
to the erasure of Indigenous ways of knowing and understandings of
maize history. In fact, through its major global brand, Mission, it might
be argued that GRUMA has perpetuated and profited from the ongoing
assault on the lives of Indigenous peoples that began with European set-
tlement and consequent genocide that the mission period represents.
However, GRUMA is not alone in this form of corporate branding and
capture.

CHAPTER 5

THE GRAN FAMILIA BIMBO
Catholic Patriarchy, Industrial Bread, and Whiteness

Few Mexican companies have been able to make the leap from national manufacturer to global producer with such fury as the Grupo Bimbo. During the first four decades since its establishment in Mexico in 1945, the packaged bread producer aggressively expanded its product lines and developed distribution routes throughout Mexico. With its iconic cartoon character logo, the Bimbo Bear, it is one of Mexico's most recognized companies. In 2020 it was estimated that Bimbo products were used in 98.9 percent of Mexican households, and it was the second most purchased food brand by Mexican consumers, after Coca-Cola.[1] With the beginning of Mexico's economic structural reforms in the 1980s, Bimbo was poised to make the leap to become a global producer. In the 1990s, it began acquiring companies in Central America, the United States, and South America and soon expanded to Asia, Europe, and Africa. It is a leading company in each of the countries in which it operates. In the United States, for example, it owns several of the most iconic bakery brands, such as Sara Lee, Entenmanns, Thomas' English Muffins, and Nature's Harvest, and commands 31 percent of the baked goods market.[2] A little more than thirty years after it initiated its international expansion, Grupo Bimbo has 214 production plants in thirty-four countries and is the world's largest bakery goods company.

The Grupo Bimbo attributes this growth to its emphasis on nurturing the values established by the founders over the years. Established in Mexico City in 1945 under the leadership of Lorenzo Servitje Sendra and his two friends, all three of them sons of Spanish immigrants, along with Sevitje Sendra's Spanish-born uncle and cousin, Bimbo began by making sliced, packaged bread at a time when it was virtually unknown in Mexico. The close-knit group operated like a family and stressed paternalism, hard work, and efficiency. The founders argue that they were mission-oriented from the outset and emphasize that they created a company that is "highly productive and fully human." Their golden rule is to treat everyone with respect, fairness, justice, trust, and care.[3] Grupo Bimbo's Global V.P. of Sustainability recently explained that "Grupo Bimbo was born to be much more than a business. Our company's purpose is to nourish a better world."[4]

However, viewed another way, Grupo Bimbo's rise and market dominance in Mexico and the world can be seen as a successful case of marketing a form of modernity that reinforces and modernizes racialized class and gendered hierarchies. Building upon colonial and capitalist ideologies, Grupo Bimbo centers modernity, efficiency, and cleanliness to sell a modern form of gendered whiteness that directly contrasts with traditional markets, indigeneity, and, though generally unspoken, Blackness. Bimbo exerts control over its workforce through paternalism; workers are referred to as associates and the company works closely with union bosses. Women are the targets of its advertising campaigns yet take a back seat to men who head the family and the business. Imbued with a conservative Catholic set of values that emphasizes solidarity among unequals, Grupo Bimbo's leaders use their business to transform social and moral societal relations. This can take the form of using their power to attack the media for exposing the sexual violence of the priest and founder of the Legonaries of Christ, Marcial Maciel, or implementing "socially responsible" business practices.

This chapter examines the rise and expansion of Grupo Bimbo within Mexico and throughout the globe. While Grupo Bimbo has long been an iconic Mexican consumer company with a deep political, social, and cultural footprint, it has been virtually ignored in discussions of Mexican history and political economy.[5] This chapter centers Grupo Bimbo in the political, economic, and cultural history of Mexico since 1945 to demonstrate how, through its commercial and political alliances, its global connections, and paternalistic control of its production, distribution, and marketing, it has shaped what Mexicans eat and created a political and economic empire in the process.

Wheat Bread and Modernity in Postrevolutionary Mexico

Wheat bread has been a staple of Mexican elites since the conquest. Its consumption grew over time as wheat came to dominate much of the agricultural lands surrounding Mexico's large cities.[6] As discussed in chapters 1 and 2, wheat bread was constructed by the ruling class as a marker of civilization. This racial chauvinism was expanded in the late nineteenth century with the development of pseudoscientific approaches that influenced research and became codified in social policy during the Porfiriato and persisted, in modified forms, throughout much of the twentieth century. This thinking is best represented by Francisco Bulnes's 1899 book that argued that "the race of wheat is the only truly progressive one" and "maize has been the eternal pacifier of America's Indigenous races and the foundation of their refusal to become civilized."[7]

In his social history of bread in Mexico, the historian Robert Weis demonstrates the role of Spanish immigration in the creation of the bread-baking industry at the turn of the twentieth century. The Spanish immigrant population of Mexico consisted of "privileged immigrants," merchants, land owners, and professionals who, due to their familial and regional networks and capital, had an outsized impact on the Mexican economy during those years.[8] The tight-knit community of bakers from Spain came to form a virtual monopoly on bread production.[9] In the last twenty-three years of the nineteenth century the number of *panaderías* (bread bakeries) grew from 68 to 150, and the number of bakers grew from 873 in 1877 to 2,286 in 1895.[10] As the market for bread grew, competition among bakeries became fierce, which drove down prices, wages, and working conditions. The deterioration of working conditions made already crowded and hot working spaces even more tense, leading to increased workplace injuries, diseases, and violence.[11] After workers responded through union organizing and carrying out a series of strikes, the state was forced to intervene, improving working conditions. By 1937 the Cárdenas administration began subsidizing wheat for mills and bakers to offset inflation, thus boosting wheat and bread consumption in urban areas. Government subsidies continued during downturns in the wheat shortages during World War II, and with the support of the Rockefeller Foundation, the Mexican state actively promoted wheat production and consumption by the middle of the 1950s.

It is in this context that Juan Servitje, a young Catalán migrant, came to Mexico City in 1903 to work at the La Flor de México bakery, which his uncle had established in 1901. The young Servitje slept on the couch in the office of the bakery, slowly worked his way up, and eagerly learned about all aspects of the business. From 1909 to 1912, he expanded his experience and bakery education by going to Buenos Aires, where he worked making candy and cakes at an Italian style café and bakery and then later at the Argentine oligarchy's Jockey Club. He returned to La Flor de México, where he worked from 1912 to 1917. In 1916 he married Josefina Sendra Grimau, also a Catalán immigrant, and began working in sales and traveling to different countries. Josefina began to rent out rooms in their house, and through her boarding house operations she accumulated a nice savings. Juan returned to the bakery business and worked for Pan Ideal, which was owned and frequented by members of Mexico City's Spanish community. When the owner told him that he could no longer work there since a family member would take over the daily operations, he consulted with his wife and with her savings they established El Molino bakery in 1928.[12] The bakery did well, and in 1931 they established a restaurant, also called El Molino, three blocks away on 16 de Septiembre Street in downtown Mexico City. The restaurant was run by Josefina, and their fourteen-year-old son Lorenzo began working at the bakery. Lorenzo worked from sunup to sundown but dreamed of something bigger.[13]

During the 1920s, the bread-baking industry was undergoing profound transformations. In the United States, according to Aaron Bobrow-Strain, approximately 90 percent of bread was baked at home by women in 1890, but by the 1930s this had largely ended as industrial bakers were delivering bread to the growing supermarkets throughout the United States.[14] In 1928, the first commercial slicing machine led to the first automatically sliced bread filling store shelves. By 1939, 90 percent of all bread sold in stores was sliced bread.[15] Packaged bread was among the first large-scale industrialized foods developed in the first half of the twentieth century.

Given its proximity to the United States and the competitiveness of the bakery industry, Mexican bakeries closely followed developments in the U.S. industry. Sliced packaged bread soon began to appear in Mexico after it took off in the United States. Pan Ideal—established by Martín Velasco, a Spanish immigrant, in 1922—purchased the packaged bread–making equipment and introduced packaged bread loafs into the Mexican market.[16] However, by 1924 Martín Velasco's investments in the mining sector went under and he was forced to sell Pan Ideal to Pablo Diez, another Spanish immigrant and a founder of the Modelo brewery.[17] Other smaller packaged bread producers soon emerged, "such as La Condesa White Bread, that sold under the Tip Top label, and Pan Lara, that used to advertise on XEQK radio station" with catchy slogans.[18] In 1918, Juan Servitje bought a mechanical bolillo maker and patented it with the name Higienica Múltiple Póo. He later sold the patent for 30,000 gold pesos. Juan Servitje had hoped that his machine would increase efficiency and hygiene in bread making. However, it never caught on since consumers wanted fresh and warm bread when they purchased it, not bread made earlier in the day.[19]

Following the death of Juan Servitje in 1936, his oldest son, Lorenzo, ran El Molino and continued looking for other opportunities. He modernized the bakery and began advertising to reach a broader clientele. He subscribed to U.S. baking trade publications such as *Baker's Helper* to learn about the latest baking methods and technologies. Lorenzo decided to remodel El Molino and purchased new bakery equipment from U.S. suppliers who suggested that he speak to Pan Ideal's engineer Alfonso Velasco, the son of the company's original owner, since Pan Ideal had recently installed the latest equipment for sliced bread production. Given the close ties between the Velasco and Servitje families, Alfonso Velasco provided advice to El Molino. The Servitje and Velasco association soon became a profitable business relationship.[20]

Lorenzo began to develop the idea for a new company in the early 1940s. With his cousin Jaime Jorba, a salesman who had traveled throughout Latin America and Europe, and his childhood friend José Trinidad Mata, he developed an import-export business during World War II that netted a significant sum. After the war, his uncle suggested setting up a bread bakery. They reached out again to Alfonso Velasco, who had studied at the American Bakery Institute in Kansas City:

> [H]e had the technical know-how and had studied the latest baking methods, the operation and maintenance of industrial machines, that included the cutting and the packaging process. He wasn't only the best trained bakery engineer in Mexico but his practical experience at Pan Ideal taught him the ins and outs of the production and the marketing process.[21]

With this know-how and some startup capital in 1945, the twenty-seven-year-old Lorenzo Servitje Sendra, his cousin Jaime Jorba, his uncle Jaime Sendra, his friend José Trinidad Mata, and the engineer Alfonso Velasco founded Bimbo Bakery.[22] They had been looking to purchase land for the factory. However, Lorenzo's new father-in-law, Daniel Montull, who owned the La Imperial and La Central match factories, offered him a larger piece of land.

The close-knit Spanish community in Mexico City that Juan Servitje and Josefina Sendra were part of afforded them numerous opportunities to build a business. The prosperous business that their oldest son, Lorenzo, inherited, coupled with his social networks within his extended family and in the Spanish community, set the stage for the development of Bimbo Bakery.

Super Pan Bimbo: Marketing Modernity, Hygiene, and Gendered Whiteness

Grupo Bimbo was established amid growing urbanization, food scarcity, and rising prices during World War II. In 1943, wheat production fell by nearly 125,000 tons or 26 percent and Mexico was forced to import 296,891 tons of wheat nearly 150 percent more than it did the previous year.[23] Newspapers reported widespread accusations of food adulteration and merchants tampering with scales in order to stretch ingredients in short supply.[24] While maize production also plummeted, Mexican officials, in line with racialized discussions of modernity, saw wheat as the future of the Mexican diet and therefore worthy of subsidies for increased production.[25] In fact, according to Tore Olsson, Secretary of Agriculture, Marte R. Gómez stunned Rockefeller Foundation officials in February 1943 when he

"designated the improvement and pathology of wheat as 'the most important single problem' confronting Mexican agriculture."[26]

As sons of Spanish immigrants in close contact with the baking industry in the United States and Europe, the creators of Bimbo saw the new
machinery as a solution to many of Mexico's food problems.[27] These new
baking and packaging machines were seen as "a shining temple to a new
way of thinking about food 'untouched by human hands.'"[28] As Sandra
Aguilar-Rodríguez demonstrates, government officials, cookbooks, and
women's magazines touted the value of eating wheat bread as a marker
of middle-class status, mestizaje, and good nutrition. Packaged bread was
seen as preferable to traditional French-style bread of bolillos and teleras.[29]

The branding, its name, its logo, and its marketing strategy were all
essential aspects of the Bimbo brand that is now so iconic. The founders
chose a name and logo that were unique and that would make their sliced
bread attractive and not threatening in Mexico. Initially they hoped to
call the company Súper Pan to underscore that their baking innovation
was an improvement over traditional bread, much like its competitor,
Pan Ideal, was an "ideal" bread. However, according to company lore, as
the partners went to register the full name, Súper Pan, S.A., they realized
that when the name was pronounced all together, it would sound like
Súper Panza (big belly). It was at that time that, according to Lorenzo
Servitje, Alfonso Velasco

> came one day and presented a long list of possible names: Súper Pan
> Sambo, Súper Pan Margarita, Súper Pan Lirio, Bonipan and an infinity
> more. Among the names was Súper Pan Bimbo. I don't know if it occurred
> to him to use the consonants of the movie *Bambi*, produced in 1942 and
> popular in Mexico at the time, or because of the famous game Bingo, pop-
> ularized in those days in Las Vegas Casinos. What is certain was that it
> sounded good, it was catchy, and we liked it. . . . Now we know that bam-
> bino is Italian for boy and colloquially they say bimbo, but these readings
> are a simple coincidence because in our case, the name emerged because
> of its metered sound.[30]

The business partners liked the sound and called the company Panifica-
ción Bimbo but marketed their bread as Súper Pan Bimbo to emphasize
its uniqueness and superior quality.

The Bimbo logo, a white cartoon bear in a baker's hat, would become ubiquitous throughout Mexico. The Bimbo founders were looking for an image "of a baker with the attitude of service and a smiling face. We wanted a nice animal that represented the noble profession of a baker."[31] According to Lorenzo Servitje, the idea of a bear came from Jaime Jorba's friendship with an American woman he met at Sunset High School in Dallas when he was twenty and she was fifteen. While both Lorenzo and Jaime referred to her as a friend in their oral histories, their relationship was more serious.[32] Under the stage name Linda Darnell, she would go on to be a Hollywood actress and costar with Tyrone Powers in several films. She and Jorba would maintain a long correspondence. Later she would say, "I had always expected one day to marry Jaime Jorba," but he did not want a wife in the public eye and wanted her to quit her career.[33] In December 1944, she sent him a postcard with a bear dressed in a Santa Claus suit and he showed it to his partners. They all liked the image and Lorenzo had his aunt draw a picture of the bear dressed as a baker wearing an apron and baker's hat. After Alfonso Velasco made some adjustments to the bear's nose and made the eyes bigger, Bimbo the Bear was born.[34]

The packaged bread of Súper Pan Bimbo with its white bear logo fit the national discourse that prioritized the value of wheat bread over tortillas.[35] Although the tortilla was the result of thousands of years of Indigenous knowledge and women's innovation, Europeanized elites deemed tortillas the food of the poor and of a bygone era. Traditional bread baking was often in the news for labor battles between the bakers and the bakery owners, charges of adulteration in the bread making process, and the lack of standardization of the size and weight especially during the times of severe bread shortages during the 1940s.[36] The use of packaged bread was portrayed as part of modernizing of the Mexican kitchen and training women to prepare nutritious meals.[37] Factory-produced and packaged bread became a symbol for the period of rapid industrialization known as the Mexican Miracle (1940–1970s). Bimbo's white bear in a baker's hat logo symbolized the connection between hygiene and the whitening of the Mexican population.

Images of whiteness, modernity, and hegemonic notions of family and gender were central to Bimbo's marketing strategy. The friendly smiling white Bimbo Bear cartoon in a white baker's hat and apron was a marked contrast to the image of dark working-class bakery workers and Indigenous women making tortillas at the metate. From the outset, Bimbo's founders invested up to 3 percent of Bimbo's total sales to marketing and publicity. After hiring Publicidad Continental, Bimbo advertisements aired on the radio and appeared in newspapers and in theaters to create a buzz around its soon-to-be-released bakery products. The day of Bimbo's launch, a two-page advertisement was taken out in *Excélsior* and other national newspapers announcing the company and its packaged bread, offering "a guarantee of purity, quality, and satisfaction, with quick and efficient service."[38] The Bimbo bear logo caught on and became an important icon in Mexico's growing consumer culture. Over the years, the Bimbo bear was redesigned to become whiter and fluffier with a smaller nose (figure 7).

Bimbo's advertising focused on mothers in modern kitchens using Bimbo products. In one advertisement (figure 8), a light-skinned mother with a frilly apron in a 1940s and 1950s classic middle-class U.S.-style kitchen spreads jam on Bimbo pound cake as her two well-groomed children watch in anticipation. The advertisement proclaims, "Kids love snacks 'at any hour' therefore there is nothing better than to give them a tasty slice of Panqué Bimbo . . . so fine! so tasty! so nutritious!" Another

FIGURE 7 The Bimbo Bear Across Time, 1947–2010. (Heather Taylor, "Osito Bimbo Takes Flight on the Rise and Shine Tour," Advertising Week 360.com, May 2017, https://www.advertisingweek360.com/osito-bimbo-takes-flight-rise-shine-tour/.)

A los chicos les encanta una golosina "a cualquier hora" ... entonces, nada mejor que darles una rica tajada del Panqué BIMBO ... ¡tan fino! ¡tan sabroso! ¡tan nutritivo!

El Panqué BIMBO se elabora con mantequilla, leche, huevos en abundancia y muchas pasas. Los tamaños mediano y grande llevan además una deliciosa capa de almendras tostadas

PANQUE

BiMBO

Tamaño Chico 50¢
Tamaño Mediano 90¢
Tamaño Grande $1.25

FIGURE 8 Bimbo Advertisement in 1947. (*Bimbo: Una historia de creer y crear* [Grupo Bimbo, 2005], 58.)

advertisement gave recipes for forty-seven different ways to make sandwiches using Pan Bimbo and included images of a light-skinned mother smiling and holding a sandwich. Bimbo's advertising to women appeared as cookbooks began to include recipes for making sandwiches. For example, in 1946 the well-known cookbook writer Josefina Velasquez de León published *Selecciones culinarias: Sandwiches modernas*, an entire book devoted to sandwiches.[39]

With the initial success of their packaged sliced bread, in 1954, Bimbo established a division that produced packaged cakes and sweet breads, Pasteles y Bizcochos, S.A. (PABISA), and trademarked the name Keike, a rough Spanish pronunciation of the English word "cake." Two years later, Keike was changed to Marinela, S.A, after Lorenzo Servitje's youngest daughter. The Marinela line featured the image of a smiling blonde girl

FIGURE 9 Marinela Advertisements, 1950s. (Bimbo, "The Birth of Marinela," https://grupobimbo.com/en/about-us/history/1950-1960/birth-marinela.)

dressed in a flowing blue skirt and a red blouse, holding a Chinese umbrella and a basket like Goldilocks. The Marinela character was inspired by Dolly Madison, the U.S.-packaged cake brand, and its marketing.[40] Other images show her eagerly looking at a cake to eat (figure 9). Aguilar-Rodríguez explains that cakes during this period were increasingly popular as government officials, the sugar industry, and cookbook writers emphasized the importance of cakes in celebrating birthdays. They even advocated that working-class women could learn to bake and supplement their family income through selling cakes.[41] However, since most women did not have ovens at home and bakery cakes, including Marinela's cakes at first, were often priced for middle- and upper-middle-class families, they were out of reach for working-class families. Recognizing a market niche, by the mid–1950s, Marinela began producing smaller, individually packaged cakes, but it took several years to develop the packaging for transport.

In 1957, Bimbo launched Gansito, Negrito, and Bombonete, three products in their Marinela line of cakes and pan dulce. The following year Alfonso Velasco, Bimbo partner and technical wizard, figured out how to package the cakes for easier transport and sale. Gansito was a pound cake filled with creme and jam and covered with chocolate frosting. Its logo was a little white goose character inspired by the cartoon duck logo of New York bakery company Drake's Cakes. Gansito cakes were very popular and by 1975, a million Gansitos were sold daily, accounting for 65 percent of Marinela's sales.[42]

In contrast to the blonde Marinela logo and the white Gansito, Negrito was a chocolate cake with chocolate frosting that was marketed using an image of a presumably African child clothed with only a yellow skirt and a matching anklet and choker (figure 10). The caricature had thick white

1957	1958	1973	2000	2012

FIGURE 10 The Evolution of Bimbo's Advertising for Negrito. (Adapted from "Nito Bimbo Timeline," https://www.timetoast.com/timelines/nito-bimbo.)

lips and a bone in his hair, and was holding a spear. Negrito specifically played on racist anti-Black tropes popular in the United States and long engrained in Mexican culture. The 1958 representations of Negrito underscored colonial notions of the wild jungle, savagery, and Black people. Several popular cartoons and characters stereotyping Black people emerged during this period. Among those were the comic book character Memín Pinguín, who first appeared in 1947 and has long been characterized as "a beloved figure in Mexico," and the famous children's composer Cri Cri and his song "Negrito Sandía" (little Black watermelon boy), in which the child is admonished to stay in his place and not speak up or say "naughty things."[43]

In their search for lyricism and popular culture, the Bimbo founders originally contemplated using the name Súper Pan Sambo. Alfonso Velasco suggested the name. Having spent considerable time in the United States, Velasco and Jorba were undoubtedly aware of the story of the little black Sambo, a racist caricature that was popular in United States at the time. As scholars have amply demonstrated, Sambo was used to "make the black male into an object of laughter" and "render the black male powerless. . . . [I]t was an illustration of humor as a device of oppression."[44] While Sambo was ultimately discarded as a possible name, racist alliteration was never too far from the minds of Bimbo's marketing team.

As historian Jesús Chairez-Garza has pointed out, in the 1990s, Bimbo launched a television campaign that reinforced racial stereotypes. In one advertisement for Bimbo's Toasted Bread, an actor of African descent tells the housewife that the toast is burning. He then recommends

Bimbo's Toasted Bread because it doesn't burn since "it is born toasted," presumably like him.[45] An advertisement campaign for Negrito further doubled down on the racist caricature by showing children in blackface playing in huts in the jungle while eating Negritos.[46] The legacy of the anti-Blackness in Mexican history and popular commercials persists. In a recent study, Mexican historian Cristina Masferrer León found that "Negrito Bimbo" is among the racist phrases children often use to bully each other in areas with significant populations of Afro-Mexicans, such as the Costa Chica of Guerrero and Oaxaca.[47]

Critical discussion of racism and anti-Blackness in Mexico began to occur in the first decade of the twenty-first century. This grew after President Vicente Fox's 2008 comments that Mexican immigrants in the United States do the work that not even African Americans do. He then recognized Memín Pinguín with a commemorative stamp.[48] These actions by Fox generated outrage in the United States and stimulated a lively discussion about racism in Mexico. It was during this period that the marketing of Negrito switched from a child in blackface to a lighter-skinned child who had an Afro and dressed in shorts. In 2013, Bimbo asked consumers to choose what Negrito should be named and gave a list of options for people to vote on. They included Afro, Funky, Choco, Rulos, and Nito. Nito, presumably short for Negrito, was declared the winner. Bimbo explained that the company was looking for a shorter name and did not indicate that its search was due to the problematic nature of the original name.[49] The new image of Nito was a "cool looking" lighter-skin child with an Afro, an oversized shirt, baggy pants, and sneakers (figure 10). Television commercials portrayed a light-skinned youth with an Afro wig in a more modernized form of blackface, reminiscent of minstrel shows of the past. Nevertheless, in 2014, Bimbo continued to use the Negrito label for a new product, Negrito Raztachoc, presumably a play on Rastafarian and chocolate.

Bimbo's marketing strategies and its close connection to the U.S. and European bakery industries reinforced race, class, and gendered hierarchies in Mexico. From its inception, Bimbo was a company with a global gaze that freely borrowed from the production and marketing strategies and images of other companies, including Disney, Dolly Madison, and Drake's Cakes. It also employed the machinery and packaging techniques used by U.S. bakery manufacturers.

Bimbo's Growth and Dominance of the National Market

Bimbo grew steadily in the first few decades of its operation. In 1946, a year after opening its doors, the partners were already making plans for expanding their first plant in the Santa Maria Insurgentes neighborhood of Mexico City. Key to this early success was their creation of a diverse product line to reach different tastes. By 1947 Bimbo had already created nine different products that were selling throughout Mexico City and developed distribution routes. Bimbo deliverymen were distinguished by their light-color uniforms complete with a cap and a black tie in trucks advertising the company. To reach areas outside Mexico City, managers developed relationships with newspaper deliverers to also transport Bimbo products on their early morning runs to nearby capitals cities of Puebla, Cuernavaca, Toluca, and Pachuca. By 1949 Bimbo began creating regional distribution centers, and using the growing number of highways, it developed new routes and markets.[50] Bimbo expanded its Mexico City plant twice, in 1947 and again in 1952, and by 1954 the number of employees had grown to approximately seven hundred from the initial staff of thirty-nine.[51]

Between 1956 and the end of the 1970s, Bimbo's operations expanded to Mexico's major central and northern cities (table 10). It built ten plants in different states, starting with Guadalajara in 1956 and Monterrey in 1960. In addition to Marinela's cake production, Bimbo created a pastry called Suandy in 1974.[52] It expanded into other markets by associating with Lorenzo and Roberto's brother Fernando Servitje Sendra, who was making candy at the family's El Molino bakery. In 1970 Bimbo started producing the Ricolino candy line and then in 1977 it entered the salted snack market with Barcel S.A., hoping to challenge Frito-Lay, the maker of potato and tortilla chips in Mexico.[53]

In the early 1960s, Bimbo had nearly complete control of Mexico's industrial production of packaged bread and cakes, though it still faced some challenges from Mexican and U.S. manufacturers. The first major challenge that Bimbo faced was in 1960 after opening its Monterrey plant. Alfonso Velasco oversaw the plant's construction, but while he was there, he forged a relationship with a local bakery. A few months after opening the plant, Velasco notified Servitje that he was leaving the company to form Panificadora Mexicana in Monterrey. Velasco established

TABLE 10 Grupo Bimbo Plant and Subsidiaries, 1945–1990

Year	Plants and Companies	Location	Type of Production
1945	Panificación Bimbo	Mexico City, Col. Sta María Insurgentes	Bakery
1947	Panificación Bimbo First Expansion	Mexico City	Bakery
1952	Panificación Bimbo Second Expansion	Mexico City	Bakery
1956	Bimbo de Occidente	Guadalajara, Jal.	Bakery
	Marinela Products	Mexico City	Cookies and pastries
1960	Bimbo del Norte	Monterrey, N.L.	Bakery
1963	Corporate Office	Mexico City	
1966	Bimbo Noroeste	Hermosillo, Son.	Bakery
1970	Bimbo del Golfo	Veracruz, Ver.	Bakery
1971	Ricolino Mexico	Mexico City	Confectionary
1972	Bimbo Plant Azcapotzalco	Mexico City	Bakery
	Marinela Plant Azapotzalco	Mexico City	Cookies and pastries
1973	Frexport (frozen fruit and preserves)	Zamora, Mich.	Agribusiness
1977	Nubar (Barcel)	Querétaro, Qro.	Snacks
	Marinela de Occidente	Guadalajara, Jal.	Cookies and pastries
	Bimbo del Centro	Irapuato, Gto.	Bakery
1978	Bimbo del Sureste	Villahermosa, Tab.	Bakery
1980	Sisaport (fruit processing)	Zamora, Mich.	Agribusiness
	Bimbo Público	Mexico City	Mex. Stock Mkt.
1981	Bimbo del Pacífico	Mazatlán, Sin.	Bakery

TABLE 10 *continued*

Year	Plants and Companies	Location	Type of Production
1982	Barcel del Norte	Gomez Palacio, Dgo.	Snacks
	Bimbo Chihuahua	Chihuahua, Chih.	Bakery
	Bimbo Toluca	Toluca, Edomex.	Bakery
1983	Maquindal	Mexico City	Metal Mechanics
1984	Interrefacciones	Mexico City	Metal Mechanics
1986	Wonder México	Mexico City	Bakery
	Molino San Vicente	Mexico City	Agribusiness
	Bimbo Yucatán	Mérida, Yuc.	Bakery
	Proarce	Mexico City	Metal Mechanics
1987	Distribución-E.U.A.	Los Angeles and Houston	Marketing
	Marinela del Sureste	Villahermosa, Tab.	Cookies and pastries
	Tía Rosa México	Mexico City	Bakery
1989	Productos Confitados	Atlixco, Pue.	Confectionary
1990	Marinela Baja California	Mexicali, BC	Cookies and pastries
	Barcel México	Toluca, Edomex	Snacks
	Bimbo Centroamérica	Guatemala, Guat.	Bakery

Source: *Bimbo: Una historia de creer y crear* (Grupo Bimbo, 2005), 177–178.

the packaged bread line Pan Rey in Monterrey; it became a strong competitor and pushed Bimbo deeper into the red in that region. However, in the end Velasco's venture went bankrupt and he sold Pan Rey to his former partners. Velasco then resumed working for Pan Ideal in Mexico City and helped it develop two brands of bread that provided competition for Bimbo.[54]

The second major challenge to Bimbo's national dominance came in 1964, when Pan Ideal forged a partnership with U.S.-based Continental Baking, the owner of Wonder Bread. In 1966, Continental entered the Mexican market with a similar line of products as Bimbo, sliced bread with its Wonder Bread brand, rolls, buns, and cakes such as its popular Twinkie brand. Continental's strategy was to price Wonder Bread significantly cheaper than Bimbo bread, hoping that the low price and the prestige of the U.S. brand would win over consumers. For the next two years the competition was intense, and Grupo Bimbo tried to work out an agreement with Continental, to no avail. Grupo Bimbo then turned to the Mexican government for aid in hiring Quality Bakers of America, Wonder's chief competition in the United States, to assess Grupo Bimbo's operations. After making several marketing strategy changes and buying new equipment, Grupo Bimbo purchased the Mexican rights to Quality Bakers of America's Sunbeam Bread brand, with its Little Miss Sunbeam logo of a smiling little blonde girl eating a slice of bread, to neutralize the competition from Wonder Bread. Although Continental Baking and Wonder Bread cut into its sales for three years, Bimbo received a reprieve with International Telephone and Telegraph's 1970 acquisition of Continental Baking since the Mexican bread market was not a priority for the conglomerate. A few years later, Continental was purchased by Ralston Purina, and then in 1986 Grupo Bimbo purchased it and with it the Wonder Brand in Mexico.[55]

The third major challenge to Bimbo came from another Mexican company. GRUMA approached Bimbo in 1998 to form a partnership since GRUMA wanted to expand its packaged tortilla business, which it developed in the United States, to Mexico using Bimbo's distribution network.[56] According to CEO Roberto Servitje, Bimbo already had its own brand of packaged tortillas, Milpa Real, and therefore turned down GRUMA's offer. GRUMA's founder and CEO felt snubbed by Bimbo and decided to challenge Bimbo's packaged bread market. In 1999, GRUMA created the Breddy brand and began to produce packaged bread, croissants, muffins, and conchas in Monterrey and Costa Rica. In Mexico, GRUMA focused its sale of Breddy in supermarkets in northern Mexico and quickly captured 12 percent of the regional bread market. Bimbo countered by selling Wonder Bread in those same markets at prices that undercut Breddy.[57] Both GRUMA and Bimbo began to lose money due to this competition. In the end, GRUMA sold Bimbo its two Breddy factories in 2002 for $70 million.[58]

After Roberto Servitje became CEO in the 1960s, he sought to transform Bimbo's management culture by reducing the tight control of the company held by top managers. Roberto Servitje felt that the recent departures of two founders, Alfonso Velasco and Jaime Jorba, was a sign that the company's authoritarianism was hurting operations. Bimbo hired industrial psychologists to help transform corporate culture and open the decision-making process to other managers. According to Roberto Servitje, "[a]t that point we were just accustomed to giving orders without discussion. With the support of a consultant, management began to meet and to create spaces for communication. At the beginning this was very difficult, but they gave us intense classes on how to learn to listen, dialogue, and create more solid teams based on specific objectives." They spent ten years learning new management skills and concepts that were in vogue in the United States "to break the ice and permeate the closed mindset of the company."[59]

During the 1970s and 1980s, Bimbo began vertically integrating its operations. Bimbo constructed a jam factory in 1980 to supply Marinela and began to design and build its own machinery (table 10). As Spanish economic historian Javier Moreno Lázaro argues, Bimbo's organizational strategy of market diversification and vertical integration enabled it to weather difficult storms and set the company up to take advantage of economic downturns, purchasing competitors in Mexico and abroad.[60] In 1980, Bimbo sold 25 percent of the company on the Stock Exchange and used the proceeds to reinvest in machinery, pay off its debts, build new plants, and expand its Barcel snack division. During the economic crisis of the 1980s, its sales suffered, and Bimbo went deeper into the red. The company created a cost-cutting plan, which reduced costs by 4 percent in 1987, and implemented "a total quality plan," which led to "a one-second improvement in productivity at all plants, and a total presence plan that aimed at completing the expansion objectives of reaching all Mexican territory with the Bimbo, Marinela and Barcel brands."[61] Through greater control over labor and with the support of labor unions, which granted nonwage worker benefits, as will be discussed in the next section, Bimbo improved productivity and sales picked up by 1988. As Grupo Bimbo came to dominate the bread market throughout Mexico, it was poised for growth with the neoliberal reforms of the 1980s and 1990s.

"To Believe and to Create": Catholic Paternalism and the Gran Familia Bimbo

One of Grupo Bimbo's many mottos is *"creer y crear"* (to believe and to create). While this slogan can be interpreted in many ways, for Lorenzo Servitje and his family, belief was tied to their conservative Catholicism and translated into a philosophy of business, society, and a way of life. This missionary sensibility was also a reaction to the liberal policies emanating from the early years of the Mexican Revolution and revolutionary events in Spain that forced several of Servitje's family members to migrate to Mexico. Influenced by these events, Servitje sought to create order and stability and built Bimbo around values guided by Catholic Social Doctrine that emphasized patriarchy, class harmony, and subsidiarity (solidarity among unequals). These values permeate Grupo Bimbo's operations and philosophy and can be seen throughout Bimbo's advertising materials, its business practices, its approach to workers, the public pronouncements of its founders, and its active role in philanthropy and political activities.

Bimbo's Catholic patriarchy is embodied by the company's patriarch, Lorenzo Servitje. In his telling of the history of Bimbo, Servitje emphasizes how his conservative Catholic upbringing forged Bimbo's company values. His parents sent him to El Instituto Alfonso XIII, later renamed El Instituto España, where for five years he studied religion and learned the importance of honor and "to live a clean and disciplined life."[62] At the age of fifteen, in a school article, Servitje wrote, "Honor should be at the core of all our actions. We should be honorable in our profession, we should be honorable with that which has been confided in us, in a word we should be honorable with society. . . . We should appear before God and the world with a clear conscience and right intention."[63] In these early years he began to contemplate devoting his life to a religious vocation, even as he studied accounting at the Instituto España and then at UNAM. However, when in 1936 he told his father of his desire to be a priest, the elder Servitje expressed disappointment, since he had hoped his son would eventually take over El Molino. In the end, his father's expectations and his own doubts led the young Servitje to abandon the idea of life as a priest.[64]

No longer on the path to priesthood, he developed into a Catholic lay activist. After attending a demonstration against the anticlerical policies of Socialist Education at the National Preparatory School, he and his friends passed by a demonstration in front of *El Nacional*, the official newspaper of Mexico's ruling party, where students were throwing rocks, and they "spontaneously joined in the shouting against Calles and Cárdenas." The newspaper's photographers captured Lorenzo and his friends at the unruly demonstration and their picture appeared in the paper the following day. On another occasion, Servitje tried to shut down a play at the Secretary of Education's theater by throwing stink bombs into the theater and causing a panic. He claimed that the play defamed the Virgen de Guadalupe. His best friend was arrested, but Servitje escaped.[65] His early formation as a Catholic militant would stay with him throughout his life.

Patriarchal notions of family and paternalistic hierarchy were instilled in the business culture of Bimbo from its inception. As the leader of the family following his father's death, Lorenzo also assumed leadership of the business. According to Robert Weis, "this paternal authority extended also to the entire workforce of Bimbo through what he called the 'mysticism' of the company and himself."[66] As the business grew, more male family members were given responsibility for overseeing the various operations of the business. For nine decades, the direction of the Gran Familia Bimbo remained firmly in the hands of three patriarchs, Lorenzo Servitje Sendra, his younger brother Roberto Servitje Sendra, and Lorenzo's youngest son, Daniel Servitje Montull.

In the Gran Familia Bimbo, women were seen as complementary to men. They were to be the moral foundation of the family, working behind the scenes to maintain familial harmony. Lorenzo Servitje's mother, Josefina Sendra Grimau, instilled these notions of the gran familia and ties to Spain in the development of the family in Mexico. In family lore, Servitje's mother worked behind the scenes to support the work of her husband and sons, oversaw secondary business operations, and even established businesses of her own. However, she never appeared on the masthead of the Bimbo corporation.[67] This model of womanhood was idealized in the Gran Familia Bimbo by Lorenzo Servitje and his brother Roberto. In explaining the success of his marriage, Lorenzo Servitje wrote, "Women cannot be equal to men. We are essentially equal, as people and children of God, but we are completely different, unfortunately."[68] His brother Roberto Servitje told the writer Silvia Cherem that he preferred that married women not work outside the household.[69] The main public role for the Servitje women was in the family's charity and philanthropic work, which is often closely tied to the church. For example, Roberto's daughter Lourdes Servitje Achutegui studied graphic design at the Universidad Iberoamericana and wrote her 1982 thesis on the brand design and image of Bimbo's Tía Rosa brand. However, once she married, Lourdes devoted herself to work with the Legionaries of Christ.[70]

The most publicly prominent Servitje woman was Marinela Servitje Montull, the eldest daughter of Lorenzo Servitje. From early childhood, she became a symbol of Bimbo when they named their pastry division after her in 1956. She has been involved in numerous philanthropical campaigns, most notably as the director of Papalote Museo del Niño from 1993 to 2011, which had a contract to exclusively sell Bimbo products.[71] She was also the president of the Instituto de Pedriatría, the Foundation Bosque de Chapultepec, the Walmart Foundation, and the Televisa Foundation. She is the wife of a former PRI congressman and spokesperson for President Ernesto Zedillo. Their son Fernando Lerdo de Tejada Servitje is an executive vice president of Grupo Bimbo and a member of the board of directors.[72]

Throughout the history of Grupo Bimbo, women have been a target of advertising but had little direct place in company operations. In early company pictures published on its website and in its official publications, there are relatively few women workers. By the 1990s, the company began to note that middle-class women were increasingly entering the workforce and saw this as a growth opportunity to further market its bread for sandwiches, pastries for breakfast, and various snack products to be consumed throughout the day. In 2011, with the growing international focus on gender equity in the workforce, Bimbo began to publish data on the gender breakdown of its workforce. While the data is not broken down by region or by type of employment, in 2009 only 13.8 percent of Bimbo employees internationally were women, and in 2011 this number grew to 16.1 percent; in 2019 it grew to 18.6 percent.[73]

With Lorenzo Servitje as the patriarch, Bimbo practiced forms of welfare capitalism popular among Mexican capitalists in Monterrey and nourished by Christian Social Doctrine.[74] As Alejandra Salas-Porras has argued, Christian Social Doctrine focuses on conservative Catholic social values as a response to communism and liberalism:

> Christian Social Doctrine represents a modern religious version, business version of ethical liberalism. It is an elitist version that is more concerned with the principle of solidarity, instead of equality, and in certain conservative moral values related to the family and education that reinforces community ties.[75]

Reciprocity based on unequal solidarity, referred to as subsidiarity, undergirds Bimbo's Gran Familia ideology. Subsidiarity holds that since not everyone is equal, something must bring an equilibrium to this inequality.[76] For Servitje, "the solution is that the outstanding men, the most gifted, are not paid unlimitedly . . . and that those destitute either by nature or by chance, the poorly endowed, can have the minimum for a dignified life."[77] In this notion of unequal social justice, it is the responsibility of the company to extend this "minimum for a dignified life." The well-structured company should be a model for society that emphasizes order, social harmony, and mutual respect. An efficient profit-driven company was crucial not only to produce wealth but to provide employment: "The company by the clarity of its aims, by the full integration of its men, by its constructive prosperity, and by its deep sense of humanity should be a model institution."[78] The Gran Familia Bimbo emphasizes that its workers are not just "social capital" or employees to be used; they are respected collaborators. Among the company's numerous slogans are "the business should be highly productive and fully human." However, while respect for workers is emphasized in the company literature, there is a paternalistic sense that employers need to look "beyond the salary" and see workers as part of the family.[79] Not everyone in the family is the same or treated equally.

Grupo Bimbo's culture of paternalism reinforced unequal patron-client relations under the guise of fostering class harmony in the Gran Familia Bimbo. From the company's inception, a trusted member of the Servitje family oversaw the hiring of workers to ensure that potential workers were scrutinized and that once hired they had a personal connection to the family. The rigorous selection of personnel, according to Roberto Servitje, was aimed at choosing workers who demonstrated "a good attitude . . . whose principles and philosophy did not oppose ours, since they would adapt rapidly and feel comfortable, and they would get involved more easily. By carefully choosing our collaborators we save much money, ensure the quality of our products and good service to the client and, additionally, we maintain productivity."[80] In the early years, Lorenzo Servitje's uncle, Jaime Sendra Grimau, was charged with hiring workers and orienting them into the Bimbo familia. This hands-on approach to hiring and training tightened control over the workforce and often intruded into the personal lives of workers. One employee remembered applying for a job in the 1950s. He was told that he lived too far away and to come back when he moved closer to the factory. Once the employee found housing nearby with some friends, he began his job at the factory.[81]

Once hired, employees received training with managers to learn about their job and the company's values. Employees received uniforms to instill order, cleanliness, responsibility, and a connection to the company. According to Roberto Servitje Sendra,

> When we began the business, we started with 10 vendors, very clean and dressed in a uniform that included a cap and a bow tie; they had impeccable trucks. At that time, none of our competitors had uniformed personnel, we were the first. Until today they continue dressed in uniforms driving trucks always clean on the inside and out.[82]

Bimbo's owners saw their secret recipe as "not treating employees as human resources but as people to whom it provides fair treatment and affection, security, opportunities to learn and grow using the profits from the company."[83] By cultivating a sense of community, hierarchy, and identification with the company, Bimbo managers tried to instill in workers a sense of mission, so that they would come to understand that "nobody does anything that isn't productive, useful, profitable, or satisfactory. Because those people who only cover appearances cannot be happy; it is very likely that inside they feel frustrated." The Bimbo leaders couched their work in moralist hierarchical terms, since "in a propitious, motivating climate, real work is beneficial for the company and for the person."[84]

Bimbo provided outlets to build comradery and demonstrate subsidiarity between owners, managers, and workers. The company encouraged the formation of baseball leagues where men could work together inside and outside of the factory and develop greater team identification with Bimbo and its owners. The company formed a mountaineering club to hike local mountains. During the 1950s, Bimbo owners and workers made yearly pilgrimages to the nearby Basílica of Our Lady of Guadalupe on December 12 in honor of the Virgen de Guadalupe.[85] Workers who showed promise but lacked education beyond primary school were often selected to attend classes to complete their secondary education, and teachers were brought in from the secondary school that the Bimbo owners established near the factory. In some cases, their full-time job became attending secondary school.[86]

The company's welfare capitalist and paternalistic approaches to its workforce were designed to ameliorate class conflict, contain worker organizing, and resist independent unions. Bimbo owners were quick to point out that they work with employee unions and believed in and respected the collective contract. They often boasted that in their Mexican operations, workers have never gone on strike. They attribute their successful employee relations to the Christian formation of the owners and Bimbo's values.

Despite their proclamations to the contrary, Bimbo has had numerous struggles with unions and workers. The union structure in Mexico after the 1940s was rather authoritarian, centralized, and controlled by the official Confederación de Trabajadores Mexicanos (CTM), led by Fidel Velásquez. The CTM often functioned as a protection union that kept militant workers out of the workplace and discouraged independent organizing by workers, in exchange for employer concessions. While the union created a sense of stability on the shop floor, it could also create headaches for the owners. Throughout the first forty years of Bimbo's operation, the Bimbo's Bakery union leader was Rodolfo Martínez Moreno, who, according to Servitje, exacted too many concessions and wanted to make backroom deals. Nevertheless, Bimbo learned to work with the official unions to keep its main plants from striking. In Monterrey, however, Bimbo followed the customs of the regional factory owners and kept the CTM out, working instead with employer-controlled white unions. White unions were close to the company and followed the company's policies and practices under the guise of class harmony. These unions were started by Monterrey industrialists during the Porfiriato and were weapons against more radical unionization movements during the revolution and later against the government-aligned corporatist unions that aligned themselves with the PRI.[87] After repeated attempts to break Bimbo's white unions, in 1965 the CTM organized in the plant and forced Bimbo to recognize the CTM union, much to the chagrin of the owners. In 1984 another potential strike almost broke out in the Monterrey plant as workers organized against the local manager, and independent unions began to organize in the plant. The plant manager fired sixteen workers "as infiltrators of the communist party," and workers pushed for a strike. Roberto Servitje had to come back from his vacation in Vail, Colorado, to negotiate with the unions. He worked out a deal with Fidel Velázquez and the governor of Nuevo León that led to the removal of thirty worker "agitators" who threatened to lead the plant on strike. After the firing of the militant workers, Bimbo pushed to have the union leader, Martínez Moreno, retired and installed a new union leader more in line with the company values. In 1985, a new union leader was chosen, Marco Antonio Fajardo Martínez, who started working at Bimbo at the age of fourteen and knew the Bimbo production process well. Bimbo owners and managers rejoiced with a union leader under their thumb, especially in the coming age of neoliberal global expansion.[88]

As the labor scholar Marcela Hernández Romo has demonstrated, Bimbo leaders used the ideology of conservative social justice and technological innovations on the line and on distribution routes to strengthen the company-union relationship and maintain control over workers. The development of handheld microcomputer scanners revolutionized the company's operations, allowing sales to be tracked in real time. While Bimbo managers developed the distribution routes, the union assigned the routes to workers based on seniority. By getting the union involved in these tasks, they became complicit and responsible for company operations.[89] In addition, the company was able to work through the union to measure worker productivity and regulate the aesthetic appearance of workers. Workers were incentivized with bonuses to come to work on time with a clean uniform, short hair, no tattoos, and no earrings. The highly disciplined labor culture was reinforced by the pro-management corporativist union.[90]

Lorenzo Servitje spread his business values to other employers. In 1957, with other likeminded conservative businessmen, he founded the

Unión Social de Empresarios Mexicanos (USEM). Using the ideas of Christian Social Doctrine in the context of Mexico, USEM created an educational program to reshape the values and image of businessmen by emphasizing the leadership role businesses had in addressing the country's social and political problems. USEM developed several regional organizations, and its leaders and members came to play important roles in Mexico's mainstream business organizations. According to Salas-Porras, "USEM has gradually and silently expanded its educational activities, generating a multiplier effect which created a long reach over a network of institutions."[91] In 1963, Servitje stepped away from the daily operations of Grupo Bimbo to focus on USEM activities, spreading his business philosophy and philanthropy. Among the first institutions that USEM created were schools in the neighborhood surrounding their first factory.

By the 1980s and 1990s, Bimbo's influence had grown as a leading Mexican consumer company and as a force in Mexican social and political life. The network of schools, universities, programs, civic organizations, and think tanks that it supported grew significantly too. Christian Social Doctrine and USEM's influence pervaded much of the thought of top business leaders and their organizations. With the growth of more competitive elections in the 1980s and 1990s, members of Mexico's conservative Partido de Acción Nacional (PAN) began to deepen their engagement with Christian Social Doctrine and its exponents. This was especially the case with the rise of the businessman Manuel Clouthier, who was close to Servitje and was the PAN's presidential candidate in the 1988 election. While Servitje was close to Clouthier, like many business elites, he feared what might happen if the more progressive and popular candidate of the left, Cuauhtémoc Cárdenas, was elected. Therefore, he supported the official PRI party. Servitje was impressed with the PRI candidate Carlos Salinas de Gortari and his neoliberal policies, which were ones he long advocated for, and thought they sounded more radical coming from Salinas de Gortari's mouth. He accompanied Salinas de Gortari on some campaign trips and was surprised by how well received he was. When the results of the 1988 elections were coming in live on national television, Cuauhtémoc Cárdenas was in the lead, but then the election machinery abruptly went down. When it came back up a couple of hours later, Salinas de Gortari had edged out Cárdenas and was declared the winner. The obvious irregularities of the election were on full display and even the business sector knew the results were questionable at best. However, Servitje rallied the business sector to support Salinas de Gortari and pressure Clouthier not to join with Cuauhtémoc Cárdenas to contest the election. While he knew that "Clouthier and Cárdenas were morally correct, the elections were questionable and the results dubious, but with the lack of evidence, pragmatism prevailed among the business class. Out of fear of the probable populism [of Cárdenas] we were inclined to Carlos Salinas de Gortari. I remember having insisted to Clouthier to give in for the sake of peace."[92] Bimbo's Servitje was now playing a high-profile role in the politics of the country.

With the Zapatista rebellion in 1994 and then the economic crisis of 1994 and 1995, business leaders influenced by USEM began to publicly question the rapid implementation of economic reforms without meaningful political reforms. As Servitje would later say, the Zapatista rebellion surprised him: "I was shocked and feared that the solution was impossible. The uncertainty distressed me, caused me fear."[93] Fearing how more popular uprisings would hurt their businesses and thinking about the need to grow their markets, business leaders began to think more directly about poverty and inequality. In the pages of the business magazine *Expansión*, business leaders demonstrated a specific concern for social problems and the need to expand their responsibility in providing social assistance, creating a code of ethics, and condemning the radical implementation of neoliberal policies.[94] Nevertheless, Servitje and the business elite had very little contact with the poverty of the countryside. Eight years after the Zapatista uprising, Servitje's daughter Marinela urged him to accompany her on a trip to see the conditions of poverty that Indigenous people experience, and he traveled with the support of the church to the highlands of Nayarit, where he spent two days. Based on those two days, he concluded, "Mexico is heartbreaking, there is tremendous poverty and ignorance. The wealthy classes have no idea what the poor are. . . . Those two days in which we breathed misery shook me. We decided to help the Coras and Huichols rebuild their school, and we promoted productive projects through the Center for Integral Development's Secretary of Social Development."[95] Servitje's paternalism focused on charity and moral reform, and this is the basis of his concept of social justice.

Throughout the 1990s, the Bimbo patriarch became very active in campaigns for moral reform. Among his more high-profile struggles were battles against immorality in public and on television. In 1993, the year he retired from his chairmanship on the board of Bimbo, he led a public campaign to prevent the international popstar Madonna from performing in Mexico. With the Unión Nacional de Padres de Familia (UNPF), a group that USEM helped develop, they argued that Madonna's concert, titled the Girlie Show, "promoted customs related to sexual life that we don't want for our families, such as homosexuality, sodomy, lesbianism, masturbation and representations of orgies."[96] The effort to ban Madonna's concert was unsuccessfully taken up in the legislature by the PRI congressman and husband of Marinela Servitje, Fernando Lerdo de Tejada, who argued that Madonna's concerts were antithetical to family morality.[97] Despite these efforts, all three concerts were sold out and a smashing success, with more than fifty-two thousand in attendance on the first night.[98]

In 1995, Servitje got involved in the battle against reality talk shows on Mexican television. His first target was *El Show de Cristina*, the popular talk show in the United States hosted by Cristina Saralegui. Leaders of the UNPF held a news conference to denounce the airing of the show because they believed the themes it addressed were inappropriate for children and youth. The producers of the show invited the head of UNPF, Francisco González Garza, to appear on the show and to discuss UNPF's objections. González Garza accepted, and he debated the merits of the show's contents with Cristina Saralegui. Weeks later, Servitje met with him and told him that he did poorly on the show, emphasizing that he was set up to look bad. They then decided to work together to hold meetings in Catholic schools, universities, and organizations in their networks to gather signatures to get the television networks to eliminate or at least limit shows that go against family values. Beginning in 1996, they began their campaign by meeting with groups and collecting signatures. By 1997, they had collected 4.5 million signatures and founded the organization A Favor de lo Mejor (In Favor of the Best) to promote positive and family-friendly messages on television.[99] Bimbo employees were also called on to be involved in the campaigns for A Favor de lo Mejor. Alfredo Pérez Mata, a Bimbo employee from Irapuato, recalls being asked by a company official to collect signatures for A Favor de lo Mejor's campaign for better programming on radio and television. He agreed, attended the orientation, and then proceeded to collect signatures. When he successfully collected more than 750 signatures working with his parish priest, he received a call from Lorenzo Servitje, who congratulated and thanked him for his work. For several days after, he enjoyed the congratulations of his fellow workers for having spoken to Don Lorenzo.[100] With the establishment of A Favor de lo Mejor, Servitje met with Televisa executives to discuss limiting the airing of talk shows and became an important force against what A Favor de lo Mejor saw as immorality, frivolity, and debauchery.[101]

In 1997, the Servitje family and Bimbo made an aggressive effort to stop the airing of a documentary on the Legionaries of Christ founder, Marcial Maciel. The Legionaries of Christ is a powerful religious order in the Catholic Church founded in Mexico in 1941 that was created to minister to the wealthy and powerful in order to multiply the church's impact on society. It counts many Mexican billionaires and millionaires among its congregants, including Carlos Slim, the Servitje family, and industrialists connected to the Monterrey group.[102] The documentary, a production of the independent television station Channel 40, was scheduled to air the testimonies of several former members of the Legionaries of Christ who claimed that they had been sexually abused by Marcial Maciel. This was an explosive charge, and the airing of the report was sure to challenge the moral authority of one of the most important Catholic leaders in Mexico and a darling of the Catholic Right.

A few weeks before the documentary was to be televised, the Legionaries got wind of the documentary's damning content, and they mobilized into action. Students from the Legionaries of Christ's Universidad de Anahuác and prominent Catholic activists, including Roberto Servitje, Bimbo's president of the board of directors, organized demonstrations against Channel 40. As a major supporter of the Legionaries of Christ, the Servitje family tried to pressure the owner of Channel 40. Roberto Servitje threatened to pull all of Bimbo's advertising from the station and urge other companies to do the same if Channel 40 aired the show. According to the journalist Ciro Gómez Leyva, Servitje argued that he would do so "because [airing the program] was an attack against the church, because it was an injustice, because it was a calamity, because it was a defamation." A day before the airing, Lorenzo Servitje spoke at a conference for A Favor de lo Mejor at the private Instituto Tecnológico Autónomo de México, where he stated that he was against the airing of the documentary. He also dropped a bombshell: Bimbo had pulled its advertising from the station. Given the weight that Bimbo has on Mexico's advertising market, this was sure to be a major blow to the young independent network. Following Servitje's explosive announcement, ten other companies pulled their advertising from the station.[103] Despite economic and political pressure, however, the program aired as scheduled. The fallout was tremendous. The Church protected Maciel for several more years, even as journalists revealed more evidence of his crimes. Servitje's and Bimbo's pulling of advertisements and its flexing of economic and political power was too much for Channel 40 and ultimately led to the end of its independent reporting and its takeover by television giant TV Azteca.

The efforts to suppress the revelations of the abuses by the Legionaries of Christ that led to the weakening of independent programming was a major demonstration of power by Bimbo, the Servitjes, and the Catholic Right.[104] Roberto Servitje firmly stood by Bimbo's actions and years later said, "I expressed my absolute disagreement, that matter should have never been brought to public light, that is why we withdrew. That is it, I have nothing more to clarify."[105] The high-profile public actions of Bimbo's founders and their overt ties to the Catholic Right strengthened Mexico's conservative sectors, which would contribute to the election of the Partido de Acción Nacional's candidates to the presidency in 2000 and again in 2006.

With the election of Vicente Fox in 2000, the Servitje family solidified their political position. According to the journalist Salvador Frausto Crotte, they donated heavily to First Lady Martha Fox de Sahagún's Vamos México Foundation. In return, the Servitje's foundations and organizations received significant funds from Vamos México and the government's Transforma México financed by the National Lottery. According to Frausto, between 2002 and 2004, "The Servitje family donated a million to the private foundation of the president's wife and received 100 times more from the government trust."[106] The Servitje family continued its moral campaign, leading a boycott against the airing of the Mexican version of the reality show *Big Brother* in 2002 on Televisa. While the show aired for five years in Mexico, Bimbo did not advertise on the program and got forty-five large companies to initially boycott the program. Two years later, Lorenzo Servitje teamed up with other Catholic organizations to denounce crime in Mexico City.[107]

Servitje continued his right-wing investment in politics by contributing 3.5 million pesos to Alberto Cárdenas's campaign for the precandidate election of the PAN. Even though Cárdenas had little chance of winning, Servitje contributed more money than any campaign donor during the precandidate electoral process.[108] The Servitje family continued to support Father Marcial Maciel, and Lorenzo Servitje did not express regret about supporting Maciel until well after the priest's death when he was pressed directly by Miguel Ángel Granados Chapa, the editor of *Proceso*, for his weekly column pointedly titled "And Don Lorenzo, Don't You Have Anything to Say?"[109]

In 2011, the Servitje family was once again embroiled in a national scandal related to injecting the teaching of religious values. The state of Puebla accepted donations of thousands of books for teachers from the Church of Scientology's education wing, Applied Scholastics. When teachers objected to the religious content, the Minister of Education in Puebla stated that it had come through a donation in coordination with Marinela Servitje's educational foundation. While she denied the allegation of facilitating the donation of 450,000 copies of the book *Learning to Learn* and the video *A Path Toward Happiness*, the values-based focus of the material did not seem like an aberration for the conservative Servitje family.[110] Applied Scholastics had a longer history in Puebla's education system. According to the organization, it mounted "an educational rescue mission" in Puebla with the sponsorship of the state's Minister of Education in 2010 and taught Study Technology fundamentals to nearly a thousand students and six hundred teachers received training by them.[111]

The Servitje family and Grupo Bimbo have been closely aligned with the Catholic Right and worked hard to implement a vision of Catholic social justice in its business operations and charity work. The company has also been on the forefront of evangelizing business sectors and creating organizations for moral reform in Mexico. Much of this work has been hidden from consumers, but as Grupo Bimbo aged into "corporate social responsibility," it pivoted its more high-profile charity work to funding organizations related to the environment, using its business operations to reduce Bimbo's carbon footprint and address poor nutrition.

Bimbo's Global Enterprises

International expansion was a natural process for Grupo Bimbo given its ties to the U.S. baking industry and the significant experience it had acquired over the first four decades since its founding. Throughout the late 1980s, Bimbo met the economic crisis as an opportunity to reinvest in its factories and upgrade its equipment to prepare for the opening of markets with trade liberalization. This helped the company pursue its strategy of keeping foreign competitors out of the bread market and bolstering its position in the Mexican snack market, which reached about 20 percent of the market in 1990. In addition, Bimbo worked with McDonald's as the U.S. fast-food giant expanded into Mexico and built a new $14 billion bun factory to supply McDonald's with hamburger buns to its specifications.[112] With the Mexican market firmly in its grasp, Bimbo took advantage of liberalization policies to expand globally.

Bimbo's 1990 acquisition of a bread and cake plant in neighboring Guatemala signaled the beginning of its aggressive expansion into markets throughout the Americas. In the late 1980s, it began consulting for a bakery firm in Chimaltenango, a little more than fifty kilometers from the capital city on the Pan-American highway. Bimbo then acquired the company and initiated its global operations in Guatemala during the final years of the country's civil war. Over the next several years, it began to restructure the plant and develop routes in Guatemala.[113] Bimbo followed its Guatemalan acquisition with its purchase of leading bakeries in Chile (Ideal, established in 1925) and Venezuela, while establishing production plants in Argentina, Colombia, Costa Rica, El Salvador, Peru, and commercial operations in Honduras and Nicaragua. In 1998, Bimbo made deals with a McDonald's franchiser to be the exclusive supplier of bakery products for its chain in Venezuela, Colombia, and Peru.[114]

Bimbo also began to expand aggressively in the United States. Beginning in 1987, it exported Bimbo products to Houston, where Lorenzo Servitje's eldest son lived, and then to Los Angeles. Both cities had large and growing Mexican communities. Bimbo's production operations in the United States began with its 1993 acquisition of several small tortillerías established by Mexican immigrants, in Oklahoma, Ohio, Sacramento, Houston, and Escondido.[115] In 1997, it purchased Pacific Pride Bakery in San Diego and then Texas's leading bakery in 1998, Mrs. Baird's, which was established in 1908.[116] The following year, it acquired Four-S Bakery, with its Weber's Bread brand in Southern California. In 2001, it began acquisition of the U.S. subsidiary of Canadian George Weston LTD, which included its bakery assets west of the Mississippi River, and it bought the remaining U.S. Weston bakery assets in 2009, including popular brands such as Thomas' English Muffins, Brownberry, and Entenmann's.[117]

However, operating in the U.S. context was different from operating in Mexico. In the United States, most goods were sold in supermarkets, while in Mexico Bimbo sold 80 percent of its products to mom-and-pop stores (tiendas de abarrotes) through routes it developed.[118] As Roberto Servitje explained,

> Different from Mexico, where we supply businesses based on what we think they will consume to avoid leftovers, there the large supermarket chains have the power to decide how much they want. The aisles need to be full, even if the goods are not being purchased, and the proportion of inventory not sold in the U.S. is too high. Selling two items a week and leaving six on the shelf is not good business.[119]

Consequently, in 2003, Bimbo Bakeries USA lost $40 million and the following year another $27 million. This was a major blow to Bimbo, and it searched for ways to address the low volume of sales and the return of merchandise. This included finding other outlets for its products, such as supplying fast-food companies and developing routes to reach new markets. Especially helpful was the incorporation of barcodes and handheld computers to track products at all points of the distribution process in real time so Bimbo could see what was taking place.[120] This informed its decision to reduce its product lines but expand its market. By 2005, it reported its first profits in the U.S. market and the way was paved for further growth (figure 11).

Bimbo continued its U.S. expansion over the next two decades with its acquisition of Sara Lee's Bakery Division in the United States, Spain, and Portugal for $975 billion. With the acquisition, Bimbo added dozens of regional bread brands in the United States in addition to its national Sara Lee brand of bread, and Bimbo became the top bread producer in the United States. In addition, the purchase gave Bimbo the opportunity to introduce its other products, "in every city and town in the country."[121]

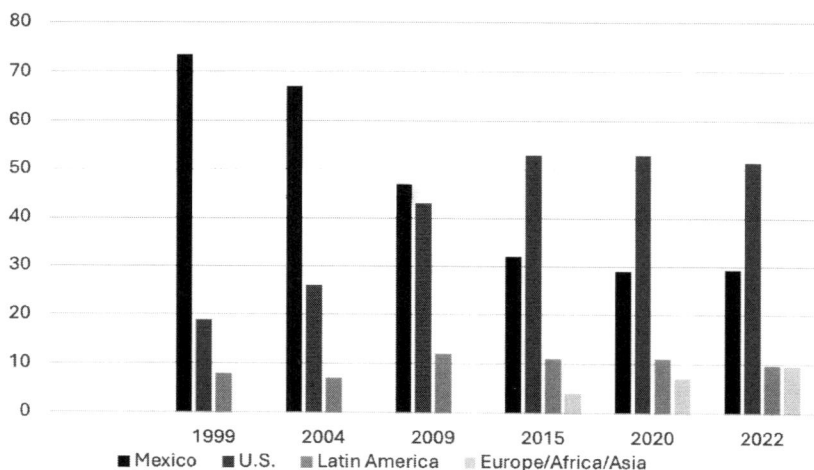

FIGURE 11 Percentage of Bimbo's Global Sales by Region, 1999–2022. (Calculated from Grupo Bimbo, *Informe Anuales*.)

Through its purchase of Sara Lee, Bimbo was catapulted into the Portuguese and Spanish markets. Although the Bimbo name was used in Spain since 1964, it was never formally part of the Grupo Bimbo. Instead, it was started by Jaime Jorba, a cousin of Lorenzo Servitje, who wanted to move back to Spain and start Bimbo there for his nuclear family to run. Jorba, who never became a Mexican citizen, had been instrumental in the early Bimbo operations but wanted to return to Europe to educate his sons and purchased a house in Cataluña. He also feared what he saw as the left-wing values in Mexico that were epitomized by President López Mateos's invitation of Cuban revolutionary leader Fidel Castro to visit Mexico City in 1962. Jorba was also tired of being under Servitje's control, though he didn't directly tell his cousin this. Together they worked out a plan where Jorba would have the business in Spain with 95 percent of the shares. He ran the operation but met tough competition. Jorba was forced to create a partnership with Campbell Taggert, a leading U.S. bakery company. Lorenzo Servitje helped steer the operations, but the company did not do well. After the death of Spanish dictator Francisco Franco, Jorba was worried by the unleashing of worker organizing and unionization that had been tightly controlled under the dictatorship, and he sold all his shares to Campbell Taggert, which came to control the Bimbo label and recipe in Spain, much to the chagrin of Servitje.[122] Less than a decade later, in 1982, Campbell Taggert was purchased by Anheuser-Busch, which spun off the new bakery sector as Earth Grains in 1996.[123] In 2001, Sara Lee purchased Earthgrains and its operations in the Iberian Peninsula.[124] Bimbo's 2010 acquisition of Sara Lee brought the company, founded by children of Spanish immigrants, back to Spain and added Portugal to its portfolio. Altogether, Sara Lee's acquisitions increased Grupo Bimbo's sales by 27 percent a year.[125]

Bimbo's surge has continued throughout the second and the beginning of the third decade of the twenty-first century with acquisitions in more than a dozen countries on four continents, bringing the total number of countries that Bimbo had plants or distribution centers in from nineteen in 2011 to thirty-four in 2023. In 2017, through its purchase of East Balt Bakeries, founded in Chicago in 1955, Bimbo acquired twenty-one bakeries and was given access to markets in ten counties in Europe, Asia, the Middle East, and Africa, in addition to brands in the United States. In that same year, it acquired three bakeries from the Adghal group in Morocco, launching Bimbo's African operations.[126]

As figure 11 illustrates, with Bimbo's transformation as a global corporation, its Mexico operations came to account for a much smaller portion of its overall operations and sales. From accounting for 100 percent of its operations in 1990, this amount dropped to 74 percent by 2000, 46 percent in 2001, and 29 percent in 2020. Its Mexican operation still grew; however, Bimbo's global operations were expanding exponentially: approximately doubling its net sales between 1994 and 2007, and then tripling them over the following seven years. By 2022, Bimbo's net sales were nearly 400 billion pesos a year, twenty-five times the amount of its 1994 sales. During this period, Bimbo's U.S. sales accounted for over half its total sales, while its Latin American operations and its Europe, Asia, and Africa sales accounted for nearly 10 percent each.

As a global enterprise with 214 factories in thirty-four countries, Bimbo is poised to make even deeper inroads into bread and bakery goods markets throughout the world. Grupo Bimbo and its iconic bear and other cartoon characters capture the hearts and stomachs of millions of consumers and profit from its contribution to the growth of low-cost sugary, salty, calorie-laden, and processed packaged foods that has accelerated rates of diet-related diseases. Bimbo has taken advantage of the nutrition crisis to produce lower-sugar-content sweets and an array of new packaged foods marketed as healthier and even nutritious.

Bimbo carefully cultivated its notions of patriarchy and religious morality through its business operations and in the public at large. While often more conservative than secular elites in the PRI, Bimbo successfully grew its business and wielded its financial clout in defense of its conservative Catholicism. Building on its moral Catholicism, the new generation of Bimbo leaders have shifted the tone of their morality to emphasize social responsibility and environmentalism, deftly co-opting the language of social movements. Grupo Bimbo is widely heralded by the corporate world as among the most innovative and sustainable companies. In 2014, it made *Forbes* magazine's coveted list of the World's Most Innovative Companies because of its development of "healthier breads as a whole [which] is a big innovation focus of the company, matching where consumer demand is moving, with multigrain variants in particular appearing across its portfolio."[127] It has aggressively worked to rebrand itself as a sustainable company committed to reducing its climate footprint by investing in windfarms and water reduction, purchasing a fleet of electric vehicles, and using suppliers involved in regenerative agriculture. By 2025, Grupo Bimbo plans to be a net-zero company.[128] On the forefront of co-opting the terms and rhetoric of social movements and the climate justice movement, Bimbo's slick repositioning of itself is illustrative of the company's long history of profiting from the basic contradictions between its business practices and the health and safety of people and the planet.

CHAPTER 6

SUPERMARKET COLONIALISM

Walmart de México and Oxxo in the Restructuring of the Food System

In September 2004, as construction workers were building a Bodega Aurrerá supermarket, part of the Walmart de México (Walmex) chain,[1] on the edge of the San Juan de Teotihuacán archaeological site in the state of Mexico, they unearthed clay pottery and the remains of a fourteenth-century wall. As they continued, the workers found nine graves, an altar, and what appeared to be a plaza. As the news spread throughout the town, it confirmed what residents and archaeologists had suspected: Walmart was building on ancestral remains. How could Walmart have been given a green light on a project that was already unpopular in the town?

Community members and small shop owners, led by poet and teacher Emmanuel D'Herrera, and the curandera Emma Ortega, formed the Frente Cívico en Defensa del Valle de Teotihuacán to stop construction and were soon joined by others. They marched on Walmart de México's corporate headquarters and blockaded the main offices of the National Institute of Anthropology and History (INAH) in Mexico City. They awoke the attention of Governor Arturo Montiel, who, on October 2, 2004, announced that the government would assist Walmex in finding another location for its store. However, Walmex sped up construction and Montiel was forced to retract his statement the following week. Mexican and international artists and intellectuals, including the artists Francisco Toledo, Leonora Carrington, Jesusa Rodríguez, and writers Homero Aridjis, Carlos Monsiváis, Elena Poniatowska, Miguel León-Portilla, and the cookbook author Diana Kennedy circulated a letter appealing to President Vicente Fox to find a political solution, since constructing the store so close to the pyramids was "a grave historical mistake."[2] Nevertheless, three weeks later, on November 4, 2004, Bodega Aurrerá in San Juan Teotihuacán opened its doors. Walmart had successfully replicated what the Spanish conquerors did nearly five hundred years before: it destroyed Indigenous community sites and used the rubble to build its own monuments on top of sites it was colonizing.

In the first decade of the twenty-first century, Walmex executives were on a mission to build as many stores as they could throughout Mexico to outpace the competition. The company's real estate development team scoured aerial photos and demographic data and found a plot of land near the entrance of San Juan de Teotihuacán in the state of Mexico, less than an hour away from Mexico City, and less than a mile from the world-renowned pyramids and archaeological site. Walmex executives thought that if they could build a Bodega Aurrerá supermarket at the town's main entrance they "would be slamming the gate on the whole town," effectively shutting out their competitors.[3]

Supermarket colonialism, supported by state policy and private capital, aimed to reshape Mexico's food system and the eating and shopping habits of Mexicans. In a more concentrated form than in the past, governments worked to marginalize traditional open-air tianguis markets and promoted the orderliness of the supermarket, with goods individually packaged on shelves organized in rows and aisles, in displays of a modern sense of order, cleanliness, consistency, and abundance. In the city of Oaxaca, for example, one scholar calculated that the "metropolitan area went from having only one small national chain supermarket twenty years ago to having sixteen large supermarkets, including nine Walmart-owned stores."[4] This pattern was repeated in many cities in a very short time. Between 1999 and 2009, the number of Mexican cities that had Walmex stores went from 38 to 265.[5] At the same time, the number of Oxxo convenience stores grew at a rate of 23 percent a year. Between 1995 and 2022, Oxxo stores grew from approximately 1,500 stores to 21,500 throughout Mexico.

Walmex's colonization of Mexico radically transformed Mexico's food system and society in less than two decades. Few organizations, save the Catholic Church and the postrevolutionary governments, have been able to conquer and colonize the expanse of Mexico physically and culturally, let alone cybernetically. The rapidity of this transformation is especially notable given Mexico's many layers of bureaucracy and regulatory red tape. Like earlier colonizing institutions, Walmex overcame these obstacles through a combination of precision demographic and logistical studies, deep pockets, and knowledge of the Mexican system.

Supermarket colonialism has expanded so rapidly that it poses an existential threat to Mexico's food system. In a few decades, supermarkets had spread throughout the country, resulting in the concentration of economic and political power in the hands of a few corporations that increasingly dictate the terms of food production and have the power to shape, and often control, working conditions in agriculture, food processing, logistics, and the retail sector. The first section of this chapter examines the origins and development of Mexico's self-service supermarkets from the mid-twentieth century to the growth of national supermarket chains in the 1980s and 1990s. I then turn my attention to Walmex and its explosion throughout Mexico in the first two decades of the twenty-first century. This chapter explains how Walmex officials were able to transform the retail landscape in such a brief period, running roughshod over Mexican laws, regulations, and even one of Mexico's most famous Indigenous monuments. In the process, Walmex adapted Walmart's logistic system, creating numerous regional distribution centers and accelerating the restructuring of the countryside. As the largest private employer in Mexico, it blends Mexican labor relations with Walmart's notorious anti-union policies, its stream-lined operations, and low wages, making Walmex the leading creator of precarious jobs for Mexico's working poor. Finally, I examine the rapid expansion of convenience stores in Mexico by focusing on Oxxo, the largest chain store in Mexico and Latin America.

From Self-Service Markets for the Elite to Supermarket Colonialism

The rise of supermarkets developed slowly in Mexico during the twentieth century. Public markets, neighborhood family stores, and open-air markets satisfied the shopping needs of consumers for centuries. As urban retail merchants began to invest in other industries, some amassed capital to expand their operations and open several retail and wholesale outlets. By the 1940s, merchants would begin to innovate their operations and adopt retail methods being developed in the United States, where the development of chain supermarkets such as Kroger, A&P, and Piggly Wiggly was taking place. These supermarkets developed with the growth of consumer capitalism and consumer movements that constructed the citizen-shopper who had the power to influence society through their purchasing power. Marketing increasingly focused on women who had growing independence and purchasing power.[6] While in the United States, supermarket chains began at the turn of the twentieth century, supermarkets came relatively late to Mexico.

As supermarkets developed, they initiated a revolution in commerce and consequently in gendered labor and social relations. Self-service supermarkets were attractive because of the large assortment of goods sold and the ability customers had to choose items themselves directly from the shelf.[7] Shoppers no longer had to ask the market proprietor for the product that was behind the counter or in the glass-display case but could instead hold the merchandise at will, creating an illusion of choice, independence, and power. The growth of self-service stores, and their capital-intensive labor processes, sped up the transformation away from women as marketers to working-class women as supermarket workers and middle- and upper-class women turned into consumers.

Many self-service stores were established by Spanish immigrants and their children. Drawing up their economic and social capital, many started as small shop owners, running neighborhood abarrote stores that sold basic foods and provided credit. Spanish merchants drew upon their networks and their proximity to the United States to develop a Spanish oligopoly in retail chain supermarket stores.[8] Of the eleven top supermarket chains in Mexico, according to Javier Moreno Lázaro, seven were established by Spanish immigrants or their children, and two were established by immigrant families from China and Lebanon (table 11). The early self-service supermarket chains were small and catered to the urban elite. In 1947, the Mexican firm Garza y Valdés established Supermercados, S.A., better known by its acronym SUMESA, which means "your table," in Monterrey in 1947. That same year, Spanish immigrants Francisco

TABLE 11 Principal Mexican Supermarkets by Year of Establishment and Owners' Background

Name	Location	Year	Owners	Family Background
SUMESA	Monterrey, N.L.	1947	Garza y Valdés	Mexican
Calimax	Tijuana, BC	1947	Familia Fimbres	Mexican
Almacenes Blanco	Mexico City	1948	Hermanos Blanco	Spanish
El Sardinero	Mexico City	1955	Jesús Fernández Torres	Spanish
Aurrerá	Mexico City	1958	Arango brothers	Mexican/Spanish
Comercial Mexicana	Mexico City	1959	González Nova brothers	Spanish
Soriana	Torreón, Coah.	1968	Martín Borque brothers	Spanish
Gigante	Mexico City	1962	Ángel Losado	Spanish
Superama	Mexico City	1963	Arango brothers	Spanish
Chedraui	Xalapa, Ver.	1970	Chedraui Obeso	Lebanese Mex.
Casa Ley	Culiacán, Sin.	1970	Juan Ley Fong	Chinese Mex.

Source: Adapted from Javier Moreno Lázaro, "Los españoles y la revolución comercial mexicana: Las cadenas de supermercados, 1921–2011," *Investigaciones de Historia Económica* 8 (2012): 71.

and Estanislao Blanco Caldevilla, who arrived in Mexico in 1943, opened Almacenes Blanco as a discount supermarket and household appliance store in Mexico City. Other stores proliferated in Mexico's major cities in the 1950s and 1960s during the Mexican Miracle, with the growth of the upper and middle classes.

In 1958, Jerónimo, Plácido, and Manuel Arango, three brothers born to Spanish immigrant parents, established a discount bulk chain store aimed at Mexican middle and working classes. Their idea for opening a store came after a trip to New York City, where they saw a long line of people waiting to enter Orbach's department store. They studied Orbach's cost-cutting discount model and felt that it could work in Mexico City. With a loan from their parents, they opened Aurrerá (Basque for forward) on the corner of Bolívar and 5 de Febrero in downtown Mexico City, selling goods at 20 to 30 percent of their retail value.[9] They soon opened stores in middle-class areas (Colonia Del Valle), an upper-income area of Colonia Lomas de Becerra, and in a lower-middle-class neighborhood of Colonia Guerrero. In 1965 the Arango brothers established a more traditional supermarket chain, Superama, which was geared toward wealthier Mexicans. As Mexico City was growing and new supermarkets were being established, the Arango brothers reached out in 1965 to the Jewel Corporation in Chicago, which provided them with a $21 million loan and logistical help for their expansion. Under Jerónimo Arango's leadership, Aurrerá became the largest retailer in Mexico and "Arango became the first merchant to put clothing, food, and hardware in one store."[10] With eight Aurrerá stores in Mexico City and one Superama, Arango established VIPS, a short-order restaurant with a small store aimed at the growing middle classes. In 1967, under Plácido Arango's direction, VIPS expanded to Madrid and was soon in twenty cities across Spain. In 1970, they established Suburbia, a clothing store with its own brand. At Suburbia, shoppers could get instant financing through Banamex.

In 1962, Ángel Losado Gómez, a migrant from Spain, established Gigante. Losado Gómez first settled in Apán in the state of Hidalgo in the 1930s and began buying and selling seeds with a local Spanish-owned company. In 1942, he "established La Comercial de Apán, which was an abarrote store, beer distribution center but above all dedicated to seed commerce."[11] According to historians Mario Cerruti and Eva Rivas Sada, he began to provide seeds for those producing malt for the growing breweries Modelo, Cuauhtémoc, and Moctezuma. La Comercial provided numerous services for agricultural producers, including operating a company store. Losado Gómez soon began to acquire nearby haciendas, expanding his operations. He moved to Mexico City and in 1963 established the largest self-service supermarket in Latin America, Gigante Mixcoac, in the south of Mexico City. Taking advantage of scale and purchasing large quantities of goods directly from producers at discounted prices, Gigante was able to reduce prices. However, initially, Gigante lost many items to theft and needed to create new administrative systems to adapt to the changing ways of operating supermarkets. It was not long before it prospered.[12]

A year before Gigante opened, Comercial Mexicana was founded by the González Nova brothers, Spanish immigrants who were merchants and textile manufacturers. They established a Comercial Mexicana in the 1930s where they sold clothing. In the 1950s, they attended several events in Dayton, Ohio, sponsored by National Cash Register, and became convinced that the self-service model of stores was the future. In 1959, they transformed their warehouse into a self-service store selling clothing and household goods. In 1962, they opened another Comercial Mexicana on Insurgentes in Mexico City as a modern supermarket selling groceries and manufactured clothing, and in 1965, they opened their second market, Comercial Asturias, followed by Comercial Pilares in Mexico City. The stores were successful and by 1972 Comercial Mexicana had fifteen megamarkets.[13]

Also in 1962, in Torreón, Coahuila, Francisco and Armando Martín Borque transformed the first of their family's several clothing and fabric stores, La Soriana, into a self-service clothing and fabric shop. Migrants from Soria in northern central Spain, they modeled their self-service store on newly built supermarkets in Mexico's capital city, Gigante and Aurrerá. Friends with both Jerónimo Arango and Ángel Losado Gómez, Francisco Martín Borque consulted with them on his new operation. Once the new Soriana fabric and clothing store opened its doors, the brothers began to transform other branches of Soriana into self-service stores.[14] As Soriana expanded and grew in popularity, in 1968 they opened their first supermarket, Centro Comercial La Soriana, which carried a variety of household items, electronics, clothing, groceries, a bakery, and a meat market, all under one roof. La Soriana soon became an important regional supermarket.[15]

Between 1970 and the 1990s, six large chain stores developed with a growing, but still limited, national presence. According to economic historian Diego López Rosado, the 1970s saw "a notable growth in supermarkets and other self-service stores that grew by 6.6 times during this decade." Nationally, in 1975 there were approximately four supermarkets for every 100,000 inhabitants and by 1980 that number doubled to eight, while in Mexico City it reached 663 per 100,000 inhabitants. By the 1980s, 51 percent of the supermarkets were concentrated in five regions: Mexico City (21%) and the states of Mexico (10%), Veracruz (10%), Jalisco (7%), and Nuevo León (3%).[16] Throughout the 1970s and

1980s, Almacenes Blanco gained popularity with its slogan, *abarata la vida,* "make life less expensive," and it built stores in cities throughout the country.[17] By 1983, Almacenes Blanco was the largest supermarket in the country, with sixty-three stores (table 12).

Three chains, Aurrerá/Superama, Comercial Mexicana, and Gigante, would overtake Almacenes Blanco in the 1990s, each with more than a hundred stores. Gigante grew from a few supermarkets in the 1960s to the largest chain store by 1992 after purchasing a chain of stores in Guadalajara, Mexico City–based El Sardinero, and acquiring the eighty-six stores of Almacenes Blanco in 1992.[18] Gigante established a chain of restaurants (Toks) and allied with U.S. companies to become the exclusive distributor of Radio Shack electronic products in Mexico. In 1999, it opened its first Gigante on the outskirts of Los Angeles and by 2004 it had a total of eight stores on the West Coast of the United States, along with stores in Costa Rica, Guatemala, and El Salvador. In 1984, Jerónimo Arango raised $53.4 million to purchase back the 36.1 percent of shares originally held by Jewel and began developing the bodega concept to sell fast-moving nonperishable goods in bulk in poor neighborhoods. The idea took off and sales grew by 20 percent in the midst of the economic crisis. Comercial Mexicana expanded its operations throughout the 1970s, and in 1981 it purchased the Monterrey supermarket chain Sumesa. Comercial Mexicana established a restaurant chain, California Restaurants, through a partnership with the Carnation company, and in 1992 with San Diego–based Price Club it created membership club warehouse stores.

While several small regional chains existed, a few grew to dominate important sections of the country. Torreón-based Soriana concentrated its operations in northeastern Mexico and in the 1980s it built supermarkets in Coahuila, Chihuahua, Durango, Aguascalientes, Zacatecas, and Baja California and by 1993, it had grown to twenty-three stores.[19] In northwestern Mexico, Casa Ley emerged as a self-service supermarket chain, building on the merchant operations of the Chinese immigrant Juan Ley Fong in Sinaloa. Upon his death in 1969, his children took over the business and by 1970 they had seventeen supermarkets. To expand their financing, they partnered with Safeway in 1981, the largest supermarket chain in the western United States, giving it a 49 percent stake in Casa Ley. By 1993, Ley had forty-two supermarkets in Sinaloa, Sonora,

TABLE 12 Mexico's Leading National Supermarket Chains, 1983–2023

Supermarket Chain	1983	1993	2000	2006	2013	2018	2023
Sumesa	31	0	0	0	0	0	0
El Sardinero	11	0	0	0	0	0	0
Aurrerá/ Superama/ Walmex	53	114	235	513	2,080	2,438	2,870
Soriana	9	23	101	234	659	815	801
Gigante	34	180	209	287	0	0	0
Comercial Mexicana/ La Comer[a]	39	120	164	205	200	65	82
Casa Ley	17[b]	42	97	117	150	180	290
Chedraui	5	20	49	94	198	260	432
H-E-B	0	0	10	21	49	65	79
Futurama/ Alsuper	n.d.	n.d.	28[c]	n.d.	44[d]	70	84
Auchan	0	0	5	0	0	0	0
Carrefour	0	0	22	0	0	0	0

Sources: Compiled from Muldoon and Servitje, *El comercio de alimentos en México*, 108; Cervantes Godoy, "The Growth of Supermarkets in Mexico," 52; Seale and Associates, Reporte de la Industria de Autoservicios, July 2018; ANTAD, *El pochteca moderno*; and various company annual reports and websites.

[a] On January 28, 2016, Soriana acquired the Comercial Mexicana brand and the majority of its stores. The remaining company rebranded as La Comer.

[b] 1978.

[c] 2003.

[d] 2010.

Baja California, and Nayarit and expanded southward to western Mexico. In Xalapa, Veracruz Grupo Chedraui established a megamarket in 1970, building off its decades of commercial activities in Xalapa and other cities in Veracruz. Originally established by the Lebanese immigrant Lázaro

Chedraui and developed by his sons and grandson, Casa Chedraui started out selling clothing until it adopted the self-service supermarket model in 1970. It expanded first throughout Veracruz and then in Tabasco, and by 1987 Chedraui had stores in twelve different states along Mexico's east coast and the interior states of Oaxaca, Puebla, and San Luis Potosí.[20]

With the neoliberal reforms of the 1980s and preparations for Mexico's entry into the North American Free Trade Agreement, government officials changed the law on direct foreign investment in 1989. The change enabled foreign-owned companies to own up to 100 percent of a company in most Mexican industries, thus overriding the 49 percent amount codified in the 1973 Law on Foreign Investment.[21] Supermarket owners, fearing an invasion by U.S. retail chains, began to step up their alliances with foreign chain stores (table 13). The first to do so was Grupo Cifra, the owners of Aurrerá and Superama, which developed a joint venture with U.S. discount chain Walmart in 1991. Initially, Cifra's partnership with Walmart focused on establishing Club Aurrerá stores, modeled on Walmart's Sam's Clubs, to serve small businesses buying in bulk. This partnership with Grupo Cifra was Walmart's first international venture as it was rapidly expanding throughout the United States and revolutionizing the retail industry through its cost-cutting strategies, control of suppliers, and innovations in logistics that enabled it to track products from purchases from suppliers to final sale to consumers.[22] The two companies later agreed that Cifra would not expand its own brand-named stores but would support the building of Walmart Supercenters. Together, they decided that most of the new stores would be opened outside of Mexico City and in most midsize cities where Cifra had little presence.[23]

The Cifra-Walmart alliance precipitated its aggressive expansion throughout Mexico. In the fall of 1993, Walmart opened is first Supercenter at the Plaza Oriental shopping center in the Mexico City borough of Iztapalapa and then a second one in 1994. The Cifra-Walmart alliance grew rapidly, and by the end of the 1994 fiscal year the partnership included twenty-three stores: seven warehouse clubs, two supermarkets, ten discount stores, two combination stores, and two supercenters.[24] At the end of the 1997 fiscal year, the joint venture included 152 businesses: 85 stores (18 Walmart Supercenters, 28 Sam's Clubs, 3 Superamas, 25 Bodegas, 4 Aurrerás, 7 Suburbia clothing stores) and 67 VIPS restaurants.[25]

Other Mexican supermarket chains forged similar partnerships with international companies, including Comercial Mexicana with Price Club and Gigante with Carrefour from France and with Fleming Companies, the largest food wholesaler in the United States at the time.[26] These deals helped keep them growing throughout the 1990s. As table 12 demonstrates, most stores nearly doubled their size between 1993 and 2000, and overall, the total number of supermarkets grew from 623 in 1993 to 1,115 in 2000.[27] This occurred even as Mexico was shocked by an economic crisis in 1994 and 1995, which led to a 70 percent devaluation of the peso.[28] The devaluation cut deeply into the value of the sales of supermarkets and increased their debts to suppliers and creditors that were owed in dollars. The crisis forced Comercial Mexicana, Gigante, Ley, Soriana, and Chedraui to cancel their immediate efforts to further integrate with foreign companies.[29] However, the crisis provided an opportunity for foreign supermarket owners. Walmart took advantage of the peso crisis to buy out the Grupo Cifra fully in 1997. After French supermarket giant Carrefour's alliance with Gigante fell apart in 1997, it had the capital to enter the Mexican market on its own. Opening stores primarily in wealthy areas, by 2005 it had twenty-nine stores and two in the process of being built when the company was purchased by Chedraui in 2005.[30] In 2007, Chedraui also expanded into the U.S. market, purchasing the seven stores that Gigante had in the United States. By 2013 it had forty-five stores in the United States, with El Super and Fiesta Foods as its flagship stores, and in 2021 it bought Smart and Final.[31]

In 2007, three years after the death of the founder of Gigante, the Martín Borque brothers who owned Soriana purchased Gigante's Mexican operations and Chedraui purchased Gigante's stores in the United States. With this purchase, Soriana became a national chain. Before the purchase it had one store in Mexico City, and the purchase of Gigante gave it forty-seven additional stores in the nation's capital and 287 new stores overall.[32] Soriana jumped from a regional supermarket to the nation's number two supermarket chain in 2008.

Between 1990 and 2010, four national chains dominated Mexico's supermarkets, along with several regional chains. Walmart, Soriana, Comercial Mexicana, and Chedraui had approximately 60 percent of all chain supermarkets, with Walmart alone accounting for 62 percent

TABLE 13 Foreign Investment in Mexican Supermarkets, 1965–2002

Year	Mexican Company	Foreign Company
1965	Aurrerá/Grupo Cifra	Jewel Corporation (1984)
1981	Casa Ley	Safeway
1989	Change in Law on Foreign Investment	
1991	Aurrerá/Grupo Cifra	Walmart
1992	Gigante	Tandy Corporation/Radio Shack (2008)
		Office Depot
		Fleming Co. (U.S.)
1994	Gigante	Carrefour (1997)
1996		Auchan (France) Opens Stores (1998)
1997		Walmart Buys Out Grupo Cifra
		Carrefour Opens Its Own Stores (2005)
		H-E-B (U.S.) Opens Store
2002	Gigante	Price Club/Costco

Sources: Compiled based on company annual reports and newspaper articles.

of sales among the top five retailers and possessing 40 percent of the country's supermarket space. In addition to the national chain supermarkets, several regional supermarkets surged. According to José Gasca and Felipe Torres, there were thirty-three regionally based chain stores, led by Casa Ley in northwestern Mexico, Alsuper in Chihuahua, Durango, the Texas-based chain H-E-B with stores in six states in northeast Mexico and the Bajío region, and Arteli in the states of Tamaulipas and Veracruz.[33]

With Soriana's acquisition of Comercial Mexicana in 2016, only three national chains remained. In 2021, Chedraui acquired U.S. discounter Smart and Final and at the end of 2022 it purchased the thirty-six stores of the Arteli supermarket chain based in Tamaulipas.[34] Walmart de México, however, was unsurpassed in its conquest of Mexican markets.

Walmart de México

With its 1997 purchase of Grupo Cifra and its Aurrerá and Superama markets, Walmart immediately solidified its dominance in Mexico's supermarket industry. In 2000 it rebranded itself as Walmart de México (Walmex) and, as a publicly traded subsidiary of Walmart, it became the showcase for the supermarket giant's international expansion. Within a few short years, Walmart built an empire in Mexico and dominated the ever-expanding retail sector. In the process, it restructured the food procurement system and accelerated the privatization of the countryside. However, it was not Walmart's ingenuity alone that set it up to be Mexico and Latin America's largest retail business.

Walmart built its Mexican empire on the success of Grupo Cifra's mixed formats that catered to both working-class and upper-income people through its discount stores (Aurrerá) and its supermarket chain (Superama). Grupo Cifra had already had extensive experience in the U.S. market through its longtime partnership with Jewel supermarkets (1965–1984) and then by aggressively partnering with Walmart. Walmart built on what it learned from Grupo Cifra's operations and brought its logistical expertise to Mexico.

After Walmart fully took over Grupo Cifra's stores it did not change their names, so for Mexican consumers, Superama and Aurrerá markets remained the same, and there were no immediate visible transformations to the stores. Instead, customers saw the continued growth and regional expansion of Bodega Aurrerá markets, which sold goods in bulk to consumers and small businesses, and a more gradual expansion of Walmart Supercenters, Sam's Clubs, and Superamas. In fact, the expansion in stores in the two decades following Walmart's buyout of Grupo Cifra was primarily seen in the construction of Bodega Aurrerá stores (figure 12). Whereas in 2000 Aurrerá stores accounted for 36 percent of all Walmex stores, by 2008 this amount jumped to 59 percent, and by 2011 it reached 74 percent. This emphasis on the expansion of Aurrerá stores continued and as of 2022 they accounted for 80 percent of all Walmart stores in Mexico.[35]

Along with expanding the number of stores, Walmex aligned the format of its self-service store to reduce duplication and maximize its efforts at

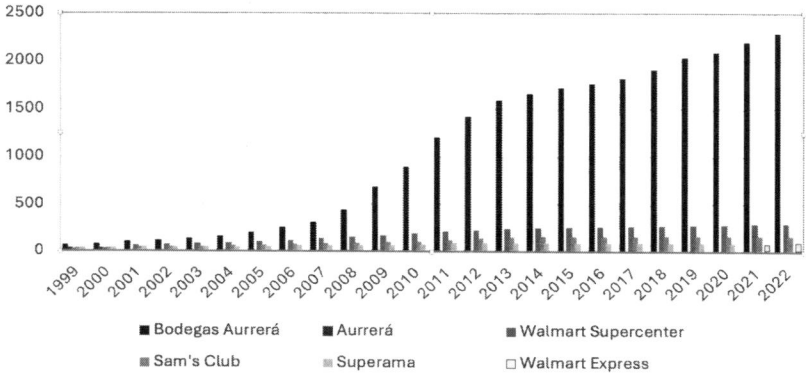

FIGURE 12 Number of Wal-Mex Stores by Type, 1999–2022. (Calculated from Walmart de México, *Informe Anuales*, 1999–2022.)

reaching consumers of different classes. For example, in 2001 it converted all Aurrerá stores (hypermarkets) into either Walmart Supercenters or Bodegas Aurrerá to concentrate on expanding only one hypermarket (Walmart Supercenters), reaching more working-class communities through Bodegas Aurrerá, and remodeling Superama supermarkets for upper-income groups.[36] Walmex then had a store in each of the major formats: in the hypermarket format, Walmart Supercenters; Sam's Club as a price club for small retailers; Superama in a supermarket format; Bodegas Aurrerá as warehouse stores; and Bodega Aurrerá Express in the small-format discount stores. This multiformat strategy made Walmex accessible to a broader market.

At the same time, Walmex started to offer credit to consumers with limited income who were generally ineligible for credit cards. Given that 40 percent of Mexicans live in poverty, extending credit served to increase consumption and forge consumer loyalty. To participate in the "So That Everyone Can Buy" program, households needed a minimum income of 1,700 pesos ($190) a month in 2002, approximately the equivalent of a little less than two minimum wages.[37] As Walmex extended credit to Mexico's working poor, store construction proliferated in working-class neighborhoods. In 2007, Walmex expanded its finance programs through the creation of the Banco de Walmart de México Adelante. Since approximately 80 percent of Mexicans did not have bank accounts, and few banks worked to attract working-class Mexicans, Walmex recognized that "there is an opportunity there," as one Walmex executive stated: "The size of the whole pie can grow for Wal-Mart and for the rest of the players."[38] The bank offered savings accounts and began to make personal loans to individual consumers and to small suppliers and business owners who shopped at Sam's Clubs and at the Bodegas Aurrerá. The goal was to support sales at Walmex stores and by 2011 it had more than a million clients and 263 branches.[39] In 2014, Walmex sold its banks to Carlos Slim's company Inbursa, which was granted access to customers in all Walmex stores.[40]

Walmex accelerated construction in different regions of Mexico.[41] Whereas in 1999, 56.2 percent of all Walmex stores were concentrated in Mexico City, by 2005 this had dropped to 33.8 percent. Walmex's presence in Mexican cities grew from 38 cities in 1999 to 172 in 2007. The growth continued in midsize and smaller cities throughout the next two decades, reaching 265 cities by 2009 and after its merger with Walmart de Centroamérica, these numbers grew to 571 in 2014, 685 by 2020, and 716 by 2023 (figure 13).[42]

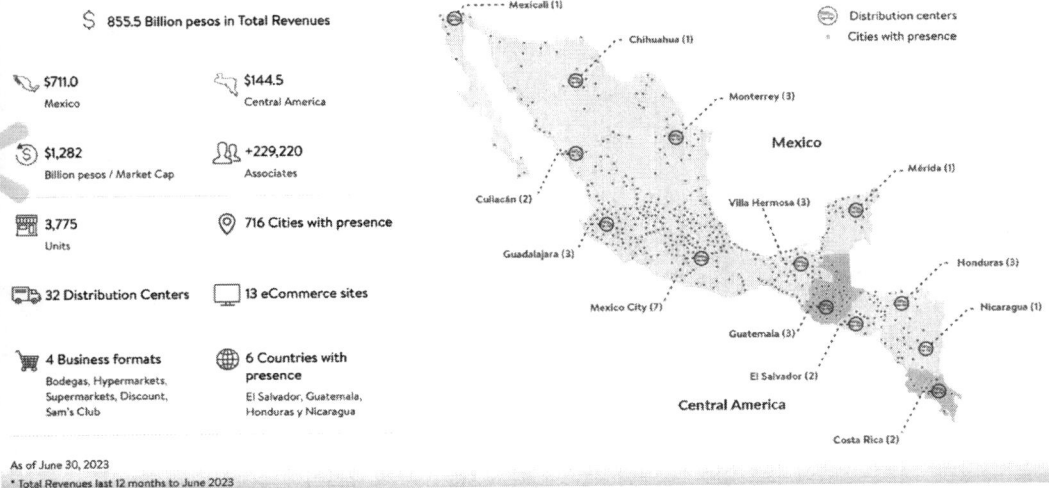

FIGURE 13 Walmart de México y Centroamérica, 2023. (https://www.walmex.mx/en/us/.)

As Walmex expanded throughout Mexico, it worked with the corporate office in Bentonville, Arkansas, to reduce its cost by centralizing its purchasing and developing its supply systems. This immediately led to cutting costs by 14 percent in 1999.[43] It then developed regional distribution centers that served as warehouses to amass food and dry goods to distribute to its proliferating number of stores. While this strategy built on Walmart's cost-cutting operations in the United States, it was an innovation in Mexico where supermarkets and other retailers procured food directly from growers and intermediaries in the production zones in the 1960s and 1970s and then by the 1990s through Mexico's publicly operated wholesale markets, Central de Abastos (CEDA). By circumventing intermediaries, either in production sites or in the CEDAs, and purchasing goods in large volumes directly from growers, Walmex could save between 10 and 20 percent on costs.[44]

By 1999, Walmex had eight distribution centers, six of which were in Mexico City and its environs and the other two in Guadalajara and Monterrey. Walmart de México quickly expanded its regional distribution centers and built store-specific distribution centers, such as one in Mexico City for Sam's Club in 2001 and another in Guadalajara for dry goods that would serve all self-service stores; others were built to supply its Suburbia clothing stores and its VIPS restaurants.[45] By 2017, Walmart had thirteen distribution centers, including one in Culiacán, two in Monterrey, and two in Villahermosa, Tabasco, in the Southeast. That same year, they announced a $36 million investment to construct a new distribution center in Mérida, to supply its thirty-six stores in Yucatán and its stores in Quintana Roo and Campeche, as part of a $1.3 billion investment to expand and strengthen its logistic infrastructure in Mexico during the 2017–2020 period.[46]

Walmart's investments in logistics led to the opening of more regional distribution centers to deepen its coverage throughout Mexico. According to a Walmart de México press release in September 2020, "A few years ago we began the enormous task of expanding our logistics network, seeking to bring products to the 2,580 stores we have in Mexico. We are becoming an agile organization by putting the customer even more at the center of decisions." In 2020, Walmart opened a 480,608 square-foot distribution center in Ciudad Chihuahua "dedicated to omni-channel logistics, which includes synchronizing product and purchasing information across physical retail stores, Walmart's e-commerce website, mobile devices, social networks and in-store kiosks and tablets."[47] In June 2022, it opened a distribution center in Villahermosa for perishables that serves seven states and nearly 230 stores, and had initiated construction of centers in Tlaxcala and the Bajío region.[48] By 2023, Walmart de México had twenty-one distribution centers throughout Mexico, as figure 13 illustrates, in addition to another eleven in Guatemala, Honduras, El Salvador, Nicaragua, and Costa Rica.

Through creating its own distributions centers, Walmex gained greater control over suppliers and began structuring production in the countryside. Several studies demonstrate how this process works for the procurement of fresh fruits, vegetables, meats, and dairy products to transform production.[49] To develop a uniform standard of appearance and quality to reduce costs, Walmex shifted the costs and burden to producers under the guise of improving quality. Walmex used its leverage to force growers to clean and pack produce on a year-round basis, maintain their own refrigerated transport, and wait up to forty-five days to receive payment. This process makes it very difficult for small producers to sell directly to Walmex and privileges larger and more organized growers. While Walmex often paid higher prices than other buyers, the strict quality control stipulations and numerous other requirements made it extremely difficult for small farms, even in co-ops and small farmer organizations, to compete for this business.[50]

Walmex's Strategy for Shutting out the Competition

Walmex's colonization of Mexico's food system, graphically mapped in figure 13, radically transformed Mexico's food system and society in less than two decades. Building upon the colonizing work of previous entities, Walmex has been able to conquer and colonize the expanse of Mexico physically, culturally, and cybernetically. The rapidity of this transformation is especially notable given Mexico's many layers of bureaucracy and regulatory red tape. However, Walmex would find innovative ways around these obstacles through a combination of its research division and a corps of fixers who knew the Mexican system.

During the first decade of the 2000s, Walmex made routine use of bribes "to subvert democratic governance—public votes, open debates, transparent procedures," according to *New York Times* Pulitzer Prize–winning investigative reporting. The *New York Times* found that "Walmart de México was not the reluctant victim of a corrupt culture that insisted on bribes at the cost of doing business. . . . Rather, Walmart de México was an aggressive and creative corrupter, offering large payoffs to get what the law otherwise prohibited."[51] In fact, this was not the first time that corruption and mismanagement by Walmex had been alleged. A 2003 investigation, funded by Walmart's corporate officials, found that Walmex "systematically increased its sales by helping favored high-volume customers evade sales taxes."[52] Walmex was adept at finding loopholes and ways around Mexican laws and cutting through red tape.

According to the testimony of Sergio Cicero Zapata, a former Walmart de México lawyer whose job included acquiring building permits in the 2000s, Walmex's CEO sought to open new stores in record time and encouraged the payments to government officials to speed up the process. "'The idea,' he said, 'was to build hundreds of new stores so fast that competitors would not have time to react.'" The *New York Times* discovered that at least $24 million in a five-year period was paid in bribes to city officials, planners, and anyone else who could possibly slow down or impede its plans. Walmex officials hired lobbyists who worked as fixers to pay up to $280,000 to facilitate a single permit. When Sergio Cicero Zapata turned whistleblower and reported to Walmart officials in Arkansas about his activities in Mexico, they sent investigators in November 2005 to conduct a preliminary investigation. Their report corroborated Cicero Zapata's claims that millions of dollars were spent on bribes with the knowledge of senior Walmex executives, including CEO Eduardo Castro-Wright. However, the investigators were not permitted to interview Castro-Wright, nor were they given access to his computer, so they were unable to see the full extent of the corruption.

Walmart corporate officials responded to the report of their investigators by rejecting a thorough independent investigation and instead turned the probe over to Walmex's general counsel, José Luis Rodríguez Macedo, one of the targets of the initial inquest. Rodríguez Macedo quickly exonerated executives for any wrongdoing and pinned corruption on the whistleblower himself. However, when Walmart's director of corporate investigation in Bentonville, Arkansas, received Rodríguez Macedo's report, he found it lacking in substance and agreed with the initial investigative report that called for a full-blown investigation. However, top Walmart executives, eager to avoid an investigation, argued that "[i]t's a Mexican issue: it's better to let it be a Mexican response." This infuriated Maritza Munich, Walmart International's general counsel, sparking her resignation. She urged that, "given the serious nature of the allegations and the need to preserve the integrity, it would seem more prudent to develop a follow-up plan of action, independent of Walmex management participation." Walmart suppressed the investigation.[53]

Several years later, the *New York Times* investigation picked up where Walmart's investigation ended and used confidential Walmart documents that investigators had gathered and conducted their own interviews. Reporters identified nineteen store sites across Mexico that were targets of bribes, and they matched the dates that permits were issued with the payments to fixers and corporate and personal "donations" given by Walmex. Walmex paid eight bribes totaling $341,000 to build a Sam's Club near the Basílica de Guadalupe in Mexico City without a construction license, environmental permit, an urban impact report, or a traffic permit. On another occasion, Walmex paid nine bribes for $765,000 total to build a refrigerated distribution center in an environmentally fragile flood basin north of Mexico City.[54] These incidents seem to be the tip of the iceberg.

The most emblematic case of Walmex's use of bribes to circumvent the law and red tape and build wherever it wanted to was the 2003–2004 construction of a Bodega Aurrerá less than a mile from the San Juan de Teotihuacán archaeological site. In its plan to build rapidly, the company's real estate development team found a plot of land, sown in alfalfa, to build a Bodega Aurrerá supermarket at the town's main entrance to effectively shut out its competitors.[55] However, there was a problem. The town was about to approve a change in the zoning policy to limit development near the pyramid. The change would make the alfalfa field zoned for housing only. Undeterred, Walmex purchased the land and prepared for construction. The city council approved the new zoning map and sent it to the state capital for review and publication in the state's official bulletin, after which it would become law.

San Juan de Teotihuacán's zoning map was published in the State of Mexico's official bulletin on September 11, 2003; however, it included a redrawn map that was not the one agreed to by the council. With this new map, Walmex's land was now zoned for commercial purposes. According to the *New York Times*, "The next day, internal Walmart de Mexico records show, Mr. Cicero authorized five bribe payments totaling $221,000. . . . One of the payments, for $52,000, was for the Bodega Aurrera in Teotihuacán, Mr. Cicero said in an interview." There were still several other permits that Walmex needed to get and numerous obstacles it needed to overcome. For example, it needed to get a traffic permit since the location of the new construction was sure to cause traffic congestion, which the city had been working to ease. Walmex worked with the town's mayor, who urged the city council to allow Walmart to start construction even though it had not received all the required permits. Through manipulation of the meeting, the mayor was able to get a general vote in favor of Walmart's project pending the receipt of the necessary permits. Construction began days later. The mayor received approximately $114,000 from Walmex fixers for his support. They also needed the approval of the National Institute of Anthropology and History (INAH) since the store was to be built within the protected archaeological zones. INAH required that excavations be done with picks and shovels and not bulldozers and backhoes, to minimize damage to any ancient ruins. While residents were pressuring INAH to stop the construction, Walmex received a permit from a top INAH official in exchange for "an 'official donation' of up to $45,000 and a 'personal gift' of up to $36,000." INAH archaeologists and residents continued trying to stop the project and queried the mayor about why Walmex was building without a construction permit. A few days later, he granted the permit. Walmex officials met with community and neighborhood leaders soliciting their support and offering money for their communities, including for a handball court, computers for the school, and money for new office for neighborhood leaders.[56]

As mentioned at the outset of this chapter, protests grew larger when INAH archaeologists found evidence that the store was built on ancient ruins. However, demonstrations and outcries from leading intellectuals were unable to stop Walmex. While the battle seemed to be over, community members continued their struggle to shut the store down. The poet and teacher Emmanuel D'Herrera and other members of the Frente Cívico en Defensa del Valle de Teotihuacán mobilized to call attention to the ways that Bodega Aurrerá would drive out local shops using its discounting method.[57] Community members worked to expose the presumed corruption of government officials who it became increasingly clear were supporting Walmex, seven years before the *New York Times* reporting would give evidence of a bribery scandal. In 2005, the Frente Cívico en Defensa del Valle de Teotihuacán continued its struggle by allying with other communities struggling against Walmex such as Indigenous communities of Pátzcuaro, Michoacán, and Juchitán, Oaxaca, where Walmex was planning new stores. As movement leader Lorenzo Trujillo declared, "We will occupy public offices and do whatever is necessary to stop the cultural plundering that Walmart carries out."[58] However, as time passed the fight seemed to be lost and Bodega Aurrerá became a fixture in the community. In 2009, in an act of desperation to rekindle attention to the social and cultural impact of Walmex, D'Herrera planted a small juice-can bomb in a shopping cart in the supermarket, causing a minor explosion. He was arrested, charged with a local crime, and then let out on bail since "all the blast did was knock him down and damage $68 worth of merchandise."[59] However, at Walmex's insistence, he was rearrested and charged with a federal crime. As he awaited trial, his health failed in part due to the poor conditions of the prison, and he died of a brain hemorrhage. The note Emmanuel D'Herrera left to his wife explained, "I am not leaving material patrimony for you and our son," he wrote. "I'm leaving you a moral and political legacy, dying as I am for a cause, in defense of the Mexican culture."[60] This legacy of fighting for justice against Walmex would be continued by many others, including Walmex employees.

Walmex strategies for rapid expansion to shut out its competition appear to have been successful. Its growth rates are historically unprecedented in Mexico. Its level of colonization of the market and Mexican territory gives it monopoly power in almost half of its stores in rural areas with less population density. Walmex dominates in 87 percent of areas in which only one supermarket exists. Throughout the country, 21 percent of Walmex stores have no other supermarket competition.[61]

The High Costs of Low Prices

Walmex exerts enormous influence in the Mexican economy. As the largest private employer in Mexico, it shapes the structure of the retail industry. With its different formats and its motto of having the lowest prices, it passes on savings to consumers across the income spectrum. Through its Bodegas Aurrerá, which are aimed at lower-income groups, it often sells products between 17 and 22 percent cheaper than other supermarkets. In all its formats, Walmart's prices are below its competition. These savings are especially significant for lower-income consumers, who generally use a much larger share of their income on food and basic goods.[62] Likewise, where Walmex stores expand to new regions, they exert a downward pressure on prices that often squeezes local markets and forces many to close. A study by Atkins, Faber, and González Navarro found that from the period of 2002 to 2014, approximately 3.9 percent of retail units were forced out of business, which translated into eighty traditional stores and one modern supermarket in the average municipality.[63] While there were definite savings on prices, this study found that these "gains are 50% larger for the richest income group compared to the poorest, primarily because of the greater valuation wealthy households place on the product variety and shopping amenities on offer at foreign stores." As early as 2002, its competitors were feeling the impact of Walmart. According to one analyst, "having seen their traditional attraction of heavy discounts and promotions upstaged by Walmart's consistently lower prices," Comercial Mexicana and Gigante were particularly impacted. Many stores cut their prices but did not have the infrastructure and "distribution and bargaining power that Walmart uses to squeeze cut-rate process out of suppliers."[64]

Walmart's lower prices also come from squeezing workers. While adapting to Mexico's labor regime Walmart brought its own labor practices to keep labor costs down and workers in check. Walmart prides itself as an aggressively anti-union shop. Hailing from Arkansas, "the first state to adopt a 'right-to-work' law—in 1944—which made illegal the union shop contract," Sam Walton "hated [unions] because they wanted to tell me how to take care of my people."[65] In the United States, Walmart employs traditional union-busting tactics coupled with southern paternalism and rural Christian evangelist roots to impose a conservative and authoritarian populism.[66] However, Walmart has learned to adjust to official unions working in collaboration with the state, such as in Mexico and China. In what appears to be an exceptional case, Walmart was forced to recognize a union after workers forged a popular grassroots movement, as Carolina Bank Muñoz demonstrates, "to mobilize its resources (autonomy, strategy, militancy, democratic participation) in a unique way, based on its own context, industry, and particular union culture of its sector."[67] The Chilean example continues to be an inspiration for Walmart workers in multiple countries but also illustrates Walmart's flexibility in its operations based on different national contexts.[68]

Following Cifra and other supermarket chains, Walmex worked with unions connected to the PRI and with company unions to negotiate protection contracts. As discussed in previous chapters, these protection contracts are deals between the employer and the union with virtually no consultation from workers. The long history of protection contracts was woven into Mexico's authoritarian structure since the 1920s. The labor lawyer José Alfonso Bouzas Ortíz argues that nine out of every ten collective contracts are protection contracts.[69] In 2021, Mexico's Ministry of Labor estimated that 85 percent of the nation's 530,000 collective contracts were employer protection contracts that strengthened company control over workers.[70] Scholars have demonstrated that in most cases, workers have little if any knowledge that a union exists.

At the onset of the twenty-first century, Walmex became Mexico's largest employer with the power to influence the nation's labor policies. Within five years of taking over from Cifra, Walmex had more than doubled the number of its employees to 92,708 in 2002, and a decade later it had grown to 238,120 employees, with more than 50,000 employees more than FEMSA, its nearest competitor.[71] As its workforce expanded, Walmex took advantage of Mexico's labor policies and practices that produced "lousy jobs and invisible unions," as researchers Chris Tilly and José Luis Álvarez Galván argue.[72] By working with the official corporatist unions, Walmex only has to deal with a few labor bosses whose jobs it is to protect the contracts that employers negotiated with them and therefore protect the employers.[73] This gives Walmex enormous power over its workforce and little recourse for its workers.

Walmex workers generally earn the equivalent of workers in other retail supermarket chains, which, given the poor conditions of work in the retail sector, is often not enough to live on. Tilly found that in 2003 and 2004, although Walmex stores paid workers the equivalent or better than other supermarkets, this amount was hardly sufficient for workers to purchase food items in Walmex stores let alone sustain their families.[74] A 2007 examination of collective contracts by Bouzas Ortíz and Reyes Ramos found that the wages of Walmex workers averaged the equivalent of two minimum wages a day ($8), the lowest-paid workers making 125 percent of the minimum wage ($5) and the highest paid making 300 percent ($12). Walmex workers are among Mexico's large working-poor population who struggle to make ends meet.[75] Bouzas Ortiz argues that collective contracts tend to be boilerplates, in which an initial template is created by the company in consultation with union bosses and then is used by all other unions, giving the appearance that the company is negotiating with multiple unions. A review of two 2018 collective contracts filed with the Local Labor Conciliation and Arbitration Board and signed by labor unions and company officials at two Bodegas Aurrerá Express in Mexico City shows the wage range for workers is approximately between 6 and 89 percent above the daily minimum wage (table 14). At least in Bodegas Aurrerá Express in Mexico City, these wages are much less than what Bouzas Ortiz and Reyes Ramos found in 2007.

TABLE 14 Daily Wages in Bodegas Aurrerá Express in Mexico City, 2018

Position	Worker Category A		Worker Category B		Wage Range/ Min Wage** (%)
	pesos	US$*	pesos	US$	
Cleaning Asst.	124.16	6.46	92.34	4.80	106–141
Maintenance Asst.	169.02	8.79	113.79	5.92	129–191
Greeter	169.02	8.79	113.79	5.92	129–191
Bakery Sales	149.04	7.75	100.77	5.24	114–169
Grocery Sales	169.02	8.79	113.79	5.92	129–191
Perishable Sales	149.04	7.75	100.77	5.24	114–169
Loading Dock	166.38	8.66	158.09	8.23	180–189

Sources: Calculated from Contratos colectivos entre Walmex and Sindicatos, January and May 2018, http://www.juntalocal.cdmx.gob.mx/ut/ut/articulos/Art _137/Fracc_VIII/1t2018/Doctos/564-CONTRATO.pdf and http://www.juntalocal .cdmx.gob.mx/ut/ut/articulos/Art_137/Fracc_VIII/1t2018/Doctos/83.pdf.

* The average exchange rate in 2018 was 19.22 pesos per dollars. See https://www .exchangerates.org.uk/USD-MXN-spot-exchange-rates-history-2018.html.

** The legal minimum wage for Mexico City was 88.06 pesos ($4.58 dollars) per day in 2018.

Working with protection unions and their managers, Walmex creates a culture of fear and subservience that stifles authentic worker organizing. Using Walmart's 1991 guide for stopping the Teamsters from organizing warehouse workers and its 1997 "A Manager's Toolbox to Remaining Union Free," Walmex maintains strict surveillance on employees, and managers are vigilant for signs of worker discontent and organizing.[76] Researcher and former Walmex worker Gabriela Victoria Alvarado argues that "the company's attempt to impose its values, principles, and behaviors is legitimized through pedagogical means or symbolic violence." This entails promoting worker identification with the company through "rituals, belief inducements, and emotional techniques intended to persuade workers to legitimize the corporation's quest for ever greater profits and lower labor costs."[77] While workplace organizing has been virtually impossible, collectives of workers, nonprofit organizations, and investigative journalists have helped uncover numerous labor and workplace violations and inhumane practices.

In 2006, small collectives of Walmex workers began to organize themselves as Trabajadores del Grupo Walmart de México. In his 2009 thesis, "The Defenseless State of Walmart de México Workers in the Federal District in the Face of Collective Protection Contracts," Esteban Conde argues that worker repression and the conditions of labor forced Walmex workers to find a way to begin to organize for their rights and transform their working conditions.[78] As a participant researcher, Conde explains how small groups of workers anonymously coalesced in Walmex worksites to discuss the poor working conditions, raise worker consciousness, and "[r]ecuperate through peaceful struggle and labor actions the DIGNITY that has been taken from them by the company that doesn't treat us as people nor as workers."[79] The workers focused on demanding a dignified living wage and working conditions. Given the low pay, Walmex often grants workers personal loans and then deducts a percentage from their paychecks, which keeps workers in a cycle of debt. An immediate goal of the organization was to get the company to reduce the number of deductions. Other key demands included allowing workers to take vacation time based on their own needs and not those of the company, and that Walmex respect the positions that workers were hired for and not shift them around based on the company's needs. By organizing themselves, the workers hoped to strengthen their position within the company, pressure the company from within, and raise national and international public awareness about the labor practices of the world's largest supermarket chain in Mexico.[80]

On Mach 15, 2007, Trabajadores del Grupo Walmart de México wrote a letter to Walmex's CEO announcing its campaign and demands for better working conditions. The company took the petition seriously and sought, unsuccessfully, to find out who the organizers were. Walmex then responded by posting its "open doors" internal policy at the entrance of managers' offices, urging workers to come forward to express their concerns with management. The company also announced the opening of new employee break rooms; in some stores the rooms included televisions and new dining facilities. However, Walmex did not address the demands for better wages and working conditions, and the worker organization scaled up its campaign.

The workers made their struggle public and went to the press. They received favorable coverage in *La Jornada* and in other outlets. Walmex immediately retaliated by announcing that it would not remodel dining rooms or create new breakrooms; it announced massive layoffs in Walmart supercenters and posted signs at the worker centers warning workers of the perils of organizing and indicating that they could quit if they did not agree with the policies. At the same time, workers were forced to attend meetings about employment policies, and Walmex security stepped up its surveillance and harassment of workers, forcing some to resign. Walmex also began to harass and intimidate journalists and the media that publicized the movement.[81] At the end of 2007, the workers allied with other organizations, including the Centro de Investigación Laboral y Asesoría Sindical (CILAS), to call for a "Day Without Walmart" boycott on December 2, 2007.[82]

In a 2007 legal challenge to Walmex's labor practices, Raúl Avila Andujo, an employee in Chihuahua, sued the company for paying him partially with store coupons to purchase goods in Walmex stores and then deducting the amount of the coupons from his paycheck. Eighteen months later, Avila Andujo's petition was heard by Mexico's Supreme Court. While Walmex argued that employees could voluntarily participate in the program that was aimed at helping workers meet their basic needs, the Supreme Court found that "this plan is similar to the practices of the old *tienda de raya* [company store] of the 19th century when workers also received their compensation through coupons to be redeemed in the company's stores, with the difference that the products were purchased for a high price."[83] The court ruled that this practice was a direct violation of Article 123 of the Mexican Constitution. In its response, Walmex underscored that its policy was aimed at helping workers and that only one person had complained.[84]

Also in 2007, a *Newsweek* exposé uncovered that Walmex hired teenagers to bag groceries for tips without receiving a wage. While the use of voluntarily unsalaried youth labor is legal in Mexico and a standard practice in the grocery industry, given Walmart's enormous profit statements and the fact that it was Mexico's largest private employer, this practice aroused many concerns in both Mexico and the United States. The report found that Walmex employed nearly 150,000 workers and an additional 19,000 unpaid youth between the ages of fourteen and sixteen. In Mexico City alone, 4,300 teenagers worked in Walmart for tips compared to 715 in Comercial Mexicana and 427 in Gigante, Walmex's two largest competitors of the day.[85] Walmex responded that it was in compliance with the agreement that stores made with the government around the bagger program and that it even gave bonuses twice a year to teens who maintained high grades. However, several studies found that many of the young workers were forced to work beyond the six-hour limit. In a 2005 study by three Mexico City university students, it was found that "Walmart abuses child labor by not giving them adequate time to rest, not allowing them to eat, not paying them extra hours, resorting to improper practices. The working condition for baggers is ideal for Walmart policies, the baggers have to comply with the schedule set by the manager, wear a uniform, but do not receive a salary and have no rights or protection."[86]

A 2008 study of youth workers at Walmex stores found that more than 60 percent of the workers interviewed reported having worked more than ten hours or more during a day. While many of the youth wanted the extra hours because their families depended on the tips they earned, approximately 23 precent were forced to work extra hours under threat of being fired.[87] Nearly half of the workers interviewed had to pay for the opportunity to volunteer at Walmex stores and the majority said that they had to pay part of the cost of their uniform, contrary to Mexican law. While not considered workers by Walmex, they were treated as workers and were often given numerous obligations.[88]

In 2012, Trabajadores del Grupo Walmart de México reappeared publicly on the heels of the *New York Times* exposé on Walmex's bribery scandal. This time Esteban Conde was identified as a cofounder of the worker rights group, and he publicly denounced the supermarket chain for violating workers' rights and paying workers unlivable wages. The organization argued that these violations included harassment of workers who demanded that their rights be respected. At a press conference, Conde showed a worker's pay stub for 5 pesos (less than 25 cents) for fifteen days of work after the company made numerous deductions from his pay. Conde also denounced Walmex's repressive policies that contributed to a 40 percent worker attrition rate.[89]

Beginning in 2013, supermarkets began to increase the number of senior citizen baggers that it voluntarily employed. While many stores had in the past voluntarily employed seniors as baggers, a 2013 agreement between the National Institute on Aging (Instituto Nacional de las Personas Adultas Mayores, INAPAM) and the Supermarket and Department Store Trade Association (Asociación Nacional de Tiendas de Autoservicios y Departamentales, ANTAD) gave tax breaks to stores that hired voluntary workers over the age of sixty. The deal was announced as a step to address the widespread poverty among senior citizens. Since only about 20 percent of senior citizens received pensions, and those that did received between $150 and $425 a month, many needed to work to survive.[90] However, as with the youth baggers, senior citizens are considered volunteer workers who only work for tips and are not paid by supermarkets. By 2020, approximately 35,000 senior citizens worked packing groceries for tips in Walmex stores. With the COVID–19 pandemic, Walmex stopped the program, arguing that senior citizens were a vulnerable population. While other supermarkets gradually had senior citizen baggers return to work if they were vaccinated in April 2021, Walmex resisted. It argued that people no longer wanted others to bag their groceries, and since stores now had more self-service checkout stands, baggers were no longer necessary. The senior baggers staged several protests in front of Walmex stores and government offices with signs stating, "We Want to Work!" Maria Guadalupe Garcia, a displaced grocery bagger, told the news, "It's not fair. I don't have anything other than this."[91] As public officials began to weigh in on the controversy, Walmex began to let vaccinated volunteers return to work in August 2021.[92]

Studies by the nongovernmental organization Proyecto de Derechos Económicos, Sociales y Culturales (PRODESC) have uncovered numerous violations of the rights of women workers. Women comprise more than half of the frontline supermarket workers, and the retail industry is one of the largest employers of women.[93] Therefore, PRODESC demonstrated that "women are disproportionately affected by Walmex's bad labor practices. The meager salaries of the industry contribute to the impoverishment of women workers."[94] The study found that at least half of women workers at Walmex stores were asked intrusive questions about their reproductive cycle, health, and plans for pregnancy. There were numerous cases of women being fired "under the pretext of safety when it was discovered that they were pregnant."[95] Walmex is by no means the lone culprit here, as women's labor rights are routinely violated in Mexico. However, as the largest private employer and one of the largest employers of women that touts its code of ethics and the "family" environment of its associates, its actions reinforce labor violations in Mexico and set the standard of contradictory workplace culture for other employers.[96]

Walmex's close work with Mexico's protection unions, its surveillance tactics, and its public relations campaign have enabled it to grow at unprecedented rates using illegal tactics at times and by keeping wages low and labor activism in check. In 2019, the U.S. Securities and Exchange Committee (SEC) completed its seven-year investigation under the Foreign Corrupt Practices Act into Walmart's international practices sparked by investigation into Walmex's bribery scandal. Walmart agreed to pay $282 million to settle the SEC charges and criminal charges brought by the U.S. Justice Department for bribing officials in Mexico, China, Brazil, and India. Walmart's CEO said they are "pleased to resolve this matter" and "committed to doing business the right way, and that means acting ethically everywhere we operate." As *Forbes* pointed out, however, Walmart got off easily: "The settlement is essentially pocket change for a company that pulled in sales of over $500 billion in 2018."[97]

Oxxo's Convenient Access to Ultra-processed Foods

As Walmex swept through Mexico and restructured the food system, labor relations, and urban and rural spaces, the convenience store chain

Oxxo was rapidly colonizing Mexican neighborhoods by displacing Mexico's ubiquitous family-run corner markets. While Walmex and other supermarkets were initially known for their megamarkets to take advantage of economies of scale, Oxxo stores became known for their small size; the nimbleness of their operation; their sale of Coca-Cola beverages, beer, and ultra-processed packaged foods; and their ubiquity throughout Mexico.

Oxxo's parent company, Fomento Económico Mexicana, S.A. (FEMSA), is allied with one of the largest companies in the world, Coca-Cola. Founded by Mexico's Grupo Visa, its history goes back to the founding of Cervecería Cuauhtémoc in 1890 and the establishment of the glass bottle factory Vidriera Monterrey in 1909. Grupo Visa then acquired local breweries and created other businesses to vertically integrate its operations and evolve into one of Mexico's largest corporations.[98] The Monterrey elite adapted to the revolutionary nationalism of the post-revolutionary period through a combination of their authoritarian control and paternalistic labor policies.[99] In 1979, Grupo Visa acquired its first Coca-Cola franchise and in 1985 merged with the brewery Cervecería Moctezuma. In 1988 it spun off FEMSA to operate its Coca-Cola bottling and commercial operations marketing, including control of its growing chain of Oxxo convenience stores.[100] Over the next several years FEMSA became the largest Coca-Cola bottler in Mexico, one of the largest per capita consumers of soda in the world. In 2002, FEMSA, with the support of Coca-Cola, purchased all of Colombia's Coca-Cola bottling plants and became the second largest bottler and marketer in the Coca-Cola system, accounting for 10 percent of all Coca-Cola sales. By 2003, FEMSA had 56 bottling plants and 249 distribution centers in nine Latin American countries and sold one-third of all Coca-Cola products in Latin America.[101]

FEMSA created Oxxo in 1978 as a convenience store to distribute its beer and Coca-Cola production. Its name evolved from the percentage sign that was initially used to announce the coming of the stores, and then it stuck as Oxxo, giving it its distinctive name.[102] Its burgeoning operations cut into the sales of locally owned abarrote stores; it has been estimated that for every new Oxxo store, five abarrote stores close.[103] Starting in Monterrey, the stores quickly expanded to other northern states and then made their way to Mexico City. By 1981, there were a hundred stores that sold the company's own products, beer, Coca-Cola, and soon sold cigarettes, candy, and packaged foods. Over the next two decades the chain spread rapidly in urban areas. In 1995, there were 767, and by 2000 their number nearly doubled to 1,468. Between 2000 and 2005, the number of Oxxo stores grew by an average of 23 percent a year.[104] The pace of growth continued throughout the next fifteen years, and by 2022, there were more than 21,500 stores throughout Mexico, and they were rapidly expanding in Brazil, Colombia, Chile, Peru, and several European countries (table 15). Since the mid-2010s, Oxxo has also successfully made its stores a virtual one-stop shop. Consumers can pick up their daily products, a snack, or lunch, get money from an ATM machine, and even pay their utility bills.[105]

Convenience stores are also the market leaders in the fast-food industry. Traditional fast-food restaurants account for only one-quarter of the market, while convenience stores such as Oxxo, 7-Eleven, and Circle K made up 55 percent of the fast-food market in 2017.[106] In 2018, 78 percent of convenience store food sales in Mexico were in Oxxo's 14,000 stores. Oxxo had nearly five times as many outlets as all the Alsea and McDonald's restaurants combined.[107] What is more, Oxxo is open 24 hours a day and 365 days a year. With its slogan, "Eat more for less," it offers an array of fast-food options, including hot dogs, pizza, sandwiches, tacos, quesadillas, gorditas, and tamales, primarily sold under its own brands Vikingo and O Sabor.[108] The second largest convenience store chain, 7-Eleven, offered free coffee in 2017 on Mondays and Thursdays. It sold its own brands of pan dulce, baguettes, sandwiches, and hot dogs for 8 pesos, or 42 cents, each. Between 2012 and 2017, the fast-food sector of the convenience stores grew by 87 percent. Circle K, which in 2014 purchased Grupo Modelo's Tiendas Extra, has similar promotions. The role of convenience stores in the fast-food sector in Mexico plays a much greater role than in the rest of the world. According to one analyst,

> Mexican consumers continue to demand time and health while they try to control their expenditures, and this benefits the convenience store chains. As a result of these factors and of the aggressive business strategies of this sector, convenience stores continue to occupy a much more important role in the food service industry in Mexico than at the global level.[109]

TABLE 15 Oxxo Convenience Stores and Pharmacies in Latin America and Europe, 2022*

Country	Oxxo and Others	Salud**	Oxxo Gas
Mexico	21,500	1,575	568
Brazil	1,468	0	
Colombia	238	712	
Chile	269	905	
Ecuador	0	903	
Peru	75	0	
Total	23,543	4,095	568
	Valora and Others		
Germany	1,430		
Switzerland	1,184		
Luxembourg	72		
The Netherlands	43		
Austria	37		
Total	2,766		

Source: FEMSA, *Informe Anual*, 2022, 21.

* Total: 30,972.

** Includes the following company names: Cruz Verde, Farmacias YZA, Moderna, Farmacón, Fybeca, SanaSana, and the beauty store chain Maicao.

Oxxo's product line makes it the largest seller of ultra-processed food and arguably contributing to Mexico's nutrition-related epidemics. Recent studies show that 30 percent of total energy intake in the Mexican diet is from ultra-processed foods, with numerous additives, colorings, flavors, stabilizers, and substances extracted from other foods. This accentuates the double burden of malnutrition, in which a growing percentage of individuals are both undernourished and overnourished. This is particularly severe in children and adolescents. Ultra-processed food consumption is shown to "reduce diet diversity and micronutrient intake in the Mexican population."[110] Studies have repeatedly demonstrated the connection between the growth of neoliberal policies, obesity, and diet-related diseases.[111] In a 2021 study of Mexico's retail food environment, one research team found "that a higher density of convenience stores within neighbourhoods is associated with higher mean BMI. Policies and programmes implemented so far in Mexico, particularly the tax on SSB and widespread health promotion campaigns, have not been enough to halt and reverse the obesity epidemic."[112] Convenience stores, packaged foods, and fast food play a central role in Mexico's nutritional public health crisis.

FEMSA has its eyes on further expanding Oxxo stores throughout Mexico, Latin America, and the world, and is developing new ways to penetrate neighborhoods where family-run markets still operate. With over 600,000 family-owned neighborhood stores in existence, FEMSA feels that it has the potential to use cost-cutting methods and economies of scale to replace these local stores. While the company acknowledges that neighborhood shop owners have personal ties with customers, it is working to make inroads into this market.[113]

Combined with its Coca-Cola operations, FEMSA employs more people than Walmex and boasts 354,000 employees in eighteen different countries.[114] Oxxo workers, like most supermarket workers, have a company protection union that is responsive to FEMSA and not to workers, keeping wages and independent organizing down. Wages at Oxxo for store workers range from slightly above the minimum wage to approximately 175 percent of the minimum wage for store managers.[115] The precarity of Oxxo's frontline workers, with long hours and low wages, means that workers often cannot afford to shop in the stores they maintain.[116]

In regions with a high degree of violence, especially along the U.S.-Mexico border, Oxxo has adapted its business practices to insulate its stores while still generating revenue. Oxxo stores have been the target of extortion by a number of criminal organizations, especially in regions where groups are fighting over territory. In 2017, four Oxxos were affected by a crime wave in Piedras, Negras, and in Apatzingán, Michoacán.[117] In 2022, twenty-seven stores were burned and firebombed in Ciudad Juárez and in the state of Guanajuato.[118] To begin to find ways to protect themselves from this violence, in 2016, Oxxo partnered with

Fujitsu Ten in Reynosa, Tamaulipas, to open its first store within a maquiladora plant. Oxxo sells the same products as other stores except for
alcohol. An Oxxo representative told the press, "The principal objective
is to bring all of our services to the employees of this company, even in
their workspaces." Within months, Oxxo stores began to open in other
maquiladoras along the border, including in the Delphi Delco maquiladora in Reynosa, and in San Luis Río Colorado, Sonora. A TikTok post in
2022 asked how many maquiladoras in Tijuana have Oxxos and dozens
of responders listed the names of several maquiladoras and posted names
of factories and even office buildings with stores in other cities along the
border.[119] As violence engulfs many regions within Mexico, Oxxo and
other corporations are finding ways to reach more consumers, while at
the same time becoming a modernized version of the company store that
captures large portions of worker's wages.

———————————

Beginning in the 1990s, supermarkets have greatly sped up the transformation of Mexico's food system. In a few decades, they have penetrated
household economies and communities of both wealthy and working-
class Mexicans. Drawing on technological innovations and targeted marketing strategies, they have found unique ways to attract consumers. The
domination of retail supermarket purchases by two mega-corporations
(Walmex and FEMSA) and two smaller but rapidly expanding companies (Chedraui and Soriana) concentrates wealth and power in the
hands of a few companies. These companies have the power to dictate
terms on producers to supply products at cut-rate prices that in turn
reinforce large agribusiness at the expense of smaller farmers, and all but
eliminates campesinos as producers of food to be sold in supermarkets.
Multinational food corporations that can meet the stringent demands of
marketers and that produce using economies of scale are the other big
winners in this system. Companies such as Bimbo, Mondelez, LALA, and
GRUMA work with these oligopolies to get prime shelf space for their
products and collect awards at the annual trade show of the Asociación
Nacional de Tiendas de Autoservicio y Departamentales (ANTAD).

The expansion of supermarkets throughout Mexico has done little to
decrease Mexico's food poverty. While supermarkets generally sell basic
foods for less than other outlets, these savings disproportionately benefit

higher-income groups. Other costs must be taken into consideration when assessing the full impact of oligopolistic control of the modern retail sector, such as wages, health, cultural, and environmental. As detailed in the next chapter, Indigenous communities, public health advocates, and social movements envision a different and more egalitarian food system.

CHAPTER 7

"PARADISE OF JUNK FOOD"

Popular Struggles, Corporate Power, and the Social Costs of Mexico's Food System

In his book *La basura que comemos* (*The Garbage That We Eat*), published in 2000, the prolific cartoonist and satirist Eduardo del Río "Rius" took aim at the corporations that have created the modern junk food diet. Through a poignant historical discussion, Rius demonstrates how colonialism and the industrialization of the food system led to the predominance of hyperprocessed foods characterized by harmful chemical additives, destroying traditional diets, health, and the environment. For Rius, "The time has come that WE NO LONGER KNOW what we are putting in our bodies. Nobody knows what percentage of chemicals we are swallowing as we eat instant soup or processed packaged cakes."[1] Throughout his analysis, Rius underscored the nutritiousness of the largely vegetarian Indigenous diet, based in maize, squash, and beans and complemented with numerous other foods that was being displaced by "Bimbo and Coca-Cola, the invaders of all corners of the Mexican republic."[2] Rius, the author of ten books on Mexican food and nutrition, including his 1973 classic book, *La panza es primero* (*The Belly Is First*), is among numerous critics of the corporate industrialization of the Mexican diet who allied themselves with campesino and working-class movements in their call to regenerate Mexican food and diets.

Rius illustrates what the previous chapters have argued: Mexico's industrial food boom has improved the wealth and the diets of a few as it
has exacerbated poverty, health disparities, and malnutrition for millions of Mexicans. Neoliberal policies have led to dwindling wages, the
slashing of the social safety net, and the expulsion of millions of Mexicans from the countryside. Contrary to the claims of policymakers, the
neoliberal food regime has not made much of a dent in chronic hunger,
and in fact, food poverty has grown in absolute numbers. As inequality
grows, working-class Mexicans find themselves with abundant access to
inexpensive ultra-processed and packaged foods. Mexico's independent
consumer rights organization El Poder del Consumidor argues that the
country is a "Paradise for Junk Food" and that corporations have radically
changed the eating habits of Mexicans, leading to rapidly growing rates
of childhood obesity and soaring numbers of deaths related to diabetes
mellitus.[3]

This chapter examines how the colonial and capitalist assault on Mexico's food system has both exacerbated inequality and brought forward
numerous popular alternatives to the industrialized corporate food system. After first examining the social impact of Mexico's neoliberal food
system and how government policies have exacerbated hunger and malnutrition, this chapter then turns to the ways that social movements and
radical intellectuals are rearticulating and enacting alternative visions
of food sovereignty. Finally, I will examine how neoliberal state policy
and corporate social responsibility programs have captured social justice
discourse, providing a modicum of relief to the poorest Mexicans while
blunting real reform and demobilizing social movements. In short, food
corporations have grabbed resources and power in Mexico.

"Permanent Food Vulnerability": The Social Costs of Neoliberal Industrial Foods

Mexico's neoliberal economic restructuring has exacerbated social and
economic inequality.[4] This process has led to a decline of higher-wage
unionized jobs and public sector jobs, an increase in lower-wage factory
work and precarious jobs, and a booming informal sector.[5] In the process, union-busting tactics and the search for more flexible labor policies have fueled inequality and insecurity. Traditional industrial centers

have been blighted due to factory closings, leading to the acceleration of women entering the labor force, and family members taking on second and third jobs.[6] For the political economists Cypher and Delgado Wise, this neoliberal shift "is carrying the nation to higher and higher levels of disarticulation, stagnation, and migration."[7] For the sociologist Sergio Zermeño, "the open economy is the enemy of our times"; it fosters anomie and despair characterized by the rise in violent crime and drug trafficking as working people and the dislocated are forced into increasingly desperate situations.[8]

The transformation of Mexico's food system and the growth of corporate dominance have done little to address poverty and social welfare. According to the Mexican government agency Consejo Nacional de Evaluación de la Política de Desarrollo Social (CONEVAL), between 1992 and 2022, the percentage of people lacking access to nutritious food averaged 22.9 percent of Mexico's total population (table 16). CONEVAL's data demonstrate that during periods of economic crisis, such as the 1995 national crisis and the 2008 global crisis, food poverty and overall rates of poverty increased significantly (69 percent in 1996 and 46.1 percent in 2010). Even when the rates of food poverty did drop, however, the absolute number remained relatively stable. The radical fluctuations in the ability of people to purchase food underscores the extreme vulnerability of the population. This vulnerability can also be seen in Mexico's overall poverty rates. While these percentages have dropped over the past few years, the number of people in poverty has grown by nearly 6 million from 2004 to 2020 (table 16).

Many analysts argue that food precarity is even worse than what the CONEVAL data indicate. Critics of CONEVAL's measurements point out that it places emphasis on access and that it does not examine whether people are able to make these purchases. Given the precarity of the lives of Mexico's poor, people have to choose what to spend their precious pesos on and this often leads to families skimping on basic necessities to cover other living costs. The work of the economist Julio Boltvinik and his Integrated Poverty Measurement Method (IPMM) demonstrated the need for multipronged approaches to poverty measurement that consider the broad range of basic needs, including housing and education. The IPMM, first developed in the 1990s, has become the standard measurement for poverty for the Mexico City government and its research

TABLE 16 CONEVAL's Measurement of Food Poverty in Mexico, 1992–2022

Population with Reduced Access to Nutritious Food		
Year	Percent	Number in Millions
1992	21.4	18.6
1994	21.2	19.0
1996	37.4	34.7
1998	33.3	31.7
2000	24.1	23.7
2002	20.0	20.1
2004	17.4	17.9
2006	13.8	14.4
2008	18.2	19.5
2010	24.8	28.4
2012	23.3	27.4
2014	23.4	28.0
2016	21.9	26.5
2018	22.2	27.5
2020	22.5	28.6
2022	18.2	23.4

Sources: Compiled from CONEVAL, "Reporte CONEVAL Cifras de Pobreza por Ingreso 2008," July 18, 2009; and CONEVAL, "Medición de Pobreza," 2014 and 2022.

arm, Evalúa Ciudad de México.[9] Whereas the CONEVAL method takes into account income and the lack of basic needs, the IPMM model includes both of those factors and relies less on variable costs that can fluctuate. The IPMM also considers the amount of available time that people have so as to account for a more holistic understanding of social well-being. Boltvinik's measurement indicates that poverty rates are much higher, hovering between 75 and 85 percent of the total population, nearly two-thirds higher than CONEVAL's calculations (table 17). The IPMM also demonstrates less variation in poverty rates. For example, whereas CONEVAL shows a growth in poverty by 17 million people as a result of the 1994–1995 peso crisis, the IPMM shows that less than 9 million people slipped into poverty during this period. Likewise, CONEVAL

TABLE 17 Estimates of Overall Poverty Rates, 1992–2022

Year	A. CONEVAL		B. Boltvinik Integrated Poverty Measurement Method		C. EVALÚA CDMEX	
	Percent	Number (millions)	Percent	Number (millions)	Percent	Number (millions)
1992	53.1	46.1	85	74.9		
1994	52.4	47	85	76.9		
1996	69.0	64	90	84.2		
1998	63.7	60.7	87	84.0		
2000	53.6	52.7	83	82.0		
2002	50	50.4	82	83.6		
2004	47.2	48.6	83	86.3		
2006	42.6	44.7	79	85.8		
2008	47.4	50.5	80	89.8	73.5	82.1
2010	46.1	52.8	82	92.8	75.7	86.7
2012	45.5	53.3	82	96.4	74.0	86.8
2014	46.2	55.3	83	100.1	74.1	88.9
2016	43.2	52.2	70.7	85.4	72.7	87.8
2018	41.9	51.9			79.1	97.9
2020	43.9	55.7			76.7	97.2
2022	36.3	46.8			75.8	97.7

Sources: A. Compiled from CONEVAL, "Reporte CONEVAL Cifras de Pobreza por Ingreso 2008," July 18, 2009; and CONEVAL, "Medición de Pobreza," 2014 and 2022; B. Julio Boltvinik and Araceli Damián, "Pobreza creciente y estructuras sociales cada vez más desiguales en México: Una vision integrada y crítica," *Acta Sociológica*, no. 70 (May–August 2016): 271–296; C. El Consejo de Evaluación del Desarrollo Social de la Ciudad de México (EVALÚA), "El Método de Medición Integrada de la Pobreza MMIP," https://www.evalua.cdmx.gob.mx/principales-atribuciones/medicion-de-la -pobreza-y-desigualdad/resultados-principales.

demonstrates a quicker rebound, with people falling in and out of poverty from year to year.[10]

In their recent survey of food security in Mexico, Felipe Torres Torres and Agustín Rojas Martínez found a steady decline in food security from 2000 to 2020. They also found that there were a growing number of municipalities and regions experiencing food insecurity. Food insecurity is especially acute in the countryside due to a combination of factors, including "the dismantling of the campesino base and the growth of rural migration, the loss of food self-sufficiency and great dependence on imports, the deficit in the agricultural trade balance, accompanied by low levels of economic growth, the fall in the purchasing power of wages, and the contraction in employment." These factors, they argued, create a "permanent food vulnerability that manifests differently throughout Mexico."[11]

Mexico's permanent food vulnerability and malnutrition rates are notoriously worse in the countryside. According to CONEVAL's 2022 estimates of poverty, "The five states with the highest percentage of the population in poverty in 2022 were Chiapas with 67.4%, Guerrero with 60.4%, Oaxaca with 58.4%, Puebla with 54.0%, and Tlaxcala with 52.5%."[12] These numbers have improved over the past decade according to CONEVAL as different administrations have targeted aid to these regions; however, the narco-related violence and the lack of access to land and high-paying jobs make these gains precarious. Chronic malnutrition among Indigenous populations is especially deleterious for infants and pregnant women. Oaxaca, for example, leads Mexico in birth defects due to a lack of folic acid in the diet of the population. In Chiapas, the poorest and most Indigenous state in Mexico, 25 percent of children under the age of five are malnourished.[13]

Rural poverty in the countryside also exists in areas where agricultural production is booming. For example, the Culiacán Valley of Sinaloa is one of Mexico's largest tomato-producing regions and accounts for approximately 33 percent of the state's agricultural production. Export agricultural production has increased since the 1990s, spurring migration from other parts of Sinaloa and other states. Recent studies of the region find that as the value of agricultural production boomed between 2000 and 2010, working and living conditions worsened for agricultural laborers.[14] While researchers found that there were improvements during the following decade, given pressures put on companies to be more socially responsible, workers still faced significant poverty and poor housing conditions. The percentage of people who lacked access to adequate food changed only slightly and comprised more than 17.3 percent of the population in Culiacán and 27.6 percent in neighboring Novolato in 2020.[15] However, given that approximately 64 percent of agricultural families' wages go toward basic food purchases, any slight shift in wages or food prices can throw their budget off-kilter, resulting in even less access to food.[16]

The export agriculture boom has also strained natural resources and the environment, severely impacting the quality of life for agriculture workers. For example, the San Quintín Valley, less than two hundred miles from the U.S.-Mexico border in Baja California, is home to some of the largest companies that produce berries and tomatoes for leading U.S. brands. Throughout the 1980s, production in San Quintín expanded to take advantage of lower labor and production costs and the relaxation of tariffs to export to the United States.[17] San Quintín is also home to thousands of workers and their families, the vast majority of whom are Indigenous people, Mixtecos, Triquis, and Zapotecos, who have been migrating from Oaxaca to the region for decades in search of seasonal employment. In the 1970s and 1980s, they began settling in the valley as the industry expanded and as neoliberal policies made working the land in their communities almost untenable. Effectively forced to migrate by neoliberal policies that favor export agriculture over food crops for domestic consumption, the population of the region more than quadrupled between 1970 and 1990 (from 8,559 to 38,151 people) and continued to expand over the next decades such that by the 2020 census approximately 117, 568 people lived the San Quintín Valley.[18] Given the rapid population growth, driven by agribusiness, the region lacks basic infrastructure for such a large population. Agribusiness has depleted the aquifers and created numerous desalination plants to water the crops. Water, however, is scarce in the neighborhoods of agricultural workers. Many complain that the water is shut off often and that it is only running once every three days. At times they go several days in a row without it.[19]

The boom in agricultural export specialization may increase profits and gross domestic product, but as Guadalajara-based researcher Humberto González demonstrates, it also leads to environmental degradation, severe exploitation of campesino and Indigenous-worker communities,

an increased dependence on transnational companies and foreign governments, and an accentuation of the deprivation of access to healthy,
nutritious, and culturally appropriate food for domestic customers.[20]
In their analysis of racialization of agricultural workers in the Mexican
Northwest between 2013 and 2019, one team of Mexican scholars found
that the national and regional press reinforced an intersectional racist
and gendered discourse of inferiority and very rarely raised deeper issues
of the structures of racism within Mexico.[21] These inequalities are deeply
rooted in anti-Indigenous and class-based policies that deprecate Indigenous people, their knowledges, and their ways of life.

Transnational food corporations have reinforced these racialized class
hierarchies and taken advantage of them through producing inexpensive
ultra-processed foods and marketing them throughout the country. The
combination of free trade, food dependency, and the rise of cheap, nutritionally poor foods has flooded the markets and entered the diets of poor
and working-class Mexicans in epidemic proportions. With more than
60 percent of the working population earning less than two minimum
wages, access to fresh healthy foods is virtually out of reach.

According to a study by Great Britain's Overseas Development Institute, the price of fruits and vegetables nearly doubled between 1990 and
2012. The prices of many industrially prepared foods, on the other hand,
fell by 20 percent during the same period.[22] Between 1999 and 2013,
Mexico's per capita annual sales of ultra-processed foods and drinks increased from 160 kilograms to nearly 220 kilograms, leading all Latin
American countries in the consumption of these foods.[23] A study by Antonio Yuñez-Naude found that the share of household food expenditures
on fresh foods fell for both urban and rural consumers between 1992
and 2012 as expenditures on processed "non-nutritional foods" more
than doubled for urban consumers and increased by one-third for rural
consumers.[24] Another team of scholars found that between 1984 and
2016, the amount of daily calories from the purchase of unprocessed
foods dropped by one-third while it increased by 84 percent for ultraprocessed foods. Within the growth of ultra-processed foods, there was
greater consumption of "cookies, pastries, sweet bread and breakfast cereals and ultra-processed tortillas, bread and meats."[25]

The sales of Coca-Cola and other sugary soft drinks also grew significantly during this period. Between 2010 and 2018, Mexican soft drink sales increased from nearly $10 billion to $16 billion even as the government waged a highly publicized public health campaign.[26] Coca-Cola and Pepsi-Cola's strategic marketing of modernity in Mexico began to reach throughout the country, including remote mountain villages in the mid-twentieth century. In many regions, especially where potable water is scarce, Coca-Cola has come to be a monopoly beverage where people rely on it for daily consumption. The most extreme examples of this consumption often occur in Indigenous communities, such as in Guerrero, where nearly 80 percent of youth drink a Coke for breakfast. In the state of Chiapas, one of the most unequal states, per capita consumption of soft drinks averaged 820 liters in 2020, five times the national average.[27]

The growth of the modern industrialized processed food industries has resulted in a public health crisis. In 1940, for the first time, diabetes was on the list of the top twenty causes of death in Mexico, accounting for approximately 1 percent of all deaths. By 1970, diabetes reached number fifteen and a decade later it was number nine, and in 1990 it reached number four on the list of the causes of death in Mexico.[28] By 2000, type 2 diabetes had become the leading cause of death in Mexico, accounting for 12.6 percent of all deaths in 2003, reaching 14 percent in 2020. In absolute numbers, diabetes-related deaths grew from approximately 47,000 a year in 2000 to 83,000 in 2010, and 151,009 in 2020.[29] These numbers are even higher when one considers other diabetes-related diseases, such as heart disease. Mexico is now plagued by what nutrition scholars refer to as the double burden of malnutrition, characterized by both undernutrition and overnutrition.[30]

The consumption of ultra-processed food was accentuated during the COVID–19 pandemic as the prices of fresh foods increased. A team of researchers affiliated with Mexico's National Health Institute found that the increase in prices of nutrient-dense foods left many of Mexico's poor to increase their consumption of foods high in energy and poor in nutrients, exacerbating food insecurity. The study found that approximately 60 percent of the population was food insecure during the pandemic, with 47 percent of these households reporting that they were reducing the expenditures on food during the pandemic.[31] Given the increase in prices of fresh food during the pandemic and the availability of shelf-stable processed packaged foods, the pandemic led to increased consumption of processed foods among precarious communities.

The power of mass marketing of processed foods, as discussed in previous chapters, has served to create a market for ultra-processed foods and to increase their ubiquity. In 2010, according to the Secretary of Health, Mexicans spent "around 240 billion pesos a year on junk food and only 10 billion dollars on basic foods."[32] In two important volumes, UNAM scholar Carola García Calderón and her colleagues demonstrated some of the ways that processed food marketers have sought to broaden their markets.[33] Through massive spending, companies have waged high-profile campaigns with leading actors and sports personalities to make their products attractive on all major media and social media outlets. In her analysis of one month of advertising on one of Mexico's popular telenovelas, *La Rosa de Guadalupe*, which has the largest audience of children and youth compared to other telenovelas, the scholar Andrea Sánchez Islas found that 30 percent of the advertisements were for food and beverages, the majority of which advertised packaged and fast foods, such as Gamesa's Emperador cookies and Domino's Pizza.[34] Videogames have also become an important avenue for advertising and companies such as Bimbo and Gamesa have created their own video games.[35] Food corporations have also enlisted social media influencers to advertise their products, enabling them to circumvent advertising restrictions.

Mexico's neoliberal food system, shaped by coloniality, capital, and state policies, has exacerbated inequality and is destroying the health of millions of Mexicans while a handful of capitalists enrich themselves, tightening their grip on the food and political systems. As capital pours into the food system, communities, organizers, and intellectuals have been underscoring the inequities in the system and struggling to create a more just system.

"Don't Touch Our Maíz": Popular Movements for Food Sovereignty

The social impact of these radical policy shifts was met by the resurgence of social movements, struggling for land, autonomy, and social and economic justice. Many of these movements center some of the ways campesinos, Indigenous communities, grassroots movements, and intellectuals are rearticulating a vision of food that is rooted in the diverse histories and cultures of Mexico's Indigenous and working-class communities.

The 1990s witnessed several social and political movements in response to the major shifts in agricultural and rural policies stemming from the 1980s and 1990s economic crises. In Jalisco in August 1993 relatively prosperous farmers who found themselves in debt during the collapse of subsidies and the liberalizing of trade in preparation for NAFTA organized themselves in a debtors' movement to fight the high interest rates and unequal banking structure. In a series of high-profile demonstrations throughout the 1990s, farmers and urban consumers denounced the banking system and liberalization of the economies and called for a more humane economic system. They named their movement El Barzón, which was the name of a popular revolutionary-era song that used the metaphor of the leather straps that bind the yoke on an ox to denounce the hacendado's control over workers through debt, high interest rates, and excessive prices at the company store.[36] Four months after El Barzón's first demonstrations, the Ejército Zapatista de Liberación Nacional (EZLN) took up arms on January 1, 1994, the same day that NAFTA went into effect. The uprising quickly captured the national and international spotlight as one of the first major attempts to halt the neoliberal economic juggernaut. The EZLN proclaimed that neoliberal policies and NAFTA would further push Indigenous Mexico into oblivion. The EZLN uprising opened the way for creative and autonomous movements to rearticulate alternative visions of food sovereignty within a more just society. These movements have also denounced the environmental and social costs of capitalist-driven food systems and the connections between climate disaster, industrial food systems, and growing inequality. The diverse approaches and goals of these movements illustrate the rich perspectives and solutions of everyday Mexicans who resisted and persisted through generations of oppression. This section explores some of these movements that are reshaping the struggle for food in more holistic ways, connecting the struggle to land, gendered labor, autonomy, and Indigenous and gendered ways of knowing.

Numerous projects have emerged through social movements in the 1990s and afterward to preserve and build upon Indigenous knowledge and foodways. Many of these were inspired by successive rural movements that united to form the El Campo no Aguanta Más (The Countryside Can Bear No More) movement in 2002–2003 and then the Sin Maíz, No Hay País (Without Maize, There Is No Country) movement in

2007.[37] The later coalition was sparked by the sudden rise in the price of tortillas, due to growing global demand, financial speculation, and the increased use of maize for ethanol; at the end of 2006 and the outset of 2007, communities were unable to purchase this most basic staple. As corporations enriched themselves, communities and popular organizations mobilized to form the Sin Maíz, No Hay País movement, underscoring the centrality of maize to Mexico.[38] The Red en Defensa del Maíz Nativo (Native Maize Defense Network, RDMN) was established by hundreds of Indigenous and smaller campesino organizations.[39]

These organizations have shifted the discourse to center Indigenous and community-based knowledges that capitalists and the Mexican state have long sought to erase, or at least neutralize, and capitalize on. Through their slogans, these networks, composed of community-based organizations, academics, public health practitioners, campesinos, and labor unions, have documented their struggles to transform Mexico's food system. Among the more high-profile campaigns has been the struggle against genetically modified maize and the multinational companies that have been patenting seeds as they usurp the lands and labor of campesinos. The largest target of these campaigns was Monsanto and its GMO maize and terminator seeds, which, given the open pollination system of maize, can spread to Indigenous communities' milpas and campesino fields and infect their crops, upending generations of seed saving and knowledges and varieties of maize. In addition, these GMO-infected crops, due to property rights laws, can be claimed as property of Monsanto and other large corporations. Over the course of the 2000s and 2010s, networks resisted GMO maize through local struggles and national and international campaigns. The RDMN and its allies declared 2013 the Year of Resistance Against Transgenic Maize and in Defense of Native Maize and of the Life and Autonomy of the People of Maize to draw attention to their struggle. Their holistic vision was developed through struggle: "maize can only be defended through continuing its planting, if we defend the life of the communities that have cared for it, if we defend the territories where Indigenous peoples, communities, and individual and collective farmers continue to carefully cultivate it in reciprocity with the environment and with each other."[40] Drawing from community struggles, RDMN uplifted Indigenous cultivation and agroecological practices and shifted the traditional model of agricultural extension to a more circular and collaborative model where campesinos drew on the traditional practices of their communities and shared methods, and incorporated innovations that they deemed ecological and socially appropriate with the help of researchers. Through this more collaborative approach, communities drew upon their knowledges of lands, seeds, plants, and their cosmological relationships to animals, the environment, and the world to share and build together in ways that strengthen individuals, communities, societies, and the earth.[41] In December 2023, after years of campesino struggle, Mexican president Andrés Manuel López Obrador banned genetically modified corn for human consumption and initiated plans to phase out the use of herbicide glyphosate. The U.S. Department of Agriculture and Monsanto and Mexican agribusiness companies have filed a complaint against the ban under the provision of the United States-Mexico-Canada Agreement, the successor to NAFTA. Claudia Sheinbaum, President López Obrador's successor, has vowed to keep up the fight.[42]

Through the political and economic transformation of the countryside, Mexican campesinos have been forced to find multiple income streams to survive and maintain their ways of life. The withdrawal of the paternalist state has allowed some communities to build on their community structures and creatively develop other structures to strengthen their autonomy and direct the growth and development of their communities. The persistence of the campesinos and the transformation of the countryside have taken on multiple forms. The scholars Mara Rosas and Mario Fuentes explained that what that they refer to as New Community-Based Rural Movements are not driven by neoliberal economic rationality but instead intentionally build upon campesino historic communitarian ways to draw on collective resources to build and strengthen their communities. They prioritize the well-being of the community first and look toward the market secondarily. Communities have shifted their focus to strengthening community ethos and producing for their needs.[43] These communities recognized the need for seeking other income streams but are intentional in using these as a campesino and Indigenous strategy to strengthen the community and "maintain their system of production and political and social organization." Strategically, it is seen as "a resistance against proletarianization by sending some people out to earn a wage to help the community maintain control of the land and the means of production."[44] The struggle for autonomy of rural and Indigenous communities in the face of neoliberal assault is a form of survival and resistance. Rosas and Fuentes argue that "resistance is not a retreat, better yet it is a proposal to construct new social structures and to reposition communities in societies incapable of integrating them in an organized process to advance prosperity."[45] This in turn has strengthened a sense of autonomy and allowed communities to build on their histories and cultures.

Among the numerous critical campesino movements that have been struggling in Mexico over the past several decades is the Consejo Nacional Urbano y Campesino (CNUC), founded in 1989 in the central-eastern state of Tlaxcala. CNUC is influenced by and linked to the national and international struggles for campesino justice and food sovereignty. However, they are rooted in the lived realities of the communities of Tlaxcala. They emphasize the importance of communal work and the importance of the ejido that emerged from Zapata's agrarian struggle during the revolution.[46] CNUC, like many campesino communities, saw Carlos Salinas de Gortari's revision of Article 27 of the Constitution and NAFTA as the last straws in neoliberal capitalism's assault on campesino communities, lands, and labor. According to Compañero Edén, a CNUC member from San Pablo Zitlatepec, "Foreign enterprises come and the government kicks us off of our lands, trying to buy us off. The government is developing an industrial corridor in this region and in San Pablo lands that the ejidos used before the reform of Article 27 are now owned by a private textile factory."[47] In 2016, Audi opened a manufacturing plant in Tlaxcala as an offshoot of its Volkswagen manufacturing operations in the neighboring state of Puebla, which impacted community lands and water resources.[48] These plants led to further industrial expansion in the once agricultural region, including a Chinese stereo speaker manufacturer that began to supply Volkswagen and Audi, a Walmart Distribution Center, and a slew of other manufacturers and warehouses.[49] CNUC founder and organizer Luz Rivera Martínez underscored what is at stake, especially since Tlaxcala is the birthplace of maize: "They take away the laws that protect us, they displace us . . . from our history, the land, the water, and our genetic heritage of maize. . . . Without land we don't have maize, without water we don't have life."[50]

Drawing on the knowledges of communities, CNUC developed a holistic approach to land, governance, and reciprocal relations in the community, the earth, and other sentient beings. One of its principal projects has been to provide work through the establishment of community projects for those who have lost jobs and land. For example, it created a fertilizer project to help wean farmers away from fifty years of dependence on chemical fertilizers and pesticides that the state forced producers to adopt. Through relearning the practice of organic composting, CNUC is trying to bring the soil back to its natural richness, since it has become sterile due to the cycle of industrial agriculture, which required the use of chemical fertilizers and pesticides. It is said that "each day the earth was poisoned . . . and as a result we have many diseases, including cancer and diabetes and kidney disease."[51] CNUC also worked to cultivate community farms and orchards to provide fresh fruits and vegetables to community members and to develop a network of greenhouses to produce tomatoes and other vegetables year-round. By recuperating their lands, communities are relearning to work collectively and be self-sufficient.

CNUC's holistic approach to community struggles is intersectional, working against capitalism, imperialism, and patriarchy at the same time. Through the creation of women's groups, they have made demands on the local government to supply basic foods and health services for the families of their members. Many women have become more active in the struggle since "they are beautiful struggles because one stops being fearful."[52] CNUC has also helped communities create workshops to discuss the causes and consequences of domestic violence and to raise awareness on women's rights. Their intersectional approach to community struggles and autonomy has shaken many communities and led to government harassment and reprisals.[53] Nevertheless, the power of the community gives them strength and builds solidarity with other movements in Mexico and throughout the world.

Autonomous movements such as CNUC and those connected to the Sin Maíz, No Hay País campaign and the RDMN emphasize the importance of the traditional milpa and the diet that it produces. The "milpa" refers to the traditional system of intercropping of maize, beans, and squash supplemented with other cultivars. The milpa diet, therefore, also emphasizes maize, beans, and squash as bases to be combined with other fresh foods. Julieta Ponce Sánchez, a nutritionist with the Centro de Orientación Alimentaria (COA) affiliated with the Sin Maíz, No Hay País campaign, argues that the milpa diet is an essential healthy diet for individuals, families, communities, and the earth. Further, she argues that with working-class Mexicans earning less than two minimum wages, a healthy milpa-based diet can be prepared relatively inexpensively.[54] She argues that the milpa "is a system of maximum nutrition and minimum cost, which means that when the milpa is displaced we have less health at maximum cost. Maize from the milpa, that which nourishes and provides sustenance, has an enemy in the household."[55] That enemy, she argues, is the myriad ultra-processed foods and sodas marketed by large corporations. The focus on the milpa diet is aimed at improving individual and collective health as part of the larger struggle for autonomy. A poster circulated in communities in 2013 by the RDMN sums up this holistic approach: "Making milpa is the indisputable way to true autonomy, it is the most certain route for not having to ask anyone's permission for the right to exist. This makes possible our defense of the territory from those who hoard lands, water, and biodiversity, from the mining and other companies that displace and destroy."[56]

In several rural communities, there has been a resurgence of local tortilla making. Feminist scholars have explained how women have fed and cared for generations, preserving and building critical knowledges in the shadows, with little recompense. For the scholar Ivonne Vizcarra Bordi, the tortilla must be turned over repeatedly, as women do when making tortillas and heating them up on the comal, to see the other side. Turning the tortilla allows us to dissect power relations and patriarchy and see how Indigenous women are holders of knowledge and know how to create a more humane world. A series of studies by a team of Mexican scholars that work with the Unión de Palmeadoras (Tortilla Makers Union), in Tlaxiaco city, Oaxaca, have underscored the resilience of Indigenous communities and their social and cultural networks that have kept Indigenous women and families in business in the Mixtec region. The Unión de Palmeadoras was established in 1990 because of the corporatist unions' efforts to organize the different sectors of the tortilla industry. Initially there were six hundred members, the majority of whom were Mixtec women who produced traditional tortillas in their households. Within a decade their numbers dropped by 50 percent, presumably due to the elimination of the tortilla subsidy and the economic crises of 1994–1995 and 2007–2010. By 2015, they were down to eighty-nine members.[57] Nevertheless, their organization has helped them assertively define their labor, its complexity, and the knowledge and skill it takes to produce and market tortillas. They have developed markets in Indigenous communities and among marginalized campesinos, helping sustain their families and communities. Their organization has enabled them "to reject the pejorative colloquial term of 'tortillería' and embrace their artisanal labor that is rooted in generations of knowledge and labor."[58]

In addition to maintaining their artisanal labor, the Palmeadoras also conserved native maize varieties and prefer to make tortillas using them. They use native varieties when they are available and buy directly from local producers, hoping to sustain their business. Unfortunately, native varieties are becoming increasingly scarce, and it is easier to purchase hybrid white maize from the state-run DICONSA store. The rapid expansion of tortillerías in this region, coupled with the expansion of GRUMA, threaten to drive these Indigenous women, who use and protect native maize varieties, out of business.[59] Despite the importance of their labor, women and their families who make and sell tortillas earn only about six dollars a day. Their livelihood is constantly under threat from the local tortillerías, which, they argue, "just want to make more money—they're not interested in what they sell. . . . We sell quality, not quantity."[60]

Popular mobilizations over the past three decades have resulted in a growing denunciation of the industrialized food system and its social impact, and the development of holistic movements throughout Mexico where campesinos and communities are developing new systems for sustainable living. Many of these fuse Indigenous ways of doing with scientific practices to reinvigorate native varieties of maize and other crops in a polyculture that works with nature. These movements envision a different food system, one that is led by Indigenous and campesino communities as "creative forces of resistance against the agro-industrial model, agribusinesses, and the neoliberal agrarian policies implemented for more than three decades by the Mexican government."[61]

From Rural Development to Famine Relief and Popular Demobilization

Neoliberal policymakers and corporate elites have worked to ameliorate the growing inequalities that they have both fueled and profited from by demobilizing social movements and intellectual critiques. Successive Mexican governments have implemented a series of social welfare policies since the 1990s that reduce aid to those defined as the most vulnerable populations while seeking to integrate them, and other disaffected communities, into the folds of the state. As discussed in chapter 3, neoliberal social policies differed significantly from the more redistributive policies of the earlier era. As these policies became more targeted, charges of political manipulation and vote buying through programs became widespread. Over time, social programs became more sophisticated in their strategy but have become less about poverty eradication and more about famine prevention.

Years of social policy nominally aimed at eradicating food poverty have been unsuccessful. Neoliberal policies in the countryside sought to transform campesinos from rural producers to the rural poor in need of social welfare policies.[62] According to analysis by UNAM's Centro de Análisis Multidisciplinario, "Federal and state governments invested 36,366,541 pesos for each poor person in the country over the 42 years (1970–2012), but instead of reducing poverty, poverty increased 58.2 percent during this same period, according to the budgets for anti-poverty programs in the three levels of government."[63] According to the study, most of the funds went to the bureaucratic apparatus and relatively little went to directly aiding the poor. Social policy has been based in top-down-driven programs that individualize poverty and shift responsibility to the poor themselves. This has translated into the "feminization of responsibility and obligation for managing poverty 'with women being made to do more to ensure household survival, when men are increasingly doing less.'"[64]

To address social movements challenging neoliberal policies and growing inequality, President Enrique Peña Nieto announced his National Crusade Against Hunger on January 21, 2013, just a month after taking office, near Zapatista communities in Las Margaritas, Chiapas. The National Crusade Against Hunger (SINHAMBRE or CNCH), reportedly modeled on Brazilian president Lula da Silva's Zero Hunger policy, was conceived as "a strategy of inclusion and social welfare that will be implemented through a broad and far-reaching participatory process to eliminate hunger through adequate nutrition for those considered poor through a multidimensional analysis of poverty, eliminate infant malnutrition and improve height and weight indicators of children, increase production of foods and income of campesinos and small producers, minimize loss of food after harvest, and increase public participation in the eradication of hunger."[65] Through focusing on aligning social policy and trying to bridge the divide between the urban and middle classes and rural campesinos, the former PRD (Partido de la Revolución Democrática) president and rural development specialist, Secretary of Social Development (SEDESOL) Rosario Robles, led the efforts of Peña Nieto's signature social policy.

According to SINHAMBRE officials, there was a disconnect between the truly poor and Mexico's middle classes. One of SINHAMBRE's first actions was to mount a public relations campaign to document and publicize the dimensions of hunger in Mexico through the arts. At a concert in Mexico City in March 2013 sponsored by SINHAMBRE, Paco Familiar from the popular band DLD shouted to the audience, "To eat is a pleasure but nutrition is a basic need for all of us. It is a universal right so raise your voice and be a part of history, of the evolution of this country. Let's end hunger."[66] In summer 2013, the photo exhibit *México sin Hambre* presented, "for the first time, images that document the problem of extreme poverty and hunger in Mexico" at the Centro Nacional de las Artes (CENART).[67] Through the public relations campaign, the government hoped to mobilize middle-class Mexicans to comprehend the realities of hunger and to donate sympathy, time, and food.

Another assumption of SINHAMBRE was that the country's food did not get to the truly needy because of inefficiency. Therefore, SINHAMBRE sought to publicize food wastage and argued that by eliminating food waste, Mexico could effectively combat hunger. In her short documentary film on the Central de Abastos in the Distrito Federal, which won first place at SINHAMBRE's film festival, Monserrat Vásquez Díaz highlighted that thirty-one million tons of vegetables and fruits are thrown out on a daily basis.[68] In September 2013, the Secretary of Social Development cited a study that showed "on average 37.44 percent of the 34 items in Mexico's basic food basket are wasted in the post-harvest food chain."[69] A similar argument was made by Robles's predecessor, Heriberto Félix Guerra, who argued that if the thirty thousand tons of food that supermarkets and restaurants waste daily could be diverted, it would be "enough to feed Mexico's 20 million nutrition poor."[70] Government agencies, however, have yet to figure out how to rescue food from garbage bins to feed the poor and hungry.[71]

SINHAMBRE targeted four hundred of Mexico's most isolated and poor municipalities to better integrate government policies and the market in the fight against hunger and nutritional poverty. SINHAMBRE worked to coordinate government programs in the crusade, including OPORTUNIDADES, DICONSA, LICONSA, and the public health sector to ensure that services were being provided. In addition, these communities received attention of other programs carried out in collaboration with the private sector. As well as providing families a package of thirteen food items at a reduced cost of 638 pesos at the government-operated DICONSA stores, they built more stores in these municipalities and started community kitchens. After ten months, SINHAMBRE proclaimed the results of its actions an unqualified success.[72] While SEDESOL officials claim that these four hundred municipalities were chosen after much study of the situation, many analysts argued that this was once again an attempt to buy votes in remote areas of the country.

SINHAMBRE and other social programs recognized the importance of taking gender into consideration as they designed programs and focused on women as co-responsible implementors of the programs. With the growth of the concept of the feminization of poverty, especially under neoliberalism, and increased male migration in the countryside, policymakers assumed that women's labor was exclusively unremunerated reproductive labor and therefore designed policies to help women monetize their labor as workers. Women received cash payments from the government and were charged with cooking and serving food provided by the programs at the community kitchens. In exchange, they had to agree to attend workshops on nutrition and other topics related to health and well-being. While in theory the programs sought to include women, they included them as customers receiving services, and not as active agents claiming their rights.[73] Instead, these policies reinforced top-down structures and used women to carry out policies. In the process, the programs often "reproduced women's traditional gender roles overloading their lives with new tasks and responsibilities, while ignoring their own agency, participation, and capacity for decision-making."[74]

As in the past, but in a much more targeted form, CNCH's social programs exercised a form of biopolitics, in which dominating classes exercised control over the poor not only through ideology but through their bodies. Social policies emphasized that the government wanted the poor "to eat in the healthiest way possible."[75] However, the "healthy" foods included in government programs were industrialized products that are accepted in urban areas but have little relevance in rural and Indigenous communities. As one campesina active in the school lunch program explained, "They send us canned foods and here we like natural foods, we have maize, potatoes, peas, beans, everything natural."[76] Government policies and food donations fostered community dependency on the government and subordinated women and communities to the government programs, threatening their food, culinary knowledges, and practices.

For example, in Indigenous communities that cultivate native maize, government programs provide the community with MASECA, GRUMA's maize flour. Indigenous women involved in community kitchens that are provisioned through these social programs are obliged to use industrialized flour, facilitating the replacement of native maize with industrialized maize, a market dominated by Mexican and international corporations. Women were also subjected to workshops on healthy eating, foods that reinforce industrialization, and narrow notions of nutrition that link obesity to eating too many tortillas. As Acuña Rodarte demonstrates, "as part of a policy that blames consumers for obesity, the nutrition talks and medical consultations many times become calls to stop the eating of tortillas."[77] Other scholars have demonstrated how government officials often blame women as the ones responsible for the poor nutrition of their families and feel that it is their role to help discipline and structure the daily lives of families.[78] These programs work to address immediate hunger but also use women to carry out an agenda to transform diet and foodways.

For many skeptics, the motives of SINHAMBRE became apparent when, in April 2013, SEDESOL contracted with PepsiCo and Nestlé to join the SINHAMBRE campaign. PepsiCo agreed to "help develop products to combat malnutrition, help develop sustainable projects in the areas SINHAMBRE is working and support the donation of Quaker products for the well-being of people in these communities." One of the first products that PepsiCo was to develop was a fortified cookie and atole that "would contribute in covering the daily nutritional needs of mothers and infants who suffer chronic malnutrition."[79] Nestlé made fortified puddings and provided recipes using Nestlé products. Many have pointed out the bitter irony that the government was enlisting the very transnational companies that were part of the problem. Víctor Suárez of the Asociación Nacional de Empresas Comercializadoras de Productoras del Campo (ANEC), for example, argued, "the agreements that Nestlé and PepsiCo have signed to participate in the National Campaign Against Hunger reflect the worst of the paths to eradicate food poverty in our country. On the contrary, this method of linking public assistance with private philanthropy is the best way to preserve inequality and poverty in Mexico."[80]

This seemingly aggressive strategy to address the hunger of millions was fraught with controversy. Early studies indicated that it promised more than it could deliver. The program had difficulty maintaining local participation by community leaders, especially when after several meetings they saw no concrete benefit. Local CNCH officials noted significant reticence and even apathy by community members, and they had to develop numerous strategies to try to gain the confidence of local communities.[81] Through focusing on eating habits and nutrition education, these programs did little to address the root causes of hunger and poor nutrition, which would require moving beyond social policy and addressing political economic factors, including land, labor, and control over resources. These material factors were ignored by social policy since this would challenge neoliberal capitalist growth and the expansion of Mexico's industrial food complex.[82]

An assessment of the National Crusade Against Hunger by the Auditoría Superior de la Federación, the nation's auditory agency to ensure the proper expenditure of public resources, found that it failed in its task to pull seven million of Mexico's poorest citizens out of poverty. On the contrary, the audit concluded that the number of people in extreme food poverty increased by nearly 13 percent. In addition, they found many irregularities in the operation of the program, including a lack of internal controls to ensure that those who were listed as receiving benefits received them. Of the more than 8 billion pesos spent during the six-year period of the campaign, only 9,700 people said that they received services.[83] In 2018, it was reported that between 2013 and 2015, nearly 80 percent of the 500 million pesos spent by the program in private contracts went to advertising the successes of the programs on the principal television channels, radio stations, and newspapers, and to making

T-shirts with the campaign logo. Its media campaign funneled nearly 143 million pesos to Televisa, a longtime supporter of the PRI and the president.[84]

Instead, SINHAMBRE continued historic anti-democratic approaches to poverty policy by taking a charity-based approach that excluded workers, consumers, and campesinos from the decision-making process. The persistence of technocratic solutions may have helped families in the short-term but were really aimed at subordinating working communities to political parties and the logic of the market.

Following the much-publicized efforts to tax junk food in the United States, Mexico began to develop similar plans to tax consumers. By punishing consumers, the idea was to change eating habits as opposed to taking a more aggressive approach to industrial food industry. The industrialized food corporations lobbied hard against any restrictions, forcing governments to weaken laws restricting the sale and advertising of junk foods, and reducing taxes levied on their sale. For example, efforts to ban the sale of colas, sugary soft drinks, and other forms of junk food were modified to limit the ban to schools. In 2014, the first national tax levied on sweetened beverages was one peso per liter and was later changed to benefit the companies.[85] A 2023 study on the impact of the tax on drink consumption found that there was a statistically significant reduction by approximately 11–14 ml in purchases because of the tax. Other studies found that consumption dropped by 7.5 percent.[86] The ban of sugary drinks and junk food in the state of Oaxaca in 2020 came during the COVID–19 pandemic, which was more likely to kill people with diet-related co-morbidities such as diabetes, obesity, and hypertension. The Oaxacan state legislator who proposed the bill argued, "It is important to finally put the brakes on this industry, which has already sickened our country and our children. . . . [The industry] gets into the most remote corners of the state where there's often not even medicines, but there's Coca-Cola."[87] However, the ban has been very difficult to enforce. Even small communities in Oaxaca that passed their own bans on junk food and sealed themselves off from deliveries during COVID–19 have seen the laws ignored.[88]

While it is still too early to assess food and social policy under the presidency of Andrés Manuel López Obrador, what is certain is that his pledge to increase the minimum wage has led to real yearly increases.

CONEVAL's 2022 data show a significant drop in the percent of people experiencing food poverty (table 16). When minimum wages are compared to the price of tortillas in tortillerías, there is a notable increase in the amount of tortillas one day's minimum wage could purchase—6.3. kilograms in 2018 to 10 kilograms each year from 2019 to 2022.[89] To be sure, these increases are not nearly enough and need to be sustained. However, they do indicate important increases. The rhetoric of López Obrador's policies also falls a bit more in line with the food sovereignty rhetoric of social movements with his creation of the office of Seguridad Alimentaria Mexicana (SEGALMEX) under the Secretary of Agriculture, which unified the government's social programs that distributed milk (LICONSA) and its chain of stores, DICONSA. SEGALMEX was initially headed by Ignacio Ovalle, a key figure in government social programs since the 1970s; however, he was removed after a scandal revealed the mismanagement of funds.[90] López Obrador also created an underfunded office of Subsecretary of Food Self-Sufficiency led by the well-respected agricultural engineer and agroecologist Victor Suárez Carrera that began to implement agroecological projects in Indigenous communities and rural areas with little access to irrigation.[91]

Corporate Power and "A New Way to Generate Wealth with Social Justice"

Mexico's food corporations have been successful at using their capital and political might to protect their interests.[92] Through their class organizing and their political connections that included raising money for candidates and putting them on their boards of directors, the food corporations have become key players in a society that has decimated the public sector and discredited public employees and politicians who are very susceptible to charges of corruption. Through their lobbying efforts, they have limited the impact of labor, economic, and consumer-related reforms. Their strategy positioned the food companies on the forefront of responding to social and economic concerns through the development of Corporate Social Responsibility (CSR) programs. These programs have allowed companies to frame their image as good corporate citizens, while at the same time enlarging their profits and doing little to address social and economic inequality or the health consequences of their products.

As we have seen in previous chapters, Mexico's capitalist class and international corporations have always had close links to political power, even if at times there were tensions between the two. Neoliberal policies beginning in the 1980s fostered many close relations between government, international foundations, and internationally competitive capitalists.[93] Strategic organizing by leading Mexican capitalists in the late 1970s and throughout the 1980s and 1990s paid off handsomely with changes to government policy that opened the economy to them. Large companies were given a series of passes on existing laws through lax enforcement and government officials looking the other way. For example, the 1982 tax law on rents (Ley del Impuesto sobre la renta) allowed Mexico's largest business groups to defer payment of taxes if their overall revenues did not meet a minimum threshold. This allowed many to distort their income by subtracting their losses from some businesses against their earnings in others. A 2009 investigative report found, "The result was that at times the 400 largest business consortiums paid 15 times less in taxes than they should have, some of these companies are strongest in their sector not only in Mexico but on the entire planet."[94] Bimbo and Walmex were high on this list. In 2008 Bimbo's actual tax payment was 2.6 percent of its sales, and it deferred 1.25 billion pesos in tax liability while Walmex paid 2.1 percent of its sales and deferred 5.5 billion pesos. After much public outrage, the PRI-controlled congress created a special commission to evaluate these special tax breaks. The commission was headed by a brother of one of the son-in-laws of Bimbo's founder, confirming for many that a serious inquiry would not take place and that crony capitalism was alive and well in Mexico.[95]

As social movements decried the growing inequality, environmental destruction, and social fallout of the rapacious neoliberal policies, capital drew upon growing trends in Europe and the United States and began to create Mexico's CSR programs. CSR became an important avenue for companies to reshape their image and "become co-responsible for social and sustainable development."[96] However, scholars of ethical consumption have demonstrated these increasingly sophisticated CSR policies are not about addressing poverty and inequality but instead serve to increase consumption and reinforce global racialized and gendered inequalities under the guise of social justice.[97]

CSR aims to get businesses to transform from a corporate philanthropy model to a model that represents the corporation as a good "global citizen." In Mexico, this transition was difficult because while there was a history of charity and philanthropy, until recently corporations had played a very limited role in this process.[98] As Mexican businessmen became more integrated in the global marketplace and the Mexican state became increasingly challenged by social movements, businesses were forced to adopt some of the philanthropic strategies of their global counterparts and competitors. In 1988, this began to change with the founding of Centro Mexicana por la Filántropia (CEMEFI) by a group of businessmen led by Manuel Arango, cofounder of the Aurrerá supermarket chain, to promote philanthropy among businesses.[99]

CEMEFI led the CSR movement in Mexico, marking a major transformation in Mexican corporate giving and responsible business practices. It created the Socially Responsible Company (ESR) program to provide an annual seal of approval for companies that incorporate CSR in their operations. According to CEMEFI, an ESR-certified company is one that

1. Operates from an ethical code, combats internal and external corruption, and contributes to the general public welfare;
2. Promotes the quality of the life of the business and provides working conditions that are favorable for quality of life of employees, suppliers, and their families, and develops practices that advance the respect for human rights and human dignity;
3. Develops a close relationship and commitment to the communities it serves;
4. Works to respect and preserve the ecology and environment and its resources for future generations.[100]

As one CEMEFI specialist put it, the goal of CSR is for "companies to achieve sustainability along three lines: financially, socially, and environmentally. . . . It is the new way to generate wealth with social justice."[101] Since the first awards were given in 2001 when seventeen companies received the distinction, it has become a highly sought after award that has spurred companies to develop CSR programs. As of 2015, more than 930 companies have received these awards. By 2023, nearly 2,300 companies received the distinction.[102] Prominent multinationals with CSR programs in their home countries became early recipients of the award. Eight of the ten companies that have received the CEMEFI CSR award for fifteen consecutive years were transnational companies, including Coca-Cola Mexico, BBVA-Bancomer, Deloitte, Hewlett Packard, Shell, Walmart, and Holcim.[103] The two nationally based companies were Bimbo and a consulting firm called Zimat. While this trend of large transnational and national firms garnering the distinction has been the rule, over the past five years or so several small- and medium-sized companies have received this distinction.

Food and beverage firms and retail outlets have a relatively high rate of participation in Corporate Social Responsibility programs. More than 20 percent of the companies who have received the distinction for more than nine consecutive years are food and beverage companies. These companies are among the most recognizable in the economy, as many are large multinationals that are consumed or frequented on a regular basis. They know the value of good public relations. Bimbo, with its company CSR slogan of "To nourish, delight, and serve our world," has long been one for the leaders in corporate welfare policies and in exercising their social responsibility.[104] As detailed in chapter 5, Bimbo's activities emerge from its founder Lorenzo Servitje's history in the Christian Social Doctrine movement and other conservative Catholic organizations, including the Legonaries of Christ and Opus Dei. This conservative activism has led the company to engage in campaigns to advocate for policies that advance conservative social mores in the media and schools. Servitje was also a big campaign contributor to some of the more conservative political candidates in the conservative National Action Party.[105] Bimbo has used CSR to both advance its public image and improve its bottom line.

As table 18 shows, Bimbo and Walmart are the only two food companies to have received the ESR distinction for the entire twenty-three years of its existence. Coca-Cola received the distinction the second year and has been on the list for twenty-two years. That three of the world's largest transnational corporations that have produced, distributed, and sold the most ultra-processed food products in Mexico at the same time that type 2 diabetes has become the leading cause of death in the country says much about the power of the CSR movement. Other food and beverage companies that have joined the movement and are now on the CEMEFI list include Grupo Herdez (15 years), Jumex (14 years), and Alsea

TABLE 18 CEMEFI's Responsible Business Recipients from the Food Sector, 2023

Years Awarded with ESR Distinction	Company Name
23	Bimbo
	Walmart
22	The Coca Cola Corporation Sucursales México
21	Jugos del Valle
20	Grupo Nestlé México
	Arca Continental (Coca-Cola Bottler)
	Grupo Modelo
19	Cadena Comercial OXXO
	PepsiCo Alimentos México
18	Peñafiel Agua Minerales
	Grupo LALA
17	Granjas Carroll de México
	Restaurantes Toks (Grupo Gigante)
15	Tequila Sauza
	Grupo Herdez
	CITROFRUT S.A.P.I.
14	Jumex
	Agrana Fruit
13	Jugos de Valle
	McDonald's Mexico
12	Alsea
	Grupo Porcicola Mexican-Kekén

Source: "Empresas Socialmente Responsables," CEMEFI, 2023, https://www.cemefi .org/resultadosesr/.

(12 years). The Grupo Maseca was noticeably absent from the CEMEFI program in 2023. However, it was listed during the first decade of the program's existence, and GRUMA still lists the awards on its website.[106] Like other companies, it also has found other avenues to demonstrate its "corporate social responsibility."[107]

Another example of the industry's lobbying power is the campaign the Consejo Mexicano de la Industria de Productos de Consumo, A.C. (ConMéxico), which waged efforts against taxing junk food as part of the government's fiscal reform efforts. ConMéxico, which represents industry leaders, vigorously took to the media to denounce the proposed tax hike, arguing that there is no scientific evidence that some food products are related to the causes of obesity.[108] Coca-Cola and Pepsi used their connections with Mexico's television duopoly to block a campaign in favor of the tax proposal, enabling the industry and ConMéxico to deflect criticism of its products. The industry has positioned itself as part of the good food movement by arguing that modern sedentary life favors obesity and that a key aspect of fighting obesity is physical activity. In 2011, seventeen of the forty-four companies that are part of ConMéxico implemented nutritional labeling on many of their products and launched their campaign "Check and Choose, the Key to Nutrition."[109] In the midst of the recent debate on junk food taxation, the Secretary of Health, the food industry, and the two major television networks developed a National Strategy to Prevent and Control Obesity and Diabetes. According to the agreement, advertising of junk food would be limited, more foods would be labeled for nutritional content, and fruits and vegetables would be included in fast-food menus.[110] ConMéxico frequently discusses anemia and other nutritional deficiencies they are committed to fighting against by using existing laws and programs.[111]

Other companies have also worked to demonstrate that their foods have nutritional value and that they promote good health. This is a particularly interesting proposition since many of their food products have very little nutritive value. Nevertheless, this has not stopped companies from developing ads that address dietary fads and promote a healthy lifestyle. GRUMA, in its U.S. and European operations, for example, has marketed its tortillas as low in carbohydrates, no trans-fats, and GMO free. Bimbo advertises that it has eliminated trans-fats from 99.5 percent of its products. Much of the dietary advertising focuses not on the nutritive value of the foods but on how many products have reduced sugar and fats. However, when their products have no nutritional value, companies offer disclaimers in small print that encourage a "healthy lifestyle." For example, on the sides of Bimbo trucks and on billboards the company advertised its "choco rollos" with a large picture, while on the bottom in very small letters it advises customers to "fill yourself with energy with 30 minutes of exercise a day."[112] Companies have also been able to use the public critiques of their role in Mexico's nutrition crisis to develop new products and bolster their claims that the companies are not the problem but can be part of the solution. Through the creation of Coca-Cola Light and the development of its bottled water lines, Coca-Cola, for example, has increased its profits while showing that it is helping reduce sugar consumption.[113]

Mexico's neoliberal food regime has had a devastating impact on Mexico's poor while at the same time raising the social justice profile of Mexico's food corporations. As we have seen in this chapter, Mexico's corporate food boom has done little to address Mexico's food poverty. At the same time, the government's neoliberal food policies weakened Mexico's social safety net and blamed the poor for their bad choices. Together, the public and private sectors have accelerated Mexico's double burden of malnutrition. Communities and social movements drew upon their knowledges, histories, and struggles to reimagine and restructure their communities to confront the neoliberal assault. However, these movements have been met with co-optative strategies by the state and capital. Through elaborate public relations campaigns, social programs and food corporations have co-opted social justice discourse emanating from social movements fighting to transform inequities in the food system. In the process, Mexico has become a "a junk food paradise" for working-class Mexicans, a place where it is cheaper to eat ultra-processed foods than the healthy and nutrient-dense milpa diet that has nourished Mexicans for centuries.

CONCLUSION

The Battle for Mexico's Food System

In 2002, community activists waged a months-long campaign to prevent McDonald's from opening a restaurant on the historic main plaza of Oaxaca City. The city center had been designated a UNESCO World Heritage Site in 1987 as an example of sixteenth-century colonial architecture "representative of a cultural tradition of more than four centuries of art and history."[1] Led by the renowned Zapotec painter, sculptor, and graphic artist Francisco Toledo, students and Indigenous organizers rallied to protect their public commons from a McDonald's invasion, which they considered a corporate insult on Oaxaca's legendary cuisine.[2] In one of their creative actions, they covered the proposed location with signs proclaiming "No McZocalo" and handed out traditional Oaxacan tamales that were communally made by students, staff, and tutors from Oaxaca's popular Universidad de la Tierra.[3] Their protest turned into a festival and celebration of Oaxacan culture and tradition.

The intellectual Elena Poniatowska weighed in on the absurdity of McDonald's fast-food symbolically replacing Oaxaca's nutritious millennial cuisine:

> In whose head can the infamous bovine hamburger (that has the horrible name Big Mac and that requires you to have the mouth of a lion

to be able to take the first bite) compare with our mole from Oaxaca, our tacos de rajas and various guisados, our huitlacoche and mushroom quesadillas during the rainy season? How can a paper plate compare with fine Oaxacan crockery? Because of it we are becoming asphyxiated by plastic. How can we exalt bad foreign food instead of valuing ours, which is extraordinary?[4]

After months of protests in Oaxaca City, in December 2002, the municipal president halted McDonald's plans for the city's main plaza. The battle against McDonald's was an important victory. It demonstrated that popular mobilization could impede, if only briefly, a global corporate giant like McDonald's. To this day McDonald's has been kept out of Oaxaca's zócalo. After his death in 2019, Toledo was memorialized in part for using "Oaxacan tamales to take down McDonald's."[5]

The Oaxacan victory, however, was just a minor setback for McDonald's and other global industrial food companies. McDonald's already had nearly 250 restaurants throughout Mexico in 2002, and by 2024, it reached more than 400.[6] In the first quarter of the twenty-first century, supermarkets, convenience stores, and fast-food and chain restaurants had tentacles throughout Mexico. By selling processed foods produced by Mexican and international oligopolies, these corporations are also selling a brand of modernity through their marketing and advertising that enlists Mexican and international singers, actors, athletes, and sports teams to sell their products.

México Between Feast and Famine has argued that this story is not new. In the words of the food studies scholar Eric Holt-Gimenez, "The food system is not broken; rather, it works precisely as a capitalist food system is supposed to work."[7] As we have seen throughout this book, Mexico's food system has been constructed based on European coloniality and its notions of modernity. Since the conquest, the food system has been built upon systematic efforts to destroy Indigenous knowledges and ways of life. Europeans brought with them a chauvinism that their society, foods, beliefs, and knowledge systems were superior. In their paternalistic and destructive quest, they, and their successors, repeatedly sought to transform a pluriverse of cultures and regions into a hegemonic nation based on Europeanized notions of wealth, agriculture, and knowledge systems.

Throughout the twentieth century, policymakers argued that Mexican nutrition was deficient, sometimes because of the structures of inequality but essentially because of myths that working people and campesinos lacked knowledge on modern nutrition. Consistently, elites belittled Indigenous diets and food knowledge systems. Policymakers, social workers, and schoolteachers lectured working-class women on nutrition. They created manuals and texts for them to read so that could unlearn their "bad habits" and become modern women raising healthy children who would be good workers and citizens. In the process, they ignored and tried to erase multisensory knowledges, such as those of the cook's sazón, which relies on touch, taste, and smell and is passed down and shaped throughout the centuries.

Mexican food companies furthered the project of transforming diets and creating a modern consumer culture. Beginning in the 1940s and 1950s, during Mexico's state-led capitalist expansion, small companies grew and innovated to meet the demand of Mexico's growing middle classes. These capitalists brought transnational experiences to Mexico, whether as Spanish immigrants or as elites who spent time in the United States or Europe. Closely attuned to experiences of food companies in the United States, they adapted this knowledge to the budding Mexican market. They forged relations with companies in the United States, imported machinery, borrowed ideas, and hired consultants. They used their political and social connections to weave themselves into the fabric of Mexico's power elite, giving them access to government loans, political support and favors, and other opportunities.

With the neoliberal reforms of the 1980s and 1990s, GRUMA, Bimbo, Grupo Aurrerá / Walmart, and Oxxo were well positioned politically and economically to expand their national and global reach. As we have seen, these companies used their power to increase their market share, and each became a world leader in the food industry. They deftly took advantage of Mexico's structures of coloniality to expand their markets while reinforcing racial, class, and gender hierarchies. As companies led by men with machines, they targeted women as creators and consumers while erasing their food knowledge.

In what kind of world, paraphrasing Poniatowska, can a food system enrich a small group of food industry billionaires while doing very little to alleviate the food poverty of millions? How can a food system reward companies with exorbitant profits as these same companies produce and sell products that are a principal cause of the epidemic of diet-related diseases? In what world can food companies employ the tools of racialized and gendered capitalism to further their class assault on the food system while granting themselves awards for their "socially responsible" corporate practices? As climate catastrophe threatens the earth, the industrial food system is woefully anachronistic and unjustifiable.

Generations of struggle have taught us, however, that there are alternatives to the neoliberal food system. These alternatives live in the pluriverse of communities whose histories, knowledges, and experiences have persisted and transformed over generations. They live in the autonomous communities where, working with agroecologists, they have fused Indigenous ways of doing with scientific practices to reinvigorate native varieties of maize and other crops. As Gustavo Esteva has argued, Mexico's Indigenous and campesino communities understand food, land, and nature not as commodities, but as life. Daily meals, or comida, are created from relationships between people, nature, and other sentient beings that have developed over centuries. Esteva called for the "reembedding of Food in Agriculture," to restore these relationships as the just way to nurture the planet and the communities who live on earth.[8] To nurture these restorative relationships, however, communities, workers, campesinas, and campesinos must have control over the destinies of their communities. The food system, and society, must be democratized. The pluriverse of communities who have fed Mexico for centuries and who maintained relationships between people and the land must be at the proverbial table.

NOTES

Introduction

1. "Traditional Mexican Cuisine—Ancestral, Ongoing Community Culture, the Michoacán Paradigm," UNESCO-Intangible Cultural Heritage (2010), accessed January 2, 2019, https://ich.unesco.org/en/RL/traditional-mexican-cuisine -ancestral-ongoing-community-culture-the-michoacan-paradigm-00400.

2. Eyder Peralta, "UNESCO Designates Traditional French and Mexican Cuisines Cultural Treasures," NPR, November 17, 2010, https://www.npr.org/sections/ thetwo-way/2010/11/17/131391343/unesco-designates-traditional-french-and -mexican-cuisines-cultural-treasures; Christine Delsol, "Mexican Cuisine Among Traditions Recognized by UNESCO," *SFGATE*, May 3, 2011, https:// www.sfgate.com/travel/article/Mexican-cuisine-among-traditions-recognized -by-2361808.php.

3. Olivier De Schutter, "Report of the Special Rapporteur on the Right to Food, Addendum, Mission to Mexico," June 13–20, 2011, United Nation General Assembly, Human Rights Council, January 17, 2012, A/HRC/19/59/Add.2.

4. De Schutter, "Report of the Special Rapporteur on the Right to Food."

5. Fox News, "Mexico Becomes Destination for World's Foodies," Fox News Media, August 23, 2012, https://www.foxnews.com/lifestyle/mexico-becomes -destination-for-worlds-foodies.

6. Adriana Gomez Licon, "Seeking New Flavours, Ancient Techniques, Star Chefs Turn Eyes to Mexican High-End Cuisine," Associated Press, August 23, 2012, https://www.yahoo.com/news/seeking-flavours-ancient-techniques-star-chefs -turn-eyes-170021190.html.

7. Gustavo Esteva and Catherine Marielle, eds., *Sin maíz, no hay país* (Mexico City: Consejo Nacional para la Cultura y las Artes, 2003), 11. All translations are mine unless otherwise indicated.

8. Laura Carlson, "NAFTA Is Starving Mexico," *Foreign Policy in Focus*, October 20, 2011, https://fpif.org/nafta_is_starving_mexico/.

9. Rius, *La basura que comemos: Transgénicos y comida chatarra* (Mexico City: Grijalbo, 2000).

10. Consejo Nacional de Evaluación de la Política de Desarrollo Social, "Pobreza en México: Resultados de pobreza en México 2022," accessed August 19, 2024, https://www.coneval.org.mx/Medicion/Paginas/PobrezaInicio.aspx.

11. Consejo Nacional de Evaluación de la Política de Desarrollo Social, *Informe de evaluación de la política de desarrollo social 2018*, 42; "Asegura que se erradicará pobreza alimentaria en Méxio," *Notimex*, November 18, 2010; Consejo Nacional de Evaluación de la Política de Desarrollo Social, "Pobreza en México."

12. See James M. Cypher, "Poverty (Mexico)," and Viviane Brachet-Márquez, "Social Welfare (Mexico): Since 1867," both in *Encyclopedia of Social Welfare History in North America*, ed. John M. Herrick, Paul Stuart, John Graham, Enrique C. Ochoa, and Ruth Britton (Thousand Oaks: SAGE, 2005).

13. "Pese a la pandemia de COVID–19 y la crisis no hay hambre en México: AMLO ante la ONU," *El Financiero*, September 22, 2020; Deyra Guerrero, "Falso que no hay hambre en México en medio de la pandemia," *Verificado*, September 24, 2020, https://verificado.com.mx/falso-que-no-hay-hambre-en-mexico-en -medio-de-la-pandemia.

14. Alysha Gálvez, *Eating NAFTA: Trade, Food Policies, and the Destruction of Mexico* (Oakland: University of California Press, 2018), xvii; Marla Dickerson, "Steeped in a New Tradition," *Los Angeles Times*, October 21, 2005; Ángeles Cruz Martínez, "La diabetes ya es la primera causa de muerte," *La Jornada*, November 11, 2011; Adriana Gomez Licon, "Mexico Tackles Epidemic of Childhood Obesity," *The Guardian*, October 21, 2011.

15. Gerardo Otero, *The Neoliberal Diet: Healthy Profits, Unhealthy People* (Austin: University of Texas Press, 2018).

16. Dolia Estevez, "Mexico's 15 Billionaire-Dollar Clans," *Forbes*, May 24, 2017, https://www.forbes.com/sites/doliaestevez/2017/05/24/mexicos-15-billion -dollar-clans/#7324619221cf.

17. Estevez, "Mexico's 15 Billionaire-Dollar Clans."

18. Arnold J. Bauer, "Millers and Grinders: Technology and Household Economy in Meso-America," *Agriculture History* 64. no. 1 (Winter 1990): 7–8.

19. Miguel Badillo, ed., *Morir en la miseria: Los 14 municipios más pobres de México* (Mexico City: Océano, 2009), 13.

20. Cited in Zósimo Camacho, "Desplazados por el hambre," in Badillo, *Morir en la Miseria*, 172.

21. Jeffrey M. Pilcher, "Industrial Tortillas and Folkloric Pepsi: The Nutritional Consequences of Hybrid Cuisines in Mexico," in *Food Nations: Selling Taste*

in Consumer Societies, ed. Warren Belasco and Philip Scranton (New York: Routledge, 2001).

22. Samuel Lowenberg, "The Plight of Mexico's Indigenous Women," *The Lancet*, May 15, 2010, http://www.thelancet.com/pdfs/journals/lancet/PIIS0140673610 607210.pdf.

23. Dickerson, "Steeped in a New Tradition."

24. De Schutter, "Report of the Special Rapporteur on the Right to Food."

25. Badillo, *Morir en la miseria*.

26. Enrique C. Ochoa, "Food History," in *Oxford University Bibliographies Online: Latin American Studies*, revised and updated, ed. Ben Vinson (New York: Oxford University Press, 2021), https://www.oxfordbibliographies.com/view/ document/obo-9780199766581/obo-9780199766581-0057.xml.

27. Charles Lyle Guthrie, "Riots in Seventeenth Century Mexico City: A Study of Social and Economic Conditions," in *Greater America: Essays in Honor of Herbert Eugene Bolton*, ed. Adele Ogden and Engel Sluiter (Berkeley: University of California Press, 1945), 245–246; Raymond L. Lee, "Grain Legislation in Colonial Mexico, 1575–1585," *Hispanic American Historical Review* 27, no. 4 (November 1947): 647–660; Enrique Florescano, "El abasto y la legislación de granos en el siglo XVI," *Historia Mexicana* 56, no. 14 (April–June 1965): 567–630.

28. Enrique Florescano, *Precios del maíz y crisis agrícolas en México, 1708–1810* (Mexico City: Ediciones ERA, 1969); Ernest Feder, *El imperialismo fresa: Una investigación sobre los mecanismos de la dependencia en la agricultura mexicana* (Mexico City: Nueva Sociologia, 1977); Roger Bartra, *Campesinado y poder político en México* (Mexico City: Ediciones ERA, 1982); Gustavo Esteva, *The Struggle for Rural Mexico* (South Hadley: Bergin & Garvey, 1983); David Barkin and Blanca Suárez, *El fin de la autosuficiencia alimentaria* (Mexico City: Océano, 1985).

29. Diego López Rosado, *El abasto de productos alimenticios en la ciudad de México* (Mexico City: Fondo de Cultura Económica, 1988).

30. Dawn Keremitsis, "Del metate al molino: La mujer mexicana de 1910 a 1940," *Historia Mexicana* 33, no. 2 (October–December 1983): 285–302.

31. Jeffrey M. Pilcher, *¡Que Vivian Los Tamales! Food and the Making of Mexican Identity* (Albuquerque: University of New Mexico Press, 1998).

32. Jeffrey M. Pilcher, *Planet Taco: A Global History of Mexican Food* (New York: Oxford University Press, 2012).

33. José Luis Juárez López, *La lenta emergencia de la comida Mexicana: Ambigüedades criollas, 1750–1800* (Mexico City: Miguel Angel Porrúa, 2005); José Luis Juárez López, *Nacionalismo culinario: La cocina mexicana en el siglo XX* (Mexico City: CONACULTA, 2008); José Luis Juárez López, *Engranaje culinario: La cocina mexicana en el siglo XIX* (Mexico City: CONACULTA, 2012).

34. See, for example, Sarah Bak-Geller Corona, "Wheat Versus Maize: Civilizing Dietary Strategies and Early Mexican Republicanism," *Journal of Interdisciplinary History of Ideas* 4, no. 8 (2015): 3–25; María del Pilar Zazueta, "Milk Against

Poverty: Nutrition and the Politics of Consumption in Twentieth-Century Mexico" (PhD diss., Columbia University, 2011); Joel Vargas Domínguez, "Metabolismo y nutrición en el México posrevolucionario: Eugenesia y clasificación de la población mexicana entre 1927 y 1943" (PhD diss., Universidad Nacional Autónoma de México, 2017).

35. Sandra Aguilar Rodríguez, "Cooking Modernity: Nutrition Policies, Class, and Gender in 1940s and 1950s Mexico," *The Americas* 64, no. 2 (October 2007): 177–178.

36. Sandra Aguilar Rodríguez, "Industrias del hogar: Mujeres, raza y moral en el México posrevolucionario," *Revista de Historia Iberoamericana* 9, no. 1 (April 2016): 10–27; Sandra Aguilar Rodríguez, "'Las penas con pan son menos': Race, Modernity and Wheat in Modern Mexico," *Bulletin of Spanish Studies* 97, no. 7 (May 2020): 539–565; Sandra Aguilar Rodríguez, "Between Women: Female Health Workers and the Struggle to Transform Diets in Rural Mexico, 1920–1960," *Jahrbuch für Geschichte Lateinamerikas/Anuario de Historua de América Latina* 59 (2022): 41–63.

37. Deborah Barndt, *Tangled Routes: Women, Work, and Globalization on the Tomato Trail*, 2nd ed. (Lanham, Md.: Rowman and Littlefield, 2008).

38. Carolina Bank Muñoz, *Transnational Tortillas: Race, Gender, and Shop-Floor Politics in Mexico and the United States* (Ithaca, N.Y.: Cornell University Press, 2008).

39. Meredith E. Abarca, *Voices in the Kitchen: Views of Food and the World from Working-Class Mexican and Mexican American Women* (College Station: Texas A&M Press, 2006); Teresa Mares and Devón G. Peña, "Urban Agriculture in the Making of Insurgent Spaces in Los Angeles and Seattle," in *Insurgent Public Space: Guerrilla Urbanism and the Remaking of Contemporary Cities*, ed. J. Hou (New York: Routledge, 2010).

40. See also Corrine Hawkes, "Uneven Dietary Development: Linking the Policies and Processes of Globalization with the Nutrition Transition, Obesity and Diet Related Chronic Diseases," *Globalization and Health* 2, no. 4 (March 2006); Emily Yates-Doerr, *The Weight of Obesity: Hunger and Global Health in Postwar Guatemala* (Oakland: University of California Press, 2015).

41. Gálvez, *Eating NAFTA*, 6.

42. Harriet Friedmann and Philip McMichael, "Agriculture and the State System: The Rise and Decline of National Agricultures, 1870 to the Present," *Sociologia Ruralis* 29, no. 2 (August 1989): 93–117.

43. Philip McMichael, *Food Regimes and Agrarian Questions* (Halifax: Fernwood, 2013).

44. Gerardo Otero, "The Neoliberal Food Regime in Latin America: State, Agribusiness Transnational Corporations and Biotechnology," *Canadian Journal of Development Studies* 33, no. 3 (September 2012); Otero, *The Neoliberal Diet*.

45. Aníbal Quijano, "Coloniality of Power, Eurocentrism, and Latin American," *Nepantla: Views from the South* 1, no. 3 (2000); Walter D. Mignolo, *The Darker*

Side of Modernity: Global Futures, Decolonial Options (Durham, N.C.: Duke University Press, 2011); Zilkia Janer, "(In)edible Nature: New World Food and Coloniality," *Cultural Studies* 21 (April 2007): 2–3.

46. Mignolo, *The Darker Side of Modernity*, 9.

47. Patricia Hill Collins, *Black Feminist Thought: Knowledge, Consciousness, and the Politics of Empowerment* (Boston: Unwin Hyman, 1990).

48. Janer, "(In)edible Nature," 385.

49. Vanessa Fonseca, "Fractal Capitalism and the Latinization of the U.S. Market" (PhD diss., University of Texas, 2003), 7.

50. María Elena García, *Gastropolitics and the Specter of Race: Stories of Capital, Culture, and Coloniality in Peru* (Oakland: University of California Press, 2021), 13.

51. See, for example, Kirsten Appendini, *De la milpa a los tortibonos: La restructuración de la política alimentaria en México*, 2nd ed. (Mexico City: El Colegio de México, 2001); Barkin and Suárez, *El fin de la autosuficiencia alimentaria*; José Luis Calva, *Crisis agrícola y alimentaria en México 1982–1988* (Mexico City: Fontamara, 1988); Blanca Rubio, *Resistencia campesina y explotación rural en México* (Mexico City: Ediciones ERA, 1987); Steven E. Sanderson, *The Transformation of Mexican Agriculture: International Structure and the Politics of Rural Change* (Princeton, N.J.: Princeton University Press, 1986).

52. Gustavo Esteva, "Re-Embedding Food in Agriculture," *Culture and Agriculture*, no. 48 (Winter 1994): 2–13; Gustavo Esteva and Catherine Marielle, eds., *Sin maíz, no hay país* (Mexico City: Consejo Nacional para la Cultura y las Artes, 2003).

53. Enrique C. Ochoa, *Feeding Mexico: The Political Uses of Food Since 1910* (Wilmington: SR Books, 2000).

54. Amílcar Challú, "Agricultural Crisis and Biological Well-Being in Mexico, 1730–1835," *Historia Agraria* 47 (April 2009): 21–44; Sarah Bak-Geller Corona, "Food Shortage in Colonial Mexico: Maize, Food Policies and the Construction of a Modern Political Culture, 1785–1807," in *The Routledge History of Food*, ed. Carol Heltosky (London: Routledge, 2019); Luis González, *San José de Gracia: Mexican Village in Transition*, trans. John Upton (Austin: University of Texas Press, 1974), 130; Alan Knight, *The Mexican Revolution*, vol. 2, *Counter-Revolution and Reconstruction* (Cambridge: Cambridge University Press, 1986), 420–423.

55. Badillo, *Morir en la miseria*.

56. Cormac O'Grady, *Famine: A Short History* (Princeton, N.J.: Princeton University Press, 2009), 6.

57. Gálvez, *Eating NAFTA*, 7.

58. Georgina Olson, "Hambre mata más que Narco," *Excelsior*, February 19, 2012, http://kiosko.net/mx/2012-02-19/np/mx_excelsior.html.

59. Leo Zuckerman, anchor of "La hora de opinar" televisa, June 2014.

60. "Pese a la pandemia de COVID–19 y la crisis no hay hambre en México: AMLO ante la ONU," *El Financiero*, September 22, 2020; Deyra Guerrero, "Falso que

no hay hambre en México en medio de la pandemia," *Verificado*, September 24, 2020, https://verificado.com.mx/falso-que-no-hay-hambre-en-mexico-en-medio-de-la-pandemia.

Chapter 1

1. Marcos Sandoval, "El maíz y los pueblos indios," in *Sin maíz, no hay país*, ed. Gustavo Esteva and Catherine Marielle (Mexico City: Consejo Nacional para la Cultura y las Artes, 2007), 65.
2. Meredith Abarca, "*Sazón*: The Flavors of Culinary Epistemology," in *Voices in the Kitchen: Views of Food and the World from Working-Class Mexican and Mexican American Women* (College Station: Texas A&M Press, 2006).
3. Gustavo Esteva, "Re-embedding Food in Agriculture," *Culture and Agriculture: Bulletin of the Culture and Agriculture Group*, no. 48 (Winter 1994): 6.
4. Guillermo Bonfil Batalla, *México Profundo: Reclaiming a Civilization*, trans. Philip A. Dennis (Austin: University of Texas Press, 1993).
5. Michael Blake, *Maize for the Gods: Unearthing the 9,000-Year History of Corn* (Oakland: University of California Press, 2015), 27.
6. Alba González Jácome, "Origenes, domesticación y dispersion del maíz (Zea mays) en México," in *El maíz nativo en México: Una aproximación crítica desde los estudios rurales*, ed. Ignacio López Moreno and Ivonne Viacarra Bordi (Mexico City: Juan Pablos Editor, S.A., 2016); Blake, *Maize for the Gods*, 86–99.
7. Roberto J. González, *Zapotec Science: Farming and Food in the Northern Sierra of Oaxaca* (Austin: University of Texas Press, 2001), 2.
8. Matthew O'Leary, "Maize: From Mexico to the World," *CIMMYT* (blog), May 20, 2016, https://www.cimmyt.org/blogs/maize-from-mexico-to-the-world/.
9. Patricia Fournier García, "El maíz y la tortilla en la historia prehispánica," in *La industria de la masa y la tortilla: Desarrollo y tecnologia*, ed. Felipe Torres, Ernesto Moreno, Isabel Chong, and Juan Quintanilla (Mexico City: Universidad Autónoma de México, 1996), 102–104; David Oseguera Parra and Rafael Ortega Packza, "Gente de maíz: Historia y diversidad en la cocina mexicana del maíz," in López Moreno and Vizcarra Bordi, *El maíz nativo en México*; *Hijos del maíz: Recetario del maíz* (Mexico City: Secretaría de Desarrollo Rural y equidad para las comunidades, 2020); Luis Alberto Vargas, "El Maíz Viajero sin Equipaje," *Anales de Antropología* 48, no. 1 (2014): 124.
10. Sophie D. Coe, *America's First Cuisines* (Austin: University of Texas Press, 1994), 149; Jeffrey M. Pilcher, *¡Qué Vivan los Tamales! Food and the Making of Mexican Identity* (Albuquerque: University of New Mexico Press, 1998), 10–11.
11. Cited in Fournier García, "El maíz y la tortilla en la historia prehispánica," 97–98.
12. Arturo Warman, *Corn and Capitalism: How a Botanical Bastard Grew to Global Dominance*, trans. Nancy L. Westrate (Chapel Hill: University of North Carolina Press, 2003), 35.
13. Warman *Corn and Capitalism*, 35.

14. Alfredo López Austin, "Cuatro mitos mesoamericanos del maíz," in *Sin maíz, no hay país*, ed. Gustavo Esteva and Catherine Marielle (Mexico City: Consejo Nacional para la Cultura y las Artes, 2007), 31.

15. See Roberto Cintli Rodríguez, *Our Sacred Maíz Is Our Mother: Indigeneity and Belonging in the Americas* (Tucson: University of Arizona Press, 2014), 60–61.

16. Blake, *Maize for the Gods*, 184.

17. Arnold J. Bauer, "Millers and Grinders: Technology and Household Economy in Meso-America," *Agricultural History* 64, no. 1 (Winter 1990): 7–8. On pellagra in the U.S. South, see Alfred Jay Bollett, "Politics and Pellagra: The Epidemic of Pellagra in the U.S. in the Early Twentieth Century," *Yale Journal of Biology and Medicine* 26 (1992): 211–21; in Africa, James C. McCann, *Maize and Grace: Africa's Encounter with a New World Crop, 1500–2000* (Cambridge, Mass.: Harvard University Press, 2005), 77 and 119.

18. See Arnold J. Bauer, "Millers and Grinders: Technology and Household Economy in Meso-America," *Agricultural History* 64, no. 1 (Winter 1990), 3; Sophie D. Coe, in *America's First Cuisines* (Austin: University of Texas Press, 1994), 14; Blake, *Maize for the Gods*, 176–182.

19. Blake, *Maize for the Gods*, 185.

20. Abarca, *Voices in the Kitchen*, 51.

21. Simon Fonteyne, José B. Castillo Caamal, Santaigo Lopez-Ridaura, Jelle Van Loon, Juan Espidio Balbuena, Leodegario Osorio Alcalá, Fermin Martínez Hernández, Sylvanus Odjo, and Nele Verhulst, "Review of Agronomic Research on the Milpa, the Traditional Polyculture System of Mesoamerica," *Frontiers in Agronomy* 5 (2023).

22. John C. Super, *Food, Conquest, and Colonization in Sixteenth-Century Spanish America* (Albuquerque: University of New Mexico Press, 1988), 68.

23. Coe, *America's First Cuisines*, 45.

24. Julieta Ramos-Elorduy and José Manuel Pino Moreno, "El consumo de insectos entre los aztecas," in *Conquista y comida: Consequencias del encuentro de dos mundos*, ed. Janet Long (Mexico City: Universidad Nacional Autónoma de México, 1996).

25. Super, *Food, Conquest, and Colonization*, 68; Joyce Marcus, "The Plant World of the Sixteenth and Seventeenth Lowland Maya," in *Maya Subsistence: Studies in Memory of Dennis E. Puleston*, ed. Kent V. Flannery (New York: Academic Press, 1982).

26. Bernardo Ortiz de Montellano, *Aztec Medicine, Health, and Nutrition* (New Brunswick, N.J.: Rutgers University Press, 1990), 101.

27. Ortiz de Montellano, *Aztec Medicine, Health, and Nutrition*, 107–108; Super, *Food, Conquest, and Colonization*, 68.

28. Ortiz de Montellano, *Aztec Medicine, Health, and Nutrition*, 102–106; M. A. B. Habib, Mashuda Parvin, Tim C. Hunton, and Mohammad R. Hasan, "A Review on Culture, Production and Use of Spirulina as Food for Humans and Feeds for Domestic Animals and Fish" (Rome: Food and Agricultural Organization, 2008).

29. Christina Chaey, "All About Spirulina, the Smoothie-Boosting Superfood of the Sea," *Bon Appétit*, May 15, 2015.

30. Sherburne F. Cook and Woodrow Borah, "Indian Food Production and Consumption in Central Mexico Before and After the Conquest (1500–1650)," in *Essays in Population History*, vol. 3, *Mexico and California* (Berkeley: University of California Press, 1979), 150.

31. See Saskia Sassen, *Expulsions: Brutality and Complexity in the Global Economy* (Cambridge, Mass.: Belknap Press of Harvard University Press, 2014); and Eric Holt-Giménez, *A Foodie's Guide to Capitalism: Understanding the Political Economy of What We Eat* (New York: Monthly Review Press, 2017).

32. Alfred Crosby, *The Columbian Exchange: Biological and Cultural Consequences of 1492* (Westport: Greenwood, 1972).

33. Sherburne F. Cook and Woodrow Norah, *The Indian Population of Central Mexico* (Berkeley: University of California Press, 1960); Alexander Koch, Chris Brierley, Mark M. Maslin, and Simon L. Lewis, "Earth System Impacts of European Arrival and Great Dying in the Americas after 1492," *Quaternary Science Reviews* 207 (2019): 13–36.

34. Jacques Soustelle, *Daily Life of the Aztecs: On the Eve of the Conquest*, trans. Patrick O'Brian (Stanford: Stanford University Press, 1961), 26.

35 Rebecca Earle, *The Body of the Conquistador: Food, Race and the Colonial Experience in Spanish America, 1492–1700* (Cambridge: Cambridge University Press, 2012), 66, 78–83.

36. Super, *Food, Conquest, and Colonization*, 36.

37. Ida Altman and James Lockhart, *Provinces of Early Mexico: Variants of Spanish American Regional Evolution* (Los Angeles: UCLA Latin American Center, 1976).

38. Zilkia Janer, "(In)edible Nature: New World Food and Coloniality," *Cultural Studies* 21, no. 2–3 (2007): 385.

39. Cited in Earle, *The Body of the Conquistador*, 165.

40. Cited in Rafael Chabrán, "Dr. Francisco Hernández Ate Tacos: The Foods and Drinks of the Mexican Treasury," *Diálogo* 18, no. 1 (2015): 22.

41. Cited in Earle, *The Body of the Conquistador*, 41.

42. Elinor G.K. Melville., *A Plague of Sheep: Environmental Consequences of the Conquest of Mexico* (Cambridge: Cambridge University Press, 1997).

43. François Chevalier, *Land and Society in Colonial Mexico: The Great Hacienda*, trans. Alvin Eustis (Berkeley: University of California Press, 1963), 93.

44. Quoted in Chevalier, *Land and Society in Colonial Mexico*, 93–94.

45. Melville, *A Plague of Sheep*, 39–40.

46. Pilcher, *¡Qué Vivan los Tamales!*, 35.

47. Quoted in José Luis Juárez López, *La lenta emergencia de la comida Mexicana: Ambigüedades criollas, 1750–1800* (Mexico City: Miguel Ángel Porrúa, 2000), 133.

48. Quoted in Juárez López, *La lenta emergencia de la comida Mexicana*, 111.

49. Quoted in Juárez López, *La lenta emergencia de la comida Mexicana*, 112.

50. Florescano, *Precios del maíz y crisis agrícolas en México*.

51. Amílcar Eduardo Challú, "Grain Markets, Food Supply Policies and Living Standards in Late Colonial Mexico" (PhD diss., Harvard University, 2007), 120–132.

52. Challú, "Grain Markets, Food Supply Policies and Living Standards in Late Colonial Mexico."

53. Amílcar E. Challú, "The Great Decline: Biological Well-Being and Living Standards in Mexico, 1730–1840," in *Living Standards in Latin American History: Height, Welfare, and Development, 1750–2000*, ed. Ricardo D. Salvatore, John H. Coatsworth, and Amilcar E. Challú (Cambridge, Mass.: Harvard University Press, 2010).

54. John Tutino, *The Mexican Heartland: How Communities Shaped Capitalism, A Nation, and World History, 1500–2000* (Princeton, N.J.: Princeton University Press, 2018), 150–155.

55. Tutino, *The Mexican Heartland*, 181.

56. Harry Cross, "Dieta y nutrición en el medio rural de Zacatecas y San Luis Potosí (Siglos XVIII y XIX)," *Historia Mexicana* 69, no. 3 (1981): 10.

57. Cross, "Dieta y nutrición," 9–13.

58. Challú, "Grain Markets, Food Supply Policies and Living Standards in Late Colonial Mexico," 31.

59. Cited in Matlide Souto Mantecón, "De la cocina a la mesa," in *Historia de la vida cotidinana en México: Tomo IV Bienes y vivencias, el siglo XIX*, ed. Ann Staples (Mexico City: El Colegio de México, 2005), 23.

60. Souto Mantecón, "De la cocina a la mesa," 21.

61. John H. Coatsworth, *El impacto económico de los ferrocarriles en el porfiriato: Crecimiento contra desarrollo* (Mexico City: Sepsetentas, 1976); Stephen H. Haber, *Industry and Underdevelopment: The Industrialization of Mexico, 1890–1940* (Stanford: Stanford University Press, 1989).

62. John Mason Hart, *Empire and Revolution: The Americans in Mexico Since the Civil War* (Berkeley: University of California Press, 2002), 506.

63. Hart, *Empire and Revolution*, 260.

64. John H. Coatsworth, "Railroads, Landholding, and Agrarian Protest in the Early Porfiriato," *Hispanic American Historical Review* 54, no. 1 (1974): 48–71; Coatsworth, *El impacto económico*, 116–134; Paul Vanderwood, *Disorder and Progress: Bandits, Police, and Mexican Development* (Lincoln: University of Nebraska Press, 1981).

65. Alicia Hernandez Chávez, *Breve Historia de Morelos* (Mexico City: El Colegio de México, 2002); Paul Hart, *Bitter Harvest: The Social Transformation of Morelos Mexico and the Origins of the Zapatista Revolution, 1849–1910* (Albuquerque: University of New Mexico Press, 2005), 149–150.

66. John H. Coatsworth, "Anotaciones sobre la producción de alimentos durante el porfiriato," *Historia Mexicana* 26, no. 2 (October–December 1976), 167–187.

67. Simon Miller, "The Mexican Hacienda Between the Insurgency and the Revolution: Maize Production and Commercial Triumph on the *Temporal*," *Journal of Latin American Studies* 16, no. 2 (November 1984): 309–336.

68. Moramay López-Alonso, "Living Standards of the Mexican Laboring Classes, 1850–1950: An Anthropometric Approach," in *Living Standards in Latin American History*, ed. Ricardo D. Salvatore, John H. Coatsworth, and Amilcar E. Challú (Cambridge, Mass.: Harvard University Press, 2010), 93.

69. John H. Coatsworth, "Patterns of Rural Rebellion in Latin America: Mexico in Comparative Perspective," in *Riot, Rebellion, and Revolution: Rural and Social Conflict in Mexico*, ed. Friedrich Katz (Princeton, N.J.: Princeton University Press, 1988), 57.

70. Cited in Pilcher, *¡Qué Vivan los Tamales!*, 77.

71. José Luis Juárez López, *Engranaje culinario: La cocina mexicana en el siglo XIX* (Mexico City: CONACULTA, 2012), 133.

72. Juárez López, *Engranaje culinario*, 132–134.

73. Pilcher, *¡Qué Vivan los Tamales!*, 82.

74. Pilcher, *¡Qué Vivan los Tamales!*, 83. For a general discussion of the discourse of criminality and race, see Robert M. Buffington, *Criminal and Citizen in Modern Mexico* (Lincoln: University of Nebraska Press, 2000).

75. W. E. Carson, *Mexico: The Wonderland of the South* (New York: MacMillan Co., 1914), 284–285.

76. Wallace Thompson, *The People of Mexico: Who They Are and How They Live* (New York: Harper and Brothers, 1921), 283–284.

77. Jason Ruiz, *Americans in the Treasure House: Travel to Porfirian Mexico and the Cultural Politics of Empire* (Austin: University of Texas Press, 2014), 144–151 and 166–168.

78. Gilbert G. Gonzalez, *Culture of Empire: American Writers, Mexico, and Mexican Immigrants, 1880–1930* (Austin: University of Texas Press, 2004).

79. Enrique C. Ochoa, "From Tortillas to Low-Carb Wraps: Capitalism and Mexican Food in Los Angeles Since the 1920s," *Diálogo: An Interdisciplinary Journal* (Spring 2015).

80. Robert Weis, *Bakers and Basques: A Social History of Bread in Mexico* (Albuquerque: University of New Mexico Press, 2012), 64; Pilcher, *¡Qué Vivan los Tamales!*

81. Carson, *Mexico*, 139.

82. Salvador Novo, *Cocina mexicana o historia gastronómica de la Ciudad de México* (Mexico City: Editorial Porrúa, 1967), 129; Pilcher, *¡Qué Vivan los Tamales!*, 64.

83. Novo, *Cocina mexicana*, 13.

84. Haber, *Industry and Underdevelopment*.

85. Jeffrey M. Pilcher, *The Sausage Rebellion: Public Health, Private Enterprise and Meat in Mexico City, 1890–1917* (Albuquerque: University of New Mexico Press, 2006), 75–77.

86. Pilcher, *The Sausage Rebellion*, 3.

87. Pilcher, *The Sausage Rebellion*.

88. Weis, *Bakers and Basques*, 34–36.

89. Weis, *Bakers and Basques*, 44.

90. Weis, *Bakers and Basques*, 62–82.

91. Ingrid Bleynat, *Vendor's Capitalism: A Political Economy of Public Markets in Mexico City* (Stanford: Stanford University Press, 2021), 45, 50–51.

Chapter 2

1. Cited in Joseph Cotter, "Cultural Wars and New Technologies: The Discourse of Plant Breeding and Professionalisation of Mexican Agronomy, 1880–1994," *Science, Technology, and Society* 5, no. 2 (2000): 147–148.

2. Cotter, "Cultural Wars and New Technologies," 147; Joseph Cotter, "The Origins of the Green Revolution in Mexico: Continuity or Change?," in *Latin America in the 1940s: War and Postwar Transitions*, ed. David Rock (Berkeley: University of California Press, 1994), 229; see also Joseph Cotter, *Troubled Harvest: Agronomy and Revolution in Mexico, 1880–2002* (Westport: Praeger, 2003).

3. Enrique C. Ochoa, *Feeding Mexico: The Political Uses of Food Since 1910* (Wilmington: Scholarly Resources, 2000), 27; John Womack, "The Mexican Revolution, 1910–1920," in *Mexico Since Independence*, ed. Leslie Bethell (New York: Cambridge University Press, 1991), 133.

4. Ochoa, *Feeding Mexico*, 30.

5. Alan Knight, *The Mexican Revolution*, vol. 2, *Counter-Revolution and Reconstruction* (Cambridge: Cambridge University Press, 1986), 413.

6. David G. LaFrance, *Revolution in Mexico's Heartland: Politics, War, and State Building in Puebla, 1913–1920* (Wilmington: SR Books, 2003), 179.

7. Luis González, *San José de Gracia: Mexican Village in Transition*, trans. John Upton (Austin: University of Texas Press, 1974), 130–131.

8. Knight, *The Mexican Revolution*, vol. 2, 420–423.

9. Cited in Ochoa, *Feeding Mexico*, 30.

10. Enrique C. Ochoa, "Lic. Moisés T. de la Peña: The Economist on Horseback," in *The Human Tradition in Mexico*, ed. Jeffrey M. Pilcher (Wilmington: SR Books, 2003); James C. Scott, *Seeing Like a State: How Certain Schemes to Improve the Human Condition Have Failed* (New Haven, Conn.: Yale University Press, 1998).

11. See Secretaría de la Economía Nacional, Dirección General de Estadística, *Informes sobre las principales estadísticas Mexicanas* (Mexico City, 1941); Carlos Alberto Contreras and Peter L. Reich, "Numbers and the State: An Overview of Government Statistical Compilation in Mexico Since the Colonial Period," in *The Statistical Abstract of Latin America*, vol. 31, ed. James W. Wilkie, Carlos Alberto Contreras, and Catherine Komisaruk (Los Angeles: UCLA Latin American Center Publications, 1995); Leticia Mayer Celis, *Entre el infierno de una realidad y el cielo de un imaginario: Estadística y comunidad científica en el México de la primera mitad del siglo XIX* (Mexico City: El Colegio de México,

1999); Sergio de la Peña, "Visión Global de los orígenes de la estadística: Guía de Forasteros y Nativos a la historia de la estadística económica nacional," in *La estadística económica en México: Los orígenes,* ed. Sergio de la Peña and James W. Wilkie (Mexico City: Siglo XXI, 1994).

12. See, for example, Moisés T. de La Peña, *La mexicanización del indio: Un problema económico* (Mexico City: Revista de Economía, 1945); Cynthia Hewitt de Alcántara, *Anthropological perspectives on Rural Mexico* (London: Routledge & Kegan Paul, 1984), 8–29; Stephen E. Lewis, "The Nation, Education, and the 'Indian Problem' in Mexico, 1920–1940," in *The Eagle and the Virgin: Nation and Cultural Revolution in Mexico, 1920–1940,* ed. Mary Kay Vaughn and Stephen E. Lewis (Durham, N.C.: Duke University Press, 2006).

13. James W. Wilkie, *The Mexican Revolution: Federal Expenditure and Social Change Since 1910* (Berkeley: University of California Press, 1970), 160.

14. Elsie Rockwell, "Schools of the Revolution: Enacting and Contesting State Forms in Tlaxcala, 1910–1930," in *Everyday Forms of State Formation: Revolution and the Negotiation of Rule in Modern Mexico,* ed. Gilbert M. Joseph and Daniel Nugent (Durham, N.C.: Duke University Press, 1994); Mary Kay Vaughn, "Nationalizing the Countryside: Schools and Rural Communities in the 1930s," in *The Eagle and the Virgin: Nation and Cultural Revolution in Mexico, 1920–1940,* ed. Mary Kay Vaughn and Stephen E. Lewis (Durham, N.C.: Duke University Press, 2006).

15. Michael A. Ervin, "The 1930 Agrarian Census in Mexico: Agronomists, Middle Politics, and the Negotiation of Data Collection," *Hispanic American Historical Review* 87, no. 3 (2007): 537–570.

16. Cited in Ervin, "The 1930 Agrarian Census in Mexico," 548.

17. Cited in Ervin, "The 1930 Agrarian Census in Mexico," 549.

18. Cited in Ervin, "The 1930 Agrarian Census in Mexico," 550.

19. Secretaría de la Economía Nacional, *Informes sobre las principales estadísticas Mexicanas,* 79.

20. Ervin, "The 1930 Agrarian Census in Mexico," 550.

21. Calculated from Secretaría de la Economía Nacional, Dirección General de Estadística, *Medidas Regionales, Censo-Agrícola-Ganadero de 1930* (México, 1933).

22. Ervin, "The 1930 Agrarian Census in Mexico."

23. Cited in Cotter, "Cultural Wars and New Technologies," 147.

24. Miguel E. Schultz, *El cultivo del maíz: ¡Selecciona tu semilla de maíz en el campo!* (Mexico City: Editorial de Izquierda de la Cámara de Diputados, 1937), 24–40.

25. Dana Markiewicz, *The Mexican Revolution and the Limits of Agrarian Reform, 1915–1946* (Boulder: Lynn Rienner, 1993), 191.

26. "Discurso del general Cárdenas al protestar como presiente de la república ante el congreso de la union, el 30 de noviembre de 1934," in Luis González González, *Los presidentes de México ante la nación: Informes, manifiestos, y*

documentos de 1821 a 1966, vol. 4 (Mexico City: Cámara de Diputados, 1966), 11–15; Ochoa, *Feeding Mexico*, 41.

27. Ochoa, "Lic. Moisés T. de la Peña," in *The Human Tradition in Mexico*, 172.

28. Christopher R. Boyer, *Becoming Campesino: Politics, Identity, and Agrarian Struggle in Postrevolutionary Michoacán, 1920–1935* (Stanford: Stanford University Press, 2003).

29. Ochoa, *Feeding Mexico*, 14, 39–70.

30. Ochoa, *Feeding Mexico*; *La CTM en la lucha por la alimentación* (Mexico City: Sistema de Distribuidoras CONASUPO, 1987), 46–50.

31. AGN-Departamento Autónoma de Trabajo, various cajas; Ochoa, *Feeding Mexico*, 29–31.

32. Joel Vargas Domínguez, "Las estadísticas de consume y el cesto de provisiones en México en las décadas de 1920 y 1930," *Estudios Sociales del Estado* 8, no. 16 (2022): 59–64; Joel Vargas Domínguez, "The Construction of the Minimum Wage and Nutrition in the Early 20th Century," *Historia Crítica*, no. 87 (2023): 115–118.

33. Jeffrey Bortz and Marco Aguila, "Earning a Living: A History of Real Wage Studies in Twentieth-Century Mexico," *Latin American Research Review* 41, no. 2 (June 2006); Jeffrey Lawrence Bortz, *Los salarios reales industrials en la ciudad de México, 1939–1975* (Mexico City: Fondo de Cultura Económica, 1988), 11–63.

34. Gen. Rafael Sánchez Tapia, Secretaría de la Economía Nacional, *Informe de las actividades dessarrolladas por la Secretería de la Economía Nacional durante el period de 19 de Agosto de 1934 al 31 de julio de 1935* (Mexico City: Talleres Gráficos de la Nación, 1935), 10–11.

35. Ochoa, *Feeding Mexico*, 32–33; México, Secretaría de la Economía Nacional, *Revista de Estadística* 3, no. 12 (December 1940).

36. Guillermo Martínez Domínguez, *Intentos de control de precios en México* (Mexico City, 1950), ix–x.

37. Martínez Domínguez, *Intentos de control de precios en México*, 72.

38. Arnoldo Córdova, *La política de masas del cardenismo* (Mexico City: Ediciones ERA, 1974).

39. Sandra Aguilar-Rodriguez, "Cooking Modernity: Nutrition Policies, Class, and Gender in 1940s and 1950s Mexico City," *The Americas* 64, no. 2 (October 2007): 177–205.

40. Nichole Sanders, *Gender and Welfare in Mexico: The Consolidation of a Postrevolutionary State* (University Park: Penn State University Press, 2011), 45.

41. Sanders, *Gender and Welfare in Mexico*, 29.

42. Manuel Martínez Báez, *Libro para la madre mexicana* (Mexico City: Talleres Linotipográficos de la Beneficiencia Pública, 1934), 1.

43. Sanders, *Gender and Welfare in Mexico*; Aguilar-Rodriguez, "Cooking Modernity."

44. Mary Kay Vaughn, "Rural Women's Literacy and Education During the Mexican Revolution: Subverting a Patriarchal Event," in *Women of the Mexican Countryside, 1850–1990*, ed. Heather Fowler-Salamini and Mary Kay Vaughn (Tucson: University of Arizona Press, 1994), 113–114.

45. José Quintín Olascoaga, *Alimentación normal del mexicano* (Mexico City: Instituto Federal de Capacitación de Magisterio, Secretaría de Educación Pública, 1963), 7.

46. Vaughn, "Rural Women's Literacy," 113–114; Claudia Agostoni, "Instruir, confortar y cuidar: Enfermeras visitadoras y de hospitales en México, 1920–1950," *Nuevo Mundo Mundos Nuevos*, no. 19 (October 2019).

47. Cited in Sanders, *Gender and Welfare in Mexico*, 61–64.

48. Cited in Sanders, *Gender and Welfare in Mexico*, 60; María del Pilar Zazueta, "Milk Against Poverty: Nutrition and the Politics of Consumption in Twentieth-Century Mexico" (PhD diss., Columbia University, 2011), 193.

49. Sandra Aguilar-Rodríguez, "Alimentando a la nación: Género y nutrición en México (1940–1960)," *Revista de Estudios Sociales* (Bogotá), no. 29 (April 2008): 28.

50. Cited in Sanders, *Gender and Welfare in Mexico*, 60.

51. Aguilar-Rodríguez, "Cooking Modernity," 192; Sandra Aguilar Rodríguez, "Alimentando a la nación: Género y nutrición en México (1940–1960)," *Revista de Estudios Sociales* (Bogotá), no. 29 (Abril de 2008): 28.

52. Aguilar-Rodríguez, "Cooking Modernity," 200.

53. Zazueta, "Milk Against Poverty," 86–103.

54. Manuel Gamio, "Diet Reforms for Indians and Mestizos," *Boletín Indigenista* 8, no. 3–4 (December 1948): 193.

55. Richmond K. Anderson, José Calvo, Gloria Serrano, and George C. Payne, "A Study of the Nutritional Status and Food Habits of Otomi Indians in the Mezquital Valley of Mexico," *American Journal of Public Health* (August 1946): 886.

56. Anderson et al., "A Study of the Nutritional Status," 902.

57. Cited in Zazueta, "Milk Against Poverty," 99.

58. Zazueta, "Milk Against Poverty," 192; Sandra Aguilar Rodríguez, "Between Women: Female Health Workers and the Struggle to Transform Diets in Rural Mexico, 1920–1960," *Anuario de Historia de América Latina* 59 (2022): 41–63.

59. Wilkie, *The Mexican Revolution*, 227–229.

60. James V. Mestaz, *Strength from the Waters: A History of Indigenous Mobilization in Northwest Mexico* (Lincoln: University of Nebraska Press, 2022); Nicole Mottier, "Calculating Pragmatism: The High Politics of the Banco Ejidal in Twentieth-Century Mexico," *The Americas* 74, no. 3 (July 2017): 331–363.

61. See Ochoa, *Feeding Mexico*, 71–156; Cynthia Hewitt de Alcántara, *La modernización de la agricultura Mexicana, 1940–1970* (Mexico City: Siglo XXI Editores, 1978), 56–98.

62. Deborah Fitzgerald, "Exporting American Agriculture: The Rockefeller Foundation in Mexico, 1943–1953," in *Missionaries of Science: The Rockefeller Foundation and Latin America*, ed. Marco Cueto (Bloomington: Indiana University Press, 1994); Cotter, *Troubled Harvest*.

63. Cited in Gustavo Esteva, "Hosting the Otherness of the Other: The Case of the Green Revolution," in *Decolonizing Knowledge: From Development to Dialogue*, ed. Frédérique Apffel-Marglin and Stephen A. Marglin (Oxford: Clarendon Press, 1996), 255.

64. Matthew Caire-Pérez, "A Different Shade of Green: Efraím Hernández, Chapingo, and Mexico's Green Revolution, 1950–1967" (PhD diss., University of Oklahoma, 2016), 9.

65. Joseph Cotter, "The Rockefeller Foundation's Mexican Agricultural Project: A Cross-Cultural Encounter, 1943–1949," in *Missionaries of Science: The Rockefeller Foundation and Latin America*, ed. Marco Cueto (Bloomington: Indiana University Press, 1994), 107.

66. Esteva, "Hosting the Otherness of the Other," 249.

67. Ochoa, *Feeding Mexico*, 140–144; Hugo Azpeitia Gómez, *Compañía Exportadora e Importadora Mexicana, S.A. (1949–1958): Conflicto y abasto alimentario* (Mexico City: CIESAS, 1994).

68. Nathaniel Whetten, *Rural Mexico* (Chicago: University of Chicago Press, 1948), 195.

69. Hewitt de Alcántara, *La modernización de la agricultura Mexicana*, 69.

70. Gladys I. McCormick, *The Logic of Compromise in Mexico: How the Countryside Was Key to the Emergence of Authoritarianism* (Chapel Hill: University of North Carolina Press, 2016), 47.

71. John Gledhill, *Casí Nada: A Study of Agrarian Reform in the Homeland of Cardenismo* (Albany: State University of New York Press, 1991).

72. Ochoa, *Feeding Mexico*, 136–140.

73. Verónica Castillo-Muñoz, "Historical Roots of Rural Migration: Land Reform, Corn Credit, and the Displacement of Rural Farmers in Nayarit Mexico, 1900–1952," *Mexican Studies / Estudios Mexicanos* 29, no. 1 (Winter 2013): 36–60.

74. Martínez Domínguez, *Intentos de control de precios en México*, 72.

75. Ochoa, *Feeding Mexico*, 110.

76. Castillo-Muñoz, "Historical Roots of Rural Migration," 52.

77. Lourdes Arizpe, *Campesinado y migración* (Mexico City: Secretaría de Educación Pública, 1985), 9.

78. Tanalís Padilla, *Rural Resistance in the Land of Zapata: The Jaramillista Movement and the Myth of the Pax Priísta, 1940–1962* (Durham, N.C.: Duke University Press, 2008); McCormick, *The Logic of Compromise in Mexico*.

79. Olga Pellicer de Brody and José Luis Reyna, *Historia de la Revolución Mexicana, período 1952–1960: El afianzamiento de la estabilidad política* (Mexico City: El Colegio de México, 1978), 123–130.

80. Hubert C. De Grammont, "La Unión General de Obreros y Campesinos de México," in *Historia de la cuestión agraria: Política estatal y conflictos agrarios, 1950–1970* (Mexico City: Siglo XXI Editores, 1989); Gladys McCormick, "Looking for Truths in the Constructed Archive: The Case of Jacinto López and the Politics of Accommodation in Rural Mexico," *A Contracorriente* 13, no. 3 (Spring 2016): 77–100.

81. See, for example, Aleida García Aguirre, *La revolución que llegaría: Experiencias de solidaridad y redes de maestros y normalistas en el movimiento campesino y la guerrilla moderna en Chihuahua, 1960–1968* (Mexico City, 2015); Tanalís Padilla, "'Latent Sites of Agitation': Normalistas Rurales and Chihuahua's Agrarian Struggle in the 1960s," in *México Beyond 1968: Revolutionaries, Radicals, and Repression During the Global Sixties and Subversive Seventies*, ed. Jaime M. Pensado and Enrique C. Ochoa (Tucson: University of Arizona Press, 2018).

82. Alexander Aviña, *Specters of Revolution: Peasant Guerillas in the Cold War Mexican Countryside* (New York: Oxford University Press, 2014); Fernando Herrera Calderón and Adela Cedillo, eds., *Challenging Authoritarianism in Mexico: Revolutionary Struggles and the Dirty War, 1964–1982* (New York: Routledge, 2011); Pensado and Ochoa, *México Beyond 1968*; McCormick, *The Logic of Compromise in Mexico*, 133–161.

83. Alexander Aviña, "A War Against Poor People: Dirty Wars and Drug Wars in 1970s Mexico," in Pensado and Ochoa, *México Beyond 1968*; Ochoa, *Feeding Mexico*; Viviane Brachet de Márquez, *The Dynamics of Domination: State, Class, and Reform in Mexico, 1910–1990* (Pittsburgh: University of Pittsburgh Press, 1995); Paul Gillingham and Benjamin T. Smith, eds., *Dictablanda: Politics, Work, and Culture in Mexico, 1938–1968* (Durham, N.C.: Duke University Pres, 2014).

84. Ochoa, *Feeding Mexico*, 181–184.

85. Jonathan Fox, *The Politics of Food in Mexico: State Power and Social Mobilization* (Ithaca, N.Y.: Cornell University Press, 1992), 92–96.

86. Fox, *The Politics of Food in Mexico*, 193–200.

87. Fox, *The Politics of Food in Mexico*, 194.

88. Fox, *The Politics of Food in Mexico*, 196–197.

89. Fox, *The Politics of Food in Mexico*, 205.

90. Calculated from Rosa Elena Montes de Oca Luján y Gerardo Escudero Columna, "Las empresas transnacionales en la industria alimentaria mexicana," *Comercio Exterior* 31, no. 9 (September 1981); and Thomas Horst, *At Home Abroad: A Study of the Domestic and Foreign Operations of the American Food-Processing Industry* (Cambridge: Ballinger, 1974), 8.

91. Patricia Jane Hall, "Five Multinational Food Processing Firms in Mexico: A Contribution to Underdevelopment?" (PhD diss., University of Washington, 1980), 105.

92. Montes de Oca Luján and Escudero Columna, "Las empresas transnacionales," 992–993.

93. Cited in Hall, "Five Multinational Food Processing Firms in Mexico," 106.

94. Paredes López and Gallardo Navarro, "La industria alimentaria en México y la penetración," 1429.

95. Montes de Oca Luján and Escudero Columna, "Las empresas transnacionales," 988.

96. Montes de Oca Luján and Escudero Columna, "Las empresas transnacionales," 994–996.

97. Bernardo Sepúlveda and Antonio Chumacero, eds., *La inversión extranjera en México* (Mexico City: El Fondo de Cultura Económica, 1973), 58.

98. Stephen R. Niblo, *Mexico in the 1940s: Modernity, Politics, and Corruption* (Wilmington: SR Books, 1999); Julio Moreno, *Yankee Don't Go Home: Mexican Nationalism, American Business Culture, and the Shaping of Modern Mexico, 1920–1950* (Chapel Hill: University of North Carolina Press, 2003).

99. Moreno, *Yankee Don't Go Home*, 113.

100. Octavio Paredes López and Yoja Gallardo Navarro, "La industria alimentaria en México y la penetración de las empresas transnacionales," *Comercio Exterior* 26, no. 12 (December 1976): 1434.

101. Montes de Oca Luján and Escudero Columna, "Las empresas transnacionales," 992.

102. Miguel Buendía, "Papitas," *El Día*, December 6, 1966, reprinted in Manuel Buendía, *Los Empresarios* (Mexico City: Océano, 1986), 19–20.

103. Montes de Oca Luján and Escudero Columna, "Las empresas transnacionales," 995n18.

104. Cited in Bernardo Olmedo Carranza, *Capital transnacional y consumo: El caso del sistema agroalimentario en México* (Mexico City: Universidad Nacional Aútonoma de México, 1986), 113.

105. Javier Moreno Lázaro, "Los españoles y la revolución comercian mexicana: Las cadenas de supermercados, 1921–2011," *Investigaciones de Historia Económica* 8, no. 2 (June 2012): 71; Juan Muldoon and Daniel Servitje, *El comercio de alimentos en México* (Mexico City: Trillas, 1984), 106–113.

106. Rello and Sodi, *Abasto y distribución de alimentos*, 202–205.

107. Rello and Sodi, *Abasto y distribución de*, 72–75.

108. Ingrid Bleyant, *Vendors' Capitalism: A Political Economy of Public Markets* (Stanford: Stanford University Press, 2021), 136–137.

109. María del Pilar Zazueta, "Milk Against Poverty: Nutrition and the Politics of Consumption in Twentieth-Century Mexico" (PhD diss., Columbia University, 2011), 331.

110. Zazueta, "Milk Against Poverty," 332–333.

111. Louise E. Walker, *Waking from the Dream: Mexico's Middle Classes After 1968* (Stanford: Stanford University Press, 2013), 105–140.

112. CONASUPO, *Platillos Populares Mexicanos* (Mexico City: Talleres Gráficos de la Nación, 1971).

113. See Gustavo Esteva, *The Struggle for Rural Mexico* (South Hadley: Bergin & Garvey, 1983); and David Barkin and Blanca Suárez, *El fin de la autosuficiencia alimentaria* (Mexico City: Océano, 1985).

Chapter 3

1. Jenni Spinner, "Food Business Is Booming South of the Border," *Bakery & Snacks*, November 21, 2013, https://www.bakeryandsnacks.com/Article/2013/11/21/Mexican-food-processing-sector-is-growing.

2. Humberto González, "Specialization on a Global Scale and Agrifood Vulnerability: 30 Years of Export Agriculture in Mexico," *Development Studies Research* 1, no. 1 (2014): 295–310.

3. There is a voluminous literature on the impact of restructuring in Mexico since the 1980s see, for example, James M. Cypher and Raúl Delgado Wise, *Mexico's Economic Dilemma: The Developmental Failure of Neoliberalism* (Lanham, Md.: Rowman and Littlefield, 2010); Enrique Dussel Peters, *La economía de la polarización: Teoría y evolución del cambio estructural de las manufacturas mexicanas (1988–1996)* (Mexico City: Universidad Nacional Autónoma de México, 1997); Gerardo Otero, ed., *Neoliberalism Revisited: Economic Restructuring and Mexico's Political Future* (Boulder: Westview Press, 1996).

4. Elvira Concheiro Bórquez, *El gran acuerdo: Gobierno y empresarios en la modernización salinista* (Mexico City: Ediciones ERA, 1996); Celso Garrido, *Desarrollo económico y procesos de financiamiento en México: Transformaciones contemporáneas y dilemas actuales* (Mexico City: Siglo XXI editores, 2005).

5. Jorge Zepeda Patterson, ed., *Los amos de México* (Mexico City: Editorial Planeta Mexicana, 2007). For a discussion of the creation of Mexico's power elite, see Roderic Ai Camp, *Mexico's Mandarins: Crafting and Power Elite for the Twenty-First Century* (Berkeley: University of California Press, 2002).

6. Robert Jones Shafer, *Mexican Business Organizations: History and Analysis* (Syracuse: Syracuse University Press, 1973); Ben Ross Schneider, "Why Is Mexican Business So Organized?," *Latin American Research Review* 37, no. 1 (2002): 94.

7. Schneider, "Why Is Mexican Business So Organized?," 97.

8. Cristina Puga, *Los empresarios organizados y el tratado de libre comercio de América de Norte* (Mexico City: UNAM/Miguel Ángel Porrúa, 2004); Richard Roman and Edur Velasco Arregui, *Continental Crucible: Big Business, Workers and Unions in the Transformation of North America*, 2nd ed. (Halifax: Fernwood / PM Press, 2015), 32–47.

9. Jorge Basavae Kunhardt, *Los grupos de capital financiero en México (1974–1995)* (Mexico City: UNAM and El Caballito, 1996), 167–169.

10. Basavae Kunhardt, *Los grupos de capital financiero*, 169–177.

11. Judith A. Teichman, *Privitization and Political Change in Mexico* (Pittsburgh: University of Pittsburgh Press, 1995), 130–131.

12. Concheiro Bórquez, *El gran acuerdo*, 80–82; Teichman, *Privitization and Political Change in Mexico*, 130–154.

13. Cited in Concheiro Bórquez, *El gran acuerdo*, 60.

14. Basavae Kunhardt, *Los grupos de capital financiero*, 245.

15. Rafael Rodríguez Castañeda, "La cena millionaria" in *Salinas en Proceso* (Mexico City: Random House Mondadori, 2012), 150–156; Andrés Oppenheimer, *Bordering on Chaos: Mexico's Roller-Coaster Journey Toward Prosperity* (Boston: Little, Brown, 1998), 83–110.

16. Oppenheimer, *Bordering on Chaos*, 87.

17. Cited in Rodríguez Castañeda, "La cena millionaria," 154.

18. Teichman, *Privitization and Political Change in Mexico*, 25.

19. Teichman, *Privitization and Political Change in Mexico*, 188–189.

20. Dag MacLeod, *Downsizing the State: Privatization and the Limits of Neoliberal Reform in Mexico* (University Park: Penn State University Press, 2004), 98–99.

21. Sean Kilachand, "Forbes History: The Original 1987 List of International Billionaires," *Forbes*, March 21, 2012, http://www.forbes.com/sites/seankilachand/2012/03/21/forbes-history-the-original-1987-list-of-international-billionaires/2/; John Summa, "Mexico's New Super-Billionaires," *Multinational Monitor*, November 1994; Dolia Estevez, "With Carlos Slim Leading the Way, Mexico's Billionaires Have a Better Year," *Forbes*, March 3, 2015, http://www.forbes.com/sites/doliaestevez/2015/03/03/with-carlos-slim-leading-the-way-mexico's-billionaires-have-a-better-year/.

22. Calculated from Rob LaFranco and Chase Peterson-Withorn, "The Richest in 2023," *Forbes*, accessed April 28, 2023, https://www.forbes.com/real-time-billionaires/#3d68b5793d78.

23. Enrique C. Ochoa, *Feeding Mexico: The Political Uses of Food Since 1910* (Wilmington: SR Books, 2000), 207.

24. Elio Alcalá Delgado and Teófilo Reues Courtier, "El Proyecto Vaquerías: Génesis del proceso modernizador de la agricultura mexicana en tiempos del neoliberalism," *Antropología: Boletín Oficial del INAH*, no. 52 (October–December 1998): 38.

25. Alcalá Delgado and Reues Courtier, "El Proyecto Vaquerías," 37.

26. Guillermo Correa, "Acción que propiciará el resurgimiento del latifundio: Líderes campesinas," *Proceso*, November 11, 1991, 13.

27. Tim Golden, "The Dream of Land Dies Hard in Mexico," *New York Times*, November 27, 1991.

28. Correa, "Acción que propiciará el resurgimiento del latifundio," 6–13.

29. Cited in Wayne Cornelius and David Myhre, *The Transformation of Rural Mexico: Reforming the Ejido Sector* (La Jolla: Center for U.S.-Mexican Studies, UC San Diego, 1998), 5.

30. *Crónica de Gobierno de Carlos Salinas de Gortari, 1988–1994: Tercer Año—Enero 1991–Diciembre 1991* (Mexico City: Fondo de Cultura Económico, 1994), 426.

31. Kirsten Appendini, "Changing Agrarian Institutions: Interpreting the Contradictions," in Cornelius and Myhre, *The Transformation of Rural Mexico*, 25.

32. Ochoa, *Feeding Mexico*; Kenneth Edward Mitchell, *State-Society Relations in Mexico: Clientelism, Neoliberal State Reform, and the Case of CONASUPO* (Aldershot: Ashgate, 2001).

33. Mitchell, *State-Society Relations in Mexico*, 113.

34. Ochoa, *Feeding Mexico*; Kirsten Appendini, *De la milpa a los tortibonos: La restructuración de la política alimentaria en México*, 2nd ed. (Mexico City: El Colegio de México, 2001).

35. Cassio Luiselli Fernández, *Agricultura y alimentación en México: Evolución, desempeño y perspectivas* (Mexico City: Siglo XXI Editores, 2017), 227–229.

36. Laura Carlson, "NAFTA Is Starving Mexico," *Foreign Policy in Focus*, October 10, 2011, https://fpif.org/nafta_is_starving_mexico/.

37. Secretaría de Agricultura y Desarrollo Rural, *Panorama agroalimentario 2022* (Mexico City: Servicio de Información Agroalimentaria y Pesquera, 2022), 15.

38. Secretaría de Agricultura y Desarrollo Rural, *Panorama agroalimentario 2022*, 14.

39. Data compiled and calculated from the Servicio de Información Agroalimentaria y Pesquera (SIAP) of the Secretaría de Agricultura, Ganaderia, Desarrollo Rural, Pesca, y Alimentación (SAGARPA), accessed January 24, 2012, http://www.siap.gob.mx/index.php?option=com_wrapper&view=wrapper&Itemid=350.

40. Lois Sanford, "The Binational Integration of the US-Mexican Avocado Industries: Examining Responses to Economic Globalism," in *Mexico in Transition: Neoliberal Globalization, the State, and Civil Society*, ed. Gerardo Otero (London: Zed Books, 2004).

41. "Mexico Avocado Exports Grow by 44% This Year," *Fresh Plaza: Global Fresh Produce and Banana News*, November 23, 2011, www.freshplaza.com/news_detail.asp?id=89343; "Mexico's Avocado Exports Rising by a Quarter Annually," *Fresh Fruit Portal.Com*, November 22, 2011, www.freshfruitportal.com/2011/11/22/mexicos-avocado-exports-rise-by-a-quarter/.

42. Secretaría de Agricultura y Desarrollo Rural, *Panorama agroalimentario 2022*, 23.

43. David Barkin and Blanca Suárez, *El fin de la autosuficiencia alimentaria* (Mexico City: Océano, 1985); Armando Bartra, "Rebellious Cornfields: Towards Food and Labour Self-Sufficiency," in *Mexico in Transition: Neoliberal Globalization, the State, and Civil Society*, ed. Gerardo Otero (London: Zed Books, 2004).

44. Gerardo Otero, ed., *Food for the Few: Neoliberal Globalism and Biotechnology in Latin American* (Austin: University of Texas Press, 2008).

45. Manuel Poitras, "Unnatural Growth: The Political Economy of Biotechnology in Mexico," in Otero, *Food for the Few*, 115; Elizabeth Fitting, "Importing Corn, Exporting Labor: The Neoliberal Corn Regime, GMOs, and the Erosion of Mexican Biodiversity," in Otero, *Food for the Few*.

46. Xóchitl Bada and Jonathan Fox, "Persistent Rurality in Mexico and 'the Right to Stay Home,'" *Journal of Peasant Studies* 49, no. 1 (2022): 30–31.

47. Jorge G. Castañeda, *Mañana Forever: Mexico and the Mexicans* (New York: Alfred A. Knopf, 2011), 21–26.

48. Bada and Fox, "Persistent Rurality in Mexico," 31.

49. Jonathan Fox and Gaspar Rivera Salgado, eds., *Indigenous Mexican Migration in the United States* (La Jolla: Center for U.S.-Mexican Studies, UC San Diego, 2004); Laura Velasco Ortiz, *Desde que tengo memoria: Narrativas de identidad en indígenas migrantes* (Tijuana: COLEF, 2005).

50. Tania Molina Ramírez, "*Migrar o morir* evidencia el abuso laboral que padecen los jornaleros," *La Jornada*, October 2, 2009.

51. Bada and Fox, "Persistent Rurality in Mexico," 40–44.

52. See E. C. Ochoa and T. D. Wilson, eds., "Mexico in the 1990s: Economic Crisis, Social Polarization, and Class Struggle," *Latin American Perspectives* 28, no. 3 (May 2001).

53. Lourdes Casanova, *Global Latinas: Latin America's Emerging Multinationals* (London: Palgrave Macmillan, 2009), 43.

54. Garrido, *Desarrollo económico y procesos de financiamiento en México*, 97.

55. Jennifer Clapp, *Food* (Malden, Mass.: Polity Press, 2012); Eric Holt-Giménez, *A Foodie's Guide to Capitalism: Understanding the Political Economy of What We Eat* (New York: Monthly Review Press, 2017); Gerardo Otero, *The Neoliberal Diet: Healthy Profits, Unhealthy People* (Austin: University of Texas Press, 2018).

56. Michelle Chauvet and Rosa Luz González, "Globalización y estrategias de grupos empresariales agroalimentarios de México," *Comercio Exterior* 51, no. 12 (2001): 1079–1088; Alfredo Manuel Coehlo and Victor Manuel Castillo-Girón, "Fusiones, adquisiciones y alianzas estratégicas en la industria alimentaria mexicana: Balance y perspectivas," *Análisis Económico* 25, no. 59 (2010): 121–142.

57. Basavae Kunhardt, *Los grupos de capital financiero*, 212–219.

58. Chauvet and González, "Globalización y estrategias," 1082.

59. For a historical overview of the Grupo Herdez, see "Nuestro legado," on its website, https://grupoherdez.com.mx/grupo-herdez/#legado.

60. Chris Tilly, "Wal-Mart in Mexico: The Limits of Growth," in *Wal-Mart: The Face of Twenty-First-Century Capitalism*, ed. Nelson Lichtenstein (New York: New Press, 2006); Julio Moreno, "Wal-Mart y la diplomacia económica en Américan Latina," *Foreign Affairs en Español*, April–June 2004.

61. Chauvet and González, "Globalización y estrategias"; Enrique C. Ochoa, "From Tortillas to Low-Carb Wraps: Capitalism and Mexican Food in Los Angeles Since the 1920s," *Diálogo* 18, no. 1 (Spring 2015): 33–46; Araceli Rendón Trejo

and Andrés Morales Alquicira, "Grupos económicos en la industria de alimentos: Las estrategias de Gruma," *Argumentos* 21, no. 57 (May–August 2008): 87–112; Gustavo Vargas Sánchez and Luis Pérez Osnaya, "Gruma: Un análisis microeconómico," *Economía Informa* 386 (May–June 2014): 31–50.

62. "Rey Midas: Eduardo Tricio Haro-La leche está en su sangre," *Revista Sexenio*, March 12, 2012, http://www.sexenio.com.mx/articulo.php?id=13725; Brendan Case, "LALA Buoyed by IPO Seeks Americas M&A to Add to Mexico Milk Gain," *Bloomberg*, December 5, 2013.

63. Case, "LALA Buoyed by IPO"; "DFA Sells National Dairy Holdings," *Farm and Dairy*, May 13, 2009, http://www.farmanddairy.com/news/dfa-sells-national -dairy-holdings/12020.html; Elinor Comlay and Tomás Sarmiento, "Mexican Dairy Company LALA Plans Expansion, Investment," Reuters, October 17, 2013, http://reuterus.com/assets/print?aid+USBRE99G1B120131017.

64. Cinthya Bibian, Alicia Prieto, and Edmundo Sánchez, "El perfil de los ejecutivos más importantes de México, enlistados por Expansión," *Expansión*, October 29, 2013, http//www.cnnexpansion.com/especiales/2103/10/14/15-eduardo-tricio -haro.

65. Oscar Granados, "Las vacas gordas del grupo Lala," *El País*, March 2017, https:// elpais.com/economia/2017/03/03/actualidad/1488541680_378738.html.

66. "Lala en el mundo," https://www.lala.com.mx/lala-en-el-mundo.

67. "As Oxxo Grows, Abarrotes Decline. But Tijuana Franchiser Has Other Ideas," *Mexico News Daily*, July 1, 2014, http://mexiconewsdaily.com/mexicolife/Oxxo -grows-abarrotes-decline-tijuana-franchiser-ideas/.

68. FEMSA (website), accessed July 3, 2015, http://www.femsa.com/es/negocios -femsa/empresas/Oxxo.

69. Jeffrey M. Pilcher, *The Sausage Rebellion: Public Health, Private Enterprise, and Meat in Mexico City, 1890–1917* (Albuquerque: University of New Mexico Press, 2006).

70. SAGARPA Boletín de Prensa, November 12, 2012, http://www.sagarpa.gob .mx/Delegaciones/jalisco/boletines/2012/noviembre/Documents/B0502012 .PDF; Laura X. Estévez-Moreno and Génaro C. Mirandda-de la Lama, "Meat Consumption and Consumer Attitudes in México: Can Persistence Lead to Change?," *Meat Science* 194 (2022): 2; Consejo Mexicano de la Carne, *Compendio estadístico 2022*, https://comecarne.org/wp-content/uploads/2022/05/ compendio_estadistico_2022.pdf, table 2.5.

71. Derrell S. Peel, Kenneth H. Matthews Jr., and Rachel J. Johnson, *Trade, the Expanding Mexican Beef Industry, and Feedlot and Stocker Cattle Production in Mexico / LDP-M–206–01*, Economic Research Service/USDA, August 2011, p. 5; Consejo Mexicano de la Carne, *Compendio estadístico 2012 de la industria cárnica Mexicana*, accessed September 3, 2015, http://infocarne.comecarne .org/compendio/visualizar?comp=1&componente=76; Consejo Mexicano de la Carne, *Compendio estadístico 2014 de la industria cárnica Mexicana*, accessed

June 2, 2023, http://infocarne.comecarne.org/compendio/visualizar?comp=7& componente=305.

72. Sigma, *Reporte Annual 2014*, 34.

73. "Campofrío," *Estrategias de Bolsa*, accessed August 8, 2015, http://www .estrategiasdebolsa.es/acciones/mercadocontinuo/campofrio/index.php.

74. Teodora Lyubomirova, "Sigma Alimentos Acquires Majority Stake in Cheese and Cream Producer Los Altos Foods," *Dairy Reporter*, May 5, 2023, https:// www.dairyreporter.com/Article/2023/05/05/Sigma-Alimentos-acquires -majority-stake-in-Mexican-cheese-specialist-Los-Altos-Foods; Roy Graber, "Sigma Alimentos Buys Closing West Liberty Foods Plant," *Watt Poultry.com*, April 20, 2023, https://www.wattagnet.com/articles/47140-sigma-alimentos -buys-closing-west-liberty-foods-plant.

75. Michelle del Campo, "Sigma, el fabricante de Fud, invierte en startups para apalancar crecimiento," *Bloomberg en linea*, February 22, 2022, https://www .bloomberglinea.com/2022/02/22/sigma-el-fabricante-de-fud-invierte-en -startups-para-apalancar-crecimiento; Julián Tabares, "La startup Lie Green Group se asocial con multinacinal Mexicana de alimentos para promover la era de solo vegetal," *Entrepreneur en Español*, July 6, 2022, https://www .entrepreneur.com/es/noticias/la-startup-live-green-group-se-asocia-con -multinacional/430849.

76. "Mexico: Market Concentration in Selected Agricultural and Food Sub-Sectors," *The Pig Site*, June 7, 2011, http://www.thepigsite.com/articles/3497/ mexico-market-concentration-in-selected-agricultural-and-food-subsectors/; Andrew Pells, "SuKarne, S.A. de C.V.," *Business Excellence*, July 1, 2010, http:// www.bus-ex.com/article/sukarne-sa-de-cv.

77. SuKarne (website), "History and Progress," accessed August 17, 2015, http:// sukarne.com/en/page/history; Anna Miller, "SuKarne: The Mexican Processing Powerhouse," *Western Livestock Journal*, April 4, 2019.

78. Pells, "SuKarne, S.A. de C.V."

79. SuKarne (website), accessed November 13, 2023, https://www.sukarne.com/ plantas/.

80. Miller, "SuKarne."

81. Industrias Bachoco, Report to Investors, May 2014, http://bachoco.com.mx/ inversionistas/statics/archive/2014_BACHOCO_may_I.pdf.

82. "Mexico: Market Concentration in Selected Agricultural and Food Sub-Sectors."

83. Tyson Foods International, *Tyson Fiscal 2013 Fact Book*, 21, accessed May 20, 2015, http://ir.tyson.com/files/doc_downloads/Tyson%202013%20Fact %20Book.pdf; "Tyson Foods' Mexican Poultry Business Sold to JBS," *The Poultry Site*, June 3, 2015, http://www.thepoultrysite.com/poultrynews/35176/tyson -foods-mexican-poultry-business-sold-to-jbs/.

84. For a brief overview of JBS's dramatic global rise, see Keren Blankfeld, "JBS: The Story Behind the World's Biggest Meat Producer," *Forbes*, May 9, 2011. For a

discussion of JBS in the context of Brazilian political economy, see Raúl Zibechi, *The New Brazil: Regional Imperialism and the New Democracy*, trans. Ramor Ryan (Oakland: AK Press, 2014).

85. S. Batres-Márquez, Roxanne L. Clemens, and Helen H. Jensen, "Mexico's Changing Pork Industry: The Forces of Domestic and International Market Demand," *Choices: The Magazine of Food, Farm, and Resources Issues* 22, no. 1 (First Quarter 2007): 7–12; Humane Society International, "An HIS Fact Sheet: Pig Factory Farming in Mexico," 2013, http://www.hsi.org/assets/pdfs/pig_factory_farming_in_mexico.pdf.

86. Michelle Perrett, "U.S. Looks to Mexico for Pork Sales," *Global Meat News*, August 17, 2015, http://www.globalmeatnews.com/Industry-Markets/US-looks-to-Mexico-for-pork-sales; "Mexico Has Potential for Greater Pig Productivity," *The Pig Site*, August 5, 2015, http://www.thepigsite.com/swinenews/40161/mexico-has-potential-for-greater-pig-productivity/.

87. David Bacon, *The Right to Stay Home: How US Policy Drives Mexican Migration* (Boston: Beacon Press, 2013), 1–34.

88. Bacon, *The Right to Stay Home*; Karina de la Paz Reyes, "Alerta sanitaria en Veracruz y Puebla por expansion de Granjas Caroll," *Solución Política* (Veracruz), August 1, 2011. The struggles of Pueblos Unidos del Valle de Perote are documented in the film *Pueblos Unidos del Valle de Perote en contra de Granjas Carroll de México* (Departamento de Cinematografía, Universidad de Veracruz, 2013), https://www.youtube.com/watch?v=2jepg5L22WI.

89. Dana Mattiolo and Dana Cimilluca, "China Makes Biggest Y.S. Play," *Wall Street Journal*, May 30, 2013.

90. Yadira Llaven Anzures, "Conagua ortgó cinco concesiones entre 2020 y 2024 a Granjas Carroll," *La Jornada*, July 1, 2024; Kara Castillo, "Exigen 'solución política' y no judicial a conflict con Granjas Carroll," *La Jornada*, August 8, 2024.

91. Salvador Medina Ramírez, "Mexico en el mercado de cerdo," *Comercio Exterior* 63, no. 6 (November–December 2013): 7–11.

92. Rosalía Lara, "Las empresas mexicanas que ganan con el conflict entre China y Estados Unidos," *Expansión*, May 24, 2019.

93. "A Healthy Appetite for Pork in Mexico," *Pig Progress*, January 13, 2022, https://www.pigprogress.net/world-of-pigs/a-healthy-appetite-for-pork-in-mexico/.

94. Raúl Bringas Nostti, "Kentucky Fried Chicken y su incursion en México: La última de las tres grandes inovacioned de Coronel Sanders, 1890–1964," *Perspectivas: Revista de Análisis de Economía, Comercio y Negocios Internacionales* 10, no. 2 (July–December 2016): 56–63.

95. Carlos Tomasini, "Burger Boy: La extinción de los dinosaurios brontodobles," *Chilango*, January 17, 2015, http://www.chilango.com/ciudad/nota/2015/01/17/burger-boy-la-extincion-de-los-dinosaurios-brontodobles; Mara Echeverría, "Burger Boy y Tomboy: Dos cadenas de sonar conquistar México," *Expansión*, May 28, 2022.

96. "¿Eres 'así de old'? Esta es la historia de Tomboy, la competencia de Burger Boy en los 70," *El Financiero*, July 9, 2022, https://www.elfinanciero.com.mx/food-and-drink/2022/07/09/que-paso-con-tomboy-la-competencia-de-burger-boy-en-los-70/.

97. Elida Bustos, "Chairman and CEO of Arcos Dorados, Woods Stanton," *Latin Business*, December 12, 2012; Robert J. McCartney, "Mexican Union Puts Heat on McDonald's," *Washington Post*, December 20, 1985.

98. McCartney, "Mexican Union Puts Heat on McDonald's."

99. On McDonald's overall economic strategy, see Steve Penfold, "Fast Food," in *The Oxford Handbook of Food History*, ed. Jeffrey Pilcher (New York: Oxford University Press, 2012); Eric Schlosser, *Fast Food Nation: The Dark Side of the All-American Meal* (Boston: Houghton Mifflin, 2001).

100. See McDonald's Mexico (website), accessed July 28, 2015, http://www.mcdonalds.com.mx/.

101. Bustos, "Chairman and CEO of Arcos Dorados"; "Woods Stanton, el hombre Big Mac," *Semana*, November 13, 2013.

102. Arcos Dorados, "Quiénes somos," accessed August 24, 2024, https://www.arcosdorados.com/quienes-somos/.

103. "A Happy Family: Alvaro Cofiño," *CEO Magazines*, August 18, 2021.

104. Menú Alsea, *Informe Anual*, 2014, accessed July 20, 2015, https://www.annualreports.com/HostedData/AnnualReportArchive/a/OTC_ALSSF_2014.pdf.

105. Vanessa Salcido, "Food Service-Hotel Restaurant Institutional Restaurant Industry in Mexico," USDA Foreign Agricultural Service, Global Agricultural Information Network Report, GAIN Report Number MX 4312, December 19, 2014.

106. Salcido, "Food Service-Hotel Restaurant Institutional Restaurant Industry in Mexico."

107. "Los 100 empresarios más importantes de Méxcio," *CNN/Expansión*, October 14, 2013, http://www.cnnexpansion.com/especiales/2013/10/14/59-alberto-torrado-martinez.

108. Karina Hernández Mundo, "Alsea amplia su inversion en México," *El Economista*, July 26, 2015, http://eleconomista.com.mx/industrias/2015/07/26/alsea-amplia-su-inversion-mexico.

109. Alsea, 2017 Annual Report, accessed October 9, 2019, https://www.alsea.net/uploads/es/documents/annual_reports/alsea_informe_anual_2017.pdf.

110. Alsea, "Nuestras Marcas: Starbucks," accessed May 30, 2023, https://www.alsea.net/marcas-de-alsea/starbucks.

111. "Mexico's Alsea Seeking to Open 300 Starbuck Stores in Europe by 2028," *Allegra: World Coffee Portal*, April 5, 2023, https://www.worldcoffeeportal.com/Latest/News/2023/April/Alsea-seeking-to-open-300-new-Starbucks-stores-in.

112. Elisa Pineda, Eric J. Brunner, Clare H. Llewellyn, and Jennifer S. Mindell, "The Retail Food Environment and Its Association with Body Mass Index in Mexico," *International Journal of Obesity* 45, no. 6 (2021): 1215–1228.

Chapter 4

1. Yester California Adventures at Yesterland, "Mission Tortilla Factory Hosted by Mission Foods," accessed May 1, 2023, http://www.yesterland.com/tortilla .html.

2. Gruma's History (website), accessed March 23, 2020, https://www.gruma.com/ en/we-are-gruma/history.aspx?sec=8836.

3. Enrique C. Ochoa, "From Tortillas to Low-Carb Wraps: Capitalism and Mexican Food in Los Angeles Since the 1920s," *Diálogo: An Interdisciplinary Journal* (Spring 2015).

4. Gruma's History (website), accessed March 23, 2020, https://www.gruma.com/ en/we-are-gruma/history.aspx?sec=8836.

5. "Impulsa Carlos Hank González crecimiento de GRUMA," *Excelsior*, July 15, 2014.

6. Aurora Gómez-Galvarriato, "Female Entrepreneurship as a Survival Strategy: Women During the Early Mechanisation of Corn Tortilla Production in Mexico City," *Continuity and Change* 35, no. 1 (May 2020).

7. Enrique C. Ochoa, "Lazaro Cardenas and the Politics of State Intervention, 1934–1940," in *Feeding Mexico: The Political Uses of Food Since 1910* (Wilmington: Scholarly Resources, 2000).

8. Vanessa Fonseca, "Fractal Capitalism and the Latinization of the US Market" (PhD diss., University of Texas at Austin, 2003), 27–30.

9. Fonseca, "Fractal Capitalism," 47–48.

10. Nacional Financiera, *La industria de la harina de maíz* (Mexico City: NAFINSA, 1982), 13–14; Jeffrey M.Pilcher, *¡Que Vivan los Tamales! Food and the Making of Mexican Identity* (Albuquerque: University of New Mexico Press, 1998), 105.

11. Alberto Bello, "Roberto González Barrera, el banquero improbable," in *Los amos de México*, 2nd ed., ed. Jorge Zepeda Patterson (Mexico City: Editorial Planeta Mexicana, 2007), 399.

12. Cited in Bello, "Roberto González Barrera, el banquero improbable," 399.

13. GRUMA, "Historia," accessed March 24, 2015, http://www.gruma.com/somos -gruma/historia.aspx?sec=1051; Nacional Financiera, *La industria de la harina de maíz*, 13.

14. Bello, "Roberto González Barrera, el banquero improbable," 410.

15. Robert Jones Schafer, *Mexico Business Organizations: History and Analysis* (Syracuse: Syracuse University Press, 1973); Roderic A. Camp, *Entrepreneurs and Politics in Twentieth Century Mexico* (New York: Oxford University Press, 1989); Ben Ross Schneider, *Business Politics and the State in Twentieth-Century Latin* America (Cambridge: Cambridge University Press, 2004), 59; Ben Ross Schneider, "Why Is Mexican Business So Organized?," *Latin American Research Review* 37, no. 1 (2002).

16. Camp, *Entrepreneurs and Politics in Twentieth-Century Mexico*, 115–116.

17. Bello, "Roberto González Barrera, el banquero improbable," 394–396.

18. Raymundo Riva Palacio, "Un hombre llamado Maseco," *Vanguardia*, July 21, 2012, https://vanguardia.com.mx/columnas-unhombrellamadomaseco-1336474 .html.

19. Camp, *Entrepreneurs and Politics in Twentieth-Century Mexico*, 58.

20. Roderic A. Camp, *Mexican Political Biographies, 1935–2009*, 4th ed. (Austin: University of Texas Press, 2009), 871–872; Thomas Rath, *Myths of Demilitarization in Postrevolutionary Mexico, 1920–1960* (Chapel Hill: University of North Carolina Press, 2013), 90.

21. Rath, *Myths of Demilitarization*, 101–102.

22. Thomas Rath, "Camouflaging the State: The Army and the Limits of Hegemony in PRIísta Mexico, 1940–1960," in *Dictablanda: Politics, Work, and Culture in Mexico, 1938–1968* (Durham, N.C.: Duke University Pres, 2014), 97. According to Rath, "military corruption was well-hidden but remained visible."

23. Bello, "Roberto González Barrera, el banquero improbable," 400.

24. Bello, "Roberto González Barrera, el banquero improbable," 400–401; Ochoa, *Feeding Mexico*, 134; Hugo Azpeitia Gómez, *Compañía Exportadora e Importadora Mexicana, S.A. (1949–1958): Conflicto y abasto alimentario* (Mexico City: CIESAS, 1994), 110–111.

25. Bello, "Roberto González Barrera, el banquero improbable," 401.

26. Raúl Salinas Lozano, *La intervención del estado y la cuestión de los precios* (Mexico City: Editorial America, 1944); Camp, *Mexican Political Biographies*, 872.

27. Bello, "Roberto González Barrera, el banquero improbable," 402.

28. Bello, "Roberto González Barrera, el banquero improbable," 401–402.

29. Bello, "Roberto González Barrera, el banquero improbable," 390.

30. Rogelio Hernández Rodríguez, "Challenging Caciquismo: An Analysis of the Leadership of Carlos Hank González," in *Caciquismo in Twentieth Century Mexico*, ed. Alan Knight and Wil Pansters (London: Institute for the Study of the Americas, 2005).

31. Bello, "Roberto González Barrera, el banquero improbable," 390.

32. John Ross, "The Politics of Greed Poison Mexico's Daily Diet: Tortillas of Blood," *Anderson Valley Advertiser*, April 5, 1995, http://www.eco.utexas.edu/ ~archive/chiapas95/1995.04/msg00150.html; Ricardo J. Galarza, "Carlos Hank González, el nieto pródigo," *Expansión*, May 11, 2009.

33. Bello, "Roberto González Barrera, el banquero improbable," 410.

34. Bello, "Roberto González Barrera, el banquero improbable," 387–388.

35. Jaime M. Pensado and Enrique C. Ochoa, eds., *México Beyond 1968: Revolutionaries, Radicals, and Repression During the Global Sixties and Subversive Seventies* (Tucson: University of Arizona Press, 2018).

36. Ochoa, *Feeding Mexico*, 167–171.

37. Bello, "Roberto González Barrera, el banquero improbable," 388–389.

38. Bello, "Roberto González Barrera, el banquero improbable," 389.

39. Ochoa, "Rural Crisis and the Creeping Hand of the State in the Countryside, 1958–1970," in *Feeding Mexico*.

40. Bello, "Roberto González Barrera, el banquero improbable," 405.

41. Nacional Financiera, *La industria de la harina de maíz*, 16; Ochoa, *Feeding Mexico*, 192.

42. Ochoa, *Feeding Mexico*, 180–182.

43. Yoja Gallardo Navarro, Edith Figueroa García, and Carlos Roldán Esparza, *La industría de alimentos procesados en México: Analisis y tendencias* (Mexico City: Instituto Politécnico Nacional, 1982), 96; Ochoa, *Feeding Mexico*.

44. Kirsten Appendini, *De la milpa a los tortibonos: La restructuración de la política alimentaria en México*, 2nd ed. (Mexico City: El Colegio de Mexico, 2001), 194.

45. Nacional Financiera, *La industria de la harina de maíz*, 51–52, 54.

46. Appendini, *De la milpa a los tortibonos*, 194.

47. Nacional Financiera, *La industria de la harina de maíz*, 76–77.

48. Alva Senzek, "Mexican Food Is a Goodwill Ambassador," *El Financiero International*, February 16–22, 1998; Roberto González Amador, "Liberan el precio de la torilla: $4 por kilogramo a partir de ayer," *La Jornada*, January 2, 1999; "Mexicans Lament Lifting of Price Controls on Tortillas," *Mexico City News*, January 3, 1999.

49. Anthony De Palma, "Graft Inquiry in Mexico Ties Zedillo to Disputed Payment," *New York Times*, July 6, 1996.

50. Calculated from Appendini, *De la milpa a los tortibonos*, 195.

51. Appendini, *De la milpa a los tortibonos*, 192–199; Ana María Rosas Peña, "Un mercado hecho bolas," *La Jornada en la Economía*, January 17, 2005.

52. Judith Maldonado, "Maseca duplicará su capacidad instalada," *El Financiero*, April 28, 1995.

53. Rosas Peña, "Un Mercado Hecho Bolas."

54. Araceli Rendón Trejo and Andrés Morales Alquicira, "Grupos económicos en la industria de alimientos: Las estrategias de GRUMA," *Argumentos* 21, no. 57 (May–August 2008): 101.

55. Anthony De Palma, "Graft Inquiry in Mexico Ties Zedillo to Disputed Payment," *New York Times*, July 6, 1996; Jim Carson and David Brooks, "Secofi autorizó pago dudoso a Maseca en 88: Fuente official," *La Jornada*, July 5, 1996.

56. Bello, "Roberto González Barrera, el banquero improbable," 413.

57. Elvira Concheiro Bórquez, *El gran acuerdo: Gobierno y empresarios en la modernización salinista* (Mexico City: Ediciones ERA, 1996), 156–158; Joel Millman, "Shares in Mexican Bus Maker and Tortilla Firm Attract Interest Again, but Caution Is Advised," *Wall Street Journal*, April 1, 1998; Joel Millman, "In Mexico's Ruling Party, Old Faces Tout New Image," *Wall Street Journal*, April 24, 2000.

58. Roberto Gonzalez Amador and Susana Gonzalez G., "Gruma y BaNorte, ejemplos de éxito aun en tiempos dificiles," *La Jornada*, October 2, 2010.

59. Bello, "Roberto González Barrera, el banquero improbable," 416; Eduardo Gitli, "La inversion directa Mexicana en Centroamérica: Eslabonamientos productivos y transferencia de technología," Departamento de Economía de la Universi-

dad Autónoma Metropolitana-Azcapotzalco y Centro Internacional de Política Económica para el Desarrollo Sostenible de la Universidad Nacional (Heredia, Costa Rica), November 2000, p. 27; González Amador and González G., "Gruma y BaNorte."

60. Gruma DEMASA (website), accessed May 22, 2020, https://www.gruma.com/es/nuestras-marcas/empresas/demasa.aspx.

61. Celso Garrido, "Inversión productive de grandes empresas mexicanas en centroamerica y su impacto tecnologico en la region," Departamento de Economía de la Universidad Autónoma Metropolitana-Azcapotzalco y Centro Internacional de Política Económica para el Desarrollo Sostenible de la Universidad Nacional (Heredia, Costa Rica), November 2000, p. 34–35. http://www.azc.uam.mx/csh/economia/empresas/archivosparadescarga/cinpeuam.pdf.

62. Gitli, "La inversion directa Mexicana en Centroamérica," 30.

63. Roberto Gonzalez Amador y Susana Gonzalez G., "Gruma y BaNorte, ejemplos de éxito aun en tiempos dificiles," *La Jornada*, October 2, 2010.

64. "100% Tortilla Market Share," *Tortilla Topics: The Newsletter for the Tortilla Industry*, November 1, 2002.

65. GRUMA, *Informe Anual*, 1998, 11, accessed April 6, 2015, http://www.gruma.com/media/149789/informe_anual_1998_esp.pdf.

66. Marla Dickerson, "Tortilla Makers Try Not to Get Flattened," *Los Angeles Times*, October 28, 2003.

67. "Integraron Maseca y Archer Daniels la mayor productora mundial de tortillas," *La Jornada*, August 23, 1996; Scott Kilman and Joel Millman, "ADM, Showing New Interest in Mexico, Agrees to Buy 22% Stake in Gruma SA," *Wall Street Journal*, August 23, 1993.

68. Daniel J. McCosh, "The Maseca Maize," *Latin CEO: Executive Strategies for the Americas*, June 2001.

69. Daniel J. McCosh, "The Maseca Maize" and "Gruma Writes off Venezuela Business," *Worldgrain.com*, April 29, 2013.

70. Gustavo Vargas Sánchez and Luis Pérez Osnaya, "Gruma: Un análisis microeconómico," *Economía Informa*, no. 386 (May–June 2014): 36.

71. For the case of Guatemala, see Juan Pablo Ozaeta, *Tratado de libre comercio entre Centroamérica, Repúbica Dominicana y Estados Unidos (TLC-CAUSA): Informe a cinco años de vigencia: su impacto en el campo* (Guatemala: Instituto de Estudios Agrarios y Rurales, 2011).

72. Susana Gauster and Alberto Alonso Fradejas, *GRUMA—MASECA: La emperadora translatina de la tortilla de harina en Centroamérica* (Guatemala: Instituto de Estudios Agrarios y Rurales, 2007), 16–29. For earlier data, see Ma. Dolores Ortega, "Domina Maseca mercado salvadoreño," *El Norte*, July 16, 2003.

73. "Maseca instalará planta en Nicaragua," *El Economista*, August 17, 2011.

74. José Manuel López, "Apuntala Gruma su expansion internacional," *El Norte*, August 9, 2004; Roberto González Amador, "Calienta Grupo Maseca 'tacos de arroz' en Asia," *La Jornada*, November 23, 2004; Gustavo Vargas Sánchez and

Luis Pérez Osnaya, "Gruma: Un análisis microeconómico," *Economía Informa*, no. 386 (May–June 2014): 36–37.

75. Juan Carlos Miranda, "Maseca es ya el principal proveedor de tortillas en cadenas de comida rápida," *La Jornada*, July 2, 2010.

76. "Global Presence," GRUMA, accessed March 23, 2020, https://www.gruma.com/en/we-are-gruma/global-presence.aspx?sec=8836.

77. Gabriela Cabrera y Daniela Clavijo, "GRUMA: La mejor defensa," *Expansion*, June 25 and July 8, 2012, pp. 207–212; "BaNorte, la mezcla de las familias González y Hank," *El Financiero*, October 25, 2017.

78. "History," GRUMA, accessed March 23, 2020, https://www.gruma.com/en/we-are-gruma/history.aspx?sec=8836.

79. Roberto González Barrera, "Proponencia de agradezcimiento por el Premio Internacional PROFMEX de Política Global," *Mexico and the World* 4, no. 3 (Summer 1999), http://www.profmex.org/mexicoandtheworld/volume4/3summer99/ponencia.html.

80. González Barrera, "Proponencia de agradezcimiento por el Premio Internacional PROFMEX de Política Global."

81. González Barrera, "Proponencia de agradezcimiento por el Premio Internacional PROFMEX de Política Global."

82. José Peralta, "(De)Stabilizing The Neoliberal Food Regime: The Struggle for the Defense of Corn in Mexico" (PhD diss., University of Illinois at Urbana-Champaign, 2012), 129; "MASECA Celebrates MASECA en la Cocina Con Las Estrellas with the 100th Celebrity: MASECA Gives Back to the Hispanic Community Via Television Segments," *Hispanic PR Wire*, April 29, 2009, https://hispanicprwire.com/en/masecar-celebra-100-estrellas-en-masecar-en-la-cocina-con-las-estrellas/.

83. "Del Promocional MASECA 2007, Lucero MASECA Spot," accessed May 31, 2024, https://www.youtube.com/watch?v=GFrFsFtUoMA.

84. Ochoa, "From Tortillas to Low-Carb Wraps."

85. Guerrero's website, accessed September 17, 2009, http://www.tortillasguerrero.com/.

86. Guerrero's website, accessed June 12, 2023, https://guerrerotortillas.com/our-products/.

87. Ochoa, "From Tortillas to Low-Carb Wraps"; Carey McWilliams, *Southern California Country: An Island on the Land* (New York: Duell, Sloan and Pearce, 1946); William Deverell, *Whitewashed Adobe: The Rise of Los Angeles and the Remaking of its Mexican Past* (Berkeley: University of California Press, 2004); Larry Gordon, "Database Tells the Stories of 100,000 Mission Indians," *Los Angeles Times*, August 8, 2006.

88. Ochoa, "From Tortillas to Low-Carb Wraps," 41.

89. "Mission Foods Revolutionizes Low Carb Tortilla; New Products Stack Up with Great Taste for Dieters and Non-Dieters Alike," *Hispanic PR Wire*, April 1, 2004, http://www.hispanicprwire.com/news.php?l=in&id=2152&cha=4.

90. E. Schroeder, "The Many Tastes of Tortillas," *BakingBusiness.com*, October 6, 2009, http://www.bakingbusiness.com.

91. "Mission Foods Rises to Meet Changing Consumer Needs with New, Great-Tasting Variety for Health-Conscious Shoppers," *Business Wire*, September 16, 2021, https://www.businesswire.com/news/home/20210916005251/en/Mission-Foods-Rises-to-Meet-Changing-Consumer-Needs-with-New-Great-Tasting-Variety-for-Health-Conscious-Shoppers.

92. Eric Schroeder, "Mission Foods unveils new Fresh Signature line," *Food Business News*, April 20, 2021, https://www.foodbusinessnews.net/articles/18421-mission-foods-unveils-new-fresh-signature-line; Lucas Cuni-Mertz, "Tortilla and Flatbread Innovation Is Trending," *Food Business News*, March 15, 2022, https://www.foodbusinessnews.net/articles/20848-tortilla-and-flatbread-innovation-is-trending.

93. Eric Schroeder, "Mission Foods Launches Zero Net Carbs Tortillas," *Food Business News*, September 27, 2022, https://www.foodbusinessnews.net/articles/22302-mission-foods-launches-zero-net-carbs-tortillas.

94. Enrique Dussel Peters and Samuel Ortiz Velásques, eds., "Tortimetro," *Monitor de la manufactura Mexicana* 10, no. 11 (February 2015): 49; Enrique C. Ochoa and Tamar Diana Wilson, introduction to "Mexico in the 1990s: Economic Crisis, Social Polarization, and Class Struggle," *Latin American Perspectives* 28, no. 3 (May 2001): 3–4.

95. Eduardo de la Rosa, "Cae consume per cápita de tortilla 22% en 3 años," *Milenio*, September 8, 2022, https://www.milenio.com/negocios/cae-consumo-per-capita-tortilla-22-3-anos.

96. Sistema Nacional de Información e Intregación de Mercados, "Información Mensual de Precios Diarios de Tortilla en Tortillerías y autoservicios de México," http://www.economia-sniim.gob.mx/TortillaAnualPorDia.asp?Cons=D&prod=T&Anio=2023&preEdo=Amb&Formato=Nor&submit=Ver+Resultados.

97. "'Precio de la tortilla seguirá subiendo si hay alza de los insumos': Productores," *Milenio Digital*, July 8, 2022, https://www.milenio.com/negocios/cnipmt-precio-tortilla-seguira-subiendo-alza-insumos?utm_medium=recommended-edt-two.

98. de la Rosa, "Cae consume per cápita de tortilla 22% en 3 años."

99. Pett, "The Fight to Save the Traditional Tortilla"; La Alianza por Nuestra Tortilla, *Del maíz a la tortilla: Lo que sabemos desde la tierra hasta la comida* (Mexico City: Alianza por Nuestra Tortilla, n.d.), accessed August 26, 2024, https://www.pornuestratortilla.org/Uploads/del-maiz-a-la-tortilla-v.1.2-pages-digital.pdf.

100. La Alianza por Nuestra Tortilla, *Del maíz a la tortilla*, 9.

101. "Industriales de la masa y la Tortilla al Borde de Desaparecer," *Milenio Digital*, May 19, 2017, https://www.milenio.com/negocios/industriales-de-la-masa-y-la-tortilla-al-borde-de-desaparecer.

102. "Industriales de la masa y la Tortilla al Borde de Desaparecer."

103. México, Secretaría de Economía-Dirección General de Industrias Básicas (SE-DGIB), "Análisis de la cadena de valor maíz-tortilla: Situación actual y factores de competencia local," April 2012, pp. 19–20, http://www.2006 -2012.economia.gob.mx/files/comunidad_negocios/industria_comercio/ informacionSectorial/20120411_analisis_cadena_valor_maiz-tortilla.pdf.

104. SE-DGIB, "Análisis de la cadena de valor maíz-tortilla," 20–21; "Se incrementa consume de tortilla en México y el mundo," *Uno más uno*, August 21, 2014, http://www.unomasuno.com.mx/se-incrementa-consumo-de-tortilla-en -mexico-y-el-mundo/.

105. Shaun Pett, "The Fight to Save the Traditional Tortilla," *New York Times*, December 21, 2018.

106. Elizabeth Dunn, "The Tortilla Cartel," *Taste*, May 15, 2018, https://tastecooking .com/the-tortilla-cartel/.

107. Gustavo Arellano, "Five Reasons to Hate GRUMA, Makers of Mission and Guerrero Tortillas, Maseca and Other Tortilla Evils," *OC Weekly*, June 26, 2012; Gustavo Arellano, "Tortilla-Washing in Action: The Case of GRUMA and Its Albuquerque Tortilla Brand," *KCRW Good Foods*, September 13, 2022, https://www .kcrw.com/culture/shows/good-food/tortilla-washing-albuquerque-grandmas.

108. Jenna Colley, "Retail Tortilla Flap Unfolds in Trial," *Houston Business Journal*, November 21, 2003.

109. Edgar Rivera, "Demandan en EU a GRUMA y Bimbo," *El Norte*, August 30, 2001; Marla Dickerson, "Tortilla Makers Try Not to Get Flattened," *Los Angeles Times*, October 28, 2003; Marla Dickerson, "Small Tortilla Makers Lose Antitrust Suit Against Rival," *Los Angeles Times*, January 6, 2004; Moises Ramirez V., "Arrecia Pleito Legal Contra GRUMA en EU," *El Norte*, February 5, 2004; "Tortilla Maker Accused of Monopoly," *Los Angeles Times*, May 28, 2004.

110. J. R. Nevarez, "Mexico's Tortilla: Selling Like Hotcakes in U.S. Market," *Los Angeles Times*, August 8, 1965.

111. Ochoa, "From Tortillas to Low-Carb Wraps," 37–38.

112. Jeffrey M. Pilcher, *Planet Taco: A Global History of Mexican Food* (New York: Oxford University Press, 2012).

113. D. A. Sylvester, "Tortillas Soon Will Become Top-Selling Bread in U.S.," *Desert News*, December 28, 2003; J. Kabbani, "Market Overview," 2010, Tortilla Industry Association Technical Conference, accessed May 25, 2014, http://www .tortilla-info.com/downloads/tech_seminar_presentations/Presentation%20- %20Market%20Overview%209-2010.pdf.

114. Dickerson, "Tortilla Makers Try Not to Get Flattened," *Los Angeles Times*, October 28, 2003.

115. Dickerson, "Tortilla Makers Try Not to Get Flattened."

116. Enrique C. Ochoa, interview with Mauro Robles, founder and CEO of La Reyna Inc., January 7, 2005; Dickerson, "Tortilla Makers Try Not to Get Flattened."

117. Alana Semuels. "Tortillas Gaining Ground in Battle for Bread Aisle," *Los Angeles Times*, November 1, 2006.

118. Pilcher, *Planet Taco.*

119. Nick Kindelsperger, "Chicago's Tortillas Are Better Than Ever Thanks to Ma-siendas Heirloom Corn from Oaxaca," *Chicago Tribune*, April 22, 2019.

120. Sarah Portnoy, "A Fast-Growing East L.A. Tortilla Business Started with Two High School Friends," *Los Angeles Times*, July 4, 2019.

Chapter 5

1. Zyanya López, "Bimbo se encuentra en la alacena de 98.9% de los hogares mex-icanos," *Expansión*, June 4, 2020, https://expansion.mx/mercadotecnia/2020/06/04/bimbo-la-marca-con-mayor-presencia-en-hogares-mexicanos.

2. LD Investments, "Grupo Bimbo: World's Leading Baking Player Worth a Look," *Seeking Alpha*, May 9, 2023, https://seekingalpha.com/article/4601805-grupo-bimbo-worlds-leading-baking-player-worth-a-look; Bimbo Bakeries USA (website), accessed June 29, 2023, https://www.bimbobakeriesusa.com/about-us.

3. Michael Distefano, "Patience, Persistence and Treating Employees Like a Fam-ily," interview with Daniel Servitje, *Korn Ferry Briefings*, no. 23 (May 15, 2015): 22–29, https://www.kornferry.com/insights/briefings-magazine/issue-23/patience-persistence-and-treating-employees-family.

4. Jon Chorley, "Entenmann's Baker Is Committed to a Sweet Future," *Forbes*, May 17, 2022, https://www.forbes.com/sites/jonchorley/2022/05/17/entenmanns-baker-is-committed-to-a-sweet-future/?sh=64c824f821a0.

5. Among the notable exceptions here is the work of Robert Weis, whose pioneer-ing M.A. thesis and articles on the early history of Bimbo have not gotten the attention they deserve. Robert Weis, "Por la verdad del Osito Bimbo: Consumo en el México contemporáneo" (M.A. thesis, Universidad Nacional Autónoma de Mexico, 2001); Robert Weis, "Bimbo," in *Icons of Mexico*, ed. Eric Zolov (Santa Barbara, Calif.: ABC-Clio, 2015).

6. Robert Weis, *Bakers and Basques: A Social History of Bread in Mexico* (Albu-querque: University of New Mexico Press, 2012), 4.

7. Cited in Jeffrey M. Pilcher, *¡Qué Vivan los Tamales! Food and the Making of Mexican Identity* (Albuquerque: University of New Mexico Press, 1998), 77.

8. Clara E. Lida, ed., *Una inmigración privilegiada: Comerciantes, empresarios y professionals españoles en México en los siglos XIX y XXI* (Madrid: Alianza Edi-torial, 1994); Pedro Pérez Herrero, "Algunas hipótesis de trabajo sobre la inmi-gración española a México: Los comerciantes," in *Tres aspectos de la presencia española en México durante el profiriato: Relaciones económicas, comerciantes y población*, ed. Clara E. Lida (Mexico City: El Colegio de México, 1981); Felipe de Jesús Bello Gómez, "Inmigración y capacidad empresarial en los albores de la industrialización de México," *Secuencia* 68 (May–August 2007): 9–54; Javier Moreno Lázaro, "Los españoles y la revolución comercial mexicana: Las cadenas de supermercados, 1921–2011," *Investigaciones de Historia Económica* 8 (2012): 69–82.

9. Weis, *Bakers and Basques*; Robert Weis, "Immigrant Entrepreneurs, Bread, and Class Negotiation in Postrevolutionary Mexico City," *Mexican Studies/Estudios Mexicanos* 25, no. 1 (Winter 2009): 71–100.

10. Weis, *Bakers and Basques*, 57 and 69.

11. Weis, "Dough Kneaded with Blood," in *Bakers and Basques*.

12. "Lorenzo Servitje, un soñador de 'imposibles,'" in *Al grano: Vida y visión de los fundadores de Bimbo*, ed. Silvia Cherem S. (Mexico City: Khalida, 2008), 35–48.

13. "Lorenzo Servitje," in Cherem S., *Al grano*, 59–60.

14. Aaron Bobrow-Strain, *White Bread: A Social History of the Store-Bought Loaf* (Boston: Beacon Press, 2012), 23–29.

15. Bobrow-Strain, *White Bread*, 55–56.

16. "Bimbo: Mucho más que una marca de pan," *Expansión*, July 4, 2008, https://expansion.mx/especiales/las-500-de-expansion-2008/el-panadero-accidental; Silvia Cherem S., *Al grano: Vida y visión de los fundadores de Bimbo* (Mexico City: Khalida, 2008).

17. Weis, "Por la verdad del Osito Bimbo."

18. "Lorenzo Servitje," in Cherem S., *Al grano*, 69.

19. *Bimbo: Una historia de creer y crear* (Grupo Bimbo, 2005), 16–17; Cherem S., *Al grano*, 8; Weis, "Immigrant Entrepreneurs," 80; Weis, "Por la verdad del Osito Bimbo."

20. "Lorenzo Servitje," in Cherem S., *Al grano*, 66–69.

21. "Bimbo: Mucho más que una marca de pan," *Expansión*, July 4, 2008, https://expansion.mx/especiales/las-500-de-expansion-2008/el-panadero-accidental; "Lorenzo Servitje," in Cherem S., *Al grano*.

22. "Lorenzo Servitje," in Cherem S., *Al grano*, 64.

23. Aída Mostkoff and Enrique C. Ochoa, "Complexities of Measuring the Food Situation in Mexico: Supply Versus Self-Sufficiency of Basic Grains, 1925–86," in *Society and Economy in Mexico*, ed. James W. Wilkie (Los Angeles: UCLA Latin American Center, 1990), 128.

24. Ochoa, "Lazaro Cardenas and the Politics of State Intervention, 1934–1940," in *Feeding Mexico*.

25. Ochoa, *Feeding Mexico*, 89–90.

26. Tore C. Olsson, *Agrarian Crossings: Reformers and the Remaking of the US and Mexican Countryside* (Princeton, N.J.: Princeton University Press, 2017), 150.

27. Weis, *Bakers and Basques*; Jeffrey M. Pilcher, *¡Qué Vivan los Tamales! Food and the Making of Mexican Identity* (Albuquerque: University of New Mexico Press, 1998).

28. Bobrow-Strain, *White Bread*, 20.

29. Sandra Aguilar-Rodríguez, "'Las penas con pan son menos': Race, Modernity, and Wheat in Modern Mexico," *Bulletin of Spanish Studies* 97, no. 7 (2020): 1–27.

30. "Lorenzo Servitje," in Cherem S., *Al grano*, 75.

31. "Lorenzo Servitje," in Cherem S., *Al grano*, 76.

32. "Lorenzo Servitje," in Cherem S., *Al grano*, 76; "Jaime Jorba a toda prueba," in Cherem S., *Al grano*, 224–227.

33. Ronald L. Davis, *Hollywood Beauty: Linda Darnell and the American Dream* (Norman: University of Oklahoma Press, 1991), 36 and 62.

34. "Lorenzo Servitje," in Cherem S., *Al grano*, 76.

35. Pilcher, "The Tortilla Discourse: Nutrition and Nation Building," in *¡Qué Vivan los Tamales!*; Enrique C. Ochoa, "From Tortillas to Low-Carb Wraps: Capitalism and Mexican Food in Los Angeles Since the 1920s," *Diálogo: An Interdisciplinary Journal* (Spring 2015).

36. Weis, "Dough Kneaded with Blood," in *Bakers and Basques*.

37. Sandra Aguilar Rodríguez, "Alimentando a la nación: Género y nutrición en México (1940–1960)," *Revista de Estudios Sociales* (Bogotá), no. 29 (April 2008): 28–41; Aguilar-Rodríguez, "Las penas con pan son menos."

38. "Lorenzo Servitje," in Cherem S., *Al grano*, 76.

39. Aguilar-Rodríguez, "Las penas con pan son menos," 15.

40. "Lorenzo Servitje," in Cherem S., *Al grano*, 91.

41. Aguilar-Rodríguez, "Las penas con pan son menos," 18–22.

42. "Lorenzo Servitje," in Cherem S., *Al grano*, 91–92.

43. See Bobby Vaughn and Ben Vinson III, "Memín Penguín, Changing Racial Debates, and Transnational Blackness," *Emisférica* 5, no. 1 (2008), https://hemisphericinstitute.org/en/emisferica-5-2-race-and-its-others/5-2-dossier/memin-penguin-changing-racial-debates-and-transnational-blackness.html#_edn9; Eduardo Cepeda, "Cri-Cri El Grillito Cantor Is Beloved by Mexican Children, But It Has an Unexamined Problematic Past," *Remezcla*, May 1, 2018, https://remezcla.com/features/music/cri-cri-el-grilito-cantor-op-ed/.

44. Joseph Boskin, *Sambo: The Rise and Demise of an American Jester* (New York: Oxford University Press, 1986), 14.

45. Jesús F. Cháirez-Garza, "A Racist Lullaby: Anti-Blackness in Mexican Popular Culture," *The Radical History Review: The Abusable Past*, July 14, 2020, https://www.radicalhistoryreview.org/abusablepast/a-racist-lullaby-anti-blackness-in-mexican-popular-culture/?fbclid=IwAR1BwURSxe6cX1ix8Oca2PoO3BJQEkkWEdakCZs71-PkVR_21V-A56iqWCs; "Comerciales mexicanos: Bimbo Pan Tostado 1996," accessed June 15, 2023, https://www.youtube.com/watch?v=u25fh74pK7w.

46. "Comercial Negrito Bimbo," accessed June 15, 2023, https://www.youtube.com/watch?v=ZyaEOWdcJeA.

47. Cristina V. Mansferrer León, "'I'm Not Sitting Next to You': Education and Racism in Afro-Mexican Communities," *Diálogos sobre Educación* 7, no. 13 (2016): 5.

48. Vaughn and Vinson, "Memín Penguín."

49. "El Negrito desapareció porque era políticamente incorrecto," *Vice*, May 17, 2016, https://www.vice.com/es/article/jpkk7y/el-negrito-desaparecio-porque-era-politicamente-incorrecto.

50. *Bimbo: Una historia de creer y crear*, 26.

51. "Lorenzo Servitje," in Cherem S., *Al grano*, 81.

52. Grupo Bimbo, *Annual Report 2009*, 22–29; "Lorenzo Servitje," in Cherem S., *Al grano*, 86.

53. "Lorenzo Servitje," in Cherem S., *Al grano*, 186–187.

54. "Lorenzo Servitje," in Cherem S., *Al grano*, 92–95.

55. Rosa Elena Montes de Oca Luján and Gerardo Escudero Columna, "Las empresas transnacionales en la industria alimentaria mexicana," *Comercio Exterior* 31, no. 9 (September 1981): 995n18; Manuel Buendía column in *El Día*, July 6, 1966; Manuel Buendía, *Los empresarios* (Mexico City: Océano, 1984), 19–20; Cherem S., *Al grano*, 293–295; Quality Baker's Association, accessed July 10, 2023, https://www.qba.com; Grupo Bimbo, *Annual Report*, 2009, 23; Salvador Frausto Crotte, "Lorenzo Servitje, una apuesta por el pan," in *Los amos de México*, 2nd ed., ed. Jorge Zepeda Patterson (Mexico City: Editorial Planeta Mexicana, 2007), 257; *Bimbo: Una historia de creer y crear*, 42.

56. Javier Moreno-Lázaro, "The Bread of the Americas. Bimbo: A Mexican Business Success Story, 1944–2010," *Revista de Historia Industrial*, no. 47 (2011): 95–96.

57. Joel Millman, "Mexican Baker Turns Up Heat on Competitors in the Americas," *Wall Street Journal*, August 27, 1999.

58. Roberto Servitje, "Altos Vuelos," in Cherem S., *Al grano*, 312; Moreno-Lázaro, "The Bread of the Americas," 95; "¿Qué fue el pan Breddy, el rival del 'Osito Bimbo' a inicios de los años 2000?," *Radio Formula*, November 20, 2022, https://www.radioformula.com.mx/estilo-de-vida/2022/11/30/que-fue-del . . . breddy-el-rival-del-osito-bimbo-inicios-de-los-anos-2000-741862.html.

59. Roberto Servitje, "Altos vuelos," in Cherem S., *Al grano*, 292.

60. Moreno-Lázaro, "The Bread of the Americas," 77.

61. Moreno-Lázaro, "The Bread of the Americas," 92–95.

62. "Lorenzo Servitje," in Cherem S., *Al grano*, 52.

63. "Lorenzo Servitje," in Cherem S., *Al grano*, 53.

64. "Lorenzo Servitje," in Cherem S., *Al grano*, 54.

65. "Lorenzo Servitje," in Cherem S., *Al grano*, 54.

66. Weis, "Por la verdad del Osito Bimbo," 12.

67. Weis, "Por la verdad del Osito Bimbo," 2.

68. Lorenzo Servitje interview with Gerardo Castillo, *Confidencias de casados famosos y felices: Claves para crecer como matrimonio* (Barcelona: Amat Editorial, 2006), 383.

69. "Roberto Servitje; Altos vuelos," in Cherem S., *Al grano*, 344.

70. "Roberto Servitje; Altos vuelos," in Cherem S., *Al grano*, 345.

71. Weis, "Por la verdad del Osito Bimbo," 12.

72. Daniela Barragán, "Los Servitje, incendiaries y conservadores, también tienen lengua que les pisen," *Sinembargo*, February 3, 2015, https://sinembargo.mx/03-02-2015/1233997; "Este es el árbol genealógico de los Servitje, el 'linaje' de Bimbo," *El CEO*, March 11, 2023, https://elceo.com/liderazgo/este-es-el-arbol-genealogico-de-los-servitje-el-linaje-de-bimbo/.

73. Grupo Bimbo, *Informe Anual*, 2011, 122–123; Grupo Bimbo, *Informe Anual*, 2019, 67.

74. For discussion on early waves of welfare capitalism in Mexico, see Michael Snodgrass, "The Birth and Consequences of Industrial Paternalism in Monterrey, Mexico, 1890–1940," *International Labor and Working-Class History*, no. 53 (Spring 1998): 115–136; and Michael Snodgrass, *Deference and Defiance in Monterrey: Workers, Paternalism, and Revolution in Mexico, 1890–1950* (Cambridge: Cambridge University Press, 2003).

75. Alejandra Salas-Porras, "Corrientes de pensamiento empresarial en México (primera parte)," *Revista Mexicana de Ciencias Políticas y Sociales* 44, no. 181 (January–April 2001): 192.

76. Efraín González Morfin, "La subsidiaridad," in *Manual de Doctrina Social Cristiana* (Mexico City: Instituto Mexicana de Doctrina Social Cristiana, 1989).

77. Cited in Weis, "Por la verdad del Osito Bimbo"; Weis, "Bimbo."

78. Lorenzo Servitje Sendra, "La revalorización de la empresa privada," in *Manual de Doctrina Social Cristiana* (Mexico City: Instituto Mexicano de Doctrina Social Crisitiana, 1989), 244.

79. Lorenzo Servitje, "Más allá del salario," in *La sociedad contemporánea y el empresario* (Mexico City: Editorial LIMUSA, 1981).

80. Roberto Servitje Sendra, *Bimbo: Estrategia de éxito empresarial*, 2nd ed. (Mexico City: Pearson Educación, 2009), 105.

81. *Bimbo: Una historia de creer y crear*, 85.

82. Servitje Sendra, *Bimbo*, 122.

83. *Bimbo: Una historia de creer y crear*, 31.

84. Servitje Sendra, *Bimbo*, 122.

85. *Bimbo: Una historia de creer y crear*, 30–31.

86. *Bimbo: Una historia de creer y crear*, 84.

87. See Miguel Angel Ramirez Sánchez, "Los sindicatos blancos de Monterrery (1931–2009)," *Frontera Norte* 23, no. 45 (July–December 2011): 177–210; Pedro S. Villegas Rojas, "El nuevo sindicalismo blanco," in *La situación del trabajo en México, 2012: El trabajo en crisis*, ed. Enrique de la Garza (Mexico City: Plaza y Valdes, 2012).

88. "Roberto Servitje, altos vuelos," in Cheram S., *Al grano*, 296–299.

89. Marcela Hernández Romo, "Las configuraciones y estrategias productivas, de relaciones laborales y sindicales en grandes corporaciones en México," in *Configuraciones productivas y relaciones laborales en empresa multinaciones en América Latina*, ed. Enrique de la Garza Toledo and Marcela Hernández Romo (Mexico City: Universdad Aútonoma Metropolitanza-Iztapalapa, 2017), 185, 190–191.

90. Hernández Romo, "Las configuraciones y estrategias productivas," 190–192.

91. Salas-Porras, "Corrientes de pensamiento empresarial en México (primera parte)," 195–96.

92. "Lorenzo Servitje," in Cheram S., *Al grano*, 160–161.

93. "Lorenzo Servitje," in Cheram S., *Al grano*, 168.

94. Alejandra Salas Porras, "Corrientes de pensamiento empresarial en México (segunda parte)," *Revista Mexicana de Ciencias Políticas y Sociales* 44, no. 182–183 (May–December 2001): 238–239.

95. "Lorenzo Servitje," in Cheram S., *Al grano*, 169.

96. Luis Granovsky, "Escándalo de la Madonna," *Cambio 16*, November 8, 1993, 10.

97. Frausto Crotte, "Lorenzo Servitje," 243.

98. Elisa Villegas de Ramirez and Ernesto Hernandez Villegas, "¡Locura! Todo lo que es una vedette: belleza, gracia, sensualidad," *El Universal*, November 11, 1993.

99. Frausto Crotte, "Lorenzo Servitje," 244–245.

100. *Bimbo: Una historia de creer y crear*, 89.

101. Frausto Crotte, "Lorenzo Servitje," 245.

102. José de Coacuterdeba, "With Elite Backing, a Catholic Order Has Pull in Mexico," *Wall Street Journal*, January 23, 2006.

103. Frausto Crotte, "Lorenzo Servitje," 246–247.

104. "Rise of the Catholic Right," *Newsweek*, June 15, 2003.

105. Roberto Servitje, "Altos vuelos," in Cheram S., *Al grano*, 344.

106. Frausto Crotte, "Lorenzo Servitje," 265–266.

107. Frausto Crotte, "Lorenzo Servitje," 247–248.

108. Frausto Crotte, "Lorenzo Servitje," 242–243.

109. "¿Y don Lorenzo no tendrá nada que decir?," *Proceso*, May 17, 2010; "El 'mea culpa' de Servitje sobre Marcial Maciel," *Proceso*, May 29, 2010.

110. Arturo Alfaro Galán, "Reparte la SEP-Puebla libros de dianética en las escuelas públicas," *La Jornada*, September 22, 2011; Juan Pablo Proat, "Dianética: la 'religión' que aniquila," *Revista Proceso*, March 18, 2012.

111. Scientology, "Academic Rescue Mission to Mexico," accessed July 12, 2023, https://www.scientology.org/how-we-help/applied-scholastics/community-actions/mexico.html.

112. Matt Moffett, "Mexico's Biggest Bread Maker Sees Opportunity in Free Trade," *Wall Street Journal*, October 3, 1991.

113. Juan Luis Fuentes Fumagalli, "Bimbo en Guatemala" (case study, Universidad Da Vinci de Guatemala, n.d.), https://udv.academia.edu/JuanLuisFuentes.

114. Grupo Bimbo, *Informe Annual*, 1999, 15.

115. Moreno-Lázaro, "The Bread of the Americas," 98; Cherem S., *Al grano*, 318–320.

116. "Mrs. Baird's About Us," accessed July 10, 2023, https://www.mrsbairds.com/about-us.

117. "Roberto Servitje, altos vuelos," in Cheram S., *Al grano*, 314–329; Dan Malovany, "The Book on Bimbo," *BakingBusiness.com*, December 8, 2010.

118. "Roberto Servitje, altos vuelos," in Cheram S., *Al grano*, 319–320; Feike de Jong, "Nueva dirreción," *Expansión*, September 30, 2005.

119. "Roberto Servitje, altos vuelos," in Cheram S., *Al grano*, 319.

120. "Roberto Servitje, altos vuelos," in Cheram S., *Al grano*, 320–321.

121. Dan Malovany, "The Book on Bimbo," *Baking Business.com*, December 8, 2010, https://www.bakingbusiness.com/articles/33766-dan-malovany-the-book-on-bimbo.

122. Moreno-Lázaro, "The Bread of the Americas," 88–92; Cherem S., *Al grano*, 247–254.

123. Bloomberg News, "Anheuser-Busch Plans Spinoff of Campbell Taggart Subsidiary," *New York Times*, July 27, 1995.

124. Ted Streuli, "There's a Bimbo on Broadway," *Journal Record*, March 20, 2012, https://journalrecord.com/2012/03/20/periscope-there's-a-bimbo-on-broadway-opinion/.

125. "Mexico's Bimbo Sees Low US Growth in Sara Lee Units," Reuters, October 24, 2011, https://www.reuters.com/article/grupobimbo-idAFN1E79N0IX20111024.

126. Gill Hyslop, "Grupo Bimbo Buys East Balt Bakeries to Expand Global Footprint," *Bakery & Snacks*, July 20, 2017, https://www.bakeryandsnacks.com/Article/2017/07/21/Grupo-Bimbo-buys-East-Balt-Bakeries-to-expand-global-footprint#; "Mexico's Bimbo Enters Africa Market with Morocco Acquisition," Reuters, April 27, 2017, https://www.reuters.com/article/grupo-bimbo-morocco/mexicos-bimbo-enters-africa-market-with-morocco-acquisition-idUSL1N1HZ2OS.

127. Kacey Culliney, "Grupo Bimbo and General Mills Make Forbes 'Most Innovative' List," *Bakery & Snacks*, September 1, 2014, https://www.bakeryandsnacks.com/Article/2014/09/01/Forbes-Most-Innovative-Grupo-Bimbo-General-Mills-make-cut.

128. Jon Chorley, "Entenmann's Baker is Committed to a Sweet Future," *Forbes*, May 18, 2022; Josh Sosland, "Grupo Bimbo Embracing Regenerative Agriculture," *Food Business News*, February 16, 2023, https://www.foodbusinessnews.net/articles/23239-grupo-bimbo-embracing-regenerative-agriculture.

Chapter 6

1. Walmart de México (Walmex) is a subsidiary of Walmart. Throughout this chapter I refer to the Mexican subsidiary as Walmex or Walmart de México to recognize the Mexican origins of the company that builds on the Aurrerá supermarket chain. Walmart is used to refer to the larger transnational company.

2. Javier Salinas and Silvia Chavez, "Piden al gobierno de Fox, 'una solución politica' al caso Walmart Teotihucán," *La Jornada*, October 15, 2004; "Mexico: Walmart canta victoria en Teotihuacan," Inter Press Service, October 14, 2004, https://ipsnoticias.net/2004/10/mexico-Walmart-canta-victoria-en-teotihuacan/.

3. David Barstow and Alejandra Xanic von Bertrab, "How Walmart Used Payoffs to Get Its Way in Mexico," *New York Times*, December 17, 2012.

4. Diana Christina Denham, "The Persistence of Indigenous Markets in Mexico's 'Supermarket Revolution'" (PhD diss., Portland State University, 2020), 9–10.

5. Walmart de México, *Informe Anual*, 2007 and 2009.

6. Tracey Deutsch, *Building a Housewife's Paradise: Gender, Politics, and American Grocery Stores in the Twentieth Century* (Chapel Hill: University of North Carolina Press, 2010).

7. See Alfred Chandler, *The Visible Hand: The Managerial Revolution in American Business* (Cambridge, Mass.: Belknap Press of Harvard University Press, 1977), 209–239; Tracey Deutsch, *Building a Housewife's Paradise: Gender, Politics, and American Grocery Stores in the Twentieth Century* (Chapel Hill: University of North Carolina Press, 2010); and Shane Hamilton, *Supermarket USA: Food and Power in the Cold War Farms Race* (New Haven, Conn.: Yale University Press, 2018).

8. Javier Moreno Lázaro, "Los españoles y la revolución comercial mexicana: Las cadenas de supermercadors, 1921–2011," *Investigaciones de Historia Económica* 8 (2012): 69–82.

9. "Aurrera-CIFRA: Siempre Adelante," in Asociación Nacional de Tiendas de Autoservicio y Departamentales (ANTAD), *El pochteca moderno: Grandes historias de los supermercados y tiendas departamentales contado por sus fundadores* (Mexico City: ANTAD, 2003), 69–73.

10. Joel Millman, "The Merchant of Mexico," *Forbes*, August 5, 1991; "Muere Jerónimo Arango, el millonario Forbes detrás de la creación de Aurrera," *Forbes México*, April 6, 2020; Moreno Lázaro, "Los españoles y la revolución Comercial Mexicana," 72; Carlos Mondragón, "Strategic Alliances in Mexico: The Case of Wal Mart-Cifra" (PhD diss., University of Texas at Austin, 1997), 62–64.

11. Mario Cerutti and Eva Rivas Sada, "El agrocomercio como escalón a las grandes cadenas urbanas: Ángel Losada Gómez y la Construcción del Grupo Gigante (1923–2004)," in *De la colonia a la globalización: Empresarios cántabros en México*, ed. Rafael Domínguez Martín and Mario Cerutti Pignat (Santander: Universidad de Cantabria, 2021), 264.

12. Cerutti and Rivas Sada, "El agrocomercio como escalón a las grandes cadenas urbanas," 268–272.

13. "Comercial Mexicana: Una tienda muy nuestra," in ANTAD, *El pochteca moderno*, 87–97.

14. *Francisco Martín Borque: Forjador incansable* (Mexico City: Miguel Ángel Porrúa, 2001), 99–204.

15. *Francisco Martín Borque*, 135–137.

16. Diego López Rosado, *El abasto de productos alimenticios en la ciudad de México* (Mexico City: Fondo de Cultura Económica, 1988), 555; Schwentesius and Gómez, "Supermarkets in Mexico," 489–490.

17. Moreno Lázaro, "Los españoles y la revolución Comercial Mexicana," 70–74; Leonardo Daniel Bernardo Aparaicio, "¿Quién era el dueño de almacenes Blanco? El icónico super de los años ochentas," *Tu Cochinita*, June 8, 2023, https://tucochinito.com/noticias/empresas-y-negocios/quien-era-dueno-de-almacenes-blanco-el-iconico-super-de-los-anos-ochentas/.

18. Moreno Lázaro, "Los españoles y la revolución comercial mexicana," 74.

19. "Casa Ley: Las grandes bateadores del comercio," in ANTAD, *El pochteca moderno*, 127–137.

20. "Grupo Chedraui: Una tradición jarocha," in ANTAD, *El pochteca moderno*, 99–105.

21. Larry Rohter, "Mexico Loosening Investment Rules," *New York Times*, May 16, 1989; Mondragón, "Strategic Alliances in Mexico," 60–61.

22. For Walmart's overall strategy, see Nelson Lichtenstein, *The Retail Revolution: How Walmart Created a Brave New World of Business* (New York: Metropolitan Books, 2009); and Bethany Moreton, *To Serve God and Walmart: The Making of Christian Free Enterprise* (Cambridge, Mass.: Harvard University Press, 2009); Chris Tilly, "Walmart in Mexico: The Limits of Growth," in *Walmart: The Face of Twenty-First-Century Capitalism* ed. Nelson Lichtenstein (New York: New Press, 2006); Julio Moreno, "Walmart y la diplomacia económica en Américan Latina," *Foreign Affairs en Español*, April–June 2004.

23. Isadore Barmash, "Walmart in Venture with Mexican Store," *New York Times*, July 11, 1991; Louise Lee and Joe Millman, "Walmart to Invest $1.2 Billion for Control of Mexican Retailer," *Wall Street Journal*, June 4, 1997; Mondragón, "Strategic Alliances in Mexico," 65–66.

24. Walmart, *Annual Report*, 1994, 9.

25. "A Walmart for Mexico City," *New York Times*, August 30, 1993; Lee and Millman, "Walmart to Invest $1.2 Billion for Control of Mexican Retailer"; Walmart, *Annual Report*, 1997, 19.

26. Mondragón, "Strategic Alliances in Mexico," 10.

27. Matilde Dalila Cervantes Godoy, "The Growth of Supermarkets in Mexico: Impacts on Production and Transaction Costs of Small-Scale Farmers" (PhD diss., University of Guelph, 2007), 52.

28. For discussion of the 1990s economic crisis, see Enrique C. Ochoa and T. D. Wilson, eds., "Mexico in the 1990s: Economic Crisis, Social Polarization, and Class Struggle," *Latin American Perspectives* 28, no. 3 (May 2001).

29. Moreno Lázaro, "Los españoles y la revolución Comercial Mexicana," 74–76.

30. Chávez, "The Transformation of Mexican Retailing," 503–513; Zacarías Ramírez Tamayo, "Chedraui adquiere Carrefour México," *El Universal*, March 13. 2005.

31. Cynthia Barrera Díaz, "Mexico's Chedraui Chases Rivals with IPO," Reuters, April 19, 2010; Erin Carlyle, "Alfredo Chedraui Obeso, Head of Mexican Walmart Competitor, Now a Billionaire," *Forbes*, January 14, 2013; Russell Redman, "Smart & Final to Be Acquired by Bodega Latina for $620 Million," *Supermarket News*, May 13, 2021, https://www.supermarketnews.com/retail-financial/smart-final-be-acquired-bodega-latina-620-million.

32. Elliot Zwieback, "Merger of Mexican Supermarkets Includes U.S. Stores," *Supermarket News*, December 17, 2007, https://www.supermarketnews.com/retail-amp-financial/merger-mexican-supermarkets-includes-us-stores.

33. José Gasca and Felipe Torres, "El control corporativo de la distribución de alimentos en México," *Revista Problemas del Desarrollo* 176, no. 45 (January–March 2014): 147–149.

34. "Chedraui duplica ganancias del 4T de 2022 tras comprar a Arteli," *El Economista*, February 21, 2023, https://www.eleconomista.com.mx/mercados/Chedraui-duplica-ganancias-del-IV-Trim.-tras-comprar-a-Arteli-20230221-0102.html.

35. Calculated from Walmart de México, *Informe Anual*, 1999–2022.

36. Walmart de México, *Informe Anual*, 2001, 2.

37. Alexander Hanrath, "Walmart Hopes to Clone Its Mexican Cash Cow," *Financial Times*, April 6. 2002.

38. Elizabeth Malkin, "Wal-mart Will Offer Retail Banking in Mexico, an Underserved Market," *New York Times*, November 24, 2006.

39. Walmart de México, *Informe Anual*, 2011, 11 and 19.

40. Amy Guthrie, "Wal-Mart de Mexico Sells Bank Business to Inbursa," *Wall Street Journal*, December 18, 2014; Walmart de México, *Informe Anual*, 2014, 89.

41. Hanrath, "Walmart Hopes to Clone Its Mexican Cash Cow."

42. Walmart de México, *Informe Anual*, 2007, 2009, 2015, and 2021.

43. Hanrath, "Walmart Hopes to Clone Its Mexican Cash Cow."

44. Schwentesius and Gómez, "Supermarkets in Mexico," 495–496.

45. Walmart de México, *Informe Anual*, 1999, 14; Walmart de México, *Informe Anual*, 2001, 3.

46. Laura Hillen, "Walmart Mexico Announces New $36 Million Distribution Center in Yucatán," *andnowuknow.com*, July 5, 2017, https://m.andnowuknow.com/quick-dish/walmart-mexico-announces-new-36-million-distribution-center-yucatan/laura-hillen/54368; "Walmart Goes Ahead with Huge New Distribution Center," *Yucatán Magazine*, July 4, 2017, https://yucatanmagazine.com/walmart-goes-ahead-with-huge-new-distribution-center/.

47. Noi Mahoney, "Walmart Opens $42 Million Distribution Center in Mexico," *Freight Waves*, September 22, 2020, https://www.freightwaves.com/news/walmart-opens-42-million-distribution-center-in-mexico.

48. "Walmart de México Builds Distribution Centers in Tlaxcala and El Bajío," *Opportimes*, September 13, 2022, https://www.opportimes.com/walmart-de-mexico-builds-distribution-centers-in-tlaxcala-and-el-bajio/.

49. Reardon and Berdegué, "The Rapid Rise of Supermarkets in Latin America," 378–384; and Thomas Reardon, Peter Timmer, and Julio Berdegué, "The Rapid Rise of Supermarkets in Developing Countries: Induced Organizational, Institutional, and Technological Change in Agrifood Systems," *eJADE: Journal of Agricultural and Development Economics* 1, no. 2 (2004): 168–183.

50. Cervantes Godoy, "The Growth of Supermarkets in Mexico"; Schwentesius and Gómez, "Supermarkets in Mexico."

51. David Barstow and Alejandra Xanic von Bertrab, "How Walmart Used Payoffs to Get Its Way in Mexico," *New York Times*, December 17, 2012.

52. David Barstow, "Vast Mexico Bribery Case Hushed Up by Walmart After Top-Level Struggle," *New York Times*, April 22, 2012.

53. Barstow, "Vast Mexico Bribery Case Hushed Up by Walmart."

54. Barstow and Xanic von Bertrab, "How Walmart Used Payoffs."

55. Barstow and Xanic von Bertrab, "How Walmart Used Payoffs."

56. Barstow and Xanic von Bertrab, "How Walmart Used Payoffs."

57. Margath A. Walker, David Walker, and Yanga Villagómez Velazquez, "The Wal-Martification of Teotihuacán: Issues of Resistance and Cultural Heritage," in *Wal-Mart World: The World's Biggest Corporation in the Global Economy*, ed. Stanley D. Brunn (New York: Routledge, 2006).

58. "Cultura-México: Walmart otra vez bajo fuego," Inter Press Service, August 25, 2005, https://ipsnoticias.net/2005/08/cultura-mexico-Walmart-otra-vez-bajo -fuego/.

59. Barstow and Xanic von Bertrab, "How Walmart Used Payoffs to Get Its Way in Mexico."

60. Barstow and Xanic von Bertrab, "How Walmart Used Payoffs to Get Its Way in Mexico"; "Fallece preso que denuncio daños de Walmart en Teotihuacán," *Proceso*, April 10, 2012, https://www.proceso.com.mx/cultura/2010/4/12/fallece -preso-que-denuncio-danos-de-Walmart-en-teotihuacan-8381.html; Adrián Ramírez López, "Walmart: El alto costo de los 'precios bajos,'" *Contralinea*, April 21, 2013, https://contralinea.com.mx/opinion/walmart-el-alto-costo-de -losprecios-bajos/.

61. COEFECE, *Estudio de competencia en el canal moderno del comercio al menudeo de alimentos y bebidas* (Mexico City: Comisión Federal de Competencia Económica, November 2020), 33–34.

62. Rubén Guerrero, Jacqueline Chacón, Elisa Mariscal, and Alexander Elbittar, "Los efectos sobre el bienestar local de la expansion de Walmart, 2009–2020," *Social Science Research Network*, November 2020, https://papers.ssrn.com/sol3/papers.cfm?abstract_id=3738400.

63. David Atkin, Benjamin Faber, and Marco Gonzalez-Navarro, "Retail Globalization and Household Welfare: Evidence from Mexico," *Journal of Political Economy* 126, no. 1 (2018): 69.

64. Alexander Hanrath, "Mexican Stores Wilt in the Face of Walmart," *Financial Times*, August 13, 2002.

65. Cited in Lichtenstein, *The Retail Revolution*, 118–119.

66. See Moreton, *To Serve God and Walmart*.

67. Carolina Bank Muñoz, *Building Power from Below: Chilean Workers Take on Walmart* (Ithaca, N.Y.: ILR Press, 2017), 57.

68. Carolina Bank Muñoz, Bridget Kenny, and Antonio Stecher, eds. *WALMART in the Global South: Workplace Culture, Labor Politics, and Supply Chains* (Austin: University of Texas Press, 2018).

69. José Alfonso Bouzas Ortíz, "Contratación colectiva de protección," *Revista Latinoamericana de Derechos Social*, no. 9 (July–December 2009): 45.

70. Gerardo Hernández, "Contratos de protección, el gran desafío para reforma laboral y el T-MEC," *El Economista*, November 22, 2021.

71. Walmart de México, *Informe Anual*, 2002, 19; "Las más grandes empleadores," *Expansión*, June 25–July 8, 2012, 316.

72. Chris Tilly and José Luis Álvarez Galván, "Lousy Jobs, Invisible Unions: The Mexican Retail Sector in the Age of Globalization," *International Labor and Working-Class History* 70 (Fall 2006): 61–85.

73. See the studies in *Contratación colectiva de protección en México: Informe a la Organización Regional Interamericana de Trabajadores (ORIT)* (Mexico City: Universidad Nacional Autónoma de México, 2007); Esteban Conde, "El estado de indefensión de los trabajadores del Grupo Walmart de México en el Distrito Federal, Ante los contractos de protección colectiva" (law thesis, Universidad Nacional Autónoma de México, June 2009).

74. Tilly, "Walmart in Mexico," 205; Chris Tilly, "Walmart and Its Workers: *NOT* the Same All Over the World," *Connecticut Law Review* 39, no. 4 (May 2007): 8–11.

75. Conde, "El estado de indefensión de los trabajadores"; José Alfonso Bouzas Ortíz and Luis Oliver Reyes Ramos, "Walmart," in *Contratación Colectiva de Protección en México: Informe a la Organización Regional Interamericana de Trabajadores (ORIT)* (Mexico City: Universidad Nacional Autónoma de México, 2007), 135.

76. Steven Greenhouse, "How Walmart Persuades Its Workers Not to Unionize," *The Atlantic*, June 8, 2015; Orson Mason, "Labor Relations and You at the Walmart Distribution Center #6022," September 1991, https://files.schuminweb .com/journal/2010/walmart-anti-union-manuals.pdf; "Walmart: A Manager's Toolbox to Remaining Union Free," May 2, 2024, http://reclaimdemocracy.org/ wordpress/wp-content/uploads/2012/08/antiunionman.pdf.

77. Gabriela Victoria Alvarado, "WALMART Culture in the Information Technologies Industry in Mexico," in *WALMART in the Global South*, ed. Carolina Bank Muñoz, Bridget Kenny, and Antonio Stecher (Austin: University of Texas Press, 2018), 170–172.

78. Conde, "El estado de indefensión de los trabajadores," 232–254.

79. Cited in Conde, "El estado de indefensión de los trabajadores," 245.

80. Conde, "El estado de indefensión de los trabajadores," 243–247.

81. Conde, "El estado de indefensión de los trabajadores," 250–252; Julio Hernández López, "¿Sindicalismo en Walmart?," *La Jornada*, June 18, 2007.

82. Subcomandate Marcos, "ONG piden boicot a Walmart por condiciones laborales de empleados," *Rebelión*, November 30, 2007, https://rebelion.org/ong -piden-boicot-a-Walmart-por-condiciones-laborales-de-empleados/.

83. Alfredo Méndez and Notimex, "Ampara la corte a un trabajador contra práctica de tienda de raya en Walmart," *La Jornada*, September 3, 2008.

84. "La Suprema Corte vs Walmart," *Expansión*, September 5, 2008.

85. Joe Contreras, "Unpaid Teens Bag Groceries for Walmart," *Newsweek*, July 30, 2007.

86. Jesús Ramirez Cuevas, "Los cerillos de Walmart," *La Jornada*, August 7, 2005; Ricardo Ramírez Bautista, Carmen Zambrano Canales, and Iván Zamora Aguilar, "Ética corporative y prática idebidas en México: Una aproximación del

trabajo de los empacadores en Walmart" (thesis, Universidad Autónoma de México, Iztapalapa, June 2005), 95.

87. Proyecto de Derechos Económicos, Sociales y Culturales (PRODESC), *Lo barato sale caro: Violaciones a los derechos humanos laborales en Walmart México* (Mexico City: Proyecto de Derechos Económicos, Sociales y Culturales, AC, 2008), 44–45.

88. PRODESC, *Lo barato sale caro*; Rosalinda Márquez García, "La justiciabilidad de los derechos humanos laborales de las mujeres y la infancia en México: Caso Walmex," *Defensor: Revista de derechos humanos*, August 2010, 18–23.

89. "Trabajadores de Walmart denuncian violaciones a sus derechos laborales," *Expansión*, April 27, 2012; "Trabajadores de Walmart destapan abusos en México y EU," *Aristegui Noticias*, August 28, 2023, https://aristeguinoticias.com/2704/mexico/trabajadores-de-walmart-destapan-abusos-en-mexico-y-eu/.

90. Yoel Esquivel, "¿Empacador voluntario? Esto se necesita para ser 'cerillito,'" *Excelsior*, June 5, 2022.

91. Mary Ellen Cagbassola, "Mexico Walmart Not Allowing Grocery Baggers Over 60 to Return to Work," *Newsweek*, June 18, 2021.

92. Blanca Juárez, "Walmart cede, admitirá de nuevo a empacadores adultos mayores en sus tiendas," *El Economista*, August 3, 2021.

93. Proyecto de Derechos Económico, Sociales y Culturales (PRODESC), *Lo barato sale caro: Violaciones a los derechos humanos laborales en Wal-Mart México* (Mexico City: PRODESC, 2008); Tilly, "Wal-Mart in Mexico," 191.

94. PRODESC, *Lo barato sale caro*, 12 and 43.

95. "Trabajo-México: Derechos sin rostro de mujer," Inter Press Services, March 3, 2009, https://ipsnoticias.net/2009/03/03/.

96. Alvarado, "WALMART Culture in the Information Technologies Industry in Mexico," 150–180.

97. Lauren Debter, "Walmart to Cough Up $282 Million to Put Years-Long Bribery Investigation Behind It," *Forbes*, June 20, 2019.

98. Alex M. Saragoza, *The Monterrey Elite and the Mexican State, 1880–1940* (Austin: University of Texas Press, 1988); Stephen H. Haber, *Industry and Underdevelopment: The Industrialization of Mexico, 1890–1940* (Stanford: Stanford University Press, 1989).

99. Michael Snodgrass, *Deference and Defiance in Monterrey: Workers, Paternalism, and Revolution in Mexico, 1890–1950* (Cambridge: Cambridge University Press, 2003).

100. "FEMSA: Our History," accessed September 2, 2023, https://www.femsa.com/en/about-femsa/our-history/.

101. Amanda Ciafone, *Counter-Cola: A Multinational History of the Global Corporation* (Oakland: University of California Press, 2019), 199–200; FEMSA, *Informe Anual*, 2002, 9; Coca-Cola FEMSA (website), accessed September 3, 2023, https://www.femsa.com/en/business-units/coca-cola-femsa/.

102. Dagnia González, "Origen del nombre de Oxxo," *América Retail*, December 19, 2022.

103. "As Oxxo Grows, Abarrotes Decline. But Tijuana Franchiser Has Other Ideas," *Mexico News Daily*, July 1, 2014, http://mexiconewsdaily.com/mexicolife/Oxxo -grows-abarrotes-decline-tijuana-franchiser-ideas/.

104. Calculated from FEMSA, *Informe Anual*, various 2002–2022.

105. "Estos son los servicios que ofrece el Oxxo que seguramente no conocías," *El Heraldo de México*, May 30, 2020.

106. Rosalía Lara, "Oxxo y 7-Eleven, los rivales a vencer en el sector de comida rápida," *Expansión*, July 27, 2017.

107. Fernanda Celis, "Oxxo vende más comida que Vips, McDonald's y Starbucks," *Forbes México*, January 4, 2019, https://www.forbes.com.mx/Oxxo-vende-mas -comida-que-vips-mcdonalds-y-starbucks/.

108. Karina Hernández Mundo, "Oxxo, el major alimentando en el sector de comida rápida," *El Economista*, June 20, 2015, https://www.eleconomista.com .mx/empresas/Oxxo-el-mejor-alimentado-en-el-sector-de-comida-rapida -20150719-0043.html.

109. Lara, "Oxxo y 7-Eleven."

110. Joaquín A. Marrón-Ponce, Tania G. Sánchez-Pimienta, Sonia Rodríguez-Ramírez, Carolina Batis, and Gustavo Cediel, "Ultra-Processed Foods Consumption Reduces Dietary Diversity and Micronutrient Intake in the Mexican Population," *Journal of Human Nutrition and Diet* 36 (2023): 241–251; Katherine D. McManus, "What Are Ultra-Processed Foods and Are They Bad for Our Health?," *Harvard Health Blog*, January 9, 2020.

111. Cecila Isabel Oviedo-Solís, Eric A, Monterrubio-Flores, Gustavo Cediel, Edgar Denova-Gutiérrez, and Simón Barquera, "Trend of Ultraprocessed Product Intake Is Associated with the Double Burden of Malnutrition in Mexican Children and Adolescents," *Nutrients* 14, no. 20 (2022).

112. Elisa Pineda, Eric J. Brunner, Clare H. Llewellyn, and Jennifer S. Mindell, "The Retail Food Environment and Its Association with Body Mass Index in Mexico," *International Journal of Obesity* 45 (2021): 1225.

113. Roberto Noguez, "No todo es Oxxo; Femsa quiere competir con 3B y abrir tienditas de barrio," *Forbes México*, February 24, 2023.

114. FEMSA, *Informe Anual*, 2022, 16.

115. "Sueldos de Oxxo en México," Indeed, accessed October 4, 2023, https://mx .indeed.com/cmp/Oxxo-8d171c32/salaries.

116. "Precarización Laboral. FEMSA/OXXO: Bajos salaries, explotación, y precarización de sus tranajadores," *La Izquierda Diario*, June 16, 2020, https:// www.laizquierdadiario.mx/FEMSA-OXXO-bajos-salarios-explotacion-y -precarizacion-de-sus-trabajadores.

117. "Van 14 asaltos con vioelencia este 2017," *Rancherita del Aire*, February 13, 2017; "Crimen organizado hacer arder Michiacán; Oxxo Cierra establecimientos en Apatzingán," *Sin Embargo*, July 4, 2017.

118. Alejandra Rodriguez, "Violencia en Guanajuato: 25 Oxxo's fueron incendiadors, asegura Femsa," *El Financiero*, August 10, 2022; "Tras quema de Oxxos y otros comercios, sector pide reforzar estado de derecho," *Forbes México*, August 12, 2022.

119. Sergio Abraham Méndez Moissen, "Instalan Oxxo en Maquila de Tamailipas: ¿El regreso de las tiendas de raya?," *La Izquierda Diario*, November 20, 2017; David Díaz, "Instalan tienda de auto servicio en parque industrial maquiladora," *EnLíneaDireta.info*, December 17, 2016; Real News Facebook post, accessed October 5, 2023, https://www.facebook.com/320936818042528/ photos/el-colmoabren-Oxxo-dentro-de-maquiladora-masimopor-deyanira -apodacaparece-que-el/1422180717918127/; suriano_juan30alonsin, TikTok, March 13, 2022, https://www.tiktok.com/@suriano_juan30alonsin/video/ 7074673858963328262.

Chapter 7

1. Rius, *La basura que comemos: Transgénicos y comida chatarra* (Mexico City: Grijalbo, 2000), 12.

2. Rius, *Mis confusiones: Memorias desmemoriadas* (Mexico City: Penguin Random House, 2014), 351.

3. "México: Paraíso de la comida chatarra," *El Poder del Consumidor*, April 22, 2007. The quotation in the title of this chapter is from this article title.

4. The quotation in this section title is from Felipe Torres Torres and Agustín Rojas Martínez, "La seguridad alimentaria en la encrucijada de las desigualdades regionales de México," *Investigaciones Regionales* 53, no. 2 (2022): 111.

5. James M. Cypher and Raúl Delgado Wise, Mexico's *Economic Dilemma: The Developmental Failure of Neoliberalism* (Lanham, Md.: Rowman and Littlefield, 2010); Richard Roman and Edur Velasco Arregui, *Continental Crucible: Big Business, Workers and Unions in the Transformation of North America* (Halifax: Fernwood / PM Press, 2015); Roberto Zepeda, *The Decline of Labor Unions in Mexico During the Neoliberal Period* (Cham: Palgrave Macmillan, 2021), 174–175.

6. See Mercedes Gonzalez de la Rocha, *The Resources of Poverty: Women and Survival in a Mexican City* (Cambridge, Mass: Blackwell, 1994); and Mercedes Gonzalez de la Rocha, "From the Resources of Poverty to the Poverty of Resources?," *Latin American Perspectives* 119 (July 2001): 72–100.

7. Cypher and Delgado Wise, *Mexico's Economic Dilemma*, 1.

8. Sergio Zermeño, *La desmodernidad Mexicana y las alternativas a la violencia y a la exclusión en nuestros días* (Mexico City: Océano, 2005), 41.

9. See Araceli Damián and Julio Boltvinik, "A Table to Eat On: The Meaning and Measurement of Poverty in Latin America," in *Latin American After Neoliberalism: Turning the Tide in the 21st Century?*, ed. Eric Hershberg and Fred Rosen (New York: New Press, 2006), 153; ad Julio Boltvinik's columns, "Economía Moral," *La Jornada*, July 29, 2011, and August 12, 2011; and Araceli Damián, "Dos modelos de medición de la pobreza en México: Resultados por entidad

federativa," November 7, 2023, https://www.evalua.cdmx.gob.mx/videos/3hNDnDNZjTw.

10. Julio Boltvinik and Araceli Damián, "Pobreza creciente y estructuras sociales cada vez más desiguales en México: Una vision integrada y crítica," *Acta Sociológica* no. 70 (May–August 2016): 271–296; Dídimo Castillo Fernández and Jorge Arzate Salgado, "Economic Crisis, Poverty and Social Policy in Mexico," *Critical Sociology* 42, no. 1 (2016): 87–104.

11. Torres Torres and Rojas Martínez, "La seguridad alimentaria," 111.

12. CONEVAL, "El CONEVAL Presenta las estimaciones de pobreza multidimensional 2022," August 10, 2023, https://www.coneval.org.mx/SalaPrensa/Comunicadosprensa/Documents/2023/Comunicado_07_Medicion_Pobreza_2022.pdf.

13. Lowenberg, "The Plight of Mexico's Indigenous Women."

14. Elisa Alejandra Martínez Rubio, Michelle Judd de la Luz, and Agustín Escobar Latapí, "Poverty and Agricultural Labor in the Culiacán Valley," *CIESAS Bulletin*, no. 4 (May 27, 2022): 2; Florencio Posadas Segura, "La situación de los trabajadores rurales en Sinaloa," *Estudios sociales* 49 (January–June 2017).

15. Martínez Rubio, Judd de la Luz, and Escobar Latapí, "Poverty and Agricultural Labor in the Culiacán Valley," 6–8.

16. Posadas Segura, "La situación de los trabajadores rurales en Sinaloa," 266.

17. Chris Kraul, "Boom in Baja: Lower Costs, Consumer Demand Year-Round Fruit Pushing Fruit, Vegetable Production South," *Los Angeles Times*, May 16, 1988.

18. Laura Velasco, Christian Zlolniski, and Marie-Laure Coubes, *De jornaleros a colonos: Residencia, trabajo e identidad en el Valle de San Quintín* (Tijuana: Colegio de la Frontera Norte, 2014), 79; INEGI, México en Cifras, accessed November 26, 2022, https://www.inegi.org.mx/app/areasgeograficas/?ag=03002.

19. Christian Zlolniski, *Made in Baja: The Lives of Farmworkers and Growers Behind Mexico's Transnational Agricultural Boom* (Oakland: University of California Press, 2019), 187.

20. Humberto González, "Specialization on a Global Scale and Agrifood Vulnerability: 30 Years of Export Agriculture in Mexico," *Development Studies Research* 1, no. 1 (2014): 295–310.

21. Gerardo Rodríguez Solis, María del Carmen Arellano Gálvez, and Patricia Aranda Gallegos, "Racialización y trabajo agrícola en el Noroeste de México: Análisis a partir de notas de prensa 2013–2019," *Noroeste de México*, no. 3 (January–June 2021): 135–163.

22. Iván Rioja-Scott, "¿Comida chatarra o cuestión de conveniencia?," *Industria Alimenticia*, September 1, 2015, http://www.industriaalimenticia.com/blogs/14-opinion/post/87954-comida-chatarra-o-cuestion-de-conveniencia.

23. Steve Wiggins and Sharada Keats, *The Rising Cost of a Healthy Diet: Changing Relative Prices of Food in High Income and Emerging Economies* (London: Overseas Development Institute, May 2015), 38.

24. Antonio Yúñez-Naude, "Old Foods and New Consumers in Mexico Under Economic Reforms," *African Journal of Agricultural and Resource Economics* 9, no. 1 (2014): 46–47.

25. Joaquín Alejandro Marrón-Ponce, Lizbeth Tolentino-Mayo, Mauricio Hernández-F., and Carolina Batis, "Trends in Ultra-Processed Food Purchases from 1984 to 2016 in Mexican Households," *Nutrients* 11, no. 1 (2019): 7–8.

26. Eduardo J Gómez, "Coca-Cola's Political and Policy Influence in Mexico: Understanding the Role of Institutions, Interests and Divided Society," *Health Policy and Planning* 34 (2019): 520–528.

27. "With Average Daily Consumption of 2.2 Liters of Coca-Cola, Chiapas Leads the World," *Mexico News Daily*, August 19, 2020; Oscar Lopez and Andrew Jacobs, "In Town with Little Water, Coca-Cola Is Everywhere. So Is Diabetes," *New York Times*, July 14, 2018.

28. Gustavo Olaiz-Fernández, Rosalba Rojas, Carlos A. Aguilar-Salinas, Juan Rauda, and Salvador Villalpando, "Diabetes mellitus en adultos mexicanos: Resultados de la Encuesta Nacional de Salud 2000," *Salud Pública de México* 49, no. 3 (January 2007).

29. Kennia Velásquez and Elizabeth Rosales, "Las fichas de Coca Cola: Táticas comerciales para incidir en políticas de salud pública" (CONNECTAS and POPLAB, 2022), accessed December 10, 2023, https://www.connectas.org/especiales/las-fichas-de-coca-cola/; R. Rojas-Martínez, C. Escamilla-Nuñez, C.A. Aguilar-Salinas, L. Castro-Porras, M. Romero-Martínez, and E. Lazcano-Ponce, "Trends in the Mortality of Diabetes in Mexico from 1998 to 2022: A Joinpoint Regression and Age-Period-Cohort Effect Analysis," *Public Health* 226 (January 2024): 128–137.

30. Barry M. Popkin, Camila Corvalan, Laurence M. Grummer-Strawn, "Dynamics of the Double Burden of Malnutrition and the Changing Nutrition Reality," *The Lancet* 395 (2020): 65–74; Maria F. Kroker-Lobos, Andrea Pedroza-Tobías, Lilia S. Pedraza, and Juan Rivera, "The Double Burden of Undernutrition and Excess Body Weight in Mexico," *American Journal of Clinical Nutrition* 100 (2014): 1652S–1658S.

31. "Inseguridad alimentaria y percepción de cambios en la alimentación en hogares mexicanos durante el confinamiento por la pandemia de Covid–19," Instituto Nacional de Salud Pública, Escuela de Salúd Publica de México, accessed December 7, 2023, https://www.espm.mx/blog/inseguridad-alimentaria-percepcion-cambios-hogares-mexicanos/.

32. Cited in Carola García Calderón, "Los alimentos chatarra en México, regulación publicitaria y autorregulación," *Derecho a Comunicar*, May–August 2011, 171–195.

33. Carola García Calderón, *Cómo engordamos: Comida chatarra, obesidad y estrategias de publicidad* (Mexico City: UNAM, 2019); Carola García Calderón, *Hábitos alimentarios, publicidad y política de salud* (Mexico City: UNAM, 2020).

34. Andrea Sánchez Islas, "Estrategias de persuasión en la publicidad de alimentos 'chatarra' en México," in *Hábitos alimentarios, publicidad y política de salud*, ed. Carola García Calderón (Mexico City: UNAM, 2020); "'La Rosa de Guadalupe' u 'Como dice el dicho,' los favoritos de niños y Jovenes," *Expansión*, April 30, 2018.

35. José Ángela Garfias Frías and Emmanuel Galicia Martínez, "Videojuegos de publicidad de comida chitarra dirigidos a niños, en elm arco de las nuevas regulaciones de salúd," in García Calderón, *Cómo engordamos*.

36. M. Guadalupe Rodríguez Gómez, "Making a Globalized Nation in the Countryside: El Barzón, a Popular Movement in Contemporary Mexico," *Urban Anthropology and Studies of Cultural Systems and World Economic Development* 27, no. 2 (Summer 1998): 197–232; Humberto González, "Convergence: Social Movements in Mexico in the Era of Neoliberal Globalization," in *Mexico in Transition: Neoliberal Globalism, the State and Civil Society*, ed. Gerardo Otero (London: Zed Books, 2004).

37. Hubert C. de Grammont and Horacio Mackinlay, "Campesino and Indigenous Social Organizations Facing Democratic Transition in Mexico, 1938–2006," *Latin American Perspectives* 36, no. 4 (July 2009): 21–40.

38. See Enrique C. Ochoa, "The Costs of Rising Tortilla Prices in Mexico," *Relay: A Socialist Project Review* (March/April 2007); "Incesante alza del precio de la tortilla; llega hasta $15 por Kilo," *La Jornada*, January 10, 2007; Luis Hernandez Navarro, "La nueva guerra de la tortilla," *La Jornada*, January 12, 2007.

39. Analiese Richard, "'Sin Maíz No Hay País': Citizenship and Environment in Mexico's Food Sovereignty Movement," in *Environment and Citizenship in Latin America: Natures, Subjects and Struggles*, ed. Alex Latta and Hannah Wittman (New York: Berghahn Books, 2012), 59.

40. GRAIN, *¡No toquen nuestro maíz! El sistema agroalimentario industrial devasta y los pueblos en México resisten* (Mexico City: GRAIN and Editorial Itaca, 2014), 8.

41. María Virginia González Santiago, *Agroecología, saberes campesinos y agricultura como forma de vida* (Chapingo: Universidad Autónoma Chapingo, 2008); Peter M. Rosset and Miguel A. Altieri, *Agroecology: Science and Politics* (Nova Scotia: Fernwood, 2017).

42. Alexander Zaitchik, "The US-Mexico Tortilla War," *The Nation*, May 28, 2024; Zósimo Camacho, "Glifosato: Perfila Poder Judicial amparar a Monsanto," *Contralinea*, November 13, 2023.

43. Mara Rosas and Mario Fuentes, "La nueva ruralidad comunitaria y las activades no-proletarias generadoras de excedentes," in *El campesinoado y su persistencia en la actualidad Mexicana*, ed. Tanalís Padilla (Mexico City: El Fondo de Cultura Económico y El Consejo Nacional Para la Cultura y las Artes, 2013).

44. Rosas and Fuentes, "La nueva ruralidad comunitaria," 445.

45. Rosas and Fuentes, "La nueva ruralidad comunitaria," 446.

46. Cited in Hannah Schmitt, *La raíz rebelde de la resistencia en la tierra del maíz: Un relato de la CNUC* (Tlaxcala, Mexico, 2016), 3.

47. Schmitt, *La raíz rebelde*, 5.

48. Enrique C. Ochoa, interview with CNUC members, July 22, 2017.

49. "Chinese Manufacturer Sonavox Builds Plant to Supply VW, Audi," *Mexico Now*, March 6, 2017, https://mexico-now.com/sonavox-sets-up-plant-in-tlaxcala/; "Tlaxcala to Encourage Industrial Development Via Route 136," *Mexico Business*, May 27, 2022, https://mexicobusiness.news/infrastructure/news/tlaxcala -encourage-industrial-development-route-136.

50. Luz Rivera Martínez, "Resisting Repression: Building Autonomy and Justice in Tlaxcala, Mexico," Cal State LA, Latin American Studies Program, March 9, 2017.

51. Schmitt, *La raíz rebelde*, 8–10.

52. Cited in Schmitt, *La raíz rebelde*, 27.

53. Mexico Solidarity Network, "Testimony from Luz Rivera Martínez (CNUC)," April 25, 2011, https://vimeo.com/22843797.

54. Ivette Lira, "Con salario de 88.36 pesos, dejen la comida chatarra y vayan por alimentos sanos, dice nutrióloga," *Sinembargo*, November 25, 2017, https://www.sinembargo.mx/25-11-2017/3355410.

55. Ivette Lira, "Los alimentos ultraprocesados arrasan con la dieta tradicional y la salud de mexicanos, alertan," *Sinembargo*, June 1, 2017, https://www.sinembargo.mx/01-06-2017/3224048.

56. GRAIN, *¡No toquen nuestro maíz!*, 19.

57. Verónica Vásquez García, Juan Felipe Nuñez Espinoza, and Tomas Ortega Ortega, "Estructura y resiliencia social en comunidades indígenas: El caso de la union de Palmeadoras de Tlaxiaco, Oaxaca, Mexico," *REDES: Revista Hispana para el Análisis de Redes Sociales* 29, no. 2 (2018): 208.

58. Vásquez García, Nuñez Espinoza, and Ortega Ortega, "Estructura y resiliencia social en comunidades indígenas," 207; Tomás Ortega Ortega et al., "Mujeres y organización comunitaria: El caso de las palmeadoras de Tlaxiaco, Oaxaca, México," *EUTOPÍA*, no. 13 (June 2018): 33–52.

59. Tomás Ortega Ortega, Verónica Vásquez García, Diego Flores Sánchez, and Juan Felipe Nuñez Espinoza, "Agrobiodiversidad, Género, y Soberanía Alimentaria en Tlaxiaco, Oaxaca," *Revista Mexicana de Ciencias Agrícolas*, no. 18 (August 12, 2017–September 17, 2017): 3673–3682.

60. Pett, "The Fight to Save the Traditional Tortilla."

61. Victor M. Toledo and Narciso Barrera-Bassols, "Political Agroecology in Mexico: A Path Toward Sustainability," *Sustainability* 9, no. 268 (2017): 11.

62. Patricia Arias, *Del arraigo a la diáspora: Dilemas de la familia rural* (Mexico City: Miguel Ángel Porrúa, 2009), 28–30.

63. Susana González G., "Absorbe burocracia recursos para el combate a la pobreza," *La Jornada*, April 7, 2013; Emir Olivares Alonso, "Pese a millionario

gasto en programas, la pobreza en al país creció 58% en 42 años," *La Jornada*, July 31, 2013.

64. Sylvia Chant cited in Maxine Molyneux, "Mothers at the Service of the New Poverty Agenda: Progresa/Oportunidades, Mexico's Conditional Transfer Programme," *Social Policy and Administration* 40, no. 4 (August 2006): 400; Sylvia Chant, "The 'Feminisation of Poverty' and the 'Feminisation' of Anti-Poverty Programmes: Room for Revision," *Journal of Development Studies* 44, no. 2 (2008): 165–197.

65. "Compartimos la música, Erradicamos el hambre," accessed December 12, 2013, http://sinhambre.gob.mx/wp-content/themes/cruzada/fragments/en-la -cruzada/ajax-post.php?postid=21301.

66. "Compartimos la música, Erradicamos el hambre," accessed December 12, 2013, http://sinhambre.gob.mx/wp-content/themes/cruzada/fragments/en-la -cruzada/ajax-post.php?postid=21301.

67. Expofoto "Mexico Sin Hambre," accessed September 9, 2013, http://sinhambre .gob.mx/.

68. Gobierno de México, "Anuncia Sedesol a los ganadores del concurso, 'En corto contra el hambre,'" July 7, 2013, https://www.gob.mx/bienestar/prensa/ anuncia-sedesol-a-los-ganadores-del-concurso-en-corto-contra-el-hambre; Enrique C. Ochoa, "The Crusade Against Hunger and the Persistence of Poverty," *NACLA Report on the Americas* (Spring 2014): 37–40.

69. "La Cruzada Nacional Contra El Hambre En Proceso de Mejora Constante," SEDESOL Comunicado de Prensa, no. 430/300913 (9/27/13).

70. "Aseguran que se erradicará pobreza alimentaria en México," Notimex, November 18, 2010, http://espanol.news.yahoo.com/s/18112010/4/n-latam-aseguran -erradicar-aacute-pobreza-alimentaria.html.

71. James Frederick and Vincent Acovino, "How This Mexico City Food Market Is Cutting Back on Food Waste," *All Things Considered*, National Public Radio, December 15, 2023, https://www.npr.org/2023/12/15/1219737644/how-this -mexico-city-food-market-is-cutting-back-on-food-waste.

72. *Informativo Sin Hambre*, no. 2 (November 2013), http://www.sedesol.gob.mx/ boletinesSinHambre/Informativo_02/.

73. See Ana María Tepichin Valle, "Género, Pobreza, y Política Social," in *Desafíos de la pobreza para la agenda del desarrollo de México*, ed. Tonatiuh Guillén López and Gerardo Ordoñez Barba (Tijuana: Colegio del Frontera Norte, 2014), 92; Molyneux, "Mothers at the Service of the New Poverty Agenda."

74. Blanca Olivia Acuña Rodarte, "De las tortillas en comal a la harina de maíz: Mujeres y política alimentaria en Acambay, Estado de México," in *Volteando la tortilla: Génaro y maíz en la alimentación actual de México*, ed. Ivonne Vizcarra Bordi (Toluca: Universidad Autónoma del Estado de México, 2018), 268.

75. Katia Yetzani García Maldonado and Ivonne Vizcarra Bordi, "Masa con o sin nixtamal: Respuestas femininas matlatincas ante los programas sociales de alimentación," in Vizcarra Bordi, *Volteando la tortilla*, 243.

76. García Maldonado and Vizcarra Bordi, "Masa con o sin nixtamal," 244.

77. Acuña Rodarte, "De las tortillas en comal a la harina de maíz," 251–272.

78. Ayari Pasquier, "Narrativas contrastantes en torno al concepto de 'seguridad alimentaria': El caso del programa Sin Hambre," in *Inseguridad alimentaria y políticas de Alivio a la pobreza: Una vision multidisciplinaria*, ed. Blanca Rubio and Ayari Pasquier (Mexico City: UNAM, 2019), 114–115.

79. "PepsiCo México se une a la Cruzada Nacional contra el Hambre," April 8, 2013, http://www.pepsico.com.mx/PressReleases/PepsiCo_Mexico_se_une_a_la_Cruzada_Nacional_contra_el_Hambre.html; Dulce Ramos, "Robles defiende participación de Pepsi y Nestlé en Cruzada contra el Hambre," *Animal Político*, April 12, 2013, https://www.animalpolitico.com/2013/04/no-privatizamos-la-cruzada-contra-el-hambre-sedesol.

80. "Capturan chatarreras Cruzada Nacional contra el Hambre," *El Poder Consumidor*, April 16, 2013, https://elpoderdelconsumidor.org/2013/04/capturan-empresas-de-comida-chatarra-la-cruzada-nacional-contra-el-hambre/.

81. Bertha Verónica Martínez-Flores and María de Lourdes Romo Aguilar, "Entre la esperanza y la desconfianza: La participación en la Cruzada Nacional contra el Hambre," *Espiral: Estudios sobre estado y sociedad*, no. 85 (September–December 2022): 157–187.

82. Blanca Olivia Acuña Rodart, "Contradicciones y límites de la política agroalimentaria en México: De la seguridad alimentaria a la Cruzada contra el hambre," *Argumentos*, no. 79 (September–December 2015): 241–263.

83. Mariana León y Ariadna Ortega, "Gastan 8,000 mdp en la Cruzada Contra el Hambre y no ayudan ni a 10,000 personas," *Expansión Política*, February 25, 2020, https://politica.expansion.mx/mexico/2020/02/24/gastan-8-000-mdp-en-la-cruzada-contra-el-hambre-y-no-ayudan-ni-a-10-000-personas.

84. Linaloe R. Flores, "De casi 500 millones para la Cruzada contra el Hambre de Peña, 386 se fueron en presumir 'sus logros,'" *Sinembargo*, July 22, 2018, https://www.sinembargo.mx/22-07-2018/3445570.

85. David Agren, "Mexico's Congress Accused of Caving to Soda Pop Industry in Tax Cut Plan," *The Guardian*, October 19, 2015.

86. J. C. Salgado Hernández, S.W. Mg, and M.A. Colchero, "Changes in Sugar-Sweetened Beverage Purchases Across the Price Distribution After the Implementation of a Tax in Mexico: A Before-and-After Analysis," *BMC Public Health* 23, no. 265 (2023); David Agren, "Mexico State Bans Sale of Sugary Drinks and Junk Food to Children," *The Guardian*, August 6, 2020.

87. Agren, "Mexico State Bans Sale."

88. Mattha Busby, "Sugar Rush: How Mexico's Addiction to Fizzy Drinks Fueled its Health Crisis," *The Guardian*, November 4, 2022.

89. See figure 6 in chapter 4.

90. Luis Miguel González, "Segalmenx y Ovalle: Los cuentos y las cuentas," *El Economista*, June 30, 2023, https://www.eleconomista.com.mx/opinion/Segalmex-y-Ovalle-los-cuentos-y-las-cuentas-20230630-0014.html.

91. See, for example, Bartra Vergés et al., *Revoluciones agroecológicos en México* (Mexico City: La Jornada del Campo, 2022).

92. The quotation in this section title is from Virdiana Díaz, "RSE, nueva forma de generar riquezas con justicia social," *El Economista*, May 18, 2015, http://eleconomista.com.mx/industrias/2015/05/18/rse-nueva-forma-generar-riquezas-justicia-social.

93. Alejandra Salas-Porras, *La economía política neoliberal en México: ¿Quién la diseñó y cómo lo hizo?* (Madrid: Ediciones Akal, S.A., 2017).

94. Fátima Monterrosa, "El verdadero hoyo fiscal: 400 grandes empresas (casi) no paguen impuestos," *Emequis*, October 26, 2009, 11.

95. Denise Dresser, *El país de uno: Reflexiones para entender y cambiar a México* (Mexico City: Santillana Ediciones, 2011), 161–165.

96. Lourdes Casanova, *Global Latinas* (New York: Palgrave Macmillan, 2009), 138.

97. See Nicki Lisa Cole, "Global Capitalism Organizing Knowledge of Race, Gender and Class: The Case of Socially Responsible Coffee," *Race, Gender, and Class* 15, no. 1–2 (2008): 170–187; Hannah Noel, "Branding Guilt: American Apparel Inc. and Latina Labor in Los Angeles," *Diálogo* 18, no. 2 (Fall 2015): 37–52.

98. For a historical overview of charity and philanthropy in Mexico, see Moisés González Navarro, *La pobreza en Méxcio* (Mexico City: El Colegio de México, 1985); and Silvia Marina Arrom, *Containing the Poor: The Mexico City Poor House, 1774–1871* (Durham, N.C.: Duke University Press, 2000).

99. Enrique C. Ochoa, "Philanthropy (Mexico)," in *Encyclopedia of Social Welfare History of North America*, ed. John Herrick and Paul Stuart (Thousand Oaks: SAGE, 2004), 270–272; Manuel Arango, "Philanthropy in Mexico," *ReVista: Harvard Review of Latin America* (Spring 2002).

100. Roberto Delgado Gallart, "El Cemefi y el Distintivo de ESR," *El Economista*, January 26, 2015; CEMEFI, "Decálogo Empresa Socialmente Responsable," accessed July 18, 2015, http://www.cemefi.org/esr/index.php.

101. Virdiana Díaz, "RSE, nueva forma de generar riquezas con justicia social," *El Economista*, May 18, 2015, http://eleconomista.com.mx/industrias/2015/05/18/rse-nueva-forma-generar-riquezas-justicia-social.

102. Gallart, "El Cemefi y el Distintivo de ESR"; Gerardo Lozano, Christian Ehrlich, and Lizeth Leal, "Corporate Social Responsibility Status in Mexico," Working Paper, Escuela de Graduados en Administración y Dirección de Empresas, Tecnológico de Monterrey, October 2005, 3–4, https://www.apec.org/docs/default-source/publications/2005/12/corporate-social-responsiblity-in-the-apec-region-current-status-and-implications-december-2005/toc/mexico.pdf?sfvrsn=91e104f_1; "CEMEFI Empresas socialmente responables, 2023," accessed December 26, 2023, https://www.cemefi.org/resultadosesr/.

103. "CEMEFI Empresas socialmente responables, 2023," accessed December 26, 2023, https://www.cemefi.org/resultadosesr/.

104. Grupo Bimbo, "Alimentar, deleitar y servir a nuestro mundo," *Informe de Responsabilidad Social y Sustentabilidad 2010*, 5.

105. Alejandra Salas-Porras, "Corrientes de pensamiento empresarial en México (primera parte)," *Revista Mexicana de Ciencias Políticas y Sociales* (January–April 2001): 181–210; Alejandra Salas-Porras, "Corrientes de pensamiento empresarial en México (segunda parte)," *Revista Mexicana de Ciencias Políticas y Sociales* (May–December 2001): 227–257.

106. GRUMA, "Socially Responsible for Over 70 years," accessed December 26, 2023, https://www.gruma.com/en/sustainability/vision-of-social-responsibility.aspx.

107. Victor Cardoso and Reuters, "Gruma fue reconocida como mejor empresa para trabajar," *La Jornada*, May 2, 2013.

108. "ConMéxico rechaza impuesto a 'chatarra,'" *CNN Expansión*, October 17, 2013, http://www.cnnexpansion.com/economia/2013/10/17/conmexico-rechaza -impuesto-a-refrescos.

109. Ramiro Alonso, "ConMéxico implementa etiquetas contra la obesidad," *El Universal*, March 16, 2011.

110. Gabriela Rivera, "Pacto Salud con empresas luchar contra la obesidad," *24 Horas*, October 24, 2013, http://www.24-horas.mx/concerta-salud-con -empresas-estrategia-contra-la-obesidad/.

111. "ConMéxico: Anemia Continues to be Serious Health Problem," *NutraIngredients*, June 21, 2019, https://www.nutraingredients-latam.com/Article/2019/06/ 21/ConMexico-Anemia-continues-to-be-serious-public-health-problem#.

112. Enrique Ochoa, field notes in Mexico City, August 2012.

113. Pablo Cabañas Díaz, "La obesidad como Fuente de ganancia: Coca light y agua embotellada," in García Calderón, *Hábitos alimentarios, publicidad y política de salud*.

Conclusion

1. UNESCO World Heritage Convention, "Historic Centre of Oaxaca and Archaeological Site of Monte Albán," accessed May 27, 2024, https://whc.unesco.org/ en/list/415.

2. Reed Johnson, "McDonald's Loses a Round to Oaxacan Cultural Pride," *Los Angeles Times*, January 5, 2003.

3. Madhu Suri Prakash and Dana Stuchul, "McEducation, Marginalized: Multiverse of Learning-Living in Grassroots Commons," *Education Studies* 36, no. 1 (August 2004): 58–72.

4. Elena Poniatowska, "Toledo Versus McDonald's," *La Jornada*, November 13, 2002.

5. Patrick J. McDonnell, "Appreciation: Francisco Toledo, a Colossus of Mexican Culture," *Los Angeles Times*, September 6, 2019; "La historia de cuando los tamales oaxaqueños 'tumbaron' a McDonald's," *Radio Formula.mx*, September 7, 2022, https://www.radioformula.com.mx/estilo-de-vida/2022/9/7/la-historia -de-cuando-los-tamales-oaxaquenos-tumbaron-mcdonalds-730686.html.

6. World Population Review, "Most McDonald's by Country 2024," accessed June 4, 2024, https://worldpopulationreview.com/country-rankings/most -mcdonalds-by-country.

7.   Eric Holt-Giménez, *A Foodie's Guide to Capitalism: Understanding the Political Economy of What We Eat* (New York: Monthly Review Press, 2017), 56.

8.   Gustavo Esteva, "Re-Embedding Food in Agriculture," *Culture and Agriculture*, no. 48 (Winter 1994): 2–13; Gustavo Esteva and Catherine Marielle, eds., *Sin maíz, no hay país* (Mexico City: Consejo Nacional para la Cultura y las Artes, 2003).

BIBLIOGRAPHY

Primary Sources

Government Studies and Publications

COEFECE. *Estudio de competencia en el canal moderno del comercio al menudeo de alimentos y bebidas.* Mexico City: Comisión Federal de Competencia Económica, November 2020.

CONASUPO. *La CTM en la lucha por la alimentación.* Mexico City: Sistema de Distribuidoras, 1987.

CONASUPO. *Platillos Populares Mexicanos.* Mexico City: Talleres Gráficos de la Nación, 1971.

CONEVAL. "Medición de Pobreza." 2014 and 2022. http://www.coneval.org.mx/Medicion/MP/Paginas/Pobreza_2014.aspx.

CONEVAL. "Reporte CONEVAL Cifras de Pobreza por Ingreso 2008." July 18, 2009.

Crónica de Gobierno de Carlos Salinas de Gortari, 1988–1994: Tercer Año—Enero 1991–Dicienbre 1991. Mexico City: Fondo de Cultura Económico, 1994.

González González, Luis, ed. *Los presidentes de México ante la nación: Informes, manifiestos, y documentos de 1821 a 1966.* Vol. 4. Mexico City: Cámara de Diputados, 1966.

Martínez Báez, Manuel. *Libro para la madre mexicana.* Mexico City: Talleres Linotipográficos de la Beneficiencia Pública, 1934.

México, Secretaría de la Economía Nacional, Dirección General de Estadística. *Medidas regionales, Censo-Agrícola-Ganadero de 1930.* Mexico City, 1933.

México, Secretaría de la Economía Nacional. *Revista de estadística* 3, no. 12 (December 1940).

México, Secretaría de la Economía Nacional. *Informe de las actividades dessarrolladas por la Secretería de la Economía Nacional durante el period de 19 de Agosto de 1934 al 31 de julio de 1935.* Mexico City: Talleres Gráficos de la Nación, 1935.

México, Secretaría de la Economía Nacional, Dirección General de Estadística. *Informes sobre las principales estadísticas Mexicanas*. Mexico City, 1941.

México, Secretaría de Economía-Dirección General de Industrias Básicas (SE-DGIB). "Análisis de la cadena de valor maíz-tortilla: Situación actual y factores de competencia local." April 2012. http://www.2006-2012.economia.gob.mx/files/comunidad_negocios/industria_comercio/informacionSectorial/20120411_analisis_cadena_valor_maiz-tortilla.pdf.

México, Secretaría de Agricultura y Desarrollo Rural. *Panorama agroalimentario 2022*. Mexico City: Servicio de Información Agroalimentaria y Pesquera, 2022.

México, Servicio de Información Agroalimentaria y Pesquera (SIAP) of the Secretaría de Agricultura. Ganaderia, Desarrollo Rural, Pesca, y Alimentación (SAGARPA). http://www.siap.gob.mx/index.php?option=com_wrapper&view=wrapper&Itemid=350.

México, Nacional Financiera. *La industria de la harina de maíz*. Mexico City: NAFINSA, 1982.

Newspapers and Magazines

Animal Político
Bloomberg en linea
El Economista
El Financiero
Expansión
Forbes
La Jornada
La Jornada del Campo
Latin Business
Los Angeles Times
Milenio
New York Times
Proceso
Wall Street Journal

Company Annual Reports and Industry Publications

Alsea. Annual Reports.

Asociación Nacional de Tiendas de Autoservicio y Departamentales, A.C. *El pochteca moderno: Grandes historias de los supermercados y tiendas departamentales contado por sus fundadores*. Mexico City: ANTAD, 2003.

Bakery & Snacks.

BakingBusiness.com.

Consejo Mexicano de la Carne. *Compendio estadístico 2012–2022*. https://comecarne.org.

Dairy Reporter.

FEMSA. *Informe Anual*, various 2002–2022.

Food Business News.

Grupo Bimbo. *Bimbo: Una historia de creer y crear,* 2005.

Grupo Bimbo. *Informe Anual,* 1998–2023.

GRUMA. *Informe Anual,* 1998–2022.

Industrias Bachoco. Report to Investors, May 2014.

Sigma, *Reporte Anual 2014.*

The Poultry Site.

Walmart de México. *Informe Anual,* 1999–2022.

WattPoultry.com

Nonprofit and NGO Reports

El Poder Del Consumidor.

La Alianza por Nuestra Tortilla. *Del maíz a la tortilla: Lo que sabemos desde la tierra hasta la comida.* Mexico City: Alianza por Nuestra Tortilla, n.d. https:// alianzapornuestratortilla.com.

Proyecto de Derechos Económicos, Sociales y Culturales (PRODESC). *Lo barato sale caro: Violaciones a los derechos humanos laborales en Wal-Mart México.* Mexico City: Proyecto de Derechos Económicos, Sociales y Culturales, AC, 2008.

Printed Primary Sources

Anderson, Richmond K, José Calvo, Gloria Serrano, and George C. Payne. "A Study of the Nutritional Status and Food Habits of Otomi Indians in the Mezquital Valley of Mexico." *American Journal of Public Health* (August 1946).

Carson, W. E. *Mexico: The Wonderland of the South.* New York: MacMillan Co., 1914.

Cherem S., Silvia. *Al grano: Vida y visión de los fundadores de Bimbo.* Mexico City: Khalida, 2008.

Gamio, Manuel. "Diet Reforms for Indians and Mestizos." *Boletín Indigenista* 8, no. 3–4 (December 1948).

González Barrera, Roberto. "Proponencia de Agradezcimiento por el Premio Internacional PROFMEX de Política Global." *Mexico and the World* 4, no. 3 (Summer 1999).

Manual de doctrina social cristiana. Mexico City: Instituto Mexicana de Doctrina Social Crisitiana, 1989.

Martínez Dominguez, Guillermo. *Intentos de control de precios en México.* Mexico City, 1950.

Olascoaga, José Quintín. *Alimentación normal del mexicano.* Mexico City: Instituto Federal de Capacitación de Magisterio, Secretaría de Educación Pública, 1963.

Rivas Tagle, Antonio. *El cultivo racional del maíz.* Mexico City, 1929.

Salinas en Proceso. Mexico City: Random House Mondadori, 2012.

Salinas Lozano, Raúl. *La intervención del estado y la cuestión de los precios.* Mexico City: Editorial America, 1944.

Schultz, Miguel E. *El cultivo del maíz: ¡Selecciona tu semilla de maíz en el campo!* Mexico City: Editorial de Izquierda de la Cámara de Diputados, 1937.

Servitje Sendra, Lorenzo. "La revalorización de la empresa privada." In *Manual de doctrina social cristiana*. Mexico City: Instituto Mexicana de Doctrina Social Cristiana, 1989.

Servitje Sendra, Roberto. *Bimbo: Estrategia de éxito empresarial*. 2nd ed. Mexico City: Pearson Educación, 2009.

Thompson, Wallace. *The People of Mexico: Who They Are and How They Live*. New York: Harper and Brothers, 1921.

Whetten, Nathaniel. *Rural Mexico*. Chicago: University of Chicago Press, 1948.

Secondary Sources

Abarca, Meredith. *Voices in the Kitchen: Views of Food and the World from Working-Class Mexican and Mexican American Women*. College Station: Texas A&M Press, 2006.

Acuña, Rodarte, and Blanca Olivia. "Contradicciones y límites de la política agroalimentaria en México: De la seguridad alimentaria a la cruzada contra el hambre." *Argumentos* 28, no. 79 (September–December 2015): 241–263.

Acuña, Rodarte, and Blanca Olivia. "De las tortillas en comal a la harina de maíz: Mujeres y política alimentaria en Acambay, Estado de México." In *Volteando la tortilla: Género y maíz en la alimentación actual de México*, edited by Ivonne Vizcarra Bordi. Toluca: Universidad Autónoma del Estado de México, 2018.

Aguilar-Rodriguez, Sandra. "Alimentando a la nación: Género y nutrición en México (1940–1960)." *Revista de Estudios Sociales*, no. 29 (April 2008): 28–41.

Aguilar-Rodríguez, Sandra. "Between Women: Female Health Workers and the Struggle to Transform Diets in Rural Mexico, 1920–1960." *Jahrbuch für Geschichte Lateinamerikas/Anuario de Historia de América Latina* 59 (2022): 41–63.

Aguilar-Rodriguez, Sandra. "Cooking Modernity: Nutrition Policies, Class, and Gender in 1940s and 1950s Mexico City." *The Americas* 64, no. 2 (October 2007): 177–205.

Aguilar-Rodríguez, Sandra. "'Las Penas con Pan Son Menos': Race, Modernity, and Wheat in Modern Mexico." *Bulletin of Spanish Studies* 97, no. 7 (2020): 1–27.

Alcalá Delgado, Elio, and Teófilo Reues Courtier. "El Proyecto Vaquerías: Génesis del proceso modernizador de la agricultura mexicana en tiempos del neoliberalism." *Antropología: Boletín oficial del INAH*, no. 52 (October–December 1998).

Altman, Ida, and James Lockhart. *Provinces of Early Mexico: Variants of Spanish American Regional Evolution*. Los Angeles: UCLA Latin American Center, 1976.

Alvarado, Gabriela Victoria. "WALMART Culture in the Information Technologies Industry in Mexico." In *WALMART in the Global South: Workplace Culture, Labor Politics, and Supply Chains*, edited by Carolina Bank Muñoz, Bridget Kenny, and Antonio Stecher. Austin: University of Texas Press, 2018.

Appendini, Kirsten. *De la milpa a los tortibonos: La restructuración de la política alimentaria en México*. Mexico City: El Colegio de Mexico, 2001.

Appendini, Kirsten. "Changing Agrarian Institutions: Interpreting the Contradictions." In *The Transformation of Rural Mexico: Reforming the Ejido Sector*, edited by Wayne Cornelius and David Myhre. La Jolla: Center for U.S.-Mexican Studies, UC San Diego, 1998.

Appendini, Kirsten, and Guadalupe Rodríguez Gómez, eds. *La paradoja de la calidad: Alimentos Mexicanos en América del Norte*. Mexico City: El Colegio de México, 2012.

Arellano, Gustavo. *Taco USA: How Mexican Food Conquered America*. New York: Scribner, 2012.

Arias, Patricia. *Del arraigo a la diaspora: Dilemas de la familia rural*. Mexico City: Miguel Angel Porrúa, 2009.

Arrom, Silvia Marina. *Containing the Poor: The Mexico City Poor House, 1774–1871*. Durham, N.C.: Duke University Press, 2000.

Arzipe, Lourdes. *Campesinado y migración*. Mexico City: Secretaría de Educación Pública, 1985.

Aviña, Alexander. *Specters of Revolution: Peasant Guerillas in the Cold War Mexican Countryside*. New York: Oxford University Press, 2014.

Aviña, Alexander. "A War Against Poor People: Dirty Wars and Drug Wars in 1970s Mexico." In *México Beyond 1968: Revolutionaries, Radicals, and Repression During the Global Sixties and Subversive Seventies*, edited by Jaime M. Pensado and Enrique C. Ochoa. Tucson: University of Arizona Press, 2018.

Azpeitia Gómez, Hugo. *Compañía Exportadora e Importadora Mexicana, S.A. (1949–1958): Conflicto y abasto alimentario*. Mexico City: CIESAS, 1994.

Bacon, David. *The Right to Stay Home: How US Policy Drives Mexican Migration*. Boston: Beacon Press, 2013.

Bada, Xóchitl, and Jonathan Fox. "Persistent Rurality in Mexico and 'the Right to Stay Home.'" *Journal of Peasant Studies* 49, no. 1 (2022): 29–53.

Badillo, Miguel, ed. *Morir en la miseria: Los 14 municipios más pobres de México*. Mexico City: Océano, 2009.

Bak-Geller Corona, Sarah. "Food Shortage in Colonial Mexico: Maize, Food Policies and the Construction of a Modern Political Culture, 1785–1807." In *The Routledge History of Food*, edited by Carol Heltosky. London: Routledge, 2019.

Bak-Geller Corona, Sarah. "Wheat Versus Maize: Civilizing Dietary Strategies and Early Mexican Republicanism." *Journal of Interdisciplinary History of Ideas* 4, no. 8 (2015): 1–25.

Bank Muñoz, Carolina. *Building Power from Below: Chilean Workers Take on Walmart*. Ithaca, N.Y.: ILR Press, 2017.

Bank Muñoz, Carolina. *Transnational Tortillas: Race, Gender, and Shop-Floor Politics in Mexico and the United States*. Ithaca, N.Y.: Cornell University Press, 2008.

Bank Muñoz, Carolina, Bridget Kenny, and Antonio Stecher, eds. *WALMART in the Global South: Workplace Culture, Labor Politics, and Supply Chains*. Austin: University of Texas Press, 2018.

Barkin, David, and Blanca Suárez. *El fin de la autosuficiencia alimentaria*. Mexico City: Océano, 1985.

Barndt, Deborah. *Tangled Routes: Women, Work, and Globalization on the Tomato Trail*. 2nd ed. Lanham, Md.: Rowman and Littlefield, 2008.

Bartra, Armando, "Rebellious Cornfields: Towards Food and Labour Self-Sufficiency." In *Mexico in Transition: Neoliberal Globalization, the State, and Civil Society*, edited by Gerardo Otero. London: Zed Books, 2004.

Bartra Vergés, Armando, Enrique Pérez Suárez, Milton Gabriel Hernández García, Sofía Medellín Urquiaga, Hernán García Crespo, Héctor Robles Berlanga, and Wendy Castañeda Abad, eds. *Revoluciones agroecológicos en México*. Mexico City: La Jornada del Campo, 2022.

Basavae Kunhardt, Jorge. *Los grupos de capital financiero en México (1974–1995)*. Mexico City: UNAM and El Caballito, 1996.

Bauer, Arnold J. "Millers and Grinders: Technology and Household Economy in Meso-America." *Agricultural History* 64, no. 1 (Winter 1990): 1–17.

Bello, Alberto. "Roberto González Barrera, el banquero improbable." In *Los amos de México*, edited by Jorge Zepeda Patterson. 2nd ed. Mexico City: Editorial Planeta Mexicana, 2007.

Bello Gómez, Felipe de Jesús. "Inmigración y capacidad empresarial en los albores de la industrialización de México." *Secuencia* 68 (May–August 2007): 9–54.

Besse, Susan. *Restructuring Patriarchy: The Modernization of Gender Inequality in Brazil, 1914–1950*. Chapel Hill: University of North Carolina Press, 1996.

Blake, Michael. *Maize for the Gods: Unearthing the 9,000-Year History of Corn*. Oakland: University of California Press, 2015.

Bleyant, Ingrid. *Vendors' Capitalism: A Political Economy of Public Markets*. Stanford: Stanford University Press, 2021.

Bobrow-Strain, Aaron. *White Bread: A Social History of the Store-Bought Loaf*. Boston: Beacon Press, 2012.

Bollett, Alfred Jay. "Politics and Pellagra: The Epidemic of Pellagra in the U.S. in the Early Twentieth Century." *Yale Journal of Biology and Medicine* 65, no. 3 (May–June 1992): 211–221.

Boltvinik, Julio, and Araceli Damián. "Pobreza creciente y estructuras sociales cada vez más desiguales en México: Una vision integrada y crítica." *Acta Sociológica*, no. 70 (May–August 2016): 271–296.

Bonfil Batalla, Guillermo. *México Profundo: Reclaiming a Civilization*. Translated by Philip A. Dennis. Austin: University of Texas Press, 1996.

Bortz, Jeffrey Lawrence. *Los salarios reales industrials en la ciudad de México, 1939–1975*. Mexico City: Fondo de Cultura Económica, 1988.

Bortz, Jeffrey, and Marco Aguila. "Earning a Living: A History of Real Wage Studies in Twentieth-Century Mexico." *Latin American Research Review* 41, no. 2 (June 2006).

Bouzas Ortiz, José Alfonso. "Contratación Colectiva de Protección." *Revista Latinoamericana de Derechos Social*, no. 9 (July–December 2009): 29–52.

Bouzas Ortiz, José Alfonso, and Luis Oliver Reyes Ramos. "Wal-Mart." In *Contratación Colectiva de Protección en México: Informe a la Organización Regional Interamericana de Trabajadores (ORIT)*. Mexico City: Universidad Nacional Autónoma de México, 2007.

Boyer, Christopher R. *Becoming Campesino: Politics, Identity, and Agrarian Struggle in Postrevolutionary Michoacán, 1920–1935*. Stanford: Stanford University Press, 2003.

Brachet de Márquez, Viviane. *The Dynamics of Domination: State, Class, and Reform in Mexico, 1910–1990*. Pittsburgh: University of Pittsburgh Press, 1995.

Brachet-Márquez, Viviane. "Social Welfare (Mexico): Since 1867." In *Encyclopedia of Social Welfare History in North America*, edited by John M. Herrick, Paul Stuart, John Graham, Enrique C. Ochoa, and Ruth Britton. Thousand Oaks: SAGE, 2005.

Bringas Nostti, Raúl. "Kentucky Fried Chicken y su incursion en México: La última de las tres grandes inovacioned de Coronel Sanders, 1890–1964." *Perspectivas: Revista de Análisis de Economía, Comercio y Negocios Internacionales* 10, no. 2 (July–December 2016): 56–63.

Buendía, Manuel. *Los empresarios*. Mexico City: Oceano, 1984.

Buffington, Robert M. *Criminal and Citizen in Modern Mexico*. Lincoln: University of Nebraska Press, 2000.

Caire-Pérez, Matthew. "A Different Shade of Green: Efraím Hernández, Chapingo, and Mexico's Green Revolution, 1950–1967." PhD diss., University of Oklahoma, 2016.

Calva, José Luis. *Crisis agrícola y alimentaria en México, 1988–82*. Mexico City: Fontamara, 1988.

Camp, Roderic Ai. *Entrepreneurs and Politics in Twentieth-Century Mexico*. New York: Oxford University Press, 1989.

Camp, Roderic Ai. *Mexican Political Biographies, 1935–2009*. Austin: University of Texas Press, 2009.

Camp, Roderic Ai. *Mexico's Mandarins: Crafting and Power Elite for the Twenty-First Century*. Berkeley: University of California Press, 2002.

Carlson, Laura. "NAFTA Is Starving Mexico." *Foreign Policy in Focus*, October 10, 2011. https://fpif.org/nafta_is_starving_mexico/.

Casanova, Lourdes. *Global Latinas: Latin America's Emerging Multinationals*. London: Palgrave Macmillan, 2009.

Castañeda, Jorge G. *Mañana Forever: Mexico and the Mexicans*. New York: Alfred A. Knopf, 2011.

Castillo Fernández, Dídimo, and Jorge Arzate Salgado. "Economic Crisis, Poverty and Social Policy in Mexico." *Critical Sociology* 42, no. 1 (2016): 87–104.

Castillo-Muñoz, Veronica. "Historical Roots of Rural Migration: Land Reform, Corn Credit, and the Displacement of Rural Farmers in Nayarit Mexico, 1900–1952." *Mexican Studies / Estudios Mexicanos* 29, no. 1 (Winter 2013).

Cerutti, Mario, and Eva Rivas Sada. "El agrocomercio como escalón a las grandes cadenas urbanas: Ángel Losada Gómex y la Construcción del Grupo Gigante (1923–2004)." In *De la colonia a la globalización: Empresarios cántabros en México*, edited by Rafael Domínguez Martín and Mario Cerutti Pignat. Santander: Universidad de Cantabria, 2021.

Cervantes Godoy, Matilde Dalila. "The Growth of Supermarkets in Mexico: Impacts on Production and Transaction Costs of Small-Scale Farmers." PhD diss., University of Guelph, 2007.

Chabrán, Rafael. "Dr. Francisco Hernández Ate Tacos: The Foods and Drinks of the Mexican Treasury." *Díalogo* 18, no. 1 (2015).

Cháirez-Garza, Jesús F. "A Racist Lullaby: Anti-Blackness in Mexican Popular Culture." *The Abusable Past*, July 14, 2020. https://abusablepast.org/a-racist-lullaby -anti-blackness-in-mexican-popular-culture/.

Challú, Amílicar E. "Agricultural Crisis and Biological Well-Being in Mexico, 1730–1835." *Historia Agraria* 47 (April 2009): 17–45.

Challú, Amílcar E. "Grain Markets, Food Supply Policies and Living Standards in Late Colonial Mexico." PhD diss., Harvard University, 2007.

Challú, Amílcar E. "The Great Decline: Biological Well-Being and Living Standards in Mexico, 1730–1840." In *Living Standards in Latin American History: Height, Welfare, and Development, 1750–2000*, edited by Ricardo D. Salvatore, John H. Coatsworth, and Amilcar E. Challú. Cambridge, Mass.: Harvard University Press, 2010.

Chandler, Alfred. *The Visible Hand: The Managerial Revolution in American Business*. Cambridge, Mass.: Belknap Press of Harvard University Press, 1977.

Chant, Sylvia. "The 'Feminisation of Poverty' and the 'Feminisation' of Anti-Poverty Programmes: Room for Revision." *Journal of Development Studies* 44, no. 2 (2008): 165–197.

Chauvet, Michelle, and Rosa Luz González. "Globalización y estrategias de grupos empresariales agroalimentarios de México." *Comercio Exterior* 51, no. 12 (2001): 1079–1088.

Chávez, Manuel. "The Transformation of Mexican Retailing with NAFTA." *Development Policy Review* 20, no. 4 (2002): 503–513.

Chevalier, François. *Land and Society in Colonial Mexico: The Great Hacienda*. Translated by Alvin Eustis. Berkeley: University of California Press, 1963.

Ciafone, Amanda. *Counter-Cola: A Multinational History of the Global Corporation*. Oakland: University of California Press, 2019.

Clapp, Jennifer. *Food*. Malden, Mass.: Polity Press, 2012.

Coatsworth, John H. "Anotaciones sobre la producción de alimentos durante el porfiriato." *Historia Mexicana* 26, no. 2 (October–December 1976): 167–187.

Coatsworth, John H. *El impacto ecónomico de los ferrocarriles en el porfiriato: Crecimiento contra desarrollo*. Mexico City: Sepsetentas, 1976.

Coatsworth, John H. "Patterns of Rural Rebellion in Latin America: Mexico in Comparative Perspective." In *Riot, Rebellion, and Revolution: Rural and Social Conflict in Mexico*, edited by Friedrich Katz. Princeton, N.J.: Princeton University Press, 1988.

Coatsworth, John H. "Railroads, Landholding, and Agrarian Protest in the Early Porfiriato." *Hispanic American Historical Review* 54, no. 1 (1974): 48–71.

Coehlo, Alfredo Manuel, and Victor Manuel Castillo-Girón. "Fusiones, adquisiciones y alianzas estratégicas en la industria alimentaria mexicana: Balance y perspectivas." *Análisis Económico* 25, no. 59 (2010): 121–142.

Cole, Nicki Lisa. "Global Capitalism Organizing Knowledge of Race, Gender and Class: The Case of Socially Responsible Coffee." *Race, Gender, and Class* 15, no. 1–2 (2008): 170–187.

Collins, Patricia Hill. *Black Feminist Thought: Knowledge, Consciousness, and the Politics of Empowerment*. Boston: Unwin Hyman, 1990.

Concheiro Bórquez, Elvira. *El gran acuerdo: Gobierno y empresarios en la modernización salinista*. Mexico City: Ediciones ERA, 1996.

Conde, Esteban. "El estado de indefensión de los trabajadores del Grupo Wal-Mart de México en el Distrito Federal, ante los contractos de protección colectiva," Law thesis, Universidad Nacional Autónoma de México, June 2009.

Contreras, Carlos Alberto, and Peter L. Reich. "Numbers and the State: An Overview of Government Statistical Compilation in Mexico Since the Colonial Period." *The Statistical Abstract of Latin America*, vol. 31, edited by James W. Wilkie, Carlos Alberto Contreras, and Catherine Komisaruk. Los Angeles: UCLA Latin American Center Publications, 1995.

Cook, Sherburne F., and Woodrow Borah. "Indian Food Production and Consumption in Central Mexico Before and After the Conquest (1500–1650)." In *Essays in Population History*, vol. 3, *Mexico and California*. Berkeley: University of California Press, 1979.

Cook, Sherburne F., and Woodrow Borah. *The Indian Population of Central Mexico*. Berkeley: University of California Press, 1960.

Córdova, Arnoldo. *La politica de masas del cardenismo*. Mexico City: Ediciones ERA, 1974.

Cornelius, Wayne, and David Myhre. *The Transformation of Rural Mexico: Reforming the Ejido Sector*. La Jolla: Center for U.S.-Mexican Studies, UC San Diego, 1998.

Cotter, Joseph. "Cultural Wars and New Technologies: The Discourse of Plant Breeding and Professionalisation of Mexican Agronomy, 1880–1994." *Science, Technology, and Society* 5, no. 2 (2000): 141–168.

Cotter, Joseph. "The Origins of the Green Revolution in Mexico: Continuity or Change?" In *Latin America in the 1940s: War and Postwar Transitions*, edited by David Rock. Berkeley: University of California Press, 1994.

Cotter, Joseph. "The Rockefeller Foundation's Mexican Agricultural Project: A Cross-Cultural Encounter, 1943–1949." In *Missionaries of Science: The Rockefeller Foundation and Latin America*, edited by Marco Cueto. Bloomington: Indiana University Press, 1994.

Cotter, Joseph. *Troubled Harvest: Agronomy and Revolution in Mexico, 1880–2002*. Westport: Praeger, 2003.

Cross, Harry. "Dieta y nutrición en el medio rural de Zacatecas y San Luis Potosí (Siglos XVIII y XIX)." *Historia Mexicana* 69, no. 3 (1981): 101–116.

Cross, John C. *Informal Politics: Street Vendors and the State in Mexico City*. Stanford: Stanford University Press, 1998.

Cypher, James M. "Poverty (Mexico)." In *Encyclopedia of Social Welfare History in North America*, edited by John M. Herrick, Paul Stuart, John Graham, Enrique C. Ochoa, and Ruth Britton. Thousand Oaks: SAGE, 2005.

Cypher, James M., and Raúl Delgado Wise. *Mexico's Economic Dilemma: The Developmental Failure of Neoliberalism*. Lanham, Md.: Rowman and Littlefield, 2010.

Damián, Araceli, and Julio Boltvinik. "A Table to Eat On: The Meaning and Measurement of Poverty in Latin America." In *Latin America After Neoliberalism: Turning the Tide in the 21st Century?*, edited by Eric Hershberg and Fred Rosen. New York: New Press, 2006.

de Grammont, Hubert C. "La Unión General de Obreros y Campesinos de México." In *Historia de la cuestión agraria: Política estatal y conflictos agrarios, 1950–1970*. Mexico Cityi: Siglo XXI Editores, 1989.

de Grammont, Hubert C., and Horacio Mackinlay. "Campesino and Indigenous Social Organizations Facing Democratic Transition in Mexico, 1938–2006." *Latin American Perspectives* 36, no. 4 (July 2009): 21–40.

de la Peña, Moisés T. *La mexicanización del indio: Un problema económico*. Mexico City: Revista de Economía, 1945.

de la Peña, Sergio. "Visión global de los orígenes de la estadística: Guía de Forasteros y Nativos a la historia de la estadística económica nacional." In *La estadística económica en México: Los orígenes*. Mexico City: Siglo XXI, 1994.

Denham, Diana Christina. "The Persistence of Indigenous Markets in Mexico's 'Supermarket Revolution.'" PhD diss., Portland State University, 2020.

De Schutter, Olivier. *Report of the Special Rapporteur on the Right to Food, Addendum, Mission to Mexico (13–20 June 2011)*. United Nation General Assembly: Human Rights Council, January 17, 2012. https://www.ohchr.org/sites/default/files/Documents/HRBodies/HRCouncil/RegularSession/Session19/A-HRC-19-59-Add2_en.pdf.

Deutsch, Tracey. *Building a Housewife's Paradise: gender, Politics, and American Grocery Stores in the Twentieth Century*. Chapel Hill: University of North Carolina Press, 2010.

Deverell, William. *Whitewashed Adobe: The Rise of Los Angeles and the Remaking of its Mexican Past*. Berkeley: University of California Press, 2004.

Dussel Peters, Enrique. *La economía de la polarización: Teoría y evolución del cambio estructural de las manufacturas mexicanas (1988–1996)*. Mexico City: Universidad Nacional Autónoma de México, 1997.

Dussel Peters, Enrique, and Samuel Ortiz Velásques, eds. *Monitor de la manufactura Mexicana* 10, no. 11 (February 2015).

Earle, Rebecca. *The Body of the Conquistador: Food, Race and the Colonial Experience in Spanish America, 1492–1700*. Cambridge: Cambridge University Press, 2012.

Ervin, Michael A. "The 1930 Agrarian Census in Mexico: Agronomists, Middle Politics, and the Negotiation of Data Collection." *Hispanic American Historical Review* 87, no. 3 (2007): 537–570.

Esteva, Gustavo. "Hosting the Otherness of the Other: The Case of the Green Revolution." In *Decolonizing Knowledge: From Development to Dialogue*, edited by Frédérique Apffel-Marglin and Stephen A. Marglin. Oxford: Clarendon Press, 1996.

Esteva, Gustavo. "Re-embedding Food in Agriculture." *Culture and Agriculture: Bulletin of the Culture and Agriculture Group*, no. 48 (Winter 1994): 2–12.

Esteva, Gustavo. *The Struggle for Rural Mexico*. South Hadley: Bergin & Garvey, 1983.

Esteva, Gustavo, and Catherine Marielle, eds. *Sin maíz no hay país*. Mexico City: Consejo Nacional para la Cultura y las Artes, 2007.

Feder, Ernest. *El imperialismo fresa: Una investigación sobre los mecanismos de la dependencia en la argricultura mexicana.* Mexico City: Nueva Sociologia, 1977.

Fitting, Elizabeth. "Importing Corn, Exporting Labor: The Neoliberal Corn Regime, GMOs, and the Erosion of Mexican Biodiversity." In *Food for the Few: Neoliberal Globalism and Biotechnology in Latin American,* edited by Gerardo Otero. Austin: University of Texas Press, 2008.

Fitting, Elizabeth. *The Struggle for Maize: Campesinos, Workers, and Transgenic Corn in the Mexican Countryside.* Durham, N.C.: Duke University Press, 2011.

Fitzgerald, Deborah. "Exporting American Agriculture: The Rockefeller Foundation in Mexico, 1943–1953." In *Missionaries of Science: The Rockefeller Foundation and Latin America,* edited by Marco Cueto. Bloomington: Indiana University Press, 1994.

Florescano, Enrique. "El abasto y la legislación de granos en el siglo XVI." *Historia Mexicana* 14, no. 4 (April–June 1965): 567–630.

Florescano, Enrique. *Precios del maíz y crisis agrícolas en México, 1708–1810.* Mexico City: Ediciones ERA, 1969.

Fonseca, Vanessa. "Fractal Capitalism and the Latinization of the US Market." PhD diss., University of Texas at Austin, 2003.

Fonteyne, Simon, José B. Castillo Caamal, Santaigo Lopez-Ridaura, Jelle Van Loon, Juan Espidio Balbuena, Leodegario Osorio Alcalá, Fermin Martínez Hernández, Sylvanus Odjo, and Nele Verhulst. "Review of Agronomic Research on the Milpa, the Traditional Polyculture System of Mesoamerica." *Frontiers in Agronomy* 5 (February 15, 2023).

Fournier García, Patricia. "El maíz y la tortilla en la historia prehispánica." In *La industria de la masa y la tortilla: Desarrollo y tecnologia,* edited by Felipe Torres, Ernesto Moreno, Isabel Chong, and Juan Quintanilla. Mexico City: Universidad Autónoma de México, 1996.

Fox, Jonathan. *The Politics of Food in Mexico: State Power and Social Mobilization.* Ithaca, N.Y.: Cornell University Press, 1992.

Fox, Jonathan, and Gaspar Rivera Salgado, eds. *Indigenous Mexican Migration in the United States.* La Jolla: Center for U.S.-Mexican Studies, UC San Diego, 2004.

Frausto Crotte, Salvador. "Lorenzo Servitje, una apuesta por el pan." In *Los amos de México,* edited by Jorge Zepeda Patterson. 2nd ed. Mexico City: Editorial Planeta Mexicana, 2007.

Friedmann, Harriet, and Philip McMichael. "Agriculture and the State System: The Rise and Decline of National Agricultures, 1870 to the Present." *Sociologia Ruralis* 29, no. 2 (1989): 93–117.

Gallardo Navarro, Yoja, Edith Figueroa García, and Carlos Roldán Esparza. *La industría de alimentos procesados en México: Analisis y tendencias.* Mexico City: Instituto Politécnico Nacional, 1982.

Gálvez, Alysha. *Eating NAFTA: Trade, Food Policies, and the Destruction of Mexico.* Oakland: University of California Press, 2018.

García, María Elena. *Gastropolitics and the Specter of Race: Stories of Capital, Culture, and Coloniality in Peru.* Oakland: University of California Press, 2021.

García Aguirre, Aleida. *La revolución que llegaría: Experiencias de solidaridad y redes de maestros y normalistas en el movimiento campesino y la guerrilla moderna en Chihuahua, 1960–1968.* Mexico City, 2015.

García Calderón, Carola. "Los alimentos chatarra en México, regulación publicitaria y autorregulación." *Derecho a Comunicar,* no. 2 (May–August 2011): 171–195.

García Calderón, Carola, ed. *Cómo engordamos: Comida chatarra, obesidad y estrategias de publicidad.* Mexico City: UNAM, 2019.

García Calderón, Carola, ed. *Hábitos alimentarios, publicidad y política de salud.* Mexico City: UNAM, 2020.

García Maldonado, Katia Yetzani, and Ivonne Vizcarra Bordi. "Masa con o sin nixtamal: Respuestas femininas matlatincas ante los programas sociales de alimentación." In *Volteando la tortilla: Génaro y maíz en la alimentación actual de México,* edited by Ivonne Vizcarra Bordi. Toluca: Universidad Autónoma del Estado de México, 2018.

Garfias Frías, José Ángela, and Emmanuel Galicia Martínez. "Videojuegos de publicidad de comida chitarra dirigidos a niños, en elm arco de las nuevas regulaciones de salúd." In *Cómo engordamos: Comida chatarra, obesidad y estrategias de publicidad,* edited by Carola García Calderón. Mexico City: UNAM, 2019.

Garrido, Celso. *Desarrollo económico y procesos de financiamiento en Méxcio: Transformaciones contemporáneas y dilemas actuales.* Mexico City: Siglo XXI editores, 2005.

Garrido, Celso. "Inversión productive de grandes empresas mexicanas en centroamerica y su impacto tecnologico en la region." Departamento de Economía de la Universidad Autónoma Metropolitana-Azcapotzalco, November 2000.

Gasca, José, and Felipe Torres. "El control corporativo de la distribución de alimentos en México." *Revista Problemas del Desarrollo* 176, no. 45 (January–March 2014): 133–155.

Gauster, Susana, and Alberto Alonso Fradejas. *GRUMA—MASECA: La emperadora translatina de la tortilla de harina en Centroamérica.* Guatemala: Instituto de Estudios Agrarios y Rurales, 2007.

Gillingham, Paul, and Benjamin T. Smith, eds. *Dictablanda: Politics, Work, and Culture in Mexico, 1938–1968.* Durham, N.C.: Duke University Pres, 2014.

Gitli, Eduardo. "La inversion directa Mexicana en Centroamérica: Eslabonamientos productivos y transferencia de technología." Departamento de Economía de la Universidad Autónoma Metropolitana-Azcapotzalco y Centro Internacional de Política Económica para el Desarrollo Sostenible de la Universidad Nacional (Heredia, Costa Rica), November 2000.

Gledhill, John. *Casí Nada: A Study of Agrarian Reform in the Homeland of Cardenismo.* Albany: State University of New York Press, 1991.

Gómez, Eduardo J. "Coca-Cola's Political and Policy Influence in Mexico: Understanding the Role of Institutions, Interests and Divided Society." *Health Policy and Planning* 34, no. 7 (2019): 520–528.

Gómez-Galavarriato, Aurora. "Female Entrepreneurship as a Survival Strategy: Women During the Early Mechanisation of Corn Tortilla Production in Mexico City." *Continuity and Change* 35, no. 1 (2020): 75–103.

Gonzalez, Gilbert G. *Culture of Empire: American Writers, Mexico, and Mexican Immigrants, 1880–1930*. Austin: University of Texas Press, 2004.

González, Humberto. "Convergence: Social Movements in Mexico in the Era of Neoliberal Globalization." In *Mexico in Transition: Neoliberal Globalism, the State and Civil Society*, edited by Gerardo Otero. London: Zed Books, 2004.

González, Humberto. "Specialization on a Global Scale and Agrifood Vulnerability: 30 Years of Export Agriculture in Mexico." *Development Studies Research* 1, no. 1 (2014): 295–310.

González, Luis. *San José de Gracia: Mexican Village in Transition*. Translated by John Upton. Austin: University of Texas Press, 1974.

González, Roberto J. *Zapotec Science: Farming and Food in the Northern Sierra of Oaxaca*. Austin: University of Texas Press, 2001.

González de la Rocha, Mercedes. "From the Resources of Poverty to the Poverty of Resources?" *Latin American Perspectives* 28, no. 4 (July 2001): 72–100.

González de la Rocha, Mercedes. *The Resources of Poverty: Women and Survival in a Mexican City*. Cambridge, Mass: Blackwell, 1994.

González González, Luis. *Los presidentes de México ante la nación: Informes, manifiestos, y documentos de 1821 a 1966*. Vol. 4. Mexico City: Cámara de Diputados, 1966.

González Jácome, Alba. "Origenes, domesticación y dispersion del maíz (Zea mays) en México." In *El maíz nativo en México: Una aproximación crítica desde los estudios rurales*, edited by Ignacio López Moreno and Ivonne Vizcarra Bordi. Mexico City: Juan Pablos Editor, 2016.

González Navarro, Moisés. *La pobreza en Méxcio*. Mexico City: El Colegio de México, 1985.

González Santiago, María Virginia. *Agroecología, saberes campesinos y agricultura como forma de vida*. Chapingo: Universidad Autónoma Chapingo, 2008.

GRAIN. *¡No toquen nuestro maíz! El sistema agroalimentario industrial devasta y los pueblos en México resisten*. Mexico City: GRAIN and Editorial Itaca, 2014.

Guajardo Díaz, Arnoldo, and Yaddy Milena Porras Melo. "Dime qué comunicas y te dire quién eres: Análisis de discurso de sitio web de grupo bimbo." *Razón y Palabra*, no. 84 (September–November 2013).

Guerrero, Rubén, Jacqueline Chacón, Elisa Mariscal, and Alexander Elbittar. "Los efectos sobre el bienestar local de la expansion de Walmart, 2009–2020." *Social Science Research Network*, November 2020. https://papers.ssrn.com/sol3/papers.cfm?abstract_id=3738400.

Guthrie, Charles Lyle. "Riots in Seventeenth Century Mexico City: A Study of Social and Economic Conditions." In *Greater America: Essays in Honor of Herbert Eugene Bolton*, edited by Adele Ogden and Engel Sluiter. Berkeley: University of California Press, 1945.

Haber, Stephen H. *Industry and Underdevelopment: The Industrialization of Mexico, 1890–1940*. Stanford: Stanford University Press, 1989.

Habib, M. A. B., Mashuda Parvin, Tim C. Hunton, and Mohammad R. Hasan. "A Review on Culture, Production and Use of Spirulina as Food for humans and Feeds for Domestic Animals and Fish." Rome: Food and Agricultural Organization, 2008.

Hall, Patricia Jane. "Five Multinational Food Processing Firms in Mexico: A Contribution to Underdevelopment?" PhD diss., University of Washington, 1980.

Hamilton, Shane. *Supermarket USA: Food and Power in the Cold War Farms Race.* New Haven, Conn.: Yale University Press, 2018.

Hart, John Mason. *Empire and Revolution: The Americans in Mexico Since the Civil War.* Berkeley: University of California Press, 2002.

Hart, Paul. *Bitter Harvest: The Social Transformation of Morelos Mexico and the Origins of the Zapatista Revolution, 1849–1910.* Albuquerque: University of New Mexico Press, 2005.

Hawkes, Corrine. "Uneven Dietary Development: Linking the Policies and Processes of Globalization with the Nutrition Transition, Obesity and Diet Related Chronic Diseases." *Globalization and Health* 2, no. 4 (2006)

Hernández Chávez, Alicia. *Breve historia de Morelos.* Mexico City: El Colegio de México, 2002.

Hernández Rodríguez, Rogelio. "Challenging Caciquismo: An Analysis of the Leadership of Carlos Hank González." In *Caciquismo in Twentieth Century Mexico,* edited by Alan Knight and Wil Pansters. London: Institute for the Study of the Americas, 2005.

Hernández Romo, Marcela. "Las configuraciones y estrategias productivas, de relaciones laborales y sindicales en grandes corporaciones en México." In *Configuraciones productivas y relaciones laborales en empresa multinaciones en América Latina,* edited by Enrique de la Garza Toledo and Marcela Hernández Romo. Mexico City: Universidad Autónoma Metropolitana-Iztapalapa, 2017.

Herrera Calderón, Fernando, and Adela Cedillo, eds. *Challenging Authoritarianism in Mexico: Revolutionary Struggles and the Dirty War, 1964–1982.* New York: Routledge, 2011.

Hewitt de Alcántara, Cynthia. *Anthropological Perspectives on Rural Mexico.* London: Routledge & Kegan Paul, 1984.

Hewitt de Alcántara, Cynthia. *La modernización de la agricultura Mexicana, 1940–1970.* Mexico City: Siglo XXI Editores, 1978.

Hijos del maíz: Recetario del maíz. Mexico City: Secretaría de Desarrollo Rural y Equidad para las Comunidades, 2020.

Holt-Giménez, Eric. *A Foodie's Guide to Capitalism: Understanding the Political Economy of What We Eat.* New York: Monthly Review Press, 2017.

Horst, Thomas. *At Home Abroad: A Study of the Domestic and Foreign Operations of the American Food-Processing Industry.* Cambridge: Ballinger, 1974.

Janer, Zilkia. "(In)edible Nature: New World Food and Coloniality." *Cultural Studies* 21, no. 2–3 (2007): 385–405.

Juárez López, José Luis. *Engranaje culinario: La cocina mexicana en el siglo XIX.* Mexico City: CONACULTA, 2012.

Juárez López, José Luis. *La lenta emergencia de la comida Mexicana: Ambigüedades criollas, 1750–1800.* Mexico City: Miguel Ángel Porrúa, 2000.

Juárez López, José Luis. *Nacionalismo culinario: La cocina mexicana en el siglo XX.* Mexico City: CONACULTA, 2008.

Keremitsis, Dawn. "Del metate al molino: La mujer mexicana de 1910 a 1940." *Historia Mexicana* 33, no. 2 (October–December 1983): 285–302.

Knight, Alan. *The Mexican Revolution.* Vol. 2, *Counter-Revolution and Reconstruction.* Cambridge: Cambridge University Press, 1986.

Knight, Alan. "Race, Revolution, and Indigenismo: Mexico, 1910–1940." In *The Idea of Race in Latin America,* edited by Richard Graham. Austin: University of Texas Press, 1987.

Koch, Alexander, Chris Brierley, Mark M. Maslin, and Simon L. Lewis. "Earth System Impacts of European Arrival and Great Dying in the Americas after 1492." *Quaternary Science Reviews* 207 (2019): 13–36.

Kroker-Lobos, Maria F., Andrea Pedroza-Tobías, Lilia S Pedraza, and Juan Rivera. "The Double Burden of Undernutrition and Excess Body Weight in Mexico." *American Journal of Clinical Nutrition* 100, no. 6 (2014): 1652S–1658S.

LaFrance, David G. *Revolution in Mexico's Heartland: Politics, War, and State Building in Puebla, 1913–1920.* Wilmington: SR Books, 2003.

Lee, Raymond L. "Grain Legislation in Colonial Mexico, 1575–1585." *Hispanic American Historical Review* 27, no. 4 (November 1947): 647–660.

Lewis, Stephen E. "The Nation, Education, and the 'Indian Problem' in Mexico, 1920–1940." In *The Eagle and the Virgin: Nation and Cultural Revolution in Mexico, 1920–1940,* edited by Mary Kay Vaughn and Stephen E. Lewis, 176–195. Durham, N.C.: Duke University Press, 2006.

Lichtenstein, Nelson. *The Retail Revolution: How Wal-Mart Created a Brave New World of Business.* New York: Metropolitan Books, 2009.

Lida, Clara E., ed. *Una inmigración privilegiada: Comerciantes, empresarios y professionals españoles en México en los siglos XIX y XXI.* Madrid: Alianza Editorial, 1994.

Long, Janet, ed. *Conquista y comida: Consequencias del encuentro de dos mundos.* Mexico City: Universdad Nacional Autónoma de México, 1996.

López-Alonso, Moramay. "Living Standards of the Mexican Laboring Classes, 1850–1950: An Anthropometric Approach." In *Living Standards in Latin American History: Height, Welfare, and Development, 1750–2000,* edited by Ricardo D. Salvatore, John H. Coatsworth, and Amilcar E. Challú. Cambridge, Mass.: Harvard University Press, 2010.

López Austin, Alfredo. "Cuatro mitos mesoamericanos del maíz." In *Sin maíz no hay país,* edited by Gustavo Esteva and Catherine Marielle. Mexico City: Consejo Nacional para la Cultura y las Artes, 2007.

López Rosado, Diego. *El abasto de productos alimenticios en la ciudad de México.* Mexico City: Fondo de Cultura Económica, 1988.

Lowenberg, Samuel. "The Plight of Mexico's Indigenous Women." *The Lancet* 375, no. 9727 (May 15, 2015): 1680–1682.

Luiselli Fernández, Cassio. *Agricultura y alimentación en México: Evolución, desempeño y perspectivas*. Mexico City: Siglo XXI Editores, 2017.

MacLeod, Dag. *Downsizing the State: Privatization and the Limits of Neoliberal Reform in Mexico*. University Park: Penn State University Press, 2004.

Mansferrer León, Cristina V. "'I'm Not Sitting Next to You': Education and Racism in Afro-Mexican Communities." *Diálogos sobre Educación* 7, no. 13 (2016): 1–16.

Marcus, Joyce. "The Plant World of the Sixteenth and Seventeenth Lowland Maya." In *Maya Subsistence: Studies in Memory of Dennis E. Puleston*. New York: Academic Press, 1982.

Mares, Teresa, and Devón G. Peña. "Urban Agriculture in the Making of Insurgent Spaces in Los Angeles and Seattle." In *Insurgent Public Space: Guerrilla Urbanism and the Remaking of Contemporary Cities*, edited by Jeffery Hou. New York: Routledge, 2010.

Markiewicz, Dana. *The Mexican Revolution and the Limits of Agrarian Reform, 1915–1946*. Boulder: Lynne Rienner, 1993.

Marrón-Ponce, Joaquín A., Tania G. Sánchez-Pimienta, Sonia Rodríguez-Ramírez, Carolina Batis, and Gustavo Cediel. "Ultra-Processed Foods Consumption Reduces Dietary Diversity and Micronutrient Intake in the Mexican Population." *Journal of Human Nutrition and Diet* 36, no. 1 (2023): 241–251.

Marrón-Ponce, Joaquín Alejandro, Lizbeth Tolentino-Mayo, Mauricio Hernández-F., and Carolina Batis. "Trends in Ultra-Processed Food Purchases from 1984 to 2016 in Mexican Households." *Nutrients* 11, no. 1 (2018).

Martínez-Flores, Bertha Verónica, and María de Lourdes Romo Aguilar. "Entre la esperanza y la desconfianza: La participación en la Cruzada Nacional contra el Hambre." *Espiral: Estudios Sobre Estado y Sociedad* 29, no. 85 (September–December 2022): 157–187.

Martínez Rubio, Elisa Alejandra, Michelle Judd de la Luz, and Agustín Escobar Latapí. "Poverty and Agricultural Labor in the Culiacán Valley." *CIESAS Bulletin*, no. 4 (May 27, 2022).

Mayer Celis, Leticia. *Entre el infierno de una realidad y el cielo de un imaginario: Estadística y comunidad científica en el México de la primera mitad del siglo XIX*. Mexico City: El Colegio de México, 1999.

McCann, James C. *Maize and Grace: Africa's Encounter with a New World Crop, 1500–2000*. Cambridge, Mass.: Harvard University Press, 2005.

McCormick, Gladys I. *The Logic of Compromise in Mexico: How the Countryside Was Key to the Emergence of Authoritarianism*. Chapel Hill: University of North Carolina Press, 2016.

McCormick, Gladys. "Looking for Truths in the Constructed Archive: The Case of Jacinto López and the Politics of Accommodation in Rural Mexico." *A Contracorriente* 13, no. 3 (Spring 2016): 77–100.

McManus, Katherine D. "What Are Ultra-Processed Foods and Are They Bad for Our Health?" *Harvard Health Blog*, January 9, 2020.

McMichael, Philip. *Food Regimes and Agrarian Questions*. Halifax: Fernwood, 2013.

McWilliams, Carey. *Southern California Country: An Island on the Land*. New York: Duell, Sloan and Pearce, 1946.

Medina Ramírez, Salvador. "Mexico en el mercado de cerdo." *Comercio Exterior* 63, no. 6 (November–December 2013): 7–11.

Melville, Elinor G. K. *A Plague of Sheep: Environmental Consequences of the Conquest of Mexico*. Cambridge: Cambridge University Press, 1997.

Mendiola García, Sandra. *Street Democracy: Vendors, Violence, and Public Space in Late Twentieth Century Mexico*. Lincoln: University of Nebraska Press, 2017.

Mestaz, James V. *Strength from the Waters: A History of Indigenous Mobilization in Northwest Mexico*. Lincoln: University of Nebraska Press, 2022.

Mignolo, Walter D. *The Darker Side of Modernity: Global Futures, Decolonial Options*. Durham, N.C.: Duke University Press, 2011.

Miller, Simon. "The Mexican Hacienda Between the Insurgency and the Revolution: Maize Production and Commercial Triumph on the Temporal." *Journal of Latin American Studies* 16, no. 2 (November 1984): 309–336.

Mitchell, Kenneth Edward. *State-Society Relations in Mexico: Clientelism, Neoliberal State Reform, and the Case of CONASUPO*. Aldershot: Ashgate, 2001.

Molyneux, Maxine. "Mothers at the Service of the New Poverty Agenda: Progresa/Oportunidades, Mexico's Conditional Transfer Programme." *Social Policy and Administration* 40, no. 4 (August 2006): 425–449.

Mondragón, Carlos. "Strategic Alliances in Mexico: The Case of Wal Mart-Cifra." PhD diss., University of Texas Austin, 1997.

Montes de Oca Luján Rosa Elena, and Gerardo Escudero Columna. "Las empresas transnacionales en la industria alimentaria mexicana." *Comercio Exterior* 31, no. 9 (September 1981): 986–1009.

Moreno, Julio. "Wal-Mart y la Diplomacia Económica en Américan Latina." *Foreign Affairs en Español* 4, no. 2 (April–June 2004): 166–180.

Moreno, Julio. *Yankee Don't Go Home: Mexican Nationalism, American Business Culture, and the Shaping of Modern Mexico, 1920–1950*. Chapel Hill: University of North Carolina Press, 2003.

Moreno Lázaro, Javier. "Los españoles y la revolución comercial mexicana: Las cadenas de supermercadors, 1921–2011." *Investigaciones de Historia Económica* 8, no. 2 (2012): 69–82.

Moreno-Lázaro, Javier. "The Bread of the Americas. Bimbo: A Mexican Business Success Story, 1944–2010." *Revista de Historia Industrial* 20, no. 47 (2011): 77–115.

Moreton, Bethany. *To Serve God and Wal-Mart: The Making of Christian Free Enterprise*. Cambridge, Mass.: Harvard University Press, 2009.

Mostkoff, Aída, and Enrique C. Ochoa. "Complexities of Measuring the Food Situation in Mexico: Supply Versus Self-Sufficiency of Basic Grains, 1925–86." In *Society and Economy in Mexico*, edited by James W. Wilkie. Los Angeles: UCLA Latin American Center, 1990.

Mottier, Nicole. "Calculating Pragmatism: The High Politics of the Banco Ejidal in Twentieth-Century Mexico." *The Americas* 74, no. 3 (July 2017): 331–363.

Muldoon, Juan, and Daniel Servitje. *El comercio de alimentos en México: Presente y future.* Mexico City: Editorial Trillas, 1984.

Niblo, Stephen R. *Mexico in the 1940s: Modernity, Politics, and Corruption.* Wilmington: SR Books, 1999.

Noel, Hannah. "Branding Guilt: American Apparel Inc. and Latina Labor in Los Angeles." *Diálogo* 18, no. 2 (Fall 2015): 37–52.

Novo, Salvador. *Cocina mexicana o historia gastronómica de la ciudad de México.* Mexico City: Editorial Porrúa, 1967.

Ochoa, Enrique C. "Coercion, Reform, and the Welfare State: The Campaign Against 'Begging' in Mexico City During the 1930s." *The Americas* 58, no. 1 (July 2001): 39–64.

Ochoa, Enrique C. "The Costs of Rising Tortilla Prices in Mexico." *Relay: A Socialist Project Review* 16 (March/April 2007): 50–51.

Ochoa, Enrique C. "The Crusade Against Hunger and the Persistence of Poverty." *NACLA Report on the Americas* 47, no. 1 (2014): 37–40.

Ochoa, Enrique C. *Feeding Mexico: The Political Uses of Food Since 1910.* Wilmington: Scholarly Resources, 2000.

Ochoa, Enrique C. "Food History." In *Oxford University Bibliographies Online: Latin American Studies,* edited by Ben Vinson. Revised and updated. New York: Oxford University Press, 2021.

Ochoa, Enrique C. "From Tortillas to Low-Carb Wraps: Capitalism and Mexican Food in Los Angeles Since the 1920s." *Diálogo: An Interdisciplinary Journal* 18, no. 1 (Spring 2015): 33–46.

Ochoa, Enrique C. "Lic. Moisés T. de la Peña: The Economist on Horseback." In *The Human Tradition in Mexico,* edited by Jeffrey M. Pilcher. Wilmington: SR Books, 2003.

Ochoa, Enrique C. "Philanthropy (in Mexico)." In *Encyclopedia of Social Welfare History of North America,* edited by John Herrick and Paul Stuart. Thousand Oaks: SAGE, 2004.

Ochoa, Enrique C., and Tamar Wilson, eds. "Mexico in the 1990s: Economic Crisis, Social Polarization, and Class Struggle." *Latin American Perspectives* 28, no. 3 (May 2001).

O'Grady, Cormac. *Famine: A Short History.* Princeton, N.J.: Princeton University Press, 2009.

Olaiz-Fernández, Gustavo, Rosalba Rojas, Carlos A Aguilar-Salinas, Juan Rauda, and Salvador Villalpando. "Diabetes mellitus en adultos mexicanos: Resultados de la Encuesta Nacional de Salud 2000." *Salud Pública de México* 49, no. 3 (2007): 331–337.

Olmedo Carranza, Bernardo. *Capital transnacional y consumo: El caso del sistema agroalimentario en México.* Mexico City: Universidad Nacional Autónoma de México, 1986.

Olsson, Tore C. *Agrarian Crossings: Reformers and the Remaking of the US and Mexican Countryside.* Princeton, N.J.: Princeton University Press, 2017.

Oppenheimer, Andrés. *Bordering on Chaos: Mexico's Roller-Coaster Journey Toward Prosperity*. Boston: Little, Brown, 1998.

Oseguera Parra, David, and Rafael Ortega Packza. "Gente de maíz: Historia y diversidad en la cocina mexicana del maíz." In *El maíz nativo en México: Una aproximación crítica desde los estudios rurales*, edited by Ignacio López Moreno and Ivonne Vizcarra Bordi. Mexico City: Juan Pablos Editor, S.A.

Ortega Ortega, Tomás, Juan Felipe Núñez Espinoza, Verónica Vázquez García, Ivonne Vizcarra Bordi, Paola Ma. Sesis, and Diego Flores Sánchez. "Mujeres y organización comunitaria: El caso de las palmeadoras de Tlaxiaco, Oaxaca, México." *EUTOPÍA*, no. 13 (January–June 2018): 33–52.

Ortega Ortega, Tomás, Verónica Vásquez García, Diego Flores Sánchez, and Juan Felipe Nuñez Espinoza. "Agrobiodiversidad, género, y soberanía alimentaria en Tlaxiaco, Oaxaca." *Revista Mexicana de Ciencias Agrícolas* 8, no. 18 (2017): 3673–3684.

Ortiz de Montellano, Bernardo. *Aztec Medicine, Health, and Nutrition*. New Brunswick, N.J.: Rutgers University Press, 1990.

Otero, Gerardo, ed. *Food for the Few: Neoliberal Globalism and Biotechnology in Latin American*. Austin: University of Texas Press, 2008.

Otero, Gerardo, ed. *Mexico in Transition: Neoliberal Globalization, the State, and Civil Society*. London: Zed Books, 2004.

Otero, Gerardo. *The Neoliberal Diet: Healthy Profits, Unhealthy People*. Austin: University of Texas Press, 2018.

Otero, Gerardo, ed. *Neoliberalism Revisited: Economic Restructuring and Mexico's Political Future*. Boulder: Westview Press, 1996.

Otero, Gerardo. "The Neoliberal Food Regime in Latin America: State, Agribusiness Transnational Corporations and Biotechnology." *Canadian Journal of Development Studies* 33, no. 3 (September 2012).

Oviedo-Solís, Cecila Isabel, Eric A. Monterrubio-Flores, Gustavo Cediel, Edgar Denova-Gutiérrez, and Simón Barquera. "Trend of Ultraprocessed Product Intake Is Associated with the Double Burden of Malnutrition in Mexican Children and Adolescents." *Nutrients* 14, no. 20 (2022).

Ozaeta, Juan Pablo. *Tratado de libre comercio entre Centroamérica, Repúbica Dominicana y Estados Unidos (TLC-CAUSA): Informe a cinco años de vigencia: Su impacto en el campo*. Guatemala: Instituto de Estudios Agrarios y Rurales, 2011.

Padilla, Tanalís, ed. *El campesinado y su persistencia en la actualidad Mexicana*. Mexico City: El Fondo de Cultura Económico y El Consejo Nacional Para la Cultura y las Artes, 2013.

Padilla, Tanalís. "'Latent Sites of Agitation': Normalistas Rurales and Chihuahua's Agrarian Struggle in the 1960s." In *México Beyond 1968: Revolutionaries, Radicals, and Repression During the Global Sixties and Subversive Seventies*, edited by Jaime M. Pensado and Enrique C. Ochoa. Tucson: University of Arizona Press, 2018.

Padilla, Tanalís. *Rural Resistance in the Land of Zapata: The Jaramillista Movement and the Myth of the Pax Priísta, 1940–1962*. Durham, N.C.: Duke University Press, 2008.

Paredes López, Octavio, and Yoja Gallardo Navarro. "La industria alimentaria en México y la penetración de las empresas transnacionales." *Comercio Exterior* 26, no. 12 (December 1976): 1421–1435.

Pasquier, Ayari. "Narrativas contrastantes en torno al concepto de 'seguridad alimentaria': El caso del programa Sin Hambre." In *Inseguridad alimentaria y políticas de alivio a la pobreza: Una vision multidisciplinaria*, edited by Blanca Rubio and Ayari Pasquier. Mexico City: UNAM, 2019.

Pellicer de Brody, Olga, and José Luis Reyna. *Historia de la Revolución Mexicana, período 1952–1960: El afianzamiento de la estabilidad política*. Mexico City: El Colegio de México, 1978.

Penfold, Steve. "Fast Food." In *The Oxford Handbook of Food History*, edited by Jeffrey Pilcher. New York: Oxford University Press, 2012.

Pensado, Jaime M., and Enrique C. Ochoa, eds. *México Beyond 1968: Revolutionaries, Radicals, and Repression During the Global Sixties and Subversive Seventies*. Tucson: University of Arizona Press, 2018.

Peralta, José. "(De)Stabilizing the Neoliberal Food Regime: The Struggle for the Defense of Corn in Mexico." Ph.D. diss., University of Illinois at Urbana-Champaign, 2012.

Pérez Herrero, Pedro. "Algunas hipótesis de trabajo sobre la inmigración española a México: Los comerciantes." In *Tres aspectos de la presencia española en México durante el profiriato: Relaciones económicas, comerciantes y población*, edited by Clara E. Lida. Mexico City: El Colegio de México, 1981.

Pilcher, Jeffrey M., ed. *The Oxford Handbook of Food History*. New York: Oxford University Press, 2012.

Pilcher, Jeffrey M. "Industrial Tortillas and Folkloric Pepsi: The Nutritional Consequences of Hybrid Cuisines in Mexico." In *Food Nations: Selling Taste in Consumer Societies*, edited by Warren Belasco and Philip Scranton, 222–229. New York: Routledge, 2001.

Pilcher, Jeffrey M. *Planet Taco: A Global History of Mexican Food*. New York: Oxford University Press, 2012.

Pilcher, Jeffrey M. *¡Qué Vivan los Tamales! Food and the Making of Mexican Identity*. Albuquerque: University of New Mexico Press, 1998.

Pilcher, Jeffrey M. *The Sausage Rebellion: Public Health, Private Enterprise, and Meat in Mexico City, 1890–1917*. Albuquerque: University of New Mexico Press, 2006.

Pineda, Elisa, Eric J. Brunner, Clare H. Llewellyn, and Jennifer S. Mindell. "The Retail Food Environment and its Association with Body Mass Index in Mexico." *International Journal of Obesity* 45 (2021): 1215–1228.

Poitras, Manuel. "Unnatural Growth: The Political Economy of Biotechnology in Mexico." In *Food for the Few: Neoliberal Globalism and Biotechnology in Latin American*, edited by Gerardo Otero. Austin: University of Texas Press, 2008.

Posadas Segura, Florencio. "La situación de los trabajadores rurales en Sinaloa." *Estudios sociales* 27, no. 49 (January–June 2017): 243–271.

Puga, Cristina. *Los empresarios organizados y el tratado de libre comercio de América de Norte.* Mexico City: Miguel Angel Porrúa Eds., 2004.

Quijano, Aníbal. "Coloniality of Power, Eurocentricism, and Latin American." *Nepantla: Views from the South* 1, no. 3 (2000): 533–580.

Ramírez Bautista, Ricardo, Carmen Zambrano Canales, and Iván Zamora Aguilar. "Ética corporative y prática idebidas en México: Una aproximación del trabajo de los empacadores en Wal-Mart." B.A. thesis, Universidad Autónoma de México, Iztapalapa, June 2005.

Ramirez Sánchez, Miguel Angel. "Los sindicatos blancos de Monterrery (1931–2009)." *Frontera Norte* 23, no. 45 (July–December 2011): 177–210.

Ramos-Elorduy, Julieta, and José Manuel Pino Moreno. "El consume de insectos entre los aztecas." In *Conquista y comida: Consequencias del encuenro de dos mundos,* edited by Janet Long. Mexico City: Universdad Nacional Autónoma de México, 1996.

Rath, Thomas. "Camouflaging the State: The Army and the Limits of Hegemony in PRIísta Mexico, 1940–1960." In *Dictablanda: Politics, Work, and Culture in Mexico, 1938–1968.* Durham, N.C.: Duke University Press, 2014.

Rath, Thomas. *Myths of Demilitarization in Postrevolutionary Mexico, 1920–1960.* Chapel Hill: University of North Carolina Press, 2013.

Reardon, Thomas, and Julio A. Berdegué. "The Rapid Rise of Supermarkets in Latin America: Challenges and Opportunities for Development." *Development Policy Review* 20, no. 4 (2002): 371–388.

Reardon, Thomas, Peter Timmer, and Julio Berdegué. "The Rapid Rise of Supermarkets in Developing Countries: Induced Organizational, Institutional, and Technological Change in Agrifood Systems." *eJADE: Journal of Agricultural and Development Economics* 1, no. 2 (2004): 168–183.

Rello, Fernando, and Demetri Sodi. *Abasto y distribución de alimentos en las grandes metropolis.* Mexico City: Nueva Imagen, 1989.

Rendón Trejo, Araceli, and Andrés Morales Alquicira. "Grupos económicos en la industria de alimientos: Las estrategias de GRUMA." *Argumentos* 21, no. 57 (May–August 2008): 87–112.

Richard, Analiese. "'Sin Maíz No Hay País': Citizenship and Environment in Mexico's Food Sovereignty Movement." In *Environment and Citizenship in Latin America: Natures, Subjects and Struggles,* edited by Alex Latta and Hannah Wittman. New York: Berghahn Books, 2012.

Rius. *La basura que comemos: Transgénicos y comida chatarra.* Mexico City: Grijalbo, 2000.

Rius. *La panza es primero.* Mexico City: Grijalbo, 1973.

Rius. *Mis confusiones: Memorias desmemoriadas.* Mexico City: Penguin Random House, 2014.

Rockwell, Elisie. "Schools of the Revolution: Enacting and Contesting State Forms in Tlaxcala, 1910–1930." In *Everyday Forms of State Formation: Revolution and the*

Negotiation of Rule in Modern Mexico, edited by Gilbert M. Joseph and Daniel Nugent. Durham, N.C.: Duke University Press, 1994.

Rodríguez, Roberto Cintli. *Our Sacred Maíz Is Our Mother: Indigeneity and Belonging in the Americas*. Tucson: University of Arizona Press, 2014.

Rodríguez Gómez, Guadalupe. "Supermercados, Tiendas 'de conveniencia' y de abarrotes: ¿Reto o nicho de oportunidad para los quesos tradicionales." In *La paradoja de la calidad: Alimentos mexicanos en América del Norte*, edited by Kirsten Appendini and Guadalupe Rodríguez Gómez. Mexico City: El Colegio de México, 2012.

Rodríguez Gómez, M. Guadalupe. "Making a Globalized Nation in the Countryside: El Barzón, a Popular Movement in Contemporary Mexico." *Urban Anthropology and Studies of Cultural Systems and World Economic Development* 27, no. 2 (Summer 1998): 197–232.

Rodríguez Solis, Gerardo, María del Carmern Arellano Gálvez, and Patricia Aranda Gallegos. "Racialización y trabajo agrícola en el Noroeste de México: Análisis a partir de notas de prensa 2013–2019." *Noroeste de México*, no. 3 (January–June 2021): 135–163.

Roman, Richard, and Edur Velasco Arregui. *Continental Crucible: Big Business, Workers and Unions in the Transformation of North America*. Halifax: Fernwood / PM Press, 2015.

Rosas, Mara, and Mario Fuentes. "La nueva ruralidad comunitaria y las activades no-proletarias generadoras de excedentes." In *El campesinado y su persistencia en la actualidad mexicana*, edited by Tanalís Padilla, 428–468. Mexico City: El Fondo de Cultura Económico y El Consejo Nacional Para la Cultura y las Artes, 2013.

Rosset, Peter M., and Miguel A. Altieri. *Agroecology: Science and Politics*. Nova Scotia: Fernwood, 2017.

Rubio, Blanca. *Resistencia campesina y explotación rural en México*. Mexico City: Ediciones Era, 1987.

Ruiz, Jason. *Americans in the Treasure House: Travel to Porfirian Mexico and the Cultural Politics of Empire*. Austin: University of Texas Press, 2014.

Salas-Porras, Alejandra. "Corrientes de pensamiento empresarial en México (primera parte)." *Revista Mexicana de Ciencias Politicas y Sociales* 44, no. 181 (January–April 2001): 181–206.

Salas-Porras, Alejandra. "Corrientes de pensamiento empresarial en México (segunda parte)." *Revista Mexicana de Ciencias Políticas y Sociales* 44, no. 182–183 (May–December 2001): 227–257.

Salas-Porras, Alejandra. *La economía política neoliberal en México: ¿Quién la diseñó y cómo lo hizo?* Madrid: Ediciones Akal, S.A., 2017.

Salvatore, Ricardo D., John H. Coatsworth, and Amilcar E. Challú, eds. *Living Standards in Latin American History: Height, Welfare, and Development, 1750–2000*. Cambridge, Mass.: Harvard University Press, 2010.

Sánchez Islas, Andrea. "Estrategias de persuasión en la publicidad de los alimentos 'chatarra' en México." In *Hábitos alimentarios, publicidad y política de salud*, edited by Carola García Calderón. Mexico City: UNAM, 2020.

Sanders, Nichole. *Gender and Welfare in Mexico: The Consolidation of a Postrevolutionary State*. University Park: Penn State University Press, 2011.

Sanderson, Steven E. *The Transformation of Mexican Agriculture: International Structure and the Politics of Rural Change*. Princeton, N.J.: Princeton University Press, 1986.

Sandoval, Marcos. "El maíz y los pueblos indios." In *Sin maíz, no hay país*, edited by Gustavo Esteva and Catherine Marielle. Mexico City: Consejo Nacional para la Cultura y las Artes, 2007.

Sanford, Lois. "The Binational Integration of the US-Mexican Avocado Industries: Examining Responses to Economic Globalism." In *Mexico in Transition: Neoliberal Globalization, the State, and Civil Society*, edited by Gerardo Otero. London: Zed Books, 2004.

Saragoza, Alex M. *The Monterrey Elite and the Mexican State, 1880–1940*. Austin: University of Texas Press, 1988.

Sassen, Saskia. *Expulsions: Brutality and Complexity in the Global Economy*. Cambridge, Mass.: Belknap Press of Harvard University Press, 2014.

Schafer, Robert Jones. *Mexico Business Organizations: History and Analysis*. Syracuse: Syracuse University Press, 1973.

Schmitt, Hannah. *La raiz rebelde de la resistencia en la tierra del maíz: Un relato de la CNUC*. Tlaxcala, Mexico, 2016.

Schneider, Ben Ross. *Business Politics and the State in Twentieth-Century Latin America*. Cambridge: Cambridge University Press, 2004.

Schneider, Ben Ross. "Why Is Mexican Business So Organized?" *Latin American Research Review* 37, no. 1 (2002): 77–118.

Schwentesius, Rita, and Manuel Ángel Gómez. "Supermarkets in Mexico: Impacts on Horticultural Systems." *Development Policy Review* 20, no. 4 (2002): 487–502.

Scott, James C. *Seeing Like a State: How Certain Schemes to Improve the Human Condition Have Failed*. New Haven, Conn.: Yale University Press, 1998.

Sepúlveda, Bernardo, and Antonio Chumacero, eds. *La inversión extranjera en México*. Mexico City: El Fondo de Cultura Económica, 1973.

Snodgrass, Michael. "The Birth and Consequences of Industrial Paternalism in Monterrey, Mexico, 1890–1940." *International Labor and Working-Class History*, no. 53 (Spring 1998): 115–136.

Snodgrass, Michael. *Deference and Defiance in Monterrey: Workers, Paternalism, and Revolution in Mexico, 1890–1950*. Cambridge: Cambridge University Press, 2003.

Soustelle, Jacques. *Daily Life of the Aztecs: On the Eve of the Conquest*. Translated by Patrick O'Brian. Stanford: Stanford University Press, 1961.

Souto Mantecón, Matlide. "De la cocina a la mesa." In *Historia de la vida cotidinana en México: Tomo IV Bienes y vivencias, el siglo XIX*, edited by Ann Staples, 15–49. Mexico City: El Colegio de México, 2005.

Super, John C. *Food, Conquest, and Colonization in Sixteenth-Century Spanish America*. Albuquerque: University of New Mexico Press, 1988.

Teichman, Judith A. *Privatization and Political Change in Mexico*. Pittsburgh: University of Pittsburgh Press, 1995.

Tepichin Valle, Ana María. "Género, pobreza, y política social." In *Desafíos de la pobreza para la agenda del desarrollo de México*, edited by Tonatiuh Guillén López and Gerardo Ordoñez Barba. Tijuana: Colegio del Frontera Norte, 2014.

Tilly, Chris. "Wal-Mart and Its Workers: *NOT* the Same All Over the World." *Connecticut Law Review* 39, no. 4 (May 2007): 3–19.

Tilly, Chris. "Wal-Mart in Mexico: The Limits of Growth." In *Wal-Mart: The Face of Twenty-First-Century Capitalism*, edited by Nelson Lichtenstein. New York: New Press, 2006.

Tilly, Chris, and José Luis Álvarez Galván. "Lousy Jobs, Invisible Unions: The Mexican Retail Sector in the Age of Globalization." *International Labor and Working-Class History* 70 (Fall 2006): 61–85.

Torres, Felipe, Ernesto Moreno, Isabel Chong, and Juan Quintanilla, eds. *La industria de la masa y la tortilla: Desarrollo y tecnologia*. Mexico City: Universidad Autónoma de México, 1996.

Torres Torres, Felipe, and Agustín Rojas Martínez. "La seguridad alimentaria en la encrucijada de las desigualidades regionales de México." *Investigaciones Regionales* 53, no. 2 (2022): 91–115.

Tutino, John. *The Mexican Heartland: How Communities Shaped Capitalism, A Nation, and World History, 1500–2000*. Princeton, N.J.: Princeton University Press, 2018.

Vanderwood, Paul. *Disorder and Progress: Bandits, Police, and Mexican Development*. Lincoln: University of Nebraska Press, 1981.

Vargas, Luis Alberto. "El maíz viajero sin equipaje." *Anales de Antropología* 48, no. 1 (2014): 123–137.

Vargas Domínguez, Joel. "Metabolismo y nutrición en el México posrevolucionario: Eugenesia y clasificación de la población mexicana entre 1927 y 1943." PhD diss., Universidad Nacional Autónoma de México, 2017.

Vargas Domínguez, Joel. "Las estadísticas de consume y el cesto de provisiones en México en las décadas de 1920 y 1930." *Estudios Sociales del Estado* 8, no. 16 (2022): 45–80.

Vargas Domínguez, Joel. "The Construction of the Minimum Wage and Nutrition in the Early 20th Century." *Historia Crítica*, no. 87 (2023): 101–125.

Vásquez García, Verónica, Juan Felipe Nuñez Espinoza, and Tomas Ortega Ortega. "Estructura y resiliencia social en comunidades indígenas: El caso de la union de Palmeadoras de Tlaxiaco, Oaxaca, Mexico." *REDES: Revista Hispana para el Análisis de Redes Sociales* 29, no. 2 (2018): 206–225.

Vargas Sánchez, Gustavo, and Luis Pérez Osnaya. "Gruma: Un análisis microeconómico." *Economía Informa*, no. 386 (May–June 2014): 31–50.

Vaughn, Bobby, and Ben Vinson III. "Memín Penguín, Changing Racial Debates, and Transnational Blackness." *Emisférica* 5, no. 1 (2008).

Vaughn, Mary Kay. "Nationalizing the Countryside: Schools and Rural Communities in the 1930s." In *The Eagle and the Virgin: Nation and Cultural Revolution in*

Mexico, 1920–1940, edited by Mary Kay Vaughn and Stephen E. Lewis. Durham, N.C.: Duke University Press, 2006.

Vaughn, Mary Kay. "Rural Women's Literacy and Education During the Mexican Revolution: Subverting a Patriarchal Event." In *Women of the Mexican Countryside, 1850–1990*, edited by Heather Fowler-Salamini and Mary Kay Vaughn. Tucson: University of Arizona Press, 1994.

Velasco Ortiz, Laura. *"Desde que tengo memoria": Narrativas de identidad en indígenas migrantes*. Tijuana: COLEF, 2005.

Velasco Ortiz, Laura, Christian Zlolniski, and Marie-Laure Coubes. *De jornaleros a colonos: Residencia, trabajo e identidad en el Valle de San Quintín*. Tijuana: Colegio de la Frontera Norte, 2014.

Villegas Rojas, Pedro S. "El nuevo sindicalismo blanco." In *La situación del trabajo en México, 2012: El trabajo en crisis*, edited by Enrique de la Garza. Mexico City: Plaza y Valdes Eds., 2012.

Vizcarra Bordi, Ivonne, ed. *Volteando la tortilla: Génaro y maíz en la alimentación actual de México*. Toluca: Universidad Autónoma del Estado de México, 2018.

Walker, Louise E. *Waking from the Dream: Mexico's Middle Classes After 1968*. Stanford: Stanford University Press, 2013.

Walker, Margath A., David Walker, and Yanga Villagómez Velazquez. "The Wal-Martification of Teotihuacán: Issues of Resistance and Cultural Heritage." In *Wal-Mart World: The World's Biggest Corporation in the Global Economy*, edited by Stanley D. Brunn. New York: Routledge, 2006.

Warman, Arturo. *Corn and Capitalism: How a Botanical Bastard Grew to Global Dominance*. Translated by Nancy L. Westrate. Chapel Hill: University of North Carolina Press, 2003.

Weiner, Richard. *Race, Nation, and Market Economic Culture in Porfirian Mexico*. Tucson: University of Arizona Press, 2004.

Weis, Robert. *Bakers and Basques: A Social History of Bread in Mexico*. Albuquerque: University of New Mexico Press, 2012.

Weis, Robert. "Bimbo." In *Icons of Mexico*, edited by Eric Zolov. Santa Barbara, Calif.: ABC-Clio, 2015.

Weis, Robert. "Immigrant Entrepreneurs, Bread, and Class Negotiation in Postrevolutionary Mexico City." *Mexican Studies / Estudios Mexicanos* 25, no. 1 (Winter 2009): 71–100.

Weis, Robert. "La amenaza del Osito Bimbo: Los intelectuales, la cultura nacional y la industrialización de la comida en México." *Brújula revista interdisciplinaria sobre estudios latinoamericanos*, no. 1 (December 2002): 94–103.

Weis, Robert. "Por la verdad del Osito Bimbo: Consumo en el México contemporáneo." M.A. thesis, Universidad Nacional Autónoma de Mexico, 2001.

Wiggins, Steve, and Sharada Keats. *The Rising Cost of a Healthy Diet: Changing Relative Prices of Food in High Income and Emerging Economies*. London: Overseas Development Institute, May 2015.

Wilkie, James W. *The Mexican Revolution: Federal Expenditure and Social Change Since 1910*. Berkeley: University of California Press, 1970.

Womack, John. "The Mexican Revolution, 1910–1920." In *Mexico Since Independence*, edited by Leslie Bethell. New York: Cambridge University Press, 1991.

Yates-Doerr, Emily. *The Weight of Obesity: Hunger and Global Health in Postwar Guatemala*. Oakland: University of California Press, 2015.

Yúñez-Naude, Antonio. "Old Foods and New Consumers in Mexico Under Economic Reforms." *African Journal of Agricultural and Resource Economics* 9, no. 1 (2014): 33–53.

Zazueta, María Del Pilar. "De Coca-Cola a Vampi-Cola: Políticas, negocios, y el consumo de refrescos y azúcar en México (1970–1982)." *Apuntes de Investigación*, no. 22 (2012): 34–55.

Zazueta, María del Pilar. "Milk Against Poverty: Nutrition and the Politics of Consumption in Twentieth-Century Mexico." PhD diss., Columbia University, 2011.

Zepeda, Roberto. *The Decline of Labor Unions in Mexico During the Neoliberal Period*. Camden: Palgrave Macmillan, 2021.

Zepeda Patterson, Jorge, ed. *Los amos de méxico*. 2nd ed. Mexico City: Editorial Planeta Mexicana, 2007.

Zermeño, Sergio. *La desmodernidad Mexicana y las alternativas a la violencia y a la exclusión en nuestros días*. Mexico City: Océano, 2005.

Zibechi, Raúl. *The New Brazil: Regional Imperialism and the New Democracy*. Translated by Ramor Ryan. Oakland: AK Press, 2014.

Zlolniski, Christian. *Made in Baja: The Lives of Farmworkers and Growers Behind Mexico's Transnational Agricultural Boom*. Oakland: University of California Press, 2019.

INDEX

Note: Page numbers in *italics* represent illustrations.

ABOUT THE AUTHOR

Enrique C. Ochoa is an award-winning professor of Latin American studies and history at Cal State Los Angeles. A community-based public historian, Ochoa works to link community struggles to their teaching and research.